CONFLICT IN LAOS

The Politics of Neutralization

CONFLICT IN LAOS

The Politics of Neutralization

Arthur J. Dommen

Revised Edition

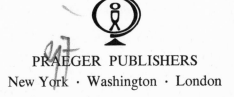

PRAEGER PUBLISHERS
New York · Washington · London

To my schoolmate,

ROBERT CAMPBELL JAMES

PRAEGER PUBLISHERS
111 Fourth Avenue, New York, N.Y. 10003, U.S.A.
5, Cromwell Place, London S.W.7, England

Published in the United States of America in 1971
by Praeger Publishers, Inc.

This is the revised edition of the book first published
in 1964 by Frederick A. Praeger, Inc.

Library of Congress Catalog Card Number: 76–145945

Printed in the United States of America

Preface to the Revised Edition

When I wrote the first edition of this book, in 1964, my hope was that it would help as a counterweight to the tendency of Americans to abdicate their natural common sense when faced with a crisis in a faraway country like Laos and to surrender willy-nilly to the simplistic formulas of ideology. We end by believing, I wrote, that all our troubles stem from an inherently aggressive enemy, forgetting that among the enemy are those who were once our friends and that much of our enemy's success is the result of our own mistaken actions. I believe that those statements are still basically applicable today, although presumably there would be less inclination today than twenty years ago in the State Department to describe Ho Chi Minh as the "mortal enemy of native independence in Indochina."

Another dismaying thought has arisen in the meantime, however. Whatever the Communists would have us believe, ideological preconceptions alone cannot account for the sending of half a million Americans to South Vietnam. The sudden dawning that the strategy of "people's war" was about to succeed in imposing the will of its originators in Hanoi on South Vietnam, fraudulent and unjust as it seemed, moved the United States to action. As a result, I have had to revise some of my rather too smug assumptions about the conflict that opposes the United States to North Vietnam in Indochina.

The conflict obviously goes a lot deeper than was previously thought. As the ambition of the men in Hanoi to acquire hegemony over Laos and Cambodia, as well as over South Vietnam, has become daily more manifest in arithmetic progression, as it were, the dilemma of the United States in deciding whether it is worth coping with this ambition has increased in geometric progression. Americans had suspected they were locked in a contest of wills; they had not suspected the contest would be pushed so far. The conclusion seems inescapable that it is harder to become friends than to become enemies. It is harder for a great and powerful country, no matter how magnanimous, to make an honorable peace—a "peace of the brave," to borrow De Gaulle's expression—with the ragged rebels it has been fighting than it is for that same country to "pacify" and "win hearts and minds" and to deal with the conduct of its own soldiers and the corruption of its allies. Consequently, I have thought it useful to the reader if, in addition to relating the events of the past years, I offered some thoughts of my own about what the deep-seated causes of this contest are.

If the contest covers all of Indochina, and if the settlement (assuming there is one) must include the neutralization of the several countries there, nonetheless, the events in Laos have been an important part of this contest. Laos has been the subject of diplomatic exchanges in such diverse places as Geneva, London, Paris, Washington, Moscow, Vienna, central Siberia, Key West, and Key Biscayne. Laos has also been the subject of clamorous debate in the U.S. Congress, for the conflict in Laos is one that has involved the United States in the dilemma of repudiating an international agreement on the grounds that it has been violated by another signatory, or of itself violating the terms of this agreement. The author of this dilemma has been North Vietnam—and not to perceive this is blindness. North Vietnam's conduct in Laos has exposed for all the world to see what must surely rank as the most monstrous confidence trick ever perpetrated—the steadfast contention by Hanoi that it is fighting a just and glorious war without having to move so much as a single soldier beyond its borders.

The intervening years have not been without their other, more personal, tragedies. I wish particularly to pay respect to the memories of two friends who were as much at home in Laos as in their own houses: Jerry A. Rose, killed in a plane crash in Quang Ngai in September, 1965, and Bernard B. Fall, killed by a mine in Quang Tri in February, 1967. In their deaths, we lost two voices for common sense that we could ill afford to lose.

Again, let me acknowledge the invaluable assistance I received from Guy Searls, who lent me the use of his library in Hong Kong; from Beth Blake, who helped me to locate materials in the Library of Congress; from Donald Wasson of the Council on Foreign Relations; from Professor A. Doak Barnett of Columbia University; from Joseph Buttinger; and from the Library of the University of Hong Kong.

Above all, my thanks go to the countless persons—Lao, Vietnamese, American, French, and of every nationality—who have in some way been connected with developments in Laos and whom I have interviewed over the past ten years. Special thanks go to Colonel William Law, former military attaché of the U.S. Embassy in Vientiane, who knew Prince Souphanouvong in the early days when he was America's friend, and who was one of the first Americans I found who understood what the United States was getting into by taking on the North Vietnamese. Although he never made the mistake of underestimating them, as so many Americans did, even he had difficulty in believing that they would be able to build and operate the Ho Chi Minh Trail.

Finally, this book would not have been possible without the keen eyes and sound sense of Phyllis Freeman of Praeger Publishers, and Shirley Zimmerman, who assisted me in the preparation of the manuscript. Mervyn W. Adams assisted me in the editing of the revised edition.

Vientiane, Laos
January, 1971

Contents

MAPS

TABLES

Introduction

The present conflict in Laos is in one sense the prolongation of a centuries-old process whereby the feudal principalities of the left bank of the Mekong were bound by ties of vassalage and forced alliances to their more powerful neighbors to the southwest and over the Annamite Mountains. In another very real sense, however, this conflict is marked by entirely new forces of attraction and subjugation, with far-reaching implications for a world in which the confrontation between the nuclear powers has reached stalemate and the gap between the have peoples and the have-not peoples is wider than it has ever been.

In 1954, when the French were fighting against defeat at the hands of the Viet Minh, the principal issue was whether the colonial power would succeed, by force of arms, in retaining its hold. For the United States, the question then was whether to lend its support to those patriots fighting for the independence of their country, as U.S. observers on the scene, both diplomatic and nondiplomatic, urged. As a result of considerations that had little to do with the justness of the harsh struggle waged by the nationalists, support was thrown instead to France.

Even then, the United States coveted no material possessions in Laos and the other countries of Indochina. It was conceivable that it might assume a new role once the colonial war ended. Americans went to Laos to establish technical-assistance missions. But the fighting did not stop. Cynically encouraged by the Vietnamese Communists across an ill-defined border, a minority faction of the nationalist movement that had been alienated by the West sought to widen its influence in Laos, using guerrilla warfare to achieve this goal.

The innocent inhabitants of Laos who came in contact with the roving agents of this guerrilla movement were told that the emphasis of the American aid program was on military armaments and training, and that the people in the villages were deriving little or no advantage from the American presence, which they had accepted on the premise that the United States promised to defend them against the aggression they feared. This aggression, furthermore, did not take place. Instead, the armed minority of the Pathet Lao arrogated to themselves the banner of nationalism and proceeded to exploit the shortcomings of a central government grown indolent and corrupt.

These developments gradually turned the balance against the United States in a situation where an open resort to American military superiority was excluded time and again because, as the State Department reminded the world, the United States was not a colonial power like France. As the exclusion of Western influence from Laos became more and more of a real possibility, the future of American policy toward other countries of Southeast Asia where, unlike Laos, the United States had committed itself by treaty to defense against aggression, was placed in jeopardy.

The Vietnamese Communists, having consolidated their authority at home, were now bringing Leninist organization and ruthless discipline to a movement "to liberate Laos from neocolonialism." Their appeals in a country of sparse population and little exploitable wealth were unorthodox: There were in Laos no groups consigned to lives of misery, as in Java; no tradition of agrarian revolt, as in China; no industrial proletariat, as in Tonkin. The political awareness of even the townspeople was far lower than in Vietnam, making it difficult to arouse potential recruits to revolutionary consciousness.

But the Vietnamese Communists made considerable progress, especially since their own regime had none of the material resources, the food surpluses, the jet-aircraft factories, or the vast fleet at sea possessed by the United States. Their agents, indoctrinated with a sense of inevitable victory, allowed themselves to be transformed into the servants of a higher political necessity; their dour, expressionless faces were their hallmark. Their subsistence was rice, a few vegetables, and an indoctrination lecture every day —nothing else.

There were many unexpected turnabouts in all this. Because a withdrawal of American aid implied an almost automatic Communist takeover, United States protection became a virtual necessity for people who had fought to rid their country of foreign entanglements. A decade after independence, a visitor to Laos could not but feel that the prestige of France, a colonial power defeated in a liberation war that took a heavy cost in French lives and honor, was actually higher than that of the United States, the champion of the self-determination of peoples. In subordinating its native belief in the liberty of peoples to what appeared to be a temporary necessity, the United States had forfeited the powerful appeal of this ideal and thereby undermined its long-range goal of assisting the construction of a politically stable society willing and able to resist the Communist "wave of the future." In contrast, the Vietnamese Communists, because they were willing to sacrifice themselves for their principles, made those principles respectable in the eyes of other Southeast Asians in the same predicament.

The conflict was bound to have repercussions in neighboring states. Infiltration and subversion by North Vietnamese agents in Laos constituted a threat to Thailand and South Vietnam. American actions in Laos harbored a threat to North Vietnam. Both the Communist powers and the non-Communist powers disregarded the spirit of the cease-fire agreements signed in Geneva in 1954, although they continued to pay lip service to the provisions of these agreements.

All this while, there existed considerations for international consent to the withdrawal of Laos from the eddies of Cold War politics. No account of foreign intervention in Laos would be complete without an analysis of the very real vectors toward neutralization.

The attempt to renegotiate a neutralization agreement came at a very late date. By then, the conflict had involved the Russians, who were caught in a dilemma of allies not exactly to their liking—most importantly, the Chinese. The confrontation between the United States and North Vietnam had produced unprecedented tensions in Laos and the other Indochinese countries. If these tensions drew in the Communist Chinese, as the rivalries of the feudal princes of centuries ago had drawn in the armies from the north, the outcome would be the imposition on a happy and carefree people of an imperialism far more pervading than any they had ever known.

The implications of the Laos conflict are clear. Given the close identity of views between the men responsible for North Vietnam's successes in Laos and the men in Peking, one may well consider whether the "inevitability of victory" in which the Communists place such faith is on the side of the guerrilla movements in Asia, Africa, and Latin America. It is these continents that have been pronounced by Peking to be the decisive battleground of the future between "imperialism" and "socialism."

The United States is accustomed to thinking of itself in the fore-

1.

The Kingdom of the Million Elephants

When the sun set on France's Indochina empire in 1954, the largest entity left by the cease-fire agreement, with an area of approximately 91,000 square miles, was the Kingdom of Laos. Of no recognizable shape, the kingdom is a sparsely inhabited, landlocked territory lying in the heart of Southeast Asia. Each of its sixteen provinces borders a more populous foreign country, as if to affirm the paramount fact that throughout its history Laos has suffered the consequences of an intimate and at times destructive involvement with powerful neighbors.

In understanding the reasons for this unhappy circumstance, however, a geophysical map will be of more use than a political one. Aside from the valley of the Mekong and its left-bank tributaries, the country's relief is one of complex mountain and plateau forms. The mountain slopes are covered by dense vegetation and are so steep, and the valley bottoms so confined, that little space remains for cultivation. Only here and there, in tiny upland clearings, men have managed to burn away the forest and establish their thatched-roof villages in a wild domain of torrents, precipices, and mist-shrouded peaks.

The Annamite Mountains stretch from southern China down to the Gulf of Siam, where they fade into vestigial hillocks in the alluvial plain of the Mekong in southernmost Vietnam. The crest of these mountains forms the eastern border of present-day Laos. From the east, the general slope of the mountains is downward to the valley of the Mekong. This crest of the Annamite chain also marks the dividing line between the two great cultures of Asia—the Indian and the Chinese. The Lao are a Hinduized people; the Vietnamese, a Sinicized people.

Generally, the rivers of Laos flow west and south toward the Mekong, and the rivers of Vietnam flow east and south toward the sea. The exceptions to this rule have provided natural routes of access across the mountains: the Ma River, which flows across northeastern Sam Neua Province and comes out in Thanh Hoa; the Song Ca, which reaches the sea near Vinh after draining the lands of Nghe An and which has its headwaters, the Mat and Mo rivers, in Laos; and, in the A Shau Valley inside what is today South Vietnam, the river draining westward to form the Kong River.

The common political border between Laos and Vietnam, which has a total length of 1,324 miles and can generally be said to reflect a natural geographic and ethnographic divide, in reality runs through a complex landscape and fails to respect accurately either the watershed or, as will be seen, the affinities of the peoples who live along it.

Tracks through the mountains have been in existence since early times in the vicinity of Dien Bien Phu, along the Ma River, at the headwaters of the Song Ca, and between Tchepone and Quang Tri at what was named the Ai Lao or Lao Bao Pass, although this was less a pass than an opening practically at sea level. The French constructed dirt roads to facilitate motor travel between Laos and Vietnam. They were Route Coloniale 7 over the Barthélémy Pass connecting the Plain of Jars and Vinh; Route Coloniale 8 over the Keo Neua Pass connecting Thakhek and Vinh; Route Coloniale 12 over the Mu Gia Pass connecting Na Phao and Ha Tinh; and Route Coloniale 9 connecting Savannakhet and Quang Tri.

Laos lies in the path of the southwesterly monsoon. For six months of the year, mist and cloud hang low over these mountains, and drenching rains turn footpaths into soggy, muddy rivulets.

At the center of northern Laos lies the Plain of Jars, a high, rolling plain of bright-green grasslands interspersed with clumps of trees on the hilltops. This plain, resembling the dairy land of southern Wisconsin, has an average elevation of 3,600 feet above sea level. It is ringed with mountains; one of these, to the immediate south, has a 9,240-foot summit, the highest in Indochina south of Hanoi. The plain takes its name from the more than 100 ancient stone jars found strewn through the meadows near its center. The jars, large enough to hold a small man in squatting position, are thought by some scholars to be funeral urns. Tests have placed their age at about 2,000 years, indicating that they were fashioned long before the Lao people entered the area. Because marks on the inside of the urns appear to have been made by iron chisels and because the only known iron-workers in this part of the world 2,000 years ago were the Chinese, some scholars believe that the jars are Chinese relics.

In southern Laos is another lofty plateau, the Bolovens, said by agronomists to contain the country's richest agricultural potential.

The great Mekong, which rises in Tibet and courses south through the gorges of China's Yünnan Province, enters Laos a few miles north of Muong Sing village, and then forms Laos' western border, first with Burma, then with Thailand. In April, just before the first monsoon storms, the Mekong is a narrow stream hiding among outcroppings of gray and black rock, its exposed bed presenting no barrier to the foot traveler. In September, the river is at its rain-swollen maximum; in the south, it is a mile-wide, thirty-foot-deep, chocolate-colored stream carrying a heavy load of mud, tree trunks, and lesser debris on a long voyage to the sea.

Most of Laos is covered by a tropical rain forest. Dark green the year round, it forms a canopy of lofty treetops. Branchless tree trunks rise straight up from the sunless forest floor, their tops festooned by giant lianas, often a foot in diameter. Scattered in the crowns are orchids, ferns, and wild figs.

Occasionally the rain forest gives way abruptly to less dense groves of smaller softwoods, their foliage not so profuse, which are mixed with a heavy undergrowth of ferns, grass, wild ginger, tropical rhododendron, and bamboo thickets. Often there is a secondary cover of wild bananas and coconut and areca palms. These are overgrown clearings, where the virgin forest was burned off long ago, either by a natural fire or by a wandering tribal family needing enough bare ground to plant a year's crop of maize or hill rice before moving on to the next valley.

These vast forests are the home of tiger, panther, and herds of wild elephant and deer. When these forests provide the hideouts of armed guerrilla bands, news dispatches most often refer to them as jungles.

The People

The oldest human inhabitants of Indochina were almost certainly men whose traces have been found in the Phou Loi Massif north of the Plain of Jars.[1] They were settled long before the first

---

[1] George Coedès, *Les Peuples de la Péninsule Indochinoise* (Paris: Dunod, 1962), pp. 28–29.

MAP 1.   Physical Features of Laos

of the migrations from the north that eventually peopled Laos; their descendants came to be known as Kha, a Lao term meaning slave. Today the Kha are especially numerous in the south and hunt and practice a shifting cultivation of rice, maize, tobacco, and cotton. They live several families to a "long house," which is set on thick wooden piles, its interior partitionless and smoke-blackened.

The Lao, who constitute less than one-half the total population today, live in the broad, fertile valley bottoms. They are descendants of a great migration of Thai peoples from southern China that occurred between the sixth and thirteenth centuries. Like the inhabitants of Thailand, they are Theravada Buddhists, and the languages of the two peoples are closely related.

Another group from the same migration—the Black Thai, White Thai, and Red Thai tribes—very early settled in the upper valleys in the mountainous areas around Muong Sing and Dien Bien Phu, between the Red River and the Mekong. They remain distinct from the lowland Lao; like them, they are rice cultivators, but unlike them, they are not Buddhists.

Subsequent arrivals were the Yao, who settled on the lower mountain slopes, followed by the Meo, who occupied the highest crests and ridges. They came from southern China in the last major migration, in the middle of the nineteenth century, which was almost as important as the earlier Thai migrations. The Meo, whose villages are not normally found in Laos anywhere below 3,500 feet, cover wide areas of Xieng Khouang Province, and in smaller numbers live in Luang Prabang, Sam Neua, Phong Saly, and Nam Tha provinces. They total between 300,000 and 500,000.

The Meo, fiercely independent and hardier than all the other tribes, are the warrior race of Laos, comparable to the Gurkhas of Nepal. They build their houses on the ground, usually not more than a dozen to a village. Indefatigable walkers and horsemen, they range the upper mountain slopes for days, hunting with their long, homemade flintlock rifles the game that keeps them alive and provides the medicinal potions that they believe bring health and long life: skin of gaur (a wild buffalo), deer's soft horn, marrow of tiger bone, gall of bear and python. The staple diet of the Meo village consists of ground fried corn, Chinese cabbage, eggplant, onions, and pork or fowl.

Two other minorities complete this picture of diverse peoples. These are the Vietnamese and the Chinese, communities of about 30,000 each, living mainly in the towns.

The Emergence of a Strong Lao State

The man who gave the territories of what is now Laos their first shape as a unified state was a fourteenth-century Thai prince named Fa Ngoun, a convert to Buddhism who had spent his youth as an exile at Angkor. He established his court at Muong Swa, on the Upper Mekong, and invited to it bonzes (Buddhist monks), scholars, and craftsmen. He acquired a 500-year-old Buddha called the Prabang, which later gave Muong Swa the name of Luang Prabang (Town of the Golden Buddha).

During this era, the rulers of the surrounding states on the east, south, and west—Annam, Champa, Angkor, Sukhothai, Ayuthia, Chieng Mai, and those of the Shans and the Burmese—were busily intriguing against one another; meanwhile, Annam was at war with China. By playing off these petty princes against one another, Fa Ngoun extended his rule to all the principalities along the Mekong, and captured Vientiane. His domain, when consolidated in 1353 under the name Lan Xang (Kingdom of the Million Elephants), reached from the crest of the Annamite Mountains on the east to the watershed division between the Mekong and the Menam, and from China in the north almost as far as Angkor Wat in the south. It included Chieng Mai and much of the Korat Plateau in what is today Thailand, and portions of present-day northern Cambodia.

Fa Ngoun was succeeded in 1373 by his son, Sam Sen Thai. In an age of warring feudal lords, his reign was one of peace, marked by the building of many *wats* (pagodas), and by the creation of a novel system of local government. Under Sam Sen Thai's system, local governors were selected by the King or by a council of notables, usually from the family of the previous incumbent. Any qualified person had the possibility of assuming a high office in the state.

The two successive kings, father and son, ruled over a group of vassal princes and exacted recognition from neighboring emperors and potentates. Their source of power was a centralized standing army of 150,000 men, divided into infantry, cavalry, and elephant corps, supported by a supply corps of 20,000 coolies. In practice, each of the local governors exerted considerable control over the soldiers recruited from his district, who also served as the local police force. With this machinery of state, the two kings preserved the independence of Lan Xang from enemies without and from dissolution within.

However, after the death of Sam Sen Thai, in 1416, the divisive forces in this early Lao kingdom proved stronger than the cohesive. The fact that the Mekong, with its alternating shallow rapids and flood-spreading crests, could not be used as an avenue of communication favored provincial autonomy rather than centralized authority. Under Sam Sen Thai's successors, his territories became prey for his more powerful neighbors.

An invasion from Annam threatened Lan Xang with extinction in 1478, when Vietnamese troops captured Luang Prabang and drove out the King, Sai Tiakaphat. However, the King's son, Prince Theng Kham, rallied his subjects and pushed the Vietnamese out of the kingdom. The father then vacated the throne in favor of his son, who began his reign under the name Souvanna Palang.

The first records of Europeans arriving in Lan Xang date from the reign of Souligna Vongsa (1637–94). They were traders and missionaries, who found the Lao a happy and carefree people but saw little prospects of either economic advantage or Christian converts. A Dutch merchant, Gerrit van Wuysthoff, arrived in 1641 and left soon thereafter. A Jesuit, Father Giovanni-Maria Leria, stayed on five years before despairing of success in his missionary work.

An interesting sidelight is provided by one notable accomplishment of Souligna Vongsa's generally peaceful reign: a boundary agreement with the empire of the Trinh in the Red River Delta. Since it was the Lao custom to build houses on stilts six to nine feet high, while the Vietnamese built their houses on the ground, a clear-cut division of territory was agreed upon: houses on stilts went to the Lao side, houses on the ground to the Vietnamese.

Souligna Vongsa died in 1694, leaving no living sons. The throne was seized by Tian Thala, the highest-ranking mandarin of the Royal Palace. Six years later he was overthrown and put to death by a provincial governor named Nantharath. Upon this, Souligna Vongsa's minor grandsons, Kitsarat and Inthasom, fled from Vientiane to Luang Prabang.

The news of this coup reached Sai Ong Hue, the son of Souligna Vongsa's brother, who had been living in exile in Annam. That same year, 1700, Sai Ong Hue marched on Vientiane at the head of an army of Vietnamese soldiers. He captured the town, had Nantharath put to death, and proclaimed himself King. He sent his half brother, Thao Long, to take possession of Luang Prabang in his name, and Kitsarat and Inthasom, once more fearing for their lives, fled northeastward to a principality ruled by a princely cousin named Khamone Noi.

In 1707, with an army of 6,000 raised by Khamone Noi, the two grandsons marched on Luang Prabang and captured it. Kitsarat was proclaimed King and sent an ultimatum to Sai Ong Hue in Vientiane that he should consider the provinces north of the Nam Thuong, or Thuong River, as a kingdom outside his sovereignty.

Sai Ong Hue's kingdom was further reduced in 1713 by the secession of a number of territories to the south along both banks of the Mekong, which grouped themselves into the Kingdom of Champassak. The old Kingdom of Lan Xang was now split up into three separate kingdoms: Vientiane, Luang Prabang, and Champassak.

Constant warfare among rival princes racked the countryside in the eighteenth and nineteenth centuries, opening it to forays by the more powerful Siam, Annam, and Burma. A Siamese army captured and sacked Vientiane in 1827, after its ruler, King Anourouth, had unsuccessfully attempted to march on Bangkok. The victorious army forcibly resettled thousands of Lao on the Korat Plateau on the right bank of the Mekong in the hope that they would cause less trouble there.

Anourouth fled across the Annamite Mountains to Hué, where the Emperor Minh Mang offered to help him reconquer his kingdom. In 1828, at the head of an expedition of Vietnamese troops, Anourouth marched back to Vientiane. However, most of the troops deserted en route, and as soon as he arrived in his ruined capital he was again chased out by the Siamese. This time he fled to the Kingdom of Xieng Khouang, a small principality centered in the Plain of Jars, which had managed to survive by paying tribute to both Lan Xang (and its successors) and Annam.

Chao Noi, King of Xieng Khouang, confronted a difficult choice, whether to offend Siam or Annam. He decided on the latter, and handed Anourouth over to the Siamese, who carried him away to Bangkok, where he died in 1835. Chao Noi's action predictably angered Minh Mang, who demanded that he come to Hué to explain his action. Instead, Chao Noi sent an envoy with rich presents, hoping to lessen the Emperor's displeasure. His gesture failed, however, and Minh Mang sent a Vietnamese force to seize him and had him publicly executed in Hué. His little kingdom then became a prefecture of the Empire of Annam, in 1832.

Annam's rule over the annexed territory of Xieng Khouang was harsh in the extreme. Its people were even compelled to wear Vietnamese dress. The outcome was a revolt, during which the Vietnamese governor was killed. After restoring order, the Vietnamese won over Chao Pho, the eldest son of Chao Noi, and in 1855 gave him the lofty title of "imperial mandatory prince" and control over the administration of Xieng Khouang. The little principality continued to pay tribute to both Annam and Luang Prabang, but after 1855 the tight grip of the Vietnamese beyond the Annamite Mountains relaxed somewhat as the emperor at Hué increasingly had to cope with the French.

The Advent of the French

In the middle of the nineteenth century, European powers were landing traders on the China coast in eager hopes of exploiting that vast, mysterious country. The traders were followed by the military, who were sent to consolidate the concessions wrested from a decadent empire. France, led by a small minority of activists envisioning control of the easiest route to the fabled wealth of Yünnan, dispatched military forces to the Red River Delta in 1872. French land and naval expeditions defeated Vietnamese troops and Chinese mercenaries and imposed a Treaty of Protectorate over the court of Hué. In 1884, France won the right to place its Residents over the mandarin administrators of Annam and Tonkin and to install a Resident-General in the citadel of Hué. French military outposts were established at Lai Chau, Son La, and Van Bu in the mountains of northwest Tonkin.

Siam, fearing that the court of Hué would invoke the Protectorate to compel the French military to reassert Annam's claims beyond the Annamite Mountains, launched its own large-scale military expedition into northern Laos in 1885. The pretext used by the Siamese was that they were protecting the inhabitants from further incursions from southern China. Indeed, for some fifteen years, Laos had been invaded by armed bands plundering and killing, and these had inflicted great suffering on the population, which called them the Ho, or Chinese.

The Siamese occupied the Plain of Jars and then dispatched two of their *commissaires* to the capital of Luang Prabang to supervise the Kingdom's affairs. Thereupon, the Quai d'Orsay sent a note to Bangkok warning that Hué claimed sovereignty over both Xieng Khouang and Luang Prabang and asking Siam to agree that a joint commission examine the boundaries of Luang Prabang on the spot. Subsequently, on May 7, 1886, Siam granted France the right to post a vice-consul to Luang Prabang. Creation of this post seemingly indicated French recognition of Siam's sovereignty over Luang Prabang, since consulates function only in foreign territories. But the matter was to end badly for the Siamese, for the Frenchman appointed to this post, Auguste Pavie, was fully alert to its prospects.

Pavie was an official of the Cochinchinese Postal and Telegraph Services who had shown considerable imagination in dealing with the peoples of southern Indochina. He departed from Bangkok with eight Cambodian bodyguards and two servants at the end of the year, and on February 11, 1887, he disembarked from his pirogue at Luang Prabang town. There the Siamese *commissaires* accorded him a polite but suspicious welcome, somewhat similar to that accorded Americans in later days by the French. The *commissaires* proceeded to frustrate his initial attempts to arrange an audience with the aged King, Oun Kham.

Four months after his arrival, at the onset of the rainy season, the Siamese troops who were the protectors of the Kingdom withdrew to Bangkok. They took along as hostages the four brothers of Deo Van Tri, a powerful White Thai chieftain at Lai Chau. In revenge, Deo Van Tri's army, composed largely of Chinese troops, descended on the undefended capital and burned it to the ground. Many of its terrified inhabitants were killed, but Pavie, acting with shrewd foresight, spirited away the septuagenarian Oun Kham to safety downstream, saving his life and preventing him from falling into hostile hands.

Thereupon Pavie persuaded the King to give up the Siamese protectorate, which had proved utterly worthless, in favor of a French protectorate. That was the beginning of French colonial rule in Laos. There is little evidence that it was the product of a grandiose and premeditated scheme. Rather, it appears to have been the accidental creation of one extraordinarily able and imaginative man.

Pavie months later returned the hostages to Deo Van Tri in perfect health, and so earned the gratitude and friendship of the Thai tribes of the Tonkin border region. And by a combination of force and skillful diplomacy, he also freed the country of the worst of the Ho marauders.

Pavie was a doer, forever clambering into his pirogue for a quick trip upstream to look into some local situation. He traveled from Luang Prabang to Hanoi, to Bangkok, to Saigon, and to most of the river junctions and outposts in between. He would sit down with his small retinue in a village headman's house and exchange tales over a jug of stiff *choum,* or rice wine, sucked through long straws, and the next day he would be off on the trail again, over mountain passes and through steaming valleys. In this way he won over the tribal leaders and could show the French tricolor in regions two weeks' march from any sizable town.[2]

In 1888, at a large gathering in the Dien Bien Phu valley, he personally received Siam's renunciation of its claim to the Douze Cantons (in Thai, Sipsong Chuthai), an extensive almond-shaped territory lying along a perpendicular drawn midway along the Luang Prabang–Hanoi axis.

Incidents between Siamese and French officials in Khammouane disturbed Pavie, and in February, 1889, he traveled there to warn the Siamese representatives to avoid any hostile moves. By now, the official French position was that this territory, which had once paid tribute to Annam, was French-protected by virtue of the Treaty of Protectorate with Annam. (This application of European legal concepts to the feuds among the principalities of Indochina has been a basic concept for later apologists for French colonization.)

After further incidents, the French dispatched a naval contingent to Bangkok. Under this pressure, Siam signed a treaty on October 3, 1893, renouncing all claims on the left bank of the Mekong, both north and south. Subsequent Franco-Siamese conventions in 1902, 1904, and 1907 attached certain right-bank territories to Luang Prabang and Champassak.

One of Pavie's last achievements before leaving Laos was the organization of the northernmost provinces, including the careful mapping of the border with Vietnam (apportioning part of the Douze Cantons to the latter and part to Luang Prabang) and joint surveys with British and Chinese commissions to establish the borders with Burma and China. The former was fixed at the Mekong by an Anglo-French declaration of January 15, 1896, and the latter by an agreement with China during 1896–97.

With these adjustments, Laos assumed its present external boundaries. Before the advent of the French, Laos had never been surveyed, and the drawing up of maps of the country was an important administrative accomplishment of French rule.

In 1889, the town of Vientiane was made the administrative capital of French Laos. From Vientiane, the Senior Resident exercised indirect control over the protected Kingdom of Luang Prabang and direct control, through Residents, over the remaining provinces.

---

[2] Pavie's journal, which reads like an adventure story, was later published: *Mission Pavie en Indochine, 1879–1895* (10 vols.; Paris, 1898–1919).

By 1905, Laos comprised the following entities:

1. The Kingdom of Luang Prabang, which included the present provinces of Luang Prabang, Sayaboury, Sam Neua, and the two southern districts of Phong Saly. The monarch retained his royal title and prerogatives under French protection, but in all important respects its administration was controlled by French officials.

2. The defunct Kingdom of Vientiane, which had not had a monarch since its plunder by a Siamese army in 1827.

3. The defunct Kingdom of Xieng Khouang, which had been annexed by the Vietnamese in 1832.

4. The defunct Kingdom of Champassak, whose royal family lost their prerogatives in 1900. (A portion of the kingdom lying on the right bank of the Mekong remained under Siamese suzerainty.)

5. The northern territories of Nam Tha and Phong Saly.

The French administration gave these territories a common front against outsiders, putting an end to the piecemeal depredations of Siam, Annam, and Burma. Internally, however, the French had to play a balancing game of shifting loyalties among the diverse tribes. At times the latent conflicts came to the surface, and in one twenty-year period the colonial administration spent ten years putting down three internal threats of armed conflict. The first occurred in 1901, when a number of Kha chiefs and sorcerers in southern Laos, apparently angered by French interference in their slave trade, whipped their people into a rebellion that was not fully quashed until 1907. In 1914, the Thai tribes in Phong Saly Province flared up in a revolt that was to occupy French colonial troops for a full two years. In the last of the three risings, the Meo in 1919 started raiding and looting the Lao, Kha, and other peoples, and were only halted two years later when the French reduced the affected area by cutting off its rice supply.

In addition to warring tribes, the thinly spread French security forces had to cope with pirate bands. In November, 1914, thirty Chinese pirates captured the town of Sam Neua and murdered the French *commissaire*.

The Lao benefited generally under the mild regime of French colonial rule, whose functionaries followed a live-and-let-live policy rather than enforcing any absolute code of behavior. In 1940, there were fewer than 600 French residents in Laos to govern slightly more than 1 million natives.

The official French *présence* manifested itself principally in fiscal control, education, and judicial organization. The tax collector became an accepted feature of French protection, but although taxatop to bottom with a small copper grater bearing three triangular points. They leave the sap to dry, and then collect it and wrap it in banana leaves. Then the raw blocks of brownish dried sap are sold.

The manufacture of opium, a lucrative monopoly under the French, bringing the Indochina Government General one-seventh of its total budgetary receipts,[5] is still the country's most valuable unofficial export. A recent estimate of production was between 50 and 100 tons annually, stated to be worth "200 francs the kilo in Xieng Khouang, or 5,000 francs in Saigon." Gross annual revenue to the Meo producers was estimated at "15 million francs, and 350 million francs to about a hundred traffickers."[6] An American anthropologist who visited Xieng Khouang Province shortly before the end of the French administration was told by an official that an estimated 60 per cent of the men of the province were addicted to the drug.[7]

Laos is less a nation state than a conglomeration of tribes and languages (eighteen major dialects are spoken in Phong Saly Province alone), less a unified society than a multiplicity of feudal societies. The family clan is all-important.

Life is punctuated by numerous festivals. A Buddhist celebration at the village *wat* means the decking of the temple and its courtyard with multicolored flags, the gathering of a large number of shaven-headed bonzes, their bright saffron robes gay in the sunshine, and ballad singers with chalked faces spinning tales of legendary heroes and divinities in songs, or *molams*. Some feast days are observed by shooting off crude rockets from wooden launching stands, others by throwing bucketfuls of water to the accompaniment of much laughter and joking. Fertility rites are performed annually in many villages of the far north, in the steep valleys of Nam Tha along the China border, in Sam Neua along the Vietnam border, and in the south.

A common ceremony honors a guest in a Lao home by tying a series of white strings around his wrists like bracelets, as a mark of friendship. Like many of the simple things of which Laos is made and which its peoples treasure, it is moving in its simple beauty.

[5] Extracted from figures in *Rapports au Grand Conseil des Interêts économiques et financiers et au Conseil du Gouvernement, 1938* (Hanoi: Taupin), p. 30.

[6] Georges Penchenier, "La Difficulté d'Etre Neutre," *Le Monde* (Paris), June 18–24, 1964 (weekly edition).

[7] George L. Barney, *The Meo of Xieng Khouang Province* (Los Angeles: University of California, Department of Anthropology and Sociology, Laos Project Paper No. 13, 1961), p. 27.

2.

Lao Issara

The beginning of the end of French control over Indochina came in 1940, when France fell to Germany.

After the French defeat, Japan obtained the right to station troops in Indochina and the right to use airfields there, and promised in return to leave intact the French civil service and security forces loyal to Vichy.

President Roosevelt tried unsuccessfully to effect the withdrawal of Japanese forces by means of a plan to make Indochina a "neutralized area." On July 24, 1941, he approached the Japanese Ambassador in Washington with this proposal: If Japan would make a commitment to regard Indochina as a "neutralized area" with the understanding that "the powers concerned would not undertake any military act of aggression against Indochina and would not exercise any military control within or over Indochina," he would do "everything within his power" to obtain from the Allies the same commitment.[1]

During these diplomatic interchanges, troops of the Bangkok government, which had failed in its efforts to obtain an Allied guarantee against Japanese aggression, occupied the portions of Luang Prabang and Champassak yielded by Siam under the conventions of 1902, 1904, and 1907. With Japanese mediation, Bangkok obtained from France the cession of this territory, which amounted to more than 21,000 square miles.

To compensate King Sisavang Vong for his territorial losses, which included the best of the royal teak forests in what is today Sayaboury Province, the Vichy Government agreed to formalize

[1] Department of State, *Peace and War: United States Foreign Policy, 1931–41* (Washington: Government Printing Office, 1943), p. 125.

the Protectorate over the Kingdom of Luang Prabang. Heretofore it had existed legally only in the cumulative provisions contained in declarations by Pavie, in Franco-Siamese agreements regarding sovereign rights over various pieces of territory, and in a number of Franco-Lao conventions, some of which had not even been ratified by the French Government. On August 29, 1941, the signatures of Marshal Henri Pétain and King Sisavang Vong put into force a solemn treaty defining the Protectorate. Under its terms, the territories of Vientiane, Xieng Khouang, and Nam Tha were included under the sovereignty of the Kingdom of Luang Prabang.

The End of the Protectorate

On March 9, 1945, the Japanese forces in Indochina ruptured their agreement with Vichy and staged a *coup de main* against the French, imprisoning all French civil servants and soldiers. A handful escaped into the mountains, managed to make their way northward over rough trails to China, and declared themselves for the Free French. The Japanese proclaimed an end to the colonial regimes in Vietnam, Laos, and Cambodia.

In Laos, King Sisavang Vong and his eldest son, Crown Prince Savang Vatthana, were served with a Japanese demand that they issue a proclamation of independence from the French. Instead, Savang Vatthana decreed a mass uprising of his people against the Japanese. The latter, determined to put down this royal truculence, which they had encountered nowhere in Indochina, sent a detachment of troops on a sixteen-day forced march from Vinh to Luang Prabang, which they occupied on April 5. They promptly packed the Crown Prince off to Saigon, and on April 8, King Sisavang Vong proclaimed the Treaty of Protectorate null and void.

The Japanese removal of the Crown Prince left a free hand to a man much less inclined to favor the French, Prince Phetsarath, the eldest of three remarkable brothers who belonged to the vice-regal branch of the Royal House of Luang Prabang.

In Laos, the title of viceroy, in existence since the establishment of the Kingdom of Lan Xang in the fourteenth century, conferred powers far broader than those associated with the title in the West. The viceroy, or *maha oupahat,* was the highest of the three grades of government officials. He functioned in executive and judicial capacities, and served as the king's most intimate consultant. The viceroy might perform any duties that the king decided on, including negotiating international agreements and leading the king's troops.

Frequently the viceroy convened a council of notables upon the death of the king to choose a successor from among the royal princes.

At various times, the viceroy had been the crown prince, or another of the king's sons, or a collateral relative of royal blood. For the three generations preceding Japan's surrender in World War II, the title had been vested in the family of Oun Keo, a brother of Anourouth, the last king of Vientiane. Oun Keo's son had been killed in the sacking of Luang Prabang in 1887, and Oun Keo's grandson, Boun Khong, had been confirmed as Viceroy by Pavie in 1895.[2] Boun Khong was the father of Phetsarath, who was born in Luang Prabang in 1890.

As was customary for princes of the royal blood under the Protectorate, Phetsarath was enrolled in schools in Hanoi and Saigon, the two seats of learning in Indochina. At the age of fifteen, he was sent to Paris to attend the Colonial College for French administrators. There, he developed an interest in planning the economic development of Laos, as well as a passion for hunting, and he spent one year at Oxford before returning to Luang Prabang in 1918.

Prince Phetsarath had a personal interest in the education of his two brothers, each of them more than ten years younger than he was. They were Souvanna Phouma, born on October 7, 1901, and Souphanouvong, born on July 12, 1912. Phetsarath and Souvanna Phouma were born of Prince Boun Khong's first wife, Princess Thongsy, a member of the reigning branch of the royal house, and Souphanouvong was born of a later wife, a fact that continues to influence his relations with Souvanna Phouma.

Both Souvanna Phouma and Souphanouvong followed in their elder brother's footsteps: secondary education in Indochina, university studies in France, and return to Indochina to enter the civil service under the French.

The young Souvanna Phouma enrolled in the sciences curriculum at the Lycée Albert Sarraut in Hanoi, the best secondary school in Indochina. Souphanouvong followed him there in 1921, and outshone his brother by becoming a formidable goalie on the soccer team and achieving a baccalaureate in both sciences and classics.

Souvanna Phouma went on to the University of Paris, and received a degree in architectural engineering from its Ecole Spéciale des Travaux Publics et du Bâtiment in 1928 and a degree in electrical engineering from the University of Grenoble in 1930. The fol-

[2] Paul Le Boulanger, *Histoire du Laos Français* (Paris: Plon, 1931), p. 202 n.

lowing year he arrived in Vientiane, and entered the bureau of architecture in the Public Works Service at an annual salary equiva- lent to about $2,300, a highly respectable figure for a Lao in the colonial civil service. With the blessing of the French, he rapidly rose to be chief of the bureau. Among his accomplishments was the restoration of the Wat Phakeo in Vientiane. On August 2, 1933, he married Aline-Claire Allard, a Roman Catholic and the daughter of a French father and a Lao mother.

In 1940, Souvanna Phouma was sent by the French to supervise construction of the Royal Road from Vang Vieng north of Vientiane through the mountains to Sala Phou Khoun, where the Routes Co- loniales 7 and 13 would link up. The engineering work earned Sou- vanna Phouma the title of principal engineer of the first class with the Indochinese Ministry of Public Works.

Meanwhile, Souphanouvong had followed him at the University of Paris. Again he surpassed his older brother, establishing a bril- liant record at the Ecole Nationale des Ponts et Chaussées, where he received a degree in civil engineering in 1937. During his summer vacation, Souphanouvong bicycled extensively about the French countryside, and after receiving his degree, he studied irrigation works in North Africa. He also worked on the docks of Le Havre and in the anti-Fascist Popular Front, where he made his first ac- quaintance with Communists. (How familiar he is with Communist dogma, however, is to this day a mystery. He prefers Greek classics to Marxist-Leninist texts as reading matter.)

Some months later, he again followed in his brother's footsteps, returning to Indochina and taking up a post in the Public Works Service. He was sent to Nha Trang in Vietnam, at a salary of $320 a year, low for Indochina and far below the standard for French engi- neers with the same qualifications. While in Nha Trang, Souphanou- vong married Le Thi Ky Nam, the daughter of a well-to-do local hotel owner. His wife soon revealed a driving ambition and anti- French nationalism. Souphanouvong spent most of the years from 1938 to 1945 building bridges along the excellent road network in central Vietnam, and at the time of the Japanese surrender was in the important communications center of Vinh.

The Lao Issara and the French Reoccupation

The imprisoning of French civil servants and security forces by the Japanese on March 9 was an awakening to Prince Phetsarath and his two brothers. It became clear to them that the French pres- ence in Laos was not necessarily a permanent one, and they acquired the hope, faint at first but encouraged by the democracies' enunciation of lofty war aims, that after the war they might govern their country in independence instead of under foreign domination.

The prestige of France suffered a major blow when it proved incapable of protecting Laos from spoliation by Japan, an Asian power. In Indochina, as in Malaya, Indonesia, and Burma, the Japanese occupation broke the myth of the white man's invincibility.

French power had been shattered by the Japanese *coup de main*. The surrender of Japan and the ending of World War II less than six months later removed at one fell stroke the single remaining cohesive force in Laos and Vietnam.

Phetsarath had held the title of Viceroy since 1941. At the time the Crown Prince was removed from Laos, Phetsarath was also Prime Minister. Clearly, he was the second most powerful political figure in Laos after King Sisavang Vong. When, on August 31, the former French Senior Resident was released from prison in Vientiane, where he had been placed by the Japanese, Phetsarath informed him that, the Vichy Government having gone out of existence, there was no possibility of his resuming his powers. The next day, without informing the King in Luang Prabang, Phetsarath officially reaffirmed the April 8 royal proclamation of independence from France. He followed this up on September 15 with a declaration proclaiming the union of the Kingdom of Luang Prabang and Champassak and the other territories of southern Laos in a single, independent Kingdom of Laos.

On September 17, however, he received a telegram signed by a high palace official informing him that the King regarded the Protectorate as still in force. According to one of Phetsarath's supporters, the King was forced to send this telegram by a French agent who had parachuted into Luang Prabang a few days previously.[3] Whatever the case, the telegram proved acutely embarrassing to Phetsarath, and it provoked considerable anger against the King when the people learned of it. A Defense Committee was established. Next, on October 10, a message from Luang Prabang informed Phetsarath that his titles of Viceroy and Prime Minister had been withdrawn. Two days later, on October 12, 1945, the Defense Committee voted a Provisional Constitution, formed a Provisional People's Assembly, and nominated a government, to be known as the Lao Issara (Free Laos), under the premiership of another princely official in Vien-

[3] Thao Katay refers to it as a *"télégramme inspiré par le colonel français Imfeld à Luang Prabang."* (*Le Laos* [Bangkok: Editions Lao Issara, 1948], p. 37.)

tiane, Phaya Khammao, who had been Governor of Vientiane Province. Souvanna Phouma was made Minister of Public Works.

Sisavang Vong steadfastly refused to endorse the Lao Issara, with the result that eight days later the Provisional People's Assembly voted to depose him. In Luang Prabang, a brief popular demonstration broke out in favor of the Lao Issara.

Meanwhile, Prince Souphanouvong, hopeful of an independent regime for Laos after the Japanese defeat and mindful of the support such a regime would require from Vietnam, had made contact with the leaders of the nationalist revolution in the newly proclaimed Vietnamese Republic. The Prince had traveled from Vinh to Hanoi via an airplane flight arranged by General Philip E. Gallagher, the chief of a small group of American military observers in Vietnam, who had been impressed by the efficiency with which the followers of the new Vietnamese President, Ho Chi Minh, had moved in to fill the vacuum left by the Japanese defeat.

Souphanouvong had an interview with Ho, and left bearing a letter signed by the President and introducing him to the Viet Minh Regional Executive Committee of Central Vietnam, the revolutionary apparatus in the region of Vietnam in which Souphanouvong had lived for the past six years. The letter stated that the Prince sought to form a Lao national government, and was to be offered all possible assistance by the Viet Minh regional representatives. When Souphanouvong reached Hué, on his way back to Laos, he was given a guard of fifty armed Viet Minh soldiers to accompany him as he set out for the Lao Bao Pass. This was the first instance of Vietnamese armed support for a Lao nationalist movement. The great importance that Ho attached to the expedition is clearly indicated by his granting the escort permission to carry off 100 of the Central Vietnam committee's stock of 240 rifles.

Souphanouvong, the young aristocrat with a grudge against the French but no experience in guerrilla organization, journeyed with his band of Viet Minh cadres across the Annamite Mountains— pausing at the Laos-Vietnam border to take a solemn oath to continue the struggle until an independent Laos had been won—to Savannakhet on the Mekong.

The first need was for loyal men. Recruits were mustered en route, some at Savannakhet, and many more at Thakhek, where Souphanouvong arrived in October. By November 1, after marching northward along the bank of the Mekong, Souphanouvong and his men arrived at Vientiane, where the Lao Issara government had just been formed. Phaya Khammao, desiring to broaden his political base, appointed Souphanouvong Commander in Chief of the Armed Forces. The Viet Minh stressed the disinterested nature of their support for the Lao Issara, pointing out that although there was military cooperation between the two governments, no Vietnamese held posts in Laos.[4]

The Lao Issara considered the Vichy-signed Treaty of Protectorate no longer binding upon Laos, as is made clear by various messages they sent to the French. Among these was this communication dated November 11, 1945, to the French *commissaire* in Vientiane, who was nervously awaiting the arrival of the French reoccupation force:

> You appear to ignore the facts of the situation in Indochina, as well as the attitude of the governments of the Allies, among whom the Government of France has no place. Your policies are supported only by the imperialistic British Government. You will run head-on into the determination of our people, whom your inhuman and hypocritical colonialism has sought to subjugate. All classes of people in Indochina are familiar with your colonial doctrines and your Protectorate, which is in reality a thinly veiled form of colonization. Only the egotists, traitors to their race, in quest of your gold and false honors, follow you. Your high promises will dissipate like smoke as soon as you have strangled our brave resistance. No, we have decided to live by the immemorial values of our ancestors, values that half a century of French tyranny has suppressed.[5]

Despite this bravado, the Lao Issara had reason to feel insecure so long as they faced the hostility of Sisavang Vong, who had signified his intent to maintain the French Protectorate before they had deposed him. A reconciliation was thus in order, and the Lao Issara dispatched a delegation to Luang Prabang. Sisavang Vong handed the leader of this delegation a statement affirming (1) that he agreed of his own free will to place himself under the authority of the provisional government and (2) that from the time of the Japanese surrender to his dethroning he had concluded no secret diplomatic agreements with any representative of the French Government.

Upon receipt of these assurances, the Lao Issara requested him to assume the throne of a unified Laos under a constitutional monarchy. Sisavang Vong agreed, and amid splendid pomp and circumstance, he was enthroned in Luang Prabang on April 23, 1946. In

---

[4] *Co Doc Lap* (*The Banner of Independence*) (Hanoi), October 28, 1945. For an evaluation of this claim, see Chapter 14, below.

[5] Quoted in Pierre Gentil, *Remous du Mékong* (Paris: Charles Lavauzelle, 1950), p. 32.

his first royal decree, the King proclaimed legal the October 12 Provisional Constitution and endorsed the government headed by Phaya Khammao.

Meanwhile, French reoccupation forces, after being held up on the lower Mekong awaiting reinforcements that had been diverted to quell an uprising in Cochinchina, were slowly making their way up the Mekong Valley against what resistance the meager Lao Issara army could muster.

The northernmost Lao province, Phong Saly, had already been reoccupied in February by the small Free French detachment that had escaped into China in 1945. The southernmost province, Champassak, with its pro-French governor, Kou Abhay, had been reoccupied without much trouble. But arriving at the town of Thakhek in March, the French forces encountered stiff resistance from the Lao Issara, who were openly assisted by Viet Minh agents. Commander in Chief Souphanouvong took personal charge of the badly outnumbered Lao Issara forces and underwent his baptism of fire from French mortars and machine guns. In the thick of the battle, he was seen walking with his son up and down the lines encouraging his men. He had set up a workshop in the town to manufacture crude grenades, an indication of the rudimentary state of the armament of the Lao Issara forces. On March 21, after bitter street fighting, the French occupied Thakhek, and Souphanouvong fled across the Mekong. In the boat, he was wounded in the left arm by a bullet from a strafing British Spitfire. Heavy fighting continued for several days along the rough track leading from Thakhek to the pass at Nape, which was the primary means of communication with the Viet Minh-controlled areas of Vietnam and so was defended against the French at the cost of many casualties. (British forces under General D. D. Gracey had received the Japanese surrender in southern Indochina.)

The French reoccupation proceeded along lines that soon formed a familiar pattern: The French forces directed their main efforts to securing control of the major towns; the resistance fighters were left free to retire to the countryside, where they embarked on a drawn-out war of attrition at the expense of an apathetic or terrorized peasant population.

The seeds for later French suspicions of American designs on Indochina were sown during these turbulent days. Agents of the Office of Strategic Services (OSS), who were the first Americans to arrive on the scene after the Japanese collapse, accorded a distinctly chilly reception to the French when the latter were liberated from prison camps. Some OSS agents made it quite clear that they opposed the reoccupation. A ten-man OSS mission arrived at Vientiane a month after the war's end and curtly ordered the handful of French personnel there to keep out of the town and to "cease their aggression" against the Lao Issara.[6] But it was principally in Hanoi that early signs of friendliness between the OSS agents and the Viet Minh aroused the French against the Americans.[7]

The French forces entered Vientiane on April 24, 1946, with only minor skirmishes. The Lao Issara government and Phetsarath set fire to a few public buildings and then fled across the Mekong to Siam, apparently intending to reach Luang Prabang. However, French forces assumed complete control of the royal capital on May 13, putting an end to that idea. On September 23, the French tricolor fluttered over Ban Houei Sai, the last provincial capital to be reoccupied.

Forced to remain in Siam, the Lao Issara undertook to harass the French with across-the-river raids into Laos. A strike in early May on the village of Pak Hin Boun, upstream from Thakhek, yielded considerable French arms and ammunition and encouraged the Lao Issara leaders to pursue these tactics. Emboldened by support from the local Siamese population, the Lao Issara attempted a raid on Vientiane. This time, however, French forces pursued them back across the river to the village of Tha Bo, killing a number of raiders and three Siamese. The French High Commissioner in Saigon blamed the deliberate violation of Siamese territory on "the obvious inability of the local Siamese authorities to control the activities of armed bands of Lao and Annamite rebels who have sought protection from these authorities."

Following a Siamese appeal to the United States and Britain to intercede with France to halt such violations, the U.S. Legation in Bangkok dispatched an OSS veteran, Major James Thompson, to make an on-the-spot inspection. At the house of the Governor of Nong Khai, across the river from Vientiane, his host said to Thompson: "Come upstairs. I have a Lao Prince you would find it interesting to meet." Upstairs, the major found a husky, square-shouldered man waiting, his left arm in a bandage, attended by two

[6] Peter Kemp, *Alms for Oblivion* (London: Cassell, 1961), p. 46. Kemp, who arrived in Laos in September, 1945, was a member of the British Force 136.

[7] Bernard B. Fall, *Le Viêt-Minh, 1945–1960* (Paris: Armand Colin, 1960), pp. 40–41. Also Fall, *The Two Viet-Nams* (New York: Frederick A. Praeger, 1963), pp. 68–71.

bodyguards. He introduced himself as Prince Souphanouvong. Souphanouvong told the American that his government wanted promises of official United States support for removal of the French from Laos. This meeting proved to be the first in a long series of contacts between the Lao Issara and Americans in territory outside Laos.

With the French reoccupation of their country a *fait accompli*, the Lao Issara leaders settled down to a life of exile in Bangkok, where they were given the tacit protection of the postwar government formed by the Free Thai leader, Pridi Phanomyong. Phetsarath had become the leader of the independence movement after the flight from Vientiane. He had had the foresight to take a fair amount of gold with him, so the Lao Issara had funds for at least a few months of operation as the Lao government in exile.

Souvanna Phouma remained Minister of Public Works, and in addition became Deputy Prime Minister. Souphanouvong still had command of the small Lao Issara forces, a responsibility that kept him in touch with the Viet Minh. (After his interview with Major Thompson at Nong Khai, he had returned in July to Hanoi, where an uneasy watchfulness prevailed between the Viet Minh and the French.) After arriving in Bangkok toward the end of 1946, he had also been made Minister of Foreign Affairs.

Phetsarath and Souphanouvong lived in the southern district of Bangkok in a walled compound containing five or six other houses. Through this compound moved a continual flow of Lao patriots, who came and went on mysterious errands connected with the Lao Issara guerrilla raids, which Souphanouvong and his Viet Minh advisers were beginning to mount in Laos. A Bangkok resident at whose house Souphanouvong's sons Ariya and Anou had been left while their father went off on a foray into Laos, recalls that he came out into his garden one morning and found the two boys eating live beetles from a tree. When he tried to stop them, they replied that this was part of their father's training to enable them to survive in the jungle. Souphanouvong and his Vietnamese wife and expanding brood of children became well-known figures in the Thai[8] capital. (By 1962, Souphanouvong had eight sons and two daughters.)

Souvanna Phouma lived modestly in Bangkok. He had taken a job with the Thai Electric Company, partly to keep himself professionally occupied but principally to provide for his family. While his wife was starting a business in Thai silk, he did the household

[8] In 1939, Siam became known officially as Thailand. In 1945, the country reverted to the name Siam, but since 1949, the official name has been Thailand.

marketing and acquired an interest in domestic affairs that he still retains. His thoughts, however, concentrated mainly on the political and economic future of his country. By May, 1947, he had formulated an ambitious project for the economic development of Laos.

(Phetsarath, a man of great intelligence and courage, was also extremely proud, and was piqued by the refusal of Sisavang Vong, the only figure in the Kingdom who outranked him, to restore his title of Viceroy and to include the position of Viceroy in the Constitution of 1947. After 1949, he voluntarily dropped from sight. He refused to return to Laos until 1957, when his title was finally restored. His death two years later deprived his country of an able and far-sighted statesman. He was also one of the few Lao who had an appreciation of the problems Laos' ethnic minorities presented, and he may have stimulated Souphanouvong's interest in the tribes. Sisavang Vong survived him by only fifteen days.)

The international crossroads that Bangkok had become after World War II enabled the princes to plead their cause with representatives of several nations and private interests. They asked the Americans and the British first for arms, then for money, and finally merely for diplomatic recognition of their government in exile. Souphanouvong, hoping to obtain a sympathetic ear from the Americans at least, tirelessly repeated President Roosevelt's statements that the French should not be allowed to go back to Indochina after the Japanese surrender, that they had done little or nothing for the inhabitants during their colonial administration, and that the backwardness of Indochina bore many resemblances to that of the Philippines at the time the islands were freed from Spanish rule. Later, after the United States had expressed its concern at the Dutch repressive action in Java and had partly cut off Marshall Plan aid to the Dutch, Souphanouvong also argued that since the Dutch had been in power in Java for more than 400 years, the French, who had been in Indochina less than 100 years, merited even less sympathy from the Americans. But for reasons of its European policy, Washington met the pleas of the Lao Issara with silence.

Souvanna Phouma believed that an important value of these contacts was that they compelled the French to take cognizance of the exiled leaders and their sentiments. He gave the French, who were ignoring the promulgation of the Provisional Constitution of October 12, 1945, an opportunity to advance an acceptable compromise.

Meanwhile, in Vientiane, in June, 1946, the French had set up a Franco-Lao joint commission to discuss the future relations between metropolitan France and its Lao Protectorate. This commission produced a document confirming the existence of a unified Laos under the sovereignty of the King of Luang Prabang but retaining all the French political, military, and economic powers over the Kingdom. These went so far as to allow the French to appoint administrators in each province. Laos became a member of the Indochinese Federation, a grouping without real autonomy created by the French in concession to the awakened nationalist aspirations of the peoples of Indochina. Elections were to be held within the year for a Constituent Assembly; in fifty-three years, this provision was the first concrete step by the French toward preparing the Lao for self-rule. The *modus vivendi* was signed by Crown Prince Savang Vatthana on August 27, 1946.

The French position in Vientiane was strengthened by the collaboration of Prince Boun Oum na Champassak, the heir to the throne of the defunct Kingdom of Champassak. Preferring the French as overlords to the Viet Minh and fearing that the latter's influence would grow in an anti-French guerrilla war, Boun Oum had organized anti-Japanese resistance in southern Laos in support of the Free French after the Japanese coup of March 9, 1945. In a protocol to the *modus vivendi,* Boun Oum's title of Chao (Prince) was confirmed and made hereditary, and he was named Inspector General of the Kingdom for life; in return, he renounced his sovereign rights over Champassak.

The French further bolstered their position by restoring to Laos, on January 19, 1947, the territories annexed by Thailand in 1941. France achieved this by taking advantage of the Bangkok government's desire to obtain membership in the United Nations and efface the stain of its collaboration with the Japanese.[9]

The *modus vivendi* of August 27, 1946, was totally unacceptable to the Lao Issara, who made further attempts before the year was out to obtain a French grant of total independence for Laos. Their hopes now rested largely on Baron Patrick Surcouf, an aristocrat who had returned to postwar Indochina as a businessman and who had great sympathy for the Lao. Through the good offices of Major Thompson, a meeting of the Breton baron and the Lao Issara leaders was brought about in November in Bangkok. At its conclusion, Surcouf assured the Lao leaders he would explain their point

[9] A commission composed of representatives of the United States, Britain, Peru, and the two disputant governments later reviewed the legality of territorial claims along the Mekong and found in favor of France on all counts. The text of the commission's report may be found in *Documentation Française* (Paris), No. 811, January 23, 1948.

of view to the French authorities in Saigon and return to see them again ten days later. However, Surcouf met an unsympathetic response in Saigon and was unable to return to Bangkok. Instead, the staff of the French High Commissioner, Vice Admiral Thierry d'Argenlieu, in no mood to deal with the pretenders to leadership of an independence movement in Laos, waited until the following March and then dispatched another man, who, predictably, achieved nothing in the way of reconciling the Lao Issara leaders.

Growth of Viet Minh Influence

Souphanouvong was beginning to pay more serious attention to his post of Commander in Chief of the Lao Issara forces and to the anti-French tribal-resistance organizers allied with the Viet Minh, whose activities showed signs of bearing fruit.

From the feeling of excitement that he generates even today in discussing these early, organized guerrilla activities against the French, it is evident that Souphanouvong threw himself wholeheartedly into the work; he has always preferred the outdoors to the office desk.

Soon he was making monthly trips into Laos to supervise directly the fight against the French. As a result of his efforts to forge them into an effective guerrilla movement, his followers in the field became skilled at ambushing French convoys and attacking French garrisons from mountain hideouts along the Thai border. Although the Lao Issara attacks were never as dangerous as those that the Viet Minh were beginning to mount in the Red River Delta, they proved a source of constant worry and annoyance to the French.

The Lao Issara guerrillas set up their own primitive arms workshops, using scrap metal taken from wrecked cars and trucks. One man working by himself could, if he was dexterous enough, fashion a crude rifle in a month's time. Souphanouvong's "factories" also turned out tools for the peasants. Out of plant material, women in villages controlled by the Lao Issara made paper to be used for propaganda purposes; one girl could produce about 10,000 pages a month. Batteries and tobacco had to be purchased across the Mekong, but except for this, the Lao Issara were virtually self-sufficient.

Their guerrilla activities in the countryside considerably hampered voting for the Constituent Assembly provided for in the *modus vivendi* of August 27, 1946. Nevertheless, forty-four delegates were elected on December 15, 1946. Over the next few months these delegates worked out, under French supervision, a constitution that

gave Laos a spurious independence bound up with yet another organization evolved in Paris, the French Union.

The Lao Issara's ability to survive and even grow despite armed
repression by the French was due in no small share to the untiring
efforts of the anonymous Viet Minh cadres, who held key advisory
posts. This Vietnamese contingent was fully aware that by tying
down French forces in Laos it was reducing French efforts to put
down the rebellion in Vietnam.

The French posed a grave threat for Ho's young republic. It was
even conceivable that all-out war could develop between his armed
partisans and the returning French forces. The more the French
evidenced their determination to reoccupy Indochina, the more Ho
felt the necessity of preserving the gains so far made. As a result,
he negotiated an accommodation with the French, the *modus vivendi* of March 6, 1946. Under its terms, France recognized the
republic as a "Free State having its own government, parliament,
army and treasury, and belonging to the Indochinese Federation
and to the French Union." In return, the French agreed to debark
a certain number of their troops at specified locations in Tonkin to
replace the Chinese Nationalist army of occupation (which, under
the terms of the Potsdam agreement, had received the Japanese surrender in all Indochina north of the Sixteenth Parallel). But Ho also
extracted the pledge that the French troops were to be progressively
withdrawn over a five-year period.

Nonetheless, an escalating frequency of incidents between the
French and the Viet Minh occurred toward the end of the year.
Alarm spread among the official French community in Tonkin, and
voices were raised for the adoption of a "hard line" toward the Viet
Minh. The irrevocable split came in December, when barricades
were thrown up and blood was spilled in the streets of Hanoi and
Haiphong. The Viet Minh staged a withdrawal of their forces from
the Red River Delta into the mountains.

"Negotiations with Ho Chi Minh are henceforth ruled out," declared Admiral d'Argenlieu, a man who had spent much of the
period between world wars as a Carmelite monk and who enter-
tained fixed ideas about the handling of colonial matters.[10] It was to
be more than seven years before the French again negotiated with
Ho, and by that time he would not trouble to attend the negotiations himself but send subordinates to approve the terms of the
French surrender.

[10] *France-Soir* (Paris), January 2, 1947.

The failure of the *modus vivendi* in Vietnam convinced Souphanouvong that nothing could be gained by negotiating with the French. They understood only one language: force of arms.

The Viet Minh assiduously encouraged Souphanouvong in this belief. Through their official representative in Bangkok, Nguyen Duc Quy, who saw Souphanouvong constantly, and through their well-placed advisers within the Lao Issara field organization, they exploited the Prince's isolation from Western sympathy and support.

The growing Viet Minh influence over Souphanouvong was eroding the unity of purpose with which the three princely brothers had begun their campaign of pressure against the French. Souvanna Phouma, dubious of the wisdom of Souphanouvong's leaning on the Viet Minh, was coming to look more favorably upon what the French were doing in Laos.

In Vientiane, the Constitution worked out by the Constituent Assembly was promulgated by King Sisavang Vong on May 11, 1947, the second Constitution he had promulgated in slightly more than a year. Its terms allowed Laos less real independence than the first. The preamble to the 1947 Constitution proclaimed the unity of the Lao provinces in a constitutional monarchy and declared Laos to be an independent state within the French Union. This entity had been created by the French Constitution of 1946 to give a voice to France's overseas territories. In fact, the French Union strongly underrepresented the peoples of the overseas territories in relation to the population of metropolitan France, and never gained any influence over the National Assembly or the French Government.

Laos now comprised twelve provinces: Phong Saly, Nam Tha, Luang Prabang, Sam Neua, Xieng Khouang, Sayaboury, Vientiane, Khammouane, Savannakhet, Saravane, Attopeu, and Champassak. (In the summer of 1963, subdivisions in a number of these provinces resulted in the formation of four additional provinces: Borikhane, Wapikanthong, Sedone, and Sithandone.)

The thirty-three deputies who constituted Laos' first National Assembly gathered in inaugural session on November 26, 1947, and invested a government headed by Prince Souvannarath, an elder half-brother of Souvanna Phouma. Laos' first constitutional government met on January 23 in a building of the Public Works Ministry that is today the French Embassy in Vientiane. The National Assembly's most important order of business in this parliamentary apprenticeship was to ratify the application of Prince Souvannarath's government for formal entry into the French Union. On the final day of the session, March 25, 1948, the

MAP 2. Political Subdivisions of Laos

deputies heard a lecture by the French *commissaire,* who paid tribute to their good will but warned them against "a certain tendency to confuse legislative with executive powers."[11]

The French, because of their growing need to maintain a quiet rear area during their military operations against the Viet Minh, granted more substantial independence to Laos in July, 1949. A Franco-Lao General Convention accorded Vientiane greater latitude in foreign affairs, including the right to apply for membership in the United Nations. Laos was to have its own Territorial army, but it was to be pooled with other French Union forces under a French commander in chief. The convention granting this independence, such as it was, was signed in an elaborate ceremony by Sisavang Vong at the Elysée Palace in Paris. For the first time, the royal flag of Laos, a white, three-headed elephant on a red field, was unfurled in the French capital.

The French were by now in serious difficulties, however, because they had failed to quell the Viet Minh rebellion by quick and decisive military counteraction. From all available indications, the rebel organization was growing stronger day by day. Sensing that greater strength lay on the Viet Minh side, Souphanouvong urged his brother not to collaborate with the French.

But Souvanna Phouma found the compromise acceptable and, against the advice of his two brothers, decided to join the King in Paris, where he was welcomed by the French.

Determined to go it alone with his guerrilla organization, and assured of Viet Minh support, Souphanouvong had established as early as February, 1949, a separate political front for the Lao Issara guerrilla army he commanded. He called this the Progressive People's Organization. By May, the split within the Lao Issara had become irrevocable. Souphanouvong was removed from his ministerial and military posts in the Lao Issara government. In Bangkok, on October 24, 1949, the Lao Issara announced its dissolution, and the following month a French transport plane brought Souvanna Phouma and twenty-five of the more moderate Lao Issara leaders back to Vientiane.

By the end of 1949, the only colonial territories remaining in Southeast Asia except for Indochina were Malaya, Singapore, the British Borneo territories, West New Guinea, and Portuguese Timor. The Philippines, Burma, India and Pakistan, and Indonesia had all regained their independence from European rule. The successful Communist revolution in China coincided with the upsurge of the

[11] *Bulletin d'Information de la France d'Outre-Mer,* May, 1948.

nationalist revolution in Indochina. The United States correctly saw that French concessions to the Indochinese peoples' aspirations for independence were the only means of defusing the rebellion and preventing its being taken over by the Communists. The State Department welcomed and encouraged the modest French steps toward granting independence to Indochina, although some American officials on the spot were convinced that these steps were too insignificant to be effective.

On January 14, 1950, from his mountain redoubt in Tonkin, Ho Chi Minh appealed to all foreign powers to recognize his republic. The appeal was taken up by the newly installed Communist government in Peking, and a few days later by Moscow. To demonstrate its desire to see self-determination put into effect in the countries of Indochina, the United States on February 7 announced its recognition of the French-sponsored, indigenous governments in Vientiane, Phnom Penh, and Saigon. Word of recognition was transmitted from the American Consul General in Saigon to the Vientiane government, now headed by Prince Boun Oum. But nearly five years were to pass before a resident American Minister, Charles W. Yost, arrived in Laos.

The following month, the United States dispatched a mission to Saigon to explore the possibility of granting economic assistance to the three governments. The mission discovered that the French were reluctant to allow the three supposedly independent governments to negotiate directly with the United States for economic aid and were completely unwilling to allow them to receive arms directly from the United States. A series of defeats by the Viet Minh in northern Tonkin in early 1950 reinforced French determination not to allow moves by the governments they sponsored to interfere with their prosecution of the war against the Viet Minh. And the French assured American observers that the war would be brought to a successful conclusion if only the United States furnished France the wherewithal.

A subsequent American mission was sent to Indochina to negotiate military and economic aid. It found that it was compelled to make serious compromises between aid for the U.S.-recognized governments of Laos, Cambodia, and Vietnam, and aid for the French in their war against the rebels. The mission achieved some bilateral arrangements, involving only the United States and the recipient country, in economic aid; these concerned outright grants of materials, which were not consigned through French intermediaries. However, the use of commercial imports to generate a counterpart fund of local currency, a successful technique of the Marshall Plan, played into France's hands. Payments for goods were critically affected by the exchange rates of the local currencies, and these rates in all three countries were controlled by France, which thus in effect exercised a veto over such aid.

In these negotiations, the exact relationship of the indigenous governments to France under the French Union became of capital importance, because its statutes stipulated that all agreements with foreign powers must be approved by its High Council. But this relationship was uncertain, as the French Union was even then the subject of protracted discussions in France. It became clear that, given the combination of French stalling in Indochina and the rapid succession of unstable ministries in the Fourth Republic, little progress was being made to implement Secretary of State Dean Acheson's statement that "It must be the policy of the United States to support free peoples."[12] The misgivings were made specific by the Far East Program Director of the Economic Cooperation Administration in a briefing he gave Acheson on May 2, in which he urged that the United States make an effort to find out from the French their exact plans for the Indochinese states and the role of the French Union in this: "These conditions have never been defined, and no one knows what the French Union means." And the Pau agreements, signed by France and the Associated States in November, 1950, did little to clarify the exact nature of the independence of the latter.

In Laos, the negotiations for economic aid ended in an agreement signed on September 9, 1951, by the government of Phoui Sananikone, which had succeeded that of Prince Boun Oum, and the American chargé d'affaires ad interim in Vientiane, Paul L. Guest. This agreement was to remain the basis for American aid to Laos for years to come.

The web of French control still extended everywhere, however. The endless discussions in France about the position of the Associated States, as Laos, Cambodia, and Vietnam were called, and about the future of the French Union were painfully slow in arriving at the complicated machinery that would shift administrative responsibility to the indigenous governments, and even more time was required to set it in motion. Gradually, however, the French handed over a number of administrative functions, namely those embracing foreign trade, communications, customs, finance, and immigration. Complicated interstate committees were established, on most of which the French retained an advisory or actual voting role.

[12] Department of State Bulletin, March 23, 1950, pp. 534–35.

Criticism that the American aid program was not fulfilling the policy objective of hastening the development of free and independent governments in the Indochinese states was met by reassurances by American officials that the French were on the verge of gaining the upper hand in the military situation and the United States must do nothing that might possibly undermine the French war effort. Also, it was pointed out, the French had primary responsibility in Indochina and the United States was not involved in the military conflict.

After the Communist attack on South Korea, Washington adopted the French line that the Indochina War was part of a common effort to contain Communist expansion. The anti-Communist emphasis was used periodically to justify to Congress the allocation of millions of dollars in military aid to the French in Indochina.

On the Fourth of July, 1950, Ho Chi Minh made what was to be his last direct appeal to the American people to "condemn the French colonial war waged under the aegis of the American government." There was no response to this appeal, as the United States found itself more and more deeply involved in the French war effort.

Negotiations for American military aid had been concluded in Saigon to the satisfaction of the French, and the first shipments of arms and ammunition began to flow in. On December 23, the United States concluded a quadripartite mutual-defense agreement that allowed deliveries to the governments of Laos, Cambodia, and non-Communist Vietnam but named the Commander in Chief of French forces in the Far East as the controlling authority for all material destined for the French Union forces fighting in Indochina. A clause prohibited the "illegal transport" of American war material out of Indochina; little of it did leave Indochina, but much of it ended up in Viet Minh hands and later became part of the basic arsenal of the Communist state of North Vietnam.

In Laos, Phoui Sananikone was succeeded as head of government in November, 1951, by Prince Souvanna Phouma. Although it was obvious that the continued French stranglehold on Laos was intolerable to the dissident Lao Issara leaders who had not returned to Vientiane, he nevertheless optimistically announced that his most immediate domestic goal was to achieve a "national union." If he could persuade his half brother to join him, the chances of freeing his government from French domination would be greater.

In response to continued pressures in the Associated States for genuine independence, the French Government on July 3, 1953, declared its intention to invite their representatives to another round of negotiations.

In contrast to vague promises, the true nature of the French motives was revealed by an exchange three weeks later at a meeting of the National Defense Committee in Paris presided over by the President of the Republic. At this meeting, Marshal Alphonse Juin proposed that the defense of Laos be entrusted to the Ministry of Foreign Affairs, which should then formally notify other foreign powers of Laos' vulnerability to Viet Minh invasion, and seek to obtain from the United States and Britain a guarantee of the territorial integrity of Laos and a warning to the Soviet Union and Communist China that such an invasion would entail dangerous consequences. Marshal Juin's proposal was not acted upon. The thought of extricating Laos from the web of ministries and subministries responsible "for relations with the Associated States" and making its territorial integrity the responsibility of an international body was repugnant to the French Government. A major share of the cost of the war was already being borne by the United States, in any case.

Fed up with French stalling on the question of independence, Souvanna Phouma on August 24, 1953, formally requested the transfer to his government of all the services that the French still retained control of, most immediately those connected with civil aviation, meteorology, fuel supplies, and border policing. Negotiations began in Paris on October 15, and a week later produced a Treaty of Amity and Association between France and Laos.

The first article proclaimed, "The French Republic recognizes and declares that the Kingdom of Laos is a fully independent and sovereign State." The second affirmed Laos' membership in the French Union, "an association of independent and sovereign peoples, with freedom and equality of rights and duties, in which all the associates place in common their resources in order to guarantee the defense of the Union as a whole." Certainly this can be interpreted to mean that France was obligated to do everything possible to defend Laos in the event of invasion.

Laos was now on the way to nationhood. But next door in Vietnam, the Viet Minh were fighting a war for independence from France. Inevitably, Laos must be caught up in this conflict.

3.

Collective Diplomacy

France did not purposefully embark upon the Indochina War. Instead, with little comprehension of the nationalist forces it sought to subdue, France undertook a police action and found itself helplessly sliding into a disastrous war without front that was to last for eight enormously costly years. The original reasons for fighting the "police action" soon became confused with such causes as the honor of the French Expeditionary Corps and the crusade against Communism. Eventually, the French goal was just to hang on.

The Viet Minh quickly revealed the efficiency of their machine and their ability to exploit issues to arouse popular support. Their organization derived from a congress of Vietnamese nationalist factions held in the south China town of Chingsi in May, 1941. The meeting had been dominated by a bearded revolutionary, Nguyen Ai Quoc, who had spent lengthy periods in Paris and Moscow. At a Comintern congress he had expressed the Leninist viewpoint on the revolutionary potential of the peasantry in underdeveloped countries, and he had been sent by that body to China in 1925. In 1930, he had become a founding member of the Indochinese Communist Party.

Out of the Chingsi congress had emerged a coalition called the League for Vietnamese Independence, or the Viet Nam Doc Lap Dong Minh Hoi, later to be known as the Viet Minh. Nguyen Ai Quoc adopted the pseudonym Ho Chi Minh, "He Who Enlightens," and he and his followers infiltrated back into Tonkin in 1944. There, they joined forces with a young history professor named Vo Nguyen Giap, who had been organizing partisan activities for the Viet Minh since 1942. Giap's guerrillas had already acquired a sizable arsenal of modern weapons, partly through ambushes of

French patrols and partly as rewards from the Japanese for spying and other forms of cooperation.

When the Japanese surrender came, Ho, Giap, and their partisans moved rapidly into Hanoi, and there, on September 2, 1945, from the balcony of the town hall, they proclaimed the republic. In the war that followed the breakdown of the *modus vivendi* between the Viet Minh and the French, the Viet Minh viewed Laos operationally as an extension of their battlefield against the French in Tonkin, Annam, and Cochinchina. A brief review of the engagements of the Indochina War that affected Laos directly is necessary here.

By the winter of 1952–53, the Viet Minh had consolidated their hold on the northern tier of provinces bordering China and were in a position to turn their attention to western Tonkin and to Laos, which was garrisoned by only 12,000 Lao Territorials and 3,000 French troops under command of Colonel Boucher de Crèvecoeur. In preparation for a spring offensive, Viet Minh guerrillas infiltrated into Laos, gathering intelligence and buying up stocks of rice that they cached along the trails leading southwest from the Tonkin border. At the same time, they sounded out tribal chiefs on their loyalties and obtained the allegiance of a small but important group of Lao agents.

The Viet Minh launched their offensive with two prongs. The first prong, comprising fifteen battalions drawn from the 308th, 312th, and 316th divisions, approached Sam Neua town in early April, 1953. The French and Lao defenders, only three battalions strong, received warning of the advancing larger forces and began withdrawing southward toward the Plain of Jars, of strategic military value because of its command of road communications in northern Laos.

Encountering no resistance, the Viet Minh entered the town of Sam Neua. There, assisted by their Lao agents, they conducted a public "trial" before a "people's tribunal" of the acting Governor of the province and the district officer of Xieng Kho, who were charged with treason because they had helped the French organize partisan resistance to the invaders. The two officials were quickly found guilty and summarily executed before a large crowd of spectators.

Meanwhile, the retreating French column, with only a half day's start on its pursuers, was struggling along a pony track through the spiny bamboo thickets, forests of wild banana trees or oaks, and arid plateaus between Sam Neua and the Plain of Jars.

About fifty miles from the Plain of Jars airfield, the Viet Minh caught up with the retreating column and staged an attack that scattered its men. Only 230 of them—one-third of the French effectives—survived the march and managed to reach the Plain. The airfield and surrounding defenses had in the meantime been reinforced by airborne troops and artillery and the pulling in of troops, including many Meo, from dozens of tiny outposts in Xieng Khouang Province.

The smaller prong of the Viet Minh offensive, consisting of five crack battalions, had departed from the region of Dien Bien Phu and were advancing toward Luang Prabang by the valley of the Hou River, a tributary of the Mekong. They captured Ban Nam Bac, and on April 28, when they were some thirty miles from the royal capital, linked up with part of the column that had captured Sam Neua.

Inside the royal capital of Luang Prabang, the French were hastily reinforcing their garrison. A blind bonze, renowned for his ability to predict events, declared that the Viet Minh would not enter Luang Prabang. The bonze's word spread rapidly. The King rejected French recommendations that he and his retinue be flown to Vientiane, and firmly announced he would remain in the Royal Palace. His son, Crown Prince Savang Vatthana, underscored his father's determination to stay by driving slowly around the town in his blue Chrysler for all to see. In expectation of the worst, all the Chinese shopkeepers locked up their establishments, but the Lao went about without sign of panic.[1]

By the first days of May, the Viet Minh had advanced to within striking distance of Luang Prabang by leaving behind their porters with their heavy mortars, ammunition, and food reserves. But then one of their advance companies fell into a French ambush seven and a half miles north of the capital, suffering about thirty casualties. Perhaps influenced by this indication of French preparedness or by the imminence of the annual monsoon season, the Viet Minh suddenly withdrew. Two days later the monsoon broke with a violent thunderstorm, and the torrential rains began, making impossible any large-scale fighting in the mountain country. Luang Prabang was saved—at least for the time being.

The Viet Minh troops in Sam Neua Province were reinforced by the arrival of the 304th Division up the Route Coloniale 7. They briefly occupied Tha Thom in Xieng Khouang Province on the upper Sane River, a Mekong tributary, but made no serious effort

[1] Henri Deydier, *Lokapâla* (Paris: Plon, 1954), pp. 164–65.

to dislodge the French from their fortified complex on the Plain of Jars. The French Foreign Legion had spent the few days before the arrival of the Viet Minh buying up the opium crop, which had just been harvested, to undercut a possible reason for the invasion.

After the monsoon season, at the end of 1953, a second threat to Laos materialized far to the south. A Viet Minh force, consisting of a division and a regiment, crossed the Annamite Mountains and, by a series of forest trails, advanced westward. They reached the Mekong on December 28 and occupied Thakhek. The French flew in reinforcements to the near-by base of Séno, and within a few days the Viet Minh abandoned Thakhek and dispersed into the hills of southern Laos, where they undertook extensive propaganda and indoctrination work among the mountain tribes. Some of them regrouped and crossed into Cambodia.

In November, 1953, the French had reoccupied, by paratroop landings, the flat-bottomed "bowl" of Dien Bien Phu, ten and one half miles long and three miles wide, transforming it into an armed camp. The French were compelled to protect Laos from invasion under the mutual-defense treaty of October 22, 1953, but at the same time the French commander in Indochina, General Henri Navarre, was under instructions not to take any action that would jeopardize the French Expeditionary Corps. Occupation of a position on the traditional Laos invasion route from which sorties could be effected against the Viet Minh seemed to comply with both conditions.

But by January, 1954, the garrison at Dien Bien Phu was all but encircled. With alarming rapidity, thirty-three battalions had occupied all the surrounding high ground, and an intricate maze of trenches had been pushed to within hailing distance of the barbed wire of the French fortifications. At the beginning of February, General Giap had completed the positioning of his batteries of 105-mm. guns, hauled by coolie labor into camouflaged emplacements on the crests overlooking the valley. He then detached the 308th Division on what he later described as a diversionary expedition toward Luang Prabang.[2] Once again, the hard-pressed air transport command of the French Expeditionary Corps flew reinforcements to Luang Prabang, and again the Viet Minh redoubled their tracks up the Hou River.

In all their operations in Laos, the Viet Minh held the initiative, fighting the war on their own terms. Never once did they allow

[2] Jules Roy, *La Bataille de Dien Bien Phu* (Paris: Julliard, 1963), p. 162.

themselves to be engaged in a full-scale confrontation in which French air supremacy or firepower superiority might be brought to bear. If the French had evacuated a town, as in the case of Sam Neua, the Viet Minh occupied it. If the French had prepared a positional stand, as at Luang Prabang on two occasions, the Viet Minh either retreated or rapidly bypassed the entrenched garrison.

The decision by the French to engage the enemy at Dien Bien Phu was systematic military thinking carried to its most pernicious extreme. When French forces in pursuit of the Viet Minh bands left the lowlands of the Red River Delta and ventured into northern and western Tonkin, they rapidly learned that the old plains system of scattered outposts manned by a platoon or less was hopeless in the mountains. These small forts could be easily picked off, one by one, in night guerrilla raids before reinforcements could be dispatched.

Following what seemed to be a logical train of thought, the French High Command decided to retain their "presence" in the Tonkin highlands by fortifying a smaller number of strongly entrenched camps, to be known as *bases aéroterrestres*. Each would be defended by several large units supported by heavy firepower and supplied by aircraft from the Red River Delta. Each would be a "hedgehog," whose bristling defenses would throw back an attacker with great casualties and without gain. That was the theory.

Accordingly, the French in 1953 had devoted considerable effort to setting up highland bases at Na San and Lai Chau. However, the French High Command consistently underestimated the Viet Minh ability to muster combat formations and engage in protracted hostilities in the rugged mountain country. Already, by August, 1953, the growing menace of Viet Minh encirclement had compelled the French to evacuate Na San. A few weeks later, Lai Chau was abandoned. Thus, at Dien Bien Phu, the French Expeditionary Corps had knowingly committed its best troops to defend a fortress hundreds of air miles from their main sources of supply and completely cut off from ground communications, at the very time the evidence pointed to the folly of such tactics.

The Viet Minh never had any doubt about winning the battle of Dien Bien Phu. They fired the first salvo from the slopes overlooking the entrenched camp with the keen awareness that they had caught the French in a deadly trap. When their fighters overran the entrenched camp, pock-marked from months of intensive mortar and artillery bombardment, there was no surprise, only shock that the French High Command had committed such an enormous error.

"People's War"

The Viet Minh victory would not have been possible without the support of the civilian population in the mountains of Tonkin and the thousands of laborers who kept the fighting men fed and supplied despite French harassment. General Giap, in an interview with Franco Calamandrei published in the Italian Communist Party newspaper *Unità* on April 21, 1954, when the trap had already been closed on the French and the chancelleries of Paris, Washington, and London were wringing their hands over the imminent disaster, declared: "We know that the struggle will still be a hard one, but we are not afraid that American air power will provide a decisive factor in this battle. The basic error committed by the imperialists has been, once again, to neglect the effort of which a people fighting for its independence is capable."

In Giap's view, the Viet Minh victory at Dien Bien Phu was the culmination of years of patient preparation. During this time, the enemy's will to resist had been imperceptibly sapped by a never-ending series of pinpricks. Meanwhile, the peasant masses had been rendered harmless to the Viet Minh cause by the constant attentions of the Viet Minh political propagandizers and organizers. Giap contends that if one is opposed by the mass of the people, nothing can be achieved; if one has their sympathy, much can be achieved; and if one attains their active collaboration, that is the best of all.

A Vietnamese who fought with the Viet Minh and later became a high civil servant in Saigon revealed that the political commissars of military units recruited from the local population had specific orders to make the commanders leave behind their wounded in retreat, even though they would certainly be massacred by French gunfire. The reason for this was simple: for each dead Viet Minh recruit, there would be, next day, five new recruits from the same village—the family of the dead man.

The Viet Minh pressed into service thousands of peasants. In groups and columns of a hundred or more, they transported rice over forest trails to feed the Viet Minh army; by moonlight and starlight, they filled in craters dug by French bombs in Viet Minh-controlled roads; finally, they hauled Viet Minh artillery pieces into positions from which they could rain down a hail of devastating fire on the incredulous French. Singly, the peasants poled rafts across rivers to transport Viet Minh matériel after the French bombed out the bridges, or housed couriers during the daylight hours when no one dared move for fear of attracting a strafing plane, or gathered intelligence on enemy operations for the Viet Minh High Command, deep in its jungle fastness. They did not do all this because they were highly paid; they were, in most cases, paid nothing. They did it because they had been persuaded that they were helping to fight for a just cause.

The war waged for eight years against the French began with small operations by a platoon or company and developed into battalion or regimental operations. "It was this process of development," Giap observes, "that enabled our army to move forward steadily on the road to victory."

He writes about a war of long duration and a war that places a premium on mobility. Giap is concerned with the mobility of the single jungle soldier, recruited from the local peasantry, armed with a crude rifle (perhaps even homemade), camouflaged with a Latania palm hat, and observing all the rules of cover and concealment that he has learned by heart, bearing enough rice to tide him over between villages. In concert with other men equally mobile and well trained, the guerrilla might successfully mount a predawn attack on a lonely outpost and capture a handful of modern rifles. Right then and there, the war would have undergone an evolution escalation comparable to that from a soldier armed with a pike to one armed with an English longbow.

"Guerrilla war is the war of the broad masses of an economically backward country standing up against a powerfully equipped and well-trained army of aggression," Giap writes.

"Is the enemy strong? One avoids him. Is he weak? One attacks him. To his modern armament one opposes a boundless heroism to vanquish either by harassing or by annihilating the enemy according to the circumstances, then by combining military operations with political and economic actions; no fixed line of demarcation, the front being wherever the enemy is found."

This analysis of the war where the front is nowhere and yet everywhere was successfully put to the test against the French Expeditionary Corps of 350,000 men, between 1946 and 1954.

Extent of American Involvement

As the Indochina War dragged on, going from bad to worse for the French, the United States found itself paying a greater and greater share of the cost. The amount spent by the United States is

46 · CONFLICT IN LAOS

variously estimated, but a reliable figure is $954 million.[3] Most of
this cost was borne in the closing months of the war; by September,
1953, the United States was estimated to be paying for fully 70 per
cent of the cost of the war.[4] A State Department report dated
August, 1953, lists the following war matériel supplied the French
Union Forces in Indochina: 170 million rounds of small-arms
ammunition, 16,000 transport vehicles and trailers, 850 combat
vehicles, 350 military planes, 250 naval craft, 10,500 radio sets,
and 90,000 small arms.[5] In response to repeated French requests,
the United States agreed toward the end of January, 1954, to send
200 ground personnel to Indochina to assist the hard-pressed
French in repairing and maintaining aircraft. When the cease-fire
was signed in Geneva, in July, American aid worth $25 million was
aboard ships bound for Indochina.

When defeat came to the French forces despite this massive
support, the United States experienced profound shock. Secretary
of State Dulles unjustly received much of the blame for the unhappy juncture in which the Administration found itself. He was
blamed, on the one hand, for failing to "do something" to prevent
the Communists from acquiring their first satellite since Czechoslovakia in 1948 and, on the other hand, for causing our allies
concern that the United States' overwhelming military power might
be launched without consultation on a sledgehammer-against-fly
mission that would risk plunging the world into a nuclear holocaust.

The truth is not so simple. The Administration of which Dulles
was a key figure had been voted into office barely two years before
on a foreign-policy platform that condemned the Democratic Party
for its handling of the China issue—specifically accusing it of having "denied the military aid that had been authorized by Congress
and which was crucially needed if China were to be saved."

Now, if the Administration had denied military aid to the French
in Indochina, it would stand accused of letting another Asian country fall, by default, to the Communists. Moreover, there was
McCarthyism, with its imputations of "softness" on the issue of
the Communist threat to American security. Its favorite target was,
of course, the State Department. These imputations served to reduce
further the already narrow field of maneuver on which the State
Department normally operates in dealing with foreign countries.

[3] Fall, *The Two Viet-Nams*, p. 458n.
[4] *Financial Times* (London), September 11, 1953.
[5] *The New York Times*, August 19, 1953.

n Intervention

ant section of the military led by Admiral Arthur Radford, tne Chairman of the Joint Chiefs of Staff, increasingly identified the Indochina War with centralized Communist planning in Moscow and Peking. The French, in this view, were fighting to defend the free world, to hold back the yellow hordes of Communist-indoctrinated peasant guerrillas bent on conquering all of Asia —first China, then Vietnam, and which country next? The analogy of a line of falling dominoes was used to illustrate the danger confronting the American defense system based on a chain of islands from Japan to Formosa and the Philippines. It was argued that intervention to meet the threat, either alone or in concert, was preferable to a negotiated surrender. As *The New York Times* put it in a dispatch printed on May 2, the Radford school argued that there should be "no agreement to cease firing or to an armistice or to any settlement that will permit the Communist Viet Minh to build up their strength and resume fighting more effectively later." The article concluded that "In essence, any solution in Indochina short of outright military defeat of the Viet Minh rebels is opposed by the men responsible for the military security of the United States."

In a speech to the Overseas Press Club in New York on March 29, Dulles himself suggested that unspecified forceful measures might be necessitated by the fighting in Indochina:

> Under the conditions of today, the imposition on Southeast Asia of the political system of Communist Russia and its Chinese Communist ally, by whatever means, must be a grave threat to the whole free community. The United States feels that that possibility should not be passively accepted but should be met by united action. This might involve serious risks. But these risks are far less than those that will face us a few years from now if we dare not be resolute today.[6]

Four days later, Dulles and Radford met with a bipartisan group of Congressional leaders and apparently put to them the idea of United States intervention in Indochina. There was no official report on that meeting, but the most likely speculation is that Dulles and Radford proposed that Congress adopt a joint resolution to permit the President to use American forces in Indochina. John W. McCormack, the minority whip in the House of Representatives, was present, and several weeks later said that there had been talk of a mass air attack on the besiegers of Dien

[6] Department of State Bulletin, April 12, 1954, p. 540.

Bien Phu[7] and a proposal that the leaders in the Congress "commit ourselves in Indochina without any assistance from any other country."[8]

At any rate, Dulles immediately set about building at top speed a coalition for intervention. He proposed to President Eisenhower that Britain be persuaded to join the United States, France, and friendly Asian nations in committing ground troops to fight the Communist forces in Indochina; if this intervention triggered the dispatch of troops by the Chinese in support of the Viet Minh, American air power would retaliate by destroying staging bases in south China. Eisenhower approved Dulles' proposal and cabled it to British Prime Minister Winston Churchill and Foreign Secretary Anthony Eden.

But there was an opposing school of thought. It held that the French were not defending the free world, but were attempting to preserve their own interests in Indochina, and that the Viet Minh were not a foreign army fighting a war of conquest but a Vietnamese army fighting for their country's independence. In this view, American intervention on the side of the French, with all the attendant risks, was not warranted.

In April, 1954, a Senate debate showed a large majority reluctant to support intervention if it meant commitment of ground troops. Senator Edwin C. Johnson summed up majority opinion in the Democratic Party by saying that he was "against sending American GI's into the mud and muck of Indochina on a bloodletting spree to perpetuate colonialism and white man's exploitation in Asia."[9] Senator John F. Kennedy quoted a report he himself had made in November, 1951: "In Indochina we have allied ourselves to the desperate effort of a French regime to hang on to the remnants of empire." He then proceeded to cite the difficulties of winning a war without popular support, and drew attention to the fact that not since the Mexican War had the United States intervened against a native population.[10]

Only a minority of Senators unequivocally endorsed intervention. William F. Knowland, the most vocal proponent of the "China Lobby," declared in an interview in early May that Indochina was vital to American security and that he was prepared to lead the Senate fight to send American forces there.[11]

[7] *The New York Times*, January 23, 1956.
[8] *Congressional Record*, February 22, 1955, p. 1655.
[9] *Ibid.*, April 19, 1954, p. 5281.
[10] *Ibid.*, April 6, 1954, pp. 4672–81.
[11] *Evening Standard* (London), May 4, 1954.

The Republicans upon coming into office had ended the Korean War. Clearly, sending American men to fight in Indochina almost immediately afterward would not be a popular step. Indeed, a Gallup poll in March, 1953, had reported 85 per cent of Americans opposed to U.S. involvement in Indochina, and Congressional mail reflected the same attitude.[12]

Within the Joint Chiefs of Staff, there was dissent from Admiral Radford's views. The Army Chief of Staff, General Matthew B. Ridgway, believed that intervention in Indochina could not succeed without committing ground troops, and that this was ruled out because the Army's overseas commitments were too much for the reduced manpower decreed by Eisenhower's "New Look" defense policy. Moreover, the malarial swamps of Indochina were an even more difficult battlefield than the hills and valleys of Korea, particularly since in Indochina it was difficult to tell friend from foe, while in South Korea the populace had been friendly. In an article published in the *Saturday Evening Post* in January, 1956, General Ridgway credited the Army's analysis of the hazards in Indochina with a considerable part in the decision against the project.

The Pentagon reportedly decided that the minimum ground force necessary would be about ten divisions, more than required in Korea. This was about half the total standing strength of the U.S. Army, six divisions of which were already committed in Europe. To support a force of this size would require a major remobilization.

Furthermore, this calculation presumed a limited and local war, on the Korean model. However, majority opinion in the Pentagon was reported to hold that such a limited intervention would be ineffectual, and that it would be essential to cut off the Viet Minh from China, their source of supply. This would probably necessitate a blockade of the China coast and destruction of the Chinese supply line. Thus, the military saw the appalling prospect that the United States would either become bogged down in a jungle war that had little prospect of decisively affecting world Communist power, or be plunged into a full-scale war involving Red China.

Secretary of the Treasury George M. Humphrey announced on May 25 that it was his hope to cut another $5 billion from expenditures during the forthcoming fiscal year. Defense Secretary Charles E. Wilson, also budget-minded, leaned in the direction of General Ridgway.

All this resulted in considerable confusion both at home and abroad. Representative McCormack, who had been privy to the debate within the Administration from the start, urged the Admin-

[12] *U.S. News & World Report,* May 7, 1954, pp. 25–26.

istration to give "to Congress and to our people some idea as to what its policy is in relation to Southeast Asia."

> The American people are confused, and I cannot blame them. When members of Congress are confused, it is only natural that our people should be. This lack of knowledge, creating uncertainty and confusion, is not confined to Democratic members alone. I have had a number of Republican members tell me they do not know where we are or where we are going.[13]

In London, the confusion in the British Government was even greater, as *The New York Times* reported on May 23:

> "You cannot ask us to agree when Cabinet ministers, senators and military leaders have not yet made up their minds about what we are to agree upon," an influential [British] official said.
>
> Ignorance of exactly what the United States wishes to do in terms of the international frontiers in Southeast Asia and its own contribution to their defense has become the principal problem facing the [British] Government.

The British, uncertain over which view had the upper hand in the councils of American policy-making, were fearful of unilateral American action in Indochina without prior consultation. But the firm British view that any action at such a late date was hopeless, and would only serve as a reckless provocation, minimized chances of any British cooperation.

Dulles has been criticized for publicly proposing united action to block aggression in Indochina before seeking French and British support. He has been accused of weakening the Western position at Geneva by going to London and Paris on the eve of the Conference to press for adoption of this policy. His efforts met with a public refusal by the British, and with a French request for immediate United States air intervention in the war, a request refused by Washington, hardly a demonstration of unity. Dulles' peculiar technique of diplomacy, which depended heavily on forceful public statements, compounded the confusion. As one account put it, "Much of what was said and done can be interpreted either as stage thunder or as a real storm brewing, and it should be borne in mind that, given Dulles' belief that loud and clear warnings may sometimes obviate the need for action, these categories are not necessarily mutually exclusive."[14]

[13] *The New York Times,* June 9, 1954.
[14] Coral Bell (ed.), *Survey of International Affairs, 1954* (London: Oxford University Press, for Royal Institute of International Affairs, 1957), pp. 25–26.

But the basic fact is that the conflicting pressures at home and abroad left Dulles, at Geneva, in a most difficult position.

At home, the Radford school talked forcefully in an effort to impress the Communists and bolster the Western bargaining position at Geneva. But the bolder this talk became, the more open were the British in their reluctance to go along with intervention and in their willingness to wait and see what developed at the Conference. And the more difficulty Dulles encountered in his efforts to secure British cooperation in "united action," the less chance he had of getting Congressional authorization to send American forces in support of the defenders of Dien Bien Phu, who were at grips with the Communists. It was a vicious circle.

Once Dien Bien Phu had fallen, the steam was let out of the great debate. Some news dispatches from Washington, obviously inspired by the State Department, even hinted that a trap had been avoided. Suspicion had been growing in Administration circles, it was reported, that Moscow or Peking would like nothing better than to get GI's committed to Indochina.

The 1954 Geneva Conference

The collapse of Dien Bien Phu was the collapse of the French effort to restore the pre-World War II *status quo* in Indochina by force. It could not be done with the resources at France's disposal, and the Americans, after lengthy and heated debate on the subject, were not going to help the French do it, after all. In May, 1954, therefore, delegates assembled in the gleaming white Palais des Nations in Geneva to fashion an acceptable peace.

Represented were France, the Communist-recognized state of Vietnam (the Democratic Republic of Vietnam, with Ho Chi Minh as its President), the non-Communist Associated State of Vietnam (the Republic of Vietnam, of former Emperor Bao Dai, resurrected by the French), Laos, Cambodia, the United States, Britain, Communist China, and the Soviet Union.

The Lao delegation was capably led by Phoui Sananikone, the scion of Vientiane's leading family, a civil servant since 1923, a leading member of the anti-Japanese resistance in northern Laos during World War II, and a minister in the first Lao Government to be formed in Vientiane.

Phoui was immediately confronted with the crucial necessity of defending the sovereignty of the Vientiane government against claims by Ho's representatives that a "resistance government" existed in Laos in the mountains of the northeastern provinces. Apparently in preparation for the seating of a separate Lao rebel delegation, the Viet Minh representatives had brought with them a handsome young Lao with angular features named Nouhak Phoumsavan, who was traveling on a Vietnamese passport.

Drawing attention to the rival Lao and Cambodians, the chief Viet Minh representative proposed that the Conference adopt a resolution declaring that "in the interests of the thorough and objective examination of the question of the cessation of hostilities and re-establishment of peace in Indochina, the Conference recognizes the necessity to invite the representatives of the governments of resistance of Khmer and Pathet Lao to take part in the work of the Conference in regard to the question of the re-establishment of peace in Indochina."[15]

In reply, Phoui declared that the "resistance government" in Laos represented "absolutely nothing." Recognizing such a body, he said, would mean that "all local leaders and party leaders and leaders of movements in all countries would consider they had the right to form governments and represent states."[16] For the Communists, of course, this was precisely the value of such "resistance governments."

Phoui successfully countered these claims, thanks to the stanch support of his efforts by the Western powers and to the halfhearted backing of Ho's gambit by Moscow and Peking. It was easier to set up a band of rebels in the jungle and proclaim them to be a resistance government than to gain recognition for them at an international conference. Recognition came with military victory, and the French still retained the upper hand in Laos. Pham Van Dong, leader of Ho's delegation, did not miss the point of the lesson.

The presence of Vietnamese soldiers in Laos and Cambodia posed a more serious problem for the Conference delegates. Early in the proceedings, the French Foreign Minister introduced the principle of regrouping foreign belligerent forces. Pham Van Dong subsequently took the position that there were no such forces in either Laos or Cambodia. However, the Chinese Foreign Minister, Chou En-lai, hinted privately to fellow delegates that the withdrawal of the Vietnamese from Laos and Cambodia should prove no insurmountable obstacle to agreement.

[15] Cmd. 9186, p. 113. For complete identification of official documents published by HMSO, London, see Bibliography.
[16] *Ibid.*, p. 116.

In the meantime, the French Government had fallen and Pierre Mendès-France, in an attempt to form a new one, had asked the National Assembly to give him until July 20 to negotiate a settlement of the Indochina War. Under this deadline, the Geneva delegates had produced by dawn on July 21 a series of agreements calling for a cease-fire in Vietnam, Laos, and Cambodia and a regrouping of belligerent forces in each country.

The agreement on Laos was signed by a French general on behalf of the commander of the French Union forces and by the Vice Minister of National Defense of the Democratic Republic of Vietnam, Ho Chi Minh's government, acting for the commander of the Viet Minh and for the commander of the army of the Lao "resistance government."

Unlike Vietnam, which was temporarily partitioned at the Seventeenth Parallel, with Ho's government in control of all territory to the north, Laos was reaffirmed as a unitary, independent state with a single government in Vientiane. The members of the forces of the Lao "resistance government" were to regroup in the two northern provinces of Sam Neua and Phong Saly pending integration into the Lao army or demobilization. The cease-fire agreement stipulated August 6 at 8 A.M. local time as the moment for hostilities to end.

From then on, introduction of fresh troops and armaments into Laos was prohibited. Within 120 days, all "Vietnamese People's Volunteers" were to be out of the country. All foreign powers except France were prohibited from establishing or maintaining bases on Lao soil. France was permitted to retain bases at Séno and at Vientiane, with a maximum effective total of 3,500 men. The French military were entrusted with training the Lao national army, and for this purpose were allowed to maintain a training mission of 1,500 officers and noncoms in Laos.

The Conference took note of two unilateral declarations by Phoui's delegation.[17] The first pledged that Laos "will never join in any agreement with other states if this agreement includes the obligation for the Royal Government of Laos to participate in a military alliance not in conformity with the principles of the Charter of the United Nations or with the principles of the agreement on the cessation of hostilities." It further stated: "During the period between the cessation of hostilities in Vietnam and the final settlement of that country's political problems, the Royal Government . . . will not request foreign aid, whether in war material, in personnel or in instructors, except for the purpose of its effective territorial de-

[17] For the texts of these declarations, see Appendix III.

fense and to the extent defined by the agreement on the cessation of hostilities."

In the second declaration, Phoui said his government "resolved to take the necessary measures to integrate all citizens, without discrimination, into the national community." Furthermore, the Royal Government would "promulgate measures to provide for special representation in the Royal Administration of the provinces of Phong Saly and Sam Neua during the interval between the cessation of hostilities and the general elections of the interests of nationals of Laos who did not support the Royal forces during hostilities."

The omission from the bilateral agreement of any details concerning how the dissidents were to be reintegrated and how the two northern provinces were to be turned back to the effective authority of the Royal Government was an advantage which the Viet Minh and their Lao agents were able to exploit in months to come.

On the other hand, the agreement left intact two important series of agreements, into which Laos had entered, with the United States and France, respectively, and which were to have considerable significance for Laos' alignment in world affairs after 1954.

The cease-fire agreement did not affect the agreements for economic and military aid negotiated by the United States and the Royal Lao Government in 1950. These agreements remained the basis of American support for the continued independence and integrity of the Vientiane government. Nor did the Geneva cease-fire abrogate the terms of the Treaty of Amity and Association between France and Laos, which obligated France to defend Laos from foreign aggression.

At the final session of the Conference, a Draft Declaration by the Conference was circulated, and the Co-Chairman, British Foreign Secretary Eden, requested the various delegates to express their views thereon. The Draft Declaration expressed the satisfaction of the participants at the conclusion of cease-fire agreements between the various belligerents, and took note of the unilateral declarations made by the Royal Government of Laos. It also stated: "In their relations with Cambodia, Laos and Vietnam, each member of the Geneva Conference undertakes to respect the sovereignty, the independence, the unity and the territorial integrity of the above-mentioned States, and to refrain from any interference in their internal affairs."[18]

18 Text in Appendix III.

All participants except the United States and non-Communist Vietnam gave their assent to this wording. American diplomacy was torn between the need to prevent further Communist territorial gains and the need to do everything possible to avoid the commitment of American ground forces to another war on the Asian mainland. As a result of this dilemma, Secretary of State John Foster Dulles had agreed to associate the United States in an armistice agreement in Indochina only under certain conditions.

As the cease-fire agreements worked out at Geneva, particularly the provisions with respect to the political future of Vietnam, reflected the strong position the Vietnamese Communists had gained for themselves, Dulles was reluctant to associate the United States with these agreements. The agreements in effect ratified Communist control over North Vietnam, at least until general elections could be held throughout Vietnam, in July, 1956, and Dulles feared that the Viet Minh with their efficacious political network would ensure that these elections would result in the extension of Communist control to the South as well.

In response to Eden's proposed draft at the final session, after Dulles had returned to the United States, the acting chief American delegate, Undersecretary of State Walter Bedell Smith, explained that his government was "not prepared to join in a Declaration by the Conference such as is submitted," and he thereupon read a declaration of the American position. The United States took note of the various cease-fire agreements and all but the final paragraph of the Draft Declaration (which provided for future consultation among the nations represented at Geneva in case of need to ensure that the cease-fire agreements were respected); also, the United States would "refrain from the threat or the use of force to disturb" the agreements arrived at in the Conference.[19]

The chief delegate from non-Communist Vietnam expressed certain reservations about the wording of the Draft Declaration and sought to have an amendment incorporated in it. To this request, Eden replied, "We cannot now amend our final act, which is a statement of the Conference as a whole, but the declaration of the representative of the State of Vietnam will be taken note of."[20]

Mendès-France has since explained privately that a principal reason that this final document of the Conference took the form of an unsigned Declaration bearing the heading of all participating nations was precisely to avoid the issue of who would sign and who

[19] Cmd. 9239, pp. 6–7.
[20] *Ibid.*, p. 9.

wouldn't. He foresaw that if signatures were required, the United States might well not sign, and then the Chinese also would not sign.

Dulles stated, two days after the final session of the Conference, that "since the United States itself was neither a belligerent in Indochina nor subject to compulsions which applied to others, we did not become a party to the Conference results."[21] It is difficult to reconcile this statement with the declaration of the American delegate that the United States would not upset the agreements reached. Furthermore, while American spokesmen continued to hint that they did not consider the United States bound by the agreements (the Chinese never claimed they were not bound by them), the Indian Government, as Chairman of the International Control Commission set up to supervise their implementation, adopted the position that the United States, as a participant in the Conference, was bound by the agreements reached.

However, given Dulles' suspicions regarding negotiations with the Communists, it is not surprising that he sought to avoid limitations on future U.S. actions in Southeast Asia. The actions he envisaged would become more apparent in the months following the Geneva Conference.

No agreement hard-won through negotiations, such as the Geneva agreements, can be absolutely foolproof. The terms can be circumvented when it comes time to apply them. While the 1954 Geneva agreements ending the fighting in Indochina were in no sense a settlement, they nevertheless provided a mutually acceptable basis for disengaging from armed conflict. The recurrence of such conflict cannot be ascribed solely to the loopholes in the cease-fire agreements. There are also the intentions of one's antagonist, the degree to which he sees it in his interest to adhere to agreements made, and, above all perhaps, the degree to which he believes *both* sides will respect the terms.

Once Dulles had accepted the fact that intervention by American forces could not possibly retrieve the position of the West in the Indochina War, he had specified for Eden the conditions he attached to American acceptance of a negotiated settlement. On June 29, Dulles stated the willingness of the United States to adhere to an agreement that:

    1. Preserves the integrity and independence of Laos and Cambodia and assures the withdrawal of Viet Minh forces therefrom.

    2. Preserves at least the southern half of Vietnam. . . .

[21] Department of State Press Release No. 400, July 23, 1954.

3. Does not impose on Laos, Cambodia, or retained Vietnam any restrictions materially impairing their capacity to maintain stable non-Communist regimes; and especially restrictions impairing their right to maintain adequate forces for internal security, to import arms and to employ foreign advisers.

4. Does not contain political provisions which would risk loss of the retained area to Communist control.

5. Does not exclude the possibility of the ultimate reunification of Vietnam by peaceful means.

6. Provides for the peaceful and humane transfer of those people desiring to be moved from one zone to another of Vietnam.

7. Provides effective machinery for international supervision of the agreement.[22]

The final agreements reached at the conclusion of the Conference provided for all these conditions. Not the least of these bright spots was the fact that the integrity and independence of Laos were reaffirmed and the Vientiane government was enabled to preserve its non-Communist character and to maintain forces adequate for its internal security.

No agreement, no matter how airtight, can of itself guarantee that its signatories, in Dulles' words, do not "risk loss of the retained area to Communist control." The Geneva agreements of 1954 did not consign Laos to inevitable Communist conquest. Its preservation from such conquest depended on the judicious application of strength and conciliation—in short, on the diplomacy of the Western powers.

[22] *The Memoirs of Anthony Eden: Full Circle* (Boston: Houghton Mifflin, 1960), p. 149.

4.

Collective Defense

The withdrawal of the French military presence from Indochina in the wake of the Geneva cease-fire threatened to create something feared by statesmen—a power vacuum on the rim of a major, expansionist state. For Secretary of State John Foster Dulles, collective security was the solution; after July 20, 1954, he devoted his energies to forging an alliance of anti-Communist governments in Southeast Asia and to extending to their territories the "umbrella" of American nuclear strategic deterrence.

The idea of an alliance of European powers and the United States to protect the small states of Southeast Asia from Communist expansion had first been suggested by the French statesman Robert Schuman in June, 1952. It had figured prominently in discussions concerning "united action" in Indochina prior to Dien Bien Phu, and had subsequently been set down on paper in draft form.

The second component in Dulles' strategy to prevent the Communists from filling the power vacuum was the principle of "massive and instant retaliation."[1] This concept was formalized in a speech delivered by Dulles before the Council on Foreign Relations in New York on January 12, 1954.

The Southeast Asian countries were to be defended not by American troops permanently garrisoned within their borders, but by a guarantee to all of swift and decisive American intervention in the event of invasion by a foreign power. The binding of the United States in a treaty with Britain and France and with the Southeast Asian countries would provide the constitutional basis in the United States for such intervention and would avoid a last-minute con-

[1] Department of State Bulletin, January 25, 1954, pp. 107–108.

frontation between the Administration and Congress when intervention by American forces was judged necessary.

The non-Communist governments of Laos, Cambodia, Vietnam, Thailand, and the Philippines shared a desire for a firm, binding arrangement with the major non-Communist power in the area, the United States. However, because of the agreements reached at the Geneva Conference, in particular the unwritten understandings that the British and French reached with Chou En-lai, it was doubtful whether Laos, Cambodia, and Vietnam could become full members of the planned alliance. On July 23, 1954, Dulles declared that it was "not clear" whether the three Associated States could join the alliance, although they could be included in the area of its protection.[2]

One of Chou's chief objectives at the Conference had been to exclude the United States military presence from Indochina. In the Chinese view, the defense alliance, which was already being talked about openly before the Conference met, would allow the United States to establish new bases on the Asian mainland, station troops there, and dispatch military training missions. During these years, Peking's preoccupation with American bases on its rim colored its entire foreign policy. At Geneva, the Chinese bent all their efforts toward securing guarantees excluding such bases, even allowing they would tolerate the continuance of French troops in the Indochina states provided the Americans were excluded.

The Chinese diplomatic objective was not incompatible with French and British desires to see these states neutralized—that is, with no foreign troops garrisoned on their soil and with no foreign bases. A few days before the Geneva Conference deadline imposed by Pierre Mendès-France, Anthony Eden, Co-Chairman of the Conference and chief representative of a nonbelligerent big power, was using his influence to bring about a cease-fire agreement between the Viet Minh and the French on the one hand, and an accommodation between the extreme demands of the Chinese and the Americans on the other. Toward this end, he held a private meeting with Chou and the French Premier. According to one reliable account,

> Mr. Eden and Mr. Mendès-France reportedly assured Mr. Chou that if an armistice were reached at Geneva that neutralized Vietnam, Laos and Cambodia there could be no question of these states joining the planned Southeast Asia alliance.[3]

[2] *Times* (London), July 24, 1954.

[3] *The New York Times,* July 18, 1954. Also see Eden's account in his memoirs, *op. cit.,* p. 145. Note that whatever Chou's engagement with

Whatever the exact understanding reached, the three Associated States were not included as members of the alliance when it was finally signed the following September in Manila. All three had been favorably disposed as early as May, 1954, toward the conclusion of the alliance, and when Viet Minh elements withdrawing from their attack on Thakhek in the spring of 1954 entered Cambodia, its government had appealed for help to the United States, Thailand, and other friendly powers.

When it became clear after Geneva that these states could not count on near-by American troops to defend them against aggression, they had to seek other alternatives. Laos retained its bilateral mutual-defense treaty with France. Cambodia began exploring the possibility of a viable *rapprochement* with Peking to guarantee its sovereignty. For Thailand, a defense alliance with the United States was the logical way of preventing a repetition of the disaster of 1941, when Bangkok had vainly sought U.S. and British aid in the face of an imminent Japanese move into the country. A close alignment with the United States had become a cornerstone of Premier Pibul Songgram's foreign policy after 1947.

When the representatives of the nations that were to form the projected Southeast Asia Collective Defense Alliance met in Manila on September 6, 1954, Thailand urged the establishment of a joint force under a supreme military commander based in Bangkok. But Dulles explained that the United States opposed earmarking troops for a standing force. In the words of one observer:

> The Americans were unwilling to commit themselves to fight battles on the ground chosen by a prospective aggressor; their right to retain freedom of action indicated less an unwillingness to undertake responsibility or to engage in a necessary fight than a refusal to be compelled to fight a ground war in Thailand or Indochina.[4]

The SEATO Pact

The final treaty was signed by the United States, Britain, France, Thailand, the Philippines, Pakistan, Australia, and New Zealand. The treaty provided:

1. Each of the parties would recognize aggression by means of armed attack in the treaty area against any of the signatories, "or

---

respect to Laos and Cambodia, he did not attempt to establish relations with the non-Communist government in Vietnam, the third Associated State.

[4] George Modelski, *SEATO: Six Studies* (Vancouver: Publications Centre, The University of British Columbia, for the Australian National University, 1962), p. 96.

against any state or territory which the parties by unanimous agreement may hereafter designate," as endangering its own peace and safety, and would act to meet it in accordance with its constitutional processes (Art. 4 [1]).

2. In the case of threats other than by armed attack in the treaty area, the parties would consult immediately on measures for the common defense (Art. 4 [2]). But no action would be taken in any designated territory or state except at the invitation or with the consent of the government concerned (Art. 4 [3]).

3. The parties would establish a council, so organized as to be able to meet at any time, to provide for consultation with regard to military and other planning (Art. 5).

4. The treaty area was designated as "the general area of Southeast Asia" and the general area of the southwest Pacific, as far as 21 degrees 30 minutes north latitude. The parties might amend the designated area by unanimous agreement (Art. 8).

5. The parties undertook to maintain and develop their individual and collective capacity to resist attack and "subversive acts from without," and to cooperate in economic measures including technical assistance (Arts. 2 and 3).

6. The treaty was to remain in force indefinitely. Other states in a position to further the objectives of the treaty might accede by unanimous agreement (Arts. 7 and 10).

To the text was added a protocol designating Laos, Cambodia, and South Vietnam as areas to which the military and economic provisions should be applicable, and an American declaration that the United States' "recognition of the effect of aggression and armed attack and its agreement with reference thereto in Article 4, para. 1, apply only to Communist aggression," although in the case of other aggression or armed attack the United States would consult with the treaty powers.[5]

The treaty made it abundantly clear that the United States would not tolerate any invasion of non-Communist territory in the area on the pattern of the Korean invasion of 1950, initiated either unilaterally by Peking or Hanoi, or in council with Moscow, whose ability to exercise over-all direction of an attack mounted by a vassal state's armed forces had been amply demonstrated in Korea.

Before the Senate Committee on Foreign Relations, Dulles explained the posture of the United States under the treaty:

[5] Text in *Southeast Asia Collective Defense Treaty and Protocol* (Department of State, Treaties and Other International Acts Series, No. 3170 [Washington: Government Printing Office, 1956]).

It is not the policy of the United States to attempt to deter attack in this area by building up a local force capable itself of defense against an all-out attack by the Communists, if it should occur. We do not expect to duplicate in this area the pattern of the North Atlantic Treaty Organization and its significant standing forces. That would require a diversion and commitment of strength which we do not think is either practical or desirable or necessary from the standpoint of the United States.

We believe that our posture in that area should be one of having mobile striking power, and the ability to use that against the sources of aggression if it occurs. We believe that is more effective than if we tried to pin down American forces at the many points around the circumference of the Communist world in that area.

It may be that other countries of the area will want to dedicate particular forces for the protection of the area under this treaty. But we made clear at Manila that it was not the intention of the United States to build up a large local force including, for example, United States ground troops for that area, but that we rely upon the deterrent power of our mobile striking force.[6]

Communist China, with its standing army of 2.5 million men, of course dominated the thoughts of the treaty signatories when they considered the threat of aggression in Southeast Asia. During the Congressional hearings on treaty ratification, Dulles reviewed all the sources of current disturbances in the territories covered by the treaty, and concluded: "All of these facts, and others which I could adduce, indicate that there persists an aggressive intention on the part of the Chinese Communists which belies their protestations of a desire for peace."[7]

The Prospect from Hanoi

Dulles' statements during the Dien Bien Phu crisis had dwelt heavily on Chinese aid to the Viet Minh and on the alleged threat of Chinese intervention in the fighting. Dulles had said less about the character of the Vietnamese Communists, and practically nothing about their methods of warfare.

American policy toward Ho's regime was based on U.S. military capability to deal with overt aggression anywhere in the world. The formal American commitment, under SEATO, to defend the non-

[6] Quoted in *Report of the Committee on Foreign Relations on Executive K,* 83d Cong., 2d sess. (Washington: Government Printing Office, 1955), p. 13.

[7] *Hearings Before the Committee on Foreign Relations, United States Senate on Executive K,* 83d Cong., 2d sess. (Washington: Government Printing Office, 1954), p. 12.

COLLECTIVE DEFENSE · 63

Communist governments of Southeast Asia, including that of South Vietnam, against such aggression was intended to set the men in Hanoi back by bringing the industrial heartland of the Red River Delta under threat of instantaneous destruction.

Against this poised threat, North Vietnam was powerless. Its army of 300,000 men, re-equipped with Soviet-bloc equipment after the 1954 victory, could do nothing against the nuclear weapons of the U.S. Seventh Fleet.

Behind the threat of military sanctions was a U.S. policy intended to isolate Ho's regime diplomatically and economically. It was the same policy that the U.S. had applied to China after Mao Tse-tung's victory in the Chinese civil war. The last American consul departed from North Vietnam, and no official relations were maintained with the regime. In Washington's view, the only legitimate government in Vietnam was the non-Communist government in Saigon.

Britain and France, however, reasoned that the Geneva Conference had established both the Hanoi and Saigon governments as temporary regimes with jurisdiction over separately defined territories pending Vietnam-wide elections, scheduled to take place in July, 1956. In accordance with this view, the two governments maintained consular representatives in Hanoi and ambassadorial representatives in Saigon.

Ho Chi Minh, who had fought to liberate all Indochina from French rule, emerged from Geneva with control over half of Vietnam. French power in Indochina was no more, but American power was rapidly replacing it. The partition had created, in North Vietnam, an entity of 16 million people in a traditionally rice-deficient territory. Its peasantry were exhausted by the long war, and much of its rice-producing land was untilled. The industrial complex of the Red River Delta, an earner of hard currency, had been crippled by warfare, sabotage, and neglect.

It was questionable whether North Vietnam would even be a viable state. The Frenchmen who for years had operated the power plants and communications networks were withdrawing, along with French tanks and troops. The victors pleaded with the vanquished to remain a few days longer in order to train Vietnamese replacements, and the French complied.

After the departure of the French, Ho had only the Communist bloc to turn to for economic assistance. American efforts to isolate North Vietnam and to obtain international diplomatic, financial, and commercial support for South Vietnam were largely successful. Ho welcomed promises of aid from the Soviet Union, Eastern Europe, and Communist China. Too great a reliance on these countries, he knew, would nullify his claim to have broken forever the bond of subservience that had held Vietnam under foreign domination for years past. Another limiting factor was that as time went on, the granting of economic aid within the bloc was based more and more on ideological allegiance and less and less on economic needs.

If the task of economic reconstruction was great, the task of social reconstruction was even greater. The sacrifices taken by the war, not the least of which was the sweeping up of thousands of peasants to battle zones often far from their native villages, left the countryside extremely unsettled. With the beginning of the land-reform program, the disruption of village life was enormous.

The deputies from the south of Vietnam who sat in the National Assembly in Hanoi were a constant reminder to the people of North Vietnam that half their people still remained to be liberated. When this was accomplished, their leaders promised them, once again they would have rice from the south in their bowls instead of rice from China; once again Vietnam would be one and prosperous.

For the men in Hanoi, the status of Laos was inextricably bound up with this unfinished revolution. Laos was strategically vital. Through Laos, agents could be sent into the South, resuming communications cut off by the establishment of the demilitarized zone along both sides of the heavily patrolled Seventeenth Parallel. In this, the control of the northern Laos provinces of Sam Neua and Phong Saly by a favorably disposed "resistance government" was of immense assistance. The existence of this Lao "resistance government" was more than an extension into Laos of North Vietnam's base area for carrying on the struggle for reunification; it was also an important means of putting pressure on the Vientiane government to prevent it from becoming completely amenable to American designs for transforming Laos into an anti-Communist "bastion."

Anyone who has traveled in the region of Laos adjoining North Vietnam can readily appreciate with what ease a determined political movement founded on guerrilla tactics can establish a liaison across these mountains. In all directions, range upon range of lofty mountain crests and saw-toothed ridges succeed one another. From the air, the ground appears matted by a never-ending carpet of green foliage. In the rain-drenched tropical forest of hardwoods laced with vines and creepers, absolutely nothing distinguishes the territory of Laos from that of North Vietnam. The only habitations are tiny hamlets, the only inhabitants are tribesmen walking single file down narrow paths tunneling beneath treetops and winding along stony mountain streams, and the only commerce is the trading of salt and opium.

The guerrillas who were to operate in this region were peasants by day and soldiers by night, using crude weapons easily concealed. Foreign observers flying over in an airplane or walking on the ground could see very little to support a contention that North Vietnamese soldiers were trespassing in Laos or that North Vietnam was sending arms across the border in violation of the Geneva cease-fire.

It will be recalled that in dealing with the mountain tribes of Laos, the French administrators had not interfered with the authority of the individual chiefs, wisely allowing the Kha, Meo, Yao, and Black, White, and Red Thai to pursue their own affairs under their traditional chiefs. These tribes had staged the only revolts against French rule in Laos. It was relatively easy for the Viet Minh to make contacts among the tribal peoples, and about the time of the Japanese surrender there were already agents in Savannakhet, Saravane, and Khammouane provinces sympathetic to their cause.

Ho Chi Minh carefully weighed American willingness to become involved in the affairs of Vietnam, Laos, and Cambodia. He was not absolutely sure that the Americans meant everything they said in their public speeches. If the post-1954 phase of the revolution started off in a low key, with maximum use of the front of the Lao "resistance government" and minimum overt involvement of the Vietnamese Communists, the United States would have no pretext for opposing him directly.

Limitations of the American Commitment

The SEATO treaty was geared to frontal invasion. It did not automatically commit the United States to go to the aid of Laos if the integrity of the Royal Lao Government was threatened by subversion. The nature of the commitment came out quite clearly during Dulles' testimony at the Senate hearings:

> Well, Article 4, paragraph 2, contemplates that if that situation arises or threatens, that we should consult together immediately in order to agree on measures which should be taken. That is an obligation for consultation. It is not an obligation for action.[8]

The problem of subversion in the treaty area was recognized immediately, but no real steps were taken to meet it head-on. Dulles did broach the idea of convening a conference of experienced leaders to thrash out means of countering subversion; the British had

[8] *Ibid.*, p. 25.

amassed a thick file of knowledge in Malaya, and President Magsay-say, in putting down the Huk rebellion in the Philippines, had dem-onstrated the ability of resourceful leadership to learn from its own mistakes.

Dulles said in his prepared remarks before the Senators:

> To go on now to the question of subversion, as I pointed out, we deal with that in this treaty more specifically than we have with any other treaty. We recognize the danger more clearly. I must admit that the mere fact of recognizing the danger does not mean that we automati-cally have found a way to meet the danger. Subversion in that area is a very difficult thing to combat. It is virulent, it is well organized, it is effectively prosecuted by trained persons, and the task of meeting that threat will tax our resources and ingenuity to the utmost.
>
> One reason why I am very anxious to have this treaty promptly con-sidered by this committee is that I hope it will be possible for us, per-haps even without awaiting the final coming into force of the treaty, to have a meeting of the signatories of the treaty, at which we will begin to think of ways and means that might be made available to combat this threat of subversion. This threat is most acute at the mo-ment in Vietnam, but, as I indicated, there are threats of the same character as to Laos, Cambodia, Thailand, and Malaya; and Burma and Indonesia are not free from that danger.
>
> Therefore, I think it is of the utmost importance that we should have an early meeting of the signatories in which we began to think of ways and means to meet this subversive threat which is recognized by the treaty as being a particular danger in this area.[9]

The Senate ratified the SEATO treaty in February, 1955. But the meeting with Magsaysay, who died in 1957, never took place.

The composition of membership in the alliance presented a di-versity of national interests that militated against effective common action. The SEATO member states had no unifying policy toward the lands they were to protect. France, the colonial power relin-quishing her hold on Indochina in a spirit of defeatism induced by a war that had cost her 172,000 casualties and the elite of her officer corps, was pursuing a transitional policy of disengagement. The arrival in power of General de Gaulle in 1958 was to reinforce French determination to avoid involvement in use of the West's mili-tary resources to fight an endless war with no well-defined political goals. Britain, concerned primarily with the security of Malaya and Singapore, had no wish to become entangled in an armed defense of the former colonial possessions of France. As the American-Euro-pean end of the SEATO alliance became more and more frayed, the

[9] *Ibid.*, p. 14.

conventional military capabilities of the United States—beginning with military advisers, leading to pilots and aircraft crews, leading in turn to the deployment of American troops—played an increasingly lonely role in the developing conflict.

The attitudes of the Asian member states reflected their small-power status and their geographical position. Pakistan was far away. The Philippines took the standoffish view traditional for an insular nation. Alone among the signatories, Thailand had a direct territorial stake in the question of who controlled Laos and Cambodia.

Thailand's motivation for becoming a founding member of SEATO, as we have seen, was its desire to commit the United States to come to its aid so that it would never again be in the lonely, helpless position it had faced when the Japanese occupied Southeast Asia in 1941. Thailand knew that if this commitment was not valid, it would rapidly have to adopt a "neutralist" foreign policy, just as Cambodia had done.

This dilemma was explained by a study group at Chatham House in London as follows:

> In assessing Siam's policy towards the Manila Treaty it should nevertheless be noted that the country's history during the past century demonstrates the flexibility of its foreign policy . . . should any signs of weakening appear on the part of the United States and its allies, a change of government might occur in Bangkok, and one more favorably inclined towards the Communist bloc might appear.[10]

Since Thailand signed the Manila Treaty, the confrontation between the United States and the Communist bloc in Laos has been the principal criterion by which the Bangkok government has judged the worth of its American alliance. Throughout the crises that were to recur in Laos between 1954 and 1962, the Bangkok government expressed forebodings about Communist gains as a polite means of reminding the Americans of this paramount fact. Finally, in March, 1962, the Bangkok government obtained from the United States a bilateral commitment to defend Thailand, which in effect removed Thai fears that the United States would not act in a crisis because of a rule adopted soon after the founding of SEATO that no action could be taken without the unanimous consent of the eight members.

This Thai attitude toward the achievement of its own security, an attitude that has been correctly called "mature and cautious,"[11]

---

[10] *Collective Defence in Southeast Asia* (London: R.I.I.A., 1956), p. 25.
[11] Modelski, *op. cit.,* p. 98.

quickly became one of the most important considerations in Washington's formulation of policy with regard to Laos. When future Thai policy depended on the demonstration of U.S. ability and willingness to meet the challenge of Communist expansion in Laos, Washington was under a continuing compulsion to take actions disproportionate to the intrinsic strategic value of Laos. In the effort to pose a "hard" opposition to Communist expansion in Laos, the United States used Thailand as a rear base: Supply depots were built, lines of communications extended to the Laos border, and strategic airfields constructed for jet aircraft.

In the decade following the Geneva Conference of 1954, there were compelling reasons on both the North Vietnamese side and the American side for actions in Laos that went beyond the requirements of achieving ends within Laos itself. These actions were to end up by making a mockery of the Geneva provisions for restoring peace in Indochina. There was to be no peace, and nowhere was the confrontation of wills between the United States and North Vietnam carried on with more stubbornness than in Laos.

Going well beyond its paper commitments to Laos, the United States took on the burden of underwriting the Royal Lao Government. With one eye on Thailand to the rear, the United States poured into Laos during that decade America's largest per capita foreign-aid disbursements in Southeast Asia.

Yet, this American involvement in Laos was drastically mismanaged. The experience acquired in countering subversion in the region was not translated into action, and the Royal Lao Army was forged on the very same pattern as the French army that had gone down to defeat at Dien Bien Phu. In a terrible repetition of history, the Lao army could not meet an aggression that was carried on clandestinely rather than frontally, that had the character of a rebellion by disaffected elements of the population rather than that of a foreign invasion, that bore a nationalist label rather than a Communist one. And when it came to a showdown, America's allies could not summon the unanimity on which action by SEATO depended.

The men who had installed themselves in Hanoi appreciated these facts from the start. The Americans would be able to bar the tiger from seizing its prey with one swift bound. But by cunning, dissimulation, and raw nerve, the tiger was soon to appear in the very midst of the people whom the SEATO powers had hoped to protect.

5.

Pathet Lao and a Red Prince

A few days after the Lao Issara announced its dissolution, in October, 1949, Souphanouvong set out from Bangkok on foot, leaving his wife and children to follow him by way of Hong Kong. He arrived some weeks later at the Viet Minh headquarters in Tonkin, then established at Tuyen Quang, seventy miles northwest of Hanoi in a zone held by guerrillas in relative security from the French. He was warmly welcomed by Ho Chi Minh, who held ambitious plans for the Lao Prince whom he had befriended some four years earlier.

A Lao civil servant and onetime confidant of the Prince, who was present at this meeting, asserts that Souphanouvong was seeking only arms and money, in that order, from the Viet Minh. Nevertheless, he also received some advice from Vo Nguyen Giap:

"Use the peasants as your eyes and ears and your main source of supply," he said. "Before cooking each meal, peasant women must take a handful of rice and put it in a basket. Even in hard times, they won't miss it, and you'd be surprised how soon it mounts up." As for the mountain tribesmen, Giap said, "Teach them to shoot, guide them in killing a French soldier and, by implicating them in a crime, you implicate them in the war."

Giap told Souphanouvong to keep away from towns. "People in towns have chairs, tables, shoes, beds—you can't eat those things. Country folk have rice, eggs, chickens, pigs. Remember, those who rule the countryside rule the country."

Giap, the history professor who in a few years was to win glory as the victor of Dien Bien Phu and become North Vietnam's Minister of Defense, made a profound impression on Souphanouvong. Both were academicians fighting a guerrilla war.

69

"Pathet Lao"

The Viet Minh sponsored Souphanouvong as head of a "Lao Liberation Committee," which was patterned on their own embryo administrative structure in those areas of Vietnam they already controlled and which distinguished his small following from the Lao who had chosen to collaborate with the French in Vientiane. On August 13, 1950, Souphanouvong presided over the "First Resistance Congress," convened in secrecy in Laos somewhere near the borders of Phong Saly, Sam Neua, and Luang Prabang provinces. The meeting was attended by "more than one hundred representatives of all strata and nationalities [i.e., tribal groups] and of various religious beliefs."[1]

The Congress, carefully steered by Viet Minh agents, organized a "national resistance government," with Souphanouvong as Prime Minister, grouping together a number of other Lao who had made independent contact with the Viet Minh, in some cases earlier than Souphanouvong, and who Ho felt would be valuable in furthering his plans in Laos.

The Congress adopted a twelve-point manifesto, at the bottom of which appeared the notation "Pathet Lao," literally "Land of the Lao," referring to the areas of Laos claimed to have been "liberated" from French rule. Pathet Lao was henceforth the name of the organization of which Souphanouvong was the titular head.

The twelve objectives in this revolutionary manifesto included the following:

> Driving out the French colonialists and opposing international imperialist intervention; forming an independent and united Pathet Lao and establishing a coalition government [with the French-sponsored government in Vientiane]; realizing democracy and freedom, realizing the equality of nationalities [tribal groups]; formally establishing the national army of Pathet Lao; implementing the national united front; developing industry, agriculture, and commerce; reducing taxes and rates of interest; wiping out illiteracy, developing national culture and uniting with the peoples of Vietnam and Khmer [Cambodia]."[2]

The Pathet Lao regarded themselves as successors to the Lao Issara, and adopted the October 12 date of the Lao Issara Provisional Constitution as the anniversary of the independence of Laos. The nationalist emphasis in all this was plain. But the Viet Minh

[1] *A Chronicle of Principal Events Relating to the Indo-China Question, 1940–1954* (Peking: World Culture Publishing House, 1954), pp. 34–35.
[2] *Ibid.,* p. 35.

adroitly merged the Pathet Lao goals with their own, so as to subordinate the Pathet Lao to themselves.

The concern of the Vietnamese Communists to manage the revolutions in Laos and Cambodia was shown as early as November 25, 1945, when the Vietnamese-dominated Indochinese Communist Party circulated to all regional executive committees a series of secret instructions under the title "Resistance and Reconstruction of the Fatherland (Instructions from the Central Executive Committee)." These instructions contained thirteen points appraising the international situation and defining an action program. Included in the latter was the formation of a united front against the French in Vietnam, Laos, and Cambodia. In the same month that these instructions were circulated, however, in accordance with his efforts to cultivate the non-Communist nationalists, Ho formally dissolved the Indochinese Communist Party.

It was reconstituted in February, 1951, as the Dang Lao Dong Viet Nam (Vietnamese Workers' Party). Souphanouvong attended the First Congress of the Lao Dong Party during February and March, as did a number of other Lao and Cambodian observers. The congress produced a platform containing the following significant clauses:

> The people of Vietnam must unite closely with the peoples of Laos and Cambodia and give them every assistance in the common struggle against imperialist aggression, for the complete liberation of Indochina and the defense of world peace.
>
> In the common interests of the three peoples, the people of Vietnam are willing to enter into long-term cooperation with the peoples of Laos and Cambodia, with a view to bringing about an independent, free, strong and prosperous federation of the states of Vietnam, Laos and Cambodia if the three peoples so desire.[3]

The Vietnamese Communist leadership's decision to establish a party calling itself specifically Vietnamese, rather than Indochinese, aroused considerable opposition among the middle-level cadres, who received the impression that the change sacrificed the interests of the Vietnamese beyond the Annamite Mountains. To allay these fears, the leadership of the Lao Dong Party explained that it was a well-known fact that the resistance against the French in Laos and Cambodia was being led by the Indochinese Communists (i.e., the Vietnamese Communists primarily), but that for local reasons in

[3] Quoted in Allan B. Cole (ed.), *Conflict in Indo-China and International Repercussions; A Documentary History, 1945–1955* (Ithaca, N.Y.: Cornell University Press, 1956), p. 105.

these two countries the resistance could not carry a Vietnamese label. After the victory had been won and the two countries liberated, the separate parties could once again be constituted into a single Indochinese Communist Party.

The Party explained the position fully to cadres by means of a circular. A copy of this document, marked "Top Secret" and dated November 1, 1951, was captured by the French. It stated:

> The creation of a separate party for each of the three states does not prejudice the revolutionary movement in Indochina. . . . The Vietnamese Party reserves the right to supervise the activities of its brother parties in Cambodia and Laos.
>
> The Central Executive Committee of the Vietnamese Workers' Party has designated a Cambodian and Laotian bureau charged with assisting the revolutionary movements in these countries. It organizes periodic assemblies of the three parties in order to discuss questions of common interest; it works toward the creation of a Vietnamese–Khmer–Laotian United Front. Militarily, Vietnam, Cambodia, and Laos constitute a combat zone; Vietnam has substantially assisted Cambodia and Laos militarily as well as from all other points of view.[4]

The decision to create a separate Communist Party in Laos seems not to have been immediately implemented. Although the sparse evidence available on this point is conflicting, a captured document intended for the training of Party members exists which gives March 22, 1955, as the official founding date.

For about a year during 1951 and 1952, we pick up Souphanouvong's camouflaged trail in Communist China. Certainly he had returned to Indochina before the firming up of Viet Minh plans for action in Laos in the spring of 1953.

As has been mentioned, Lao agents were involved in the Viet Minh actions in Sam Neua and Luang Prabang provinces. They were the first handful of guerrillas of the embryo Pathet Lao "army" to appear upon the scene.

Souphanouvong's Lieutenants

The organization of the Pathet Lao armed forces was entrusted to the Defense Minister in the resistance "government," Kaysone Phomvihan. Born in Savannakhet in either 1920 or 1925, Kaysone was the son of a Lao mother and a Vietnamese father, who, like many Vietnamese in Laos, worked for the French administration.

[4] Quoted in Department of State, *The Situation in Laos* (Washington: September, 1959), pp. 2–3.

Kaysone entered the University of Hanoi for medical studies in the early 1940's, when Souphanouvong was employed by the Indochinese civil service in Central Vietnam. Kaysone became active in the nationalist activities of the Students' Union and did some youth work under the direction of the Indochinese Communist Party. He became an active sympathizer of the Viet Minh and received both political and military training from them.

Ho heard of him, and in 1945 dispatched him back to his home town of Savannakhet with an important mission. He was to infiltrate another Lao nationalist movement that held some prospect of being useful to the Viet Minh. The rival movement was headed by Oun Sananikone, a leading member of the powerful Sananikone family of Vientiane. Oun had gone to Thailand during World War II, and his group was associated with the Free Thai movement, which was sponsoring the idea of an independent "Greater Laos" incorporating the Lao peoples on both banks of the Mekong. After Oun's return to Laos, however, his faction lost its dynamism and the project for a "Greater Laos" eventually disappeared from the platforms of the Lao leaders.

When Souphanouvong arrived at Savannakhet in 1945, he found Kaysone and a small group of followers already there. A dispute threatened briefly to erupt over formal leadership of the Lao resistance movement, but Kaysone deferred to the higher-ranking Prince and joined his band with Souphanouvong's. When the latter joined the Lao Issara government in Vientiane, Kaysone remained outside, but followed the Prince to Bangkok. Between 1950 and 1954, as Minister of Defense in the resistance "government," Kaysone had the task of recruiting partisans for the Viet Minh-style guerrilla force of the Pathet Lao. He subsequently held the post of Commander in Chief of the Pathet Lao forces from 1954 to 1957, the important period when the movement was consolidating its base area. He has held no government titles since then, although he is believed to be the most powerful figure today in the Pathet Lao movement.

A gifted linguist, Kaysone speaks fluent Thai, Shan, French, and English, in addition to his native Lao and Vietnamese. He has a strong distaste for the perquisites of military rank. This may explain why Kaysone himself has never divested himself of his name, which is a Lao transliteration of the Vietnamese "Cai Song," meaning "Corporal Song," and has never been referred to by officer's rank.

Kaysone is active in the military councils of the Lao Dong Party. In October, 1959, some months after the arrest of Souphanouvong in Vientiane, he was unanimously elected Vice Chairman of the Neo

Lao Hak Sat. He has not been seen in public in non-Communist countries since May, 1958, when he was defeated in the National Assembly elections in Attopeu, allegedly because of electoral rigging against Neo Lao Hak Sat candidates.

The Viet Minh had succeeded in enlisting the support of the ethnic minorities of northern and western Tonkin, overcoming the age-old animosity between lowland Vietnamese and mountain tribes.[5] Now, in 1950, Souphanouvong's "resistance government" was able to acquire as ministers two tribal leaders of Laos, Sithone Komadam and Phay Dang.

Sithone Komadam was the son of the great Kha chieftain of southern Laos who had led the 1901-7 Kha revolt against the French and who had finally been captured by them and executed. Perhaps more than any other member of the Lao dissidents, Sithone hated colonial domination. Even when addressing European visitors, Sithone has been known to use an interpreter rather than speak French.

Born about 1906 in either Saravane or Attopeu Province, Sithone crossed over the mountains into southern Vietnam during World War II, and there came upon the militant Communist Tran Van Giau. Slipping back into Laos, Sithone made contact with both the Viet Minh leadership in Tonkin and the Lao Issara government in Vientiane. His name appeared on lists of the Lao Issara faithful that were published in Vientiane at this time, but he never appeared in the Lao capital.

In the 1950 "government," Sithone, who eluded the French in Laos instead of settling in the relative security of Souphanouvong's compound in Bangkok, was Minister without Portfolio. But his principal sphere of influence continued to be the south. Two British doctors who in 1962 stumbled unwittingly into his "domain" reported that he rode a small pony over the countryside and was in constant touch with his soldiers and commissars through an elaborate network of messengers, which no doubt also kept him in contact with the Pathet Lao headquarters in the north.

Phay Dang, the other tribal leader in the "resistance government," had guerrilla bands in the Meo villages of Xieng Khouang Province loyal to him and hostile to the French. At the time of the

---

[5] One of Ho's first acts when he came to power in North Vietnam was to create a Thai-Meo Autonomous Region along the entire length of the Tonkin border with Phong Saly and Sam Neua. News of this undoubtedly had an impact among the mountain peoples in Laos, as did the fact that the Second North Vietnamese National Assembly included 56 mountaineers among its 362 northern deputies.

French reoccupation of Thakhek in March, 1946, Phay Dang, then a village headman, set about organizing his guerrillas into what later became known as the Meo Resistance League. He described his efforts in an interview in 1957:

"I heard there had been a great battle and that the townspeople had fought very bravely against the French. I thought it would be very good if we could fight together against the same enemy. I went down to the plains myself and tried to find this prince. He had already left and was in Thailand. I sent him a message and the reply came back: 'Arouse the people. Create a strong organization. Later we will fight together.' So I returned to the mountains and began to organize all the [Meo] villages from our own base. . . . Every village appointed organizers and formed scouts and defense corps."[6]

Before the Meo Resistance League, the Meo had no formal political organization, as the lowland villagers had; their family ties had traditionally knit them closely together. The difficulties of organizing the Meo were immense. Not only were they a people of independent will, but they were a people who shifted their villages frequently, especially in times of trouble, unlike the lowland Lao. Phay Dang later described the impact made on the Meo by the first manifesto of the Pathet Lao:

When the program of the Front was distributed among our [Meo] people, they saw it answered their deepest wishes. Equality for all races. Nobody had ever spoken of this before. A united fight against the French. We had never thought it possible. Abolition of unjust taxes. The French had burned and plundered our villages, massacred our people, taken our women in collecting taxes in the past. Of course, there were difficulties. We could not immediately improve the lives of the people. But it was not long before the people could see the benefits of our alliance with the Lao and others. They felt the efforts made by the Front and government to improve their lives. In place of our poisoned arrows and flintlocks we began to get some modern arms, some automatics and light machineguns. Great efforts were made to get salt to our villages. The opium tax was abolished and other taxes lightened. We formed women's associations and a youth movement. At first, membership was slow. Each village is on an isolated mountaintop and it was difficult to get people together. But after a few months people saw this was a very good thing and they joined up with great enthusiasm. From the self-defense corps we set up guerrilla bases, first of all in our own province of Xieng Khouang and then in the neighboring ones. We have 40,000 [Meo] in our

[6] Wilfred Burchett, *Mekong Upstream* (Hanoi: Red River Publishing House, 1957), p. 264.

province alone and later on we were able to form whole [Meo] companies from our guerrilla bases and attach them to the regular Pathet Lao forces formed by Souphanouvong.[7]

Souphanouvong's "resistance government" included, as Minister of Economy and Finance, Nouhak Phoumsavan, the young Lao later sent to the Geneva Conference by the Viet Minh. Nouhak remained in either Laos or Vietnam while Souphanouvong was in Bangkok, and meanwhile received intensive training from the Viet Minh.

The son of a peasant, Nouhak was educated only in primary school in his birthplace, Savannakhet. He was operating a bus line connecting Vinh, Savannakhet, and Thakhek when he first came in contact with the Viet Minh. They found Nouhak a valuable courier, and Nouhak threw in his lot with them.

In December, 1952, Nouhak was in the entourage of the Viet Minh delegation to the Peking Conference of the Asian and Pacific Regions. In May, 1954, he arrived at the Geneva Conference, after being given the additional portfolio of Pathet Lao Minister of Foreign Affairs.

When the first coalition government was eventually established in Vientiane in 1957 and the Pathet Lao "resistance government" was dissolved, Nouhak took up residence in Vientiane, and became a deputy to the National Assembly, representing Sam Neua. Later, in 1959, he was arrested, as was Souphanouvong, and escaped in the Prince's party in 1960. Nouhak headed the Pathet Lao delegation at the Ban Namone cease-fire talks in 1961. He is today the only ranking Pathet Lao leader from a peasant background.

As Deputy Prime Minister of the 1950 "resistance government," Souphanouvong picked a man who had been closely associated with him in Bangkok and who remains to this day one of his most trusted deputies, Phoumi Vongvichit. Born in 1910, the son of a Governor of Vientiane Province, Phoumi entered the Indochinese civil service and became secretary to the French Resident in Xieng Khouang. When the Pathet Lao took over administration of Sam Neua Province after the 1954 Geneva Conference, Phoumi was made Governor. In the first coalition formed in 1957, Phoumi, like Souphanouvong, entered the Cabinet at Vientiane. Phoumi became Minister of Cults, and as such skillfully indoctrinated a number of bonzes in the justness of the Communist view of world affairs.

Phoumi was dispatched to Geneva in 1961 to head the Pathet Lao delegation to the second conference on Laos. In the second

[7] *Ibid.,* p. 267.

coalition formed in Vientiane in 1962, Phoumi was again Souphanouvong's colleague in the Cabinet, this time as Minister of Information, Propaganda, and Tourism. He has a quiet, clerkish air, and handles the orthodox Communist jargon with perfection.

In his recruiting drive in the Mekong Valley in October, 1945, Souphanouvong enlisted certain members of the region's leading families. Two who joined the resistance against the French and fought side by side with Souphanouvong in his small Lao Issara army were Singkapo Chounlamany and Phoumi Nosavan.

Singkapo, scion of the leading family of Thakhek, which had provided administrative officials for Khammouane Province for three generations, abandoned both his wife and his teaching career to join Souphanouvong's guerrillas. Phoumi, a member of the powerful Voravong family of Savannakhet, was sent by Souphanouvong to learn guerrilla tactics from the Viet Minh, a training he completed in 1947. Phoumi was ambitious and determined on a military career.

When Souphanouvong took the Lao Issara dissidents into a tacit alliance with the Viet Minh in 1949, Singkapo and Phoumi were in the village of Do Luang, near the border of Laos and Central Vietnam. The two men had the alternative of staying on with the Prince in his new relationship with the Viet Minh or of journeying to Vientiane to cooperate with the French-sponsored government being set up there. The two men decided their fates by drawing matchsticks, it is said; the long matchstick signified Vientiane, and the short, Souphanouvong. Phoumi drew the long stick, the story goes, and Singkapo cursed his luck.

Singkapo had difficulty in relinquishing the bourgeois life, a price of membership in the Pathet Lao. Sent on travels abroad by the Pathet Lao high command, he gave disturbing signs of defecting to the Royal Government, and in Vientiane, his proclivity for nightclubbing got him in hot water. In May, 1955, Souphanouvong sent him to Communist China for some political reindoctrination. In 1961, he became a general in the Pathet Lao army. His second wife, like Souphanouvong's wife, was Vietnamese, and the two men have remained close associates.

Phoumi Nosavan was rewarded for his decision to return to Vientiane with rapid promotion in the territorial army the French were forming. He entered in October, 1950, as a lieutenant, and was soon fighting against the Viet Minh, who had instructed him in guerrilla tactics. By 1959, he was a brigadier general.

Securing a Base

In the mounting war with the French, Souphanouvong and his small band of Pathet Lao faithful dutifully followed in the footsteps of their mentors, the Viet Minh. In order to support their claim to represent a legitimate government fighting for independence, the Pathet Lao bent their efforts to establishing a "liberated" base area. A revealing newspaper article by Nouhak stated in 1953:

> We have not always had an extended operations base with which to support our long-term resistance.
> During April of this year . . . we liberated nearly 40,000 square kilometers of territory, which included the entire province of Sam Neua, a large part of Xieng Khouang, and part of Luang Prabang and Phong Saly provinces. . . .
> This victory gave us a vast, wide operational base full of obstacles, a base where paddy, forest products, and soil resources are abundant, a base which borders the free zone of the friendly country of Vietnam. In this place we will build up our armed forces, establish our territory, and reinforce our front.[8]

The passing reference to the Viet Minh hardly suggests that if 40,000 square kilometers of Lao territory were indeed "liberated" in April, 1953, it was done almost entirely by the Viet Minh guerrillas and not by the fledgling Pathet Lao, with their mixed leadership of displaced aristocrats, schoolteachers, and tribal chieftains.

Describing the Pathet Lao administration established in the wake of the Viet Minh invasion, Phoui Sananikone told the 1954 Geneva Conference:

> Mr. Pham Van Dong has told us that a "free Lao administration" was being installed in the occupied zones. For the good of the inhabitants I wish it were so. But alas, that is far from being the case. This so-called Government does not exist apart from the Viet Minh, and has no seat other than the Viet Minh military command posts.[9]

The Geneva agreement of 1954 gave the Pathet Lao what they most needed: security of their base area in order to proceed with consolidation of their armed forces and to impose their iron-clad rule. The agreement provided for regrouping areas for the belligerents, and allocated the two provinces of Sam Neua and Phong Saly to the Pathet Lao for this purpose.

This was to be a temporary measure to separate the belligerents

---

[8] Broadcast by Vietnam News Agency on April 24, 1953, of an article in *Lao Itsala (Free Laos)*.

[9] Cmd. 9186, p. 155.

and make the cease-fire a reality. But in November, 1954, Souphanouvong declared: "The Pathet Lao forces . . . have proclaimed the power of the Pathet Lao in the two provinces of Sam Neua and Phong Saly."

The Pathet Lao proceeded to set up all the trappings of a permanent administration in Sam Neua and Phong Saly. They established schools and print shops to publish their own textbooks. They appointed village headmen and district officers. They meted out justice according to rules of Communist Party discipline. They recruited a local militia. They stored arms and ammunition for the day when the enemy, no longer the French but the Vientiane government and its American backers, would resist their "liberation" of additional territory.

The signatories at Geneva had set up an International Commission for Supervision and Control (ICC), composed of representatives of India, Poland, and Canada, to oversee on the spot the implementation of the accords. Because of the priority enjoyed by Vietnam, the three commissioners of the ICC in Laos did not assemble until October 1, nearly two months after the ceasefire, by which time almost half the period allotted for withdrawal of Vietnamese and regrouping of Pathet Lao troops had elapsed.

After it began field operations, the ICC met with endless difficulties. Its efforts to inspect any part of the border region in order to supervise the withdrawal of "Vietnamese People's Volunteer Forces" and the demobilization of the Pathet Lao were systematically frustrated by the Pathet Lao's repeated failures to furnish facilities and liaison officers. On at least three occasions, the ICC complained in 1957, its inspection teams were fired on by Pathet Lao guerrillas. When members of one investigating team arrived unannounced in a village, they were promptly tied up. The Pathet Lao's standard explanation was that a "misunderstanding" had arisen because the ICC team had been taken for foreign agents.

The ICC's independent verification that the Vietnamese "volunteers" had withdrawn completely from Laos, as prescribed in Article 4 of the ceasefire agreement, was a farce, illustrated by the following extract from an official ICC report:

> It may be said that owing to difficult terrain and monsoon weather, particularly till the end of September, and mutual distrust between the two parties, and the fact that the Commission staff and its team did not get fully set up till early October, the withdrawals were not checked *in toto* by either the Joint Groups or the International Teams. . . . Finally, it is stressed that the Commission has had to

rely to some extent on the assurances given by the two parties that they have completely withdrawn their forces in accordance with the terms of the Geneva Agreement.[10]

The Vientiane government complained that ten Vietnamese "volunteer" officers were stationed in Sam Neua Province after the 120-day withdrawal period and that two of them held official posts. An investigatory ICC team in Sam Neua could neither prove nor disprove the allegation.[11]

The clause providing for a check on all arms shipments into Laos was equally susceptible to violation. The ICC reported:

> In November 1955, the Commission's team at Sam Neua investigated the Royal Government's complaint which had been lodged in June 1955 regarding reported import of war materials from Vietnam into the province of Sam Neua, which they later alleged in August 1955 were stored in the village of Ban That. Due to non-availability of a helicopter and of a Pathet Lao liaison officer at various times, investigation of this complaint was delayed. The team stated that no depot of arms, ammunition or equipment was found in the village or in the area surrounding the village.[12]

Meanwhile, in the rugged jungle country of the northern border region, the Communists went ahead with their efforts. Supply lines were mounted and extended across the border at will, then dismounted as rapidly. Agents came and went without fear of being observed.

But if the ICC was powerless to investigate the situation in the two border provinces, first-hand accounts of it began to be heard from defectors and other Lao whose families were very much involved in what was happening.

These accounts were later substantiated by diaries written by Vietnamese *can bo* (cadres) serving in Laos and by a United Nations mission that, in the summer of 1959, directly questioned many inhabitants of Sam Neua Province. The evidence proved that the

[10] Cmd. 9445, p. 15. One student of the ICC operations in Laos observes that "the neglect on the part of the ICC member countries in staffing their delegations seems inexcusable" and concludes that a unique opportunity open to an organization whose prestige was not yet tarnished to influence the pattern of subsequent events was thereby lost. The same dilatoriness was, fortunately, not repeated in 1961. See D. R. SarDesai, *Indian Foreign Policy in Cambodia, Laos, and Vietnam 1947–1964* (Berkeley and Los Angeles: University of California Press, 1968), p. 155.

[11] Cmd. 9630, p. 19.

[12] Cmnd. 314, p. 27.

Pathet Lao, far from being the patriotic, nationalist movement its propaganda portrayed, was nothing but a tool of the North Vietnamese Lao Dong Party.

One of the earliest reliable accounts of North Vietnamese domination of the Pathet Lao is attributed to Major Kavinh Koenakorn, a onetime secretary to a Pathet Lao political delegation to the Royal Government, who defected to Vientiane in September, 1955. He reported that the Vietnamese had absolute control of the Pathet Lao organization at all levels, and that Pathet Lao officials could decide nothing but had to obey *can bo* orders. He described how, after 1954, families in the Pathet Lao-controlled areas were deliberately split up and women and children removed across the border by the North Vietnamese to serve as hostages and as potential recruits. (Souphanouvong enrolled two of his sons in schools in North Vietnam.) Many of those sent to North Vietnam were later returned to Sam Neua, where they constituted something of a fifth column.

Phoui Sananikone, at the Geneva Conference, accused the Viet Minh of imposing "relentless social coercion" in the Pathet Lao zones:

> In the province of Sam Neua, which has been occupied since April 1953, children are sent to Viet Nam for Communist indoctrination; the whole population up to the age of fifty-six (including children and pregnant women) is forced to do haulage and road work, while rice, salt, etc., are requisitioned unmercifully.[13]

A defector, in an interview published in November, 1955, said:

> I thought I was fighting in and for my own country, but the discipline imposed by the Viet Minh [North Vietnamese] kept us in constant danger of deportation. The least argument, the smallest mistake, was greeted by the fatal words: "to be sent to the instruction center." These instruction centers were in [North] Vietnam, and no one who went there ever came back.[14]

Intensive political indoctrination in Sam Neua was closely modeled on that carried out by the Viet Minh in Tonkin during the Indochina War. A mimeographed instruction sheet distributed to Pathet Lao cadres contained this catechism:

> Question: Have the [Lao] Issara recruited new forces since the cease-fire?

[13] Cmd. 9186, p. 155.
[14] Lao Presse bulletin, Vientiane, November 26, 1955.

Answer: Never, there are only volunteers.
Question: Are the Issara requisitioning rice?
Answer: No, the residents give it voluntarily.[15]

After the cease-fire had been signed in Geneva on July 20, 1954, one of Souvanna Phouma's first acts was to renew contact with his brother. He took a plane to Khang Khay, a village on the Plain of Jars, and there the two men had a cordial reunion after five years of separation.

On his return to Vientiane, the Prime Minister expressed his conviction that an agreement reintegrating the Pathet Lao into the national community would soon be reached. He discounted the rumor that Souphanouvong had become a convinced Communist.

The Pathet Lao were now caught in a dilemma: Whether to consolidate their hold on their base area, in the expectation that force would prove the most effective means to power in Laos, or to press negotiations for a role in a coalition government, a course that would give them a minority voice in the Vientiane government but would almost certainly cost them their exclusive control over Sam Neua and Phong Saly.

Probably as a result of the influence of the North Vietnamese, who were primarily concerned over the security of their borders while the Lao Dong Party was consolidating its hold on the population, the first decision was in favor of consolidation. Royal Army troops who probed into the two provinces in an effort to reassert Vientiane's jurisdiction there were threatened with ambush by Pathet Lao guerrillas.

The Geneva agreement to leave the procedure for reintegrating the two provinces to later negotiations between the Royal Government and the Pathet Lao enabled the latter to retain its positions there in the interval. The Pathet Lao used this time to build up a solid core of cadres, on the Viet Minh model. By mid-1956, more than 3,000 partisans had been recruited from the populations of Sam Neua and Phong Saly, neither of which totaled more than 100,000. These troops released hard-core cadres for missions in the other provinces of Laos, which were nominally under Vientiane's control. In 1956 alone, several hundred cadres were dispatched from these base areas.

The Pathet Lao were unwilling to take part in the general elections for the country's unicameral National Assembly, scheduled

[15] Sisouk na Champassak, *Storm Over Laos* (New York: Frederick A. Praeger, 1961), p. 38.

for 1955 by the Geneva provisions. Seeking pretexts for boycotting the voting, the Pathet Lao demanded changes in the basic electoral law, including lowering the qualifying age for candidates from thirty to twenty-five and extending the franchise to women, and continuance of their exclusive administration of Sam Neua and Phong Saly until after the elections. When the Royal Government rejected these demands, the Pathet Lao refused to participate in the elections. After being postponed for four months, voting was held on December 25. At this time, the Royal Government's control over the countryside of Sam Neua and Phong Saly was so poor that to get blank ballots to some localities, it had to resort to dropping them from airplanes.

The country-wide voting gave eight seats out of thirty-nine to left-leaning candidates outside the Pathet Lao. The Pathet Lao branded the results "illegal and invalid."[16]

Souvanna Phouma had relinquished the post of Prime Minister in October, 1954, and had been succeeded by Katay Don Sasorith, a southerner and former Minister of Finance in the Lao Issara government. When he took office, Katay spoke hopefully of prevailing upon Souphanouvong's nationalism and bringing the Pathet Lao back into the national community:

> If it is left to the Lao, it can be worked out. . . . I believe Souphanouvong is a Lao nationalist. It is possible to cooperate with these people if we can get them away from the Viet Minh.[17]

No start could be made toward negotiating the Pathet Lao's reintegration into the national community, as envisaged at Geneva, until the insecurity in the two northern provinces had been settled. But Pathet Lao continued to resist attempts by the Royal Army to establish Vientiane's authority in these provinces; this would have prevented consolidation of the Pathet Lao base area, which was necessary to North Vietnam.

As a starting point, negotiations were limited to a regrouping of separate forces in the two provinces. Talks opened at the end of June, 1955, to the accompaniment of a Pathet Lao attack on the main government outpost in Sam Neua Province. After a long deadlock, agreement was reached on the regrouping of Royal Army troops, and a cease-fire line had almost been decided on when the Pathet Lao attacked and captured two of the government outposts

16 Cmnd. 314, pp. 6–9.
17 *New York Herald Tribune,* January 9, 1955.

whose status was being discussed. In October, a new cease-fire agreement was drawn up, which, since it prohibited reinforcements, could be said to favor the Pathet Lao; but again the negotiations on the details of the separation of the two sides broke down. Meanwhile, the Pathet Lao maintained their pressure by means of guerrilla pinpricks.

Later in 1955, Katay attempted to negotiate a political settlement with Pathet Lao emissaries in Rangoon, but without result. Finally the ICC, in a resolution adopted on January 7, 1956, advised the Pathet Lao that the Geneva accords meant that it was "the sovereign right of the Royal Government to establish its administration in the two northern provinces and this right is undisputed."

Coalition in Vientiane and Party Underground

When Souvanna Phouma returned to office as Prime Minister in March, 1956, after a sixteen-month interval, the atmosphere for political negotiations with the Pathet Lao improved considerably. He announced that reintegration of the Pathet Lao was the most important domestic task facing his new government, and he indicated that he was prepared to go outside the borders of Laos, to Hanoi and to Peking, to achieve it.

Meanwhile, however, an important meeting in Sam Neua had created a basic change in the Pathet Lao organization and brought a new departure in Pathet Lao policy toward Vientiane.

A conference of 160 leading Pathet Lao cadres, said to represent a diversity of ethnic minorities, political parties, religious bodies, and popular organizations, met in secrecy at the beginning of 1956. On January 6 they adopted a political manifesto that stressed the desirability of forming a united front, and by implication held out the possibility of a coalition with the Royal Government. A new organization was created to implement this program. It was called the Neo Lao Hak Sat (Lao Patriotic Front).

More significant, however, was the secret creation a short time earlier of a true Communist Party of Laos. This party, called the Phak Pasason Lao (People's Party of Laos), was modeled closely on the Lao Dong Party of North Vietnam.[18]

[18] The discovery of the existence of this party is the work of Paul F. Langer of the RAND Corporation and Professor Joseph J. Zasloff of the University of Pittsburgh, who conducted eight months of field work in Laos, interviewed a great number of persons in Laos and elsewhere, and made a thorough examination of documentary sources. Their joint study has been

The relationship between the Phak Pasason Lao and the Neo Lao Hak Sat (NLHS) is the relationship between the brain and the body. The NLHS, which claims to be a mass political party, and its adjunct, the Pathet Lao armed forces, expound and implement the program decided upon within the councils of the Phak Pasason Lao. The key policy-making organ of the latter is a Central Committee believed to consist of only about twenty members, with Kaysone as secretary general. The operating principle of the Phak Pasason Lao is the Marxist-Leninist principle of "democratic centralism" by which decisions are transmitted to lower echelons by means of cell meetings, which in turn voice their support for the Party line.

The NLHS also serves as a pool for recruits to the Phak Pasason Lao, whose total membership is unknown but probably numbers in the hundreds. The recruits are put through a probationary period of indoctrination and training, during which they are carefully screened. The cadre training system includes a command school for the military, another for political and military cadres, and an additional one for ethnic minorities. New members are admitted at a ceremony in which they swear unquestioning obedience to all orders received from their superior in the Party hierarchy, without regard for the race of the person issuing the order.

(The parallel of this organization with the Communist organization in South Vietnam is striking. There, the Marxist-Leninist Party known as the People's Revolutionary Party acts as the brain for the broader mass organization known as the National Liberation Front and its armed forces. The top leaders of the People's Revolutionary Party are reported to have extremely close ties with the Lao Dong Party of North Vietnam.)

For the Asian Communist movements, 1955–56 was a peaceable

---

published as *Revolution in Laos: The North Vietnamese and the Pathet Lao* (Santa Monica, Calif.: RAND Corporation Memorandum RM-5935-ARPA, September 1969).

Their discovery that the Phak Pasason Lao exists as a separate Communist Party, confirmed by recent Communist broadcasts, seems to prove conclusively that the thesis prevailing up to the time their study was published —that the Communist Party of Laos was a party called the Phak Khon Ngan whose leaders held simultaneous membership in the Lao Dong Party —was in error. In fact, as Langer and Zasloff point out, there probably never was such a Lao party as the Phak Khon Ngan, whose name is simply the Lao translation of Lao Dong (Workers') Party. I am grateful to Langer and Zasloff for their kind permission to use the fruit of their research to bring my own book up to date in this respect.

period, during which they used parliamentary tactics and accommodation with nationalist movements and governments. In South Vietnam, the passing of the July, 1956, date set at Geneva for the elections throughout both portions of Vietnam did not trigger the start of insurgency. The date passed without action because Ngo Dinh Diem, having won a referendum in the south for the post of head of state over the French puppet, Bao Dai, and crushed his major political opponents by force, refused to participate in Vietnam-wide elections. His refusal might have been taken by Hanoi as a provocation. But the insurgency did not begin until well after July, 1956, although the groundwork for such an eventuality had been laid when the Viet Minh withdrew from the south in 1954.[19]

In Laos, there was a noticeable decrease in the frequency of incidents between Royal Army troops and Pathet Lao guerrillas in Sam Neua and Phong Saly, and an easing of military pressure on government strongpoints. In this more favorable atmosphere, discussions between the two sides got under way in Vientiane on August 1, 1956.

The Pathet Lao proved themselves to be hard bargainers. It soon became clear Pathet Lao representation in a coalition government was the price for settlement of the factionalism within the country in accordance with Souvanna Phouma's hopes.

When it appeared that Souvanna Phouma would not allow himself to be swayed by the American Ambassador in Vientiane, J. Graham Parsons, who advised against such a coalition and pointed out that it had not been stipulated at Geneva,[20] Souphanouvong himself arrived in the capital to take charge of the Pathet Lao delegation.

Complete agreement on the details of the settlement was not reached until more than a year later, in November, 1957. Then Souvanna Phouma and Souphanouvong signed two documents, one political and one military, and declared their satisfaction at the prospect of "complete and early success of general reconciliation."

Two Pathet Lao leaders were taken into the Vientiane government: Souphanouvong, as Minister of Plans, Reconstruction, and Urbanism; and Phoumi Vongvichit, as Minister of Cults. The NLHS was to be permitted to operate as a political party, and sup-

[19] "Toward the end of 1957 and the beginning of 1958, the first armed self-defense units of the southern people came into existence." (*Hoc Tap* [*Studies*], Hanoi, February, 1964.)

[20] Parsons later remarked frankly: "I struggled for sixteen months to prevent a coalition." (*Hearings,* I, p. 195.) For complete identification of Congressional hearings, see Bibliography.

plementary elections to the National Assembly were to be held within four months.

Sam Neua and Phong Saly provinces were formally turned over to the authority of the King on November 18. The Pathet Lao retained a considerable voice in the new administration set up in these provinces. A Vientiane governor was appointed in Sam Neua, with a Pathet Lao deputy; a Pathet Lao governor was appointed in Phong Saly, with a Vientiane deputy. The mayor of Sam Neua town was a Pathet Lao, and the mayor of Phong Saly town a Vientiane official. Half the mayors and other officials of the two provinces were to be appointed from the Pathet Lao and half from Vientiane.

The military agreement provided that the Royal Government would take over the "entire personnel" and "entire equipment" of the Pathet Lao forces. But further clauses provided that, because of budgetary limitations, the number of Pathet Lao troops to be integrated into the Royal Army, whose size had been set at 23,650 men, would be limited to 1,500, including officers, noncoms, and men. The men to be integrated into the Royal Army would be selected by the Pathet Lao, and the remaining Pathet Lao troops would be demobilized.

At a ceremony held on February 18, 1958, at the Plain of Jars, 1,501 Pathet Lao soldiers were formally integrated into the Royal Army. This left 4,280 to be demobilized in the next few days. The rapid growth in the Pathet Lao forces since the 1954 cease-fire was explained to ICC observers by a Pathet Lao spokesman as the result of the incorporation of "volunteers." Shrewdly, the Pathet Lao leadership had selected the 1,501 from its best fighting men, many of them from the mountain tribes, and formed them into two battalions with their own weapons and officers while they said they were awaiting actual integration into Royal Army units.

The ICC sent off a report on March 5 stating that "complete integration of former Pathet Lao military personnel into the Lao National Army has been achieved."[21] But subsequent events were to show that ceremonial integration was very different from absorption of the Pathet Lao soldiers into the ranks of the army. Soon disputes broke out over the Pathet Lao's allotment of officer ranks in the Royal Army. Other difficulties arose. The issue of these soldiers was to drag on until May, 1959—and then it was to have a most unexpected denouement.

To the Vientiane government, the problem posed by the partisans

[21] Cmnd. 541, p. 74.

of the old Lao Issara independence movement at last appeared solved. In agreeing to integrate the Pathet Lao partisans into the national army and to accord their political leaders a minority voice in the Cabinet, Vientiane was reasoning along these lines: It would bring the "outsiders" on the inside by granting them responsibility in the affairs of the nation. Their acceptance of this responsibility would weaken their ties with North Vietnam. The Pathet Lao could not have it both ways; they could not participate in Cabinet decisions and at the same time foster their private rebellious movement in the jungle. So went the Vientiane logic.

Work at the Village Level

Through the systematic assignment of cadres by provinces, districts, and villages, the NLHS organized a country-wide network of cells. The cells provided a means for mobilizing popular support for the NLHS political program, which was decided upon in the secrecy of the Phak Pasason Lao and then passed down to the NLHS leaders for implementation. Conversely, the intimate knowledge of village happenings acquired by the cadres at the cell level provided a constant flow of intelligence to the central directorate.

The cell network as it existed toward the end of 1958 was analyzed by the anti-Communist newspaper *Lao Hakxa Sat*.[22] Horizontally, it was organized into study groups, family groups, and associations; vertically, the front organizations. Study groups were formed by hard-core, well-indoctrinated cadres, who gathered around themselves sympathizers who, by persuasion, coercion, or outright terrorism, were gradually rendered more and more susceptible to the NLHS political line. Some of these study groups would split, forming other study groups in neighboring villages and districts.

The newspaper attributed the success of the study-group organizers to their personal ascendancy, their dedication, and their tireless activity in gaining undisputed leadership and control. The hard-core organizers guided discussions and sponsored motions in accordance with a program that was carefully prepared at a higher echelon.

At the study-group level, there was little or no concern with a knowledge of Marxism-Leninism. On the contrary, the emphasis was on practical, down-to-earth matters that were readily comprehensible to the villagers and would be sure to enlist their support.

[22] *Lao Hakxa Sat* (*National Guardian*) (Vientiane), No. 5, November 1–14, 1958.

Instead of analyzing the struggle against "imperialism," NLHS propaganda pointed to the American aid program as evidence of a scheme to exploit Laos for foreign purposes. Potential converts were sent from their villages on trips to Vientiane so that they could get an eyeful of the luxurious homes and cars that Lao Government officials had bought with money meant to help Laos become economically independent. Because of Laos' sparse population, land reform was given little importance. As Phoui Sananikone commented: "The redistribution of land certainly figures on the program of popular movements in many Asian countries; but for anyone who knows Laos and its economic problems, it is almost cruel irony to talk of dividing up the land when there are too few inhabitants to cultivate the immense areas available."

The family group made use of the traditionally strong family ties among the Lao. It comprised between five and ten families led by a "responsible" (cadre), almost always a convinced Communist. The families of a group were summoned to a compulsory meeting every five days. At these meetings, the cadres gradually developed self-criticism and guided the participants' minds along lines of rigorous discipline. Besides using the family groups as effective channels for disseminating propaganda, the Communists also learned from them what was going on in the village. These family groups were reported to have been instrumental in preparing victories for several of the NLHS candidates who contested the elections prescribed in the November, 1957, reintegration agreement.

"Through intimidation and punitive measures, members are forced to participate willingly or otherwise," the *Lao Hakxa Sat* article said. "In the long run, apathy on the part of the more willing ones and inertia on the part of the others combine to place the population under the complete control of the cadres and make them obedient to their orders."

The front organizations grouped together persons of similar age or profession into associations of peasants, women, youth, and young girls. Through regular association meetings, through self-criticism conducted at these meetings, through shows of strength by "volunteer" militia forces, the Communists softened up the population. It was virtually impossible to resign from one of these associations.

The associations provided the Communists with a valuable picture of what was going on in the minds of the villagers. For example, in a family of four, the father might belong to the Peasants' Federation (Samakhom Sao Hai Na), the mother to the Women's

Federation (Samakhom Mae Nying Lao), the daughter to the Young Girls' Association (Youvannari), and the son to the Youth Federation (Samakhom Sao Num). Each member of the family was subjected to propaganda that, although adapted to each group's requirements, was aimed at a single objective. By conducting self-criticism sessions, the cadres soon learned all the undercurrents of the village, the people's state of mind, the danger signs pointing to the germination of rebellion. The child was led to denounce his parents, the wife her husband.

The strong organizational apparatus facilitated action that had been decided upon in secrecy at the center of the web, involving disobedience to the orders given by the traditional village headman (*nai ban*). In this resistance, the front organizations played a key role.

Through passive resistance, slanders, and rumors, honest village headmen quickly became discouraged and were led to resign. Alternatively, the population of a village, encouraged by one of the front organizations, might make a collective petition asking the district officer (*chao muong*) to change the village headman. This type of action was designed to effect the replacement of "undesirable" leaders by NLHS sympathizers.

In other instances, the population might be incited against village "capitalists," those whose standard of living was above average. Through boycotts and intimidation, the cadres forced such people to leave the village and seek asylum in the larger towns, where they felt safe. In some villages, certain inhabitants were made responsible for destroying all government propaganda arriving in the village, others for housing strangers and keeping them under surveillance.

All this elaborate organization was enforced by threats, made concrete by clandestine armed groups that appeared in the villages from time to time. Sometimes these groups passed death sentences, sometimes they passed out first or second warnings. As a last measure, assassination proved a highly effective way of undercutting the will to resist and of ensuring the obedience of the peasants.

Since the villagers could not easily disentangle themselves from the front organizations of which they were members, these organizations were able to mete out punishment to any who persisted in resisting the Party's orders. Three categories of punishment were known to the villagers, each more severe than the previous one. These were isolation, re-education, and trial by secret tribunal.

Under the first type, the offender was completely isolated from his fellow villagers. They were not permitted to give him food or shelter, and his family could not see or talk to him. He was treated as an outcast. Under the second type, the offender was removed from the village and placed in a special camp, where he was informed of his mistakes and "re-educated." The most severe form of punishment was the trial by secret tribunal; if the offender did not return to his home, the other villagers deduced the verdict.

Coercion was one tactic used by the NLHS in organizing the population; the other, applied with equal skill, was persuasion. A Royal Government report in July, 1957, observed:

> The Pathet Lao propagandist knows how to present himself as a friend who helps and advises and works with his own hands. He acts disinterestedly, shows honesty and enthusiasm and knows how to get along with a minimum of comfort.
>
> The success of his work lies in those qualities and in the fact that he is always there . . . and does not fear the ephemeral effect of the mobile information teams of the Royal Lao Government.
>
> The proof of the success of the propaganda methods of the Pathet Lao cadres can best be seen in the fact that they have succeeded in having the Lao population accept the Vietnamese as "brothers."[23]

Buddhism and its institutions confronted the NLHS with an interesting tactical dilemma. As Buddhism is strong among the lowland Lao and the bonzes form a considerable part of the population and wield great influence on Lao customs and habits, the NLHS was attracted by the possibility of using this influence for political ends.

Attempts were made by the NLHS to enlist the support of the bonzes and to bring them to the NLHS point of view on political matters, particularly during the tenure of Phoumi Vongvichit as Minister of Cults. The fact that Souphanouvong is a devout Buddhist has been of assistance in this effort, as indicated by a Lao bonze in Vientiane:

> He visits the monks at the wat and tells them of his troubles and the hardships suffered by his army when they were fighting in the forest. The soldiers were not paid any salary, and they had to beg rice in the villages. I like Souphanouvong and the Pathet Lao because they are honest people. Most of the monks sympathize with the Pathet Lao in their difficulties.[24]

[23] Quoted in Bernard B. Fall, "Informal Communications in Southeast Asia" (Washington: 1960), mimeographed, pt. 2, pp. 32–33.

[24] Quoted in Joel M. Halpern, *Government, Politics, and Social Structure in Laos* (Southeast Asia Studies, Monograph Series, No. 4 [New Haven, Conn.: Yale University Press, 1964]).

However, because the NLHS leaders and the Pathet Lao forces included a strong component of ethnic minorities, they could not take an unequivocal stand on Buddhism. In the mountain country, the people are not Buddhists but make sacrifices to the spirits of the forest; they regard the bonzes who come to their upland villages preaching Buddhism as subversive agents. In many such villages controlled by the Pathet Lao, the bonzes have been chased out by the population, and Buddhist temples have been desecrated.

The effect of the softening-up action carried on by the Pathet Lao cadres in the villages was first to make the villagers less amenable to the central government's orders, and then to estrange them completely from the government. They arrived at the point where they believed that the web of fronts and groups in which they were enmeshed was really their government. The French described this state as *pourriture*—rottenness.

The basic source for statements from the leadership of the NLHS was the official NLHS newspaper, *Lao Hak Sat,* until it was banned by the Royal Government on May 16, 1959. After this, a clandestine edition was quoted from with regularity by Hanoi and Peking. Important statements of attitude or policy were quoted from *Lao Hak Sat* immediately after publication, a surprising feat in a country whose communications are primitive. Even more amazing, Hanoi and Peking have quoted from *Lao Hak Sat* a full day before its publication in Vientiane. Crediting such statements to the Pathet Lao had several advantages for Hanoi and Peking: It enhanced the guerrilla movement's international prestige, and it permitted Hanoi and Peking to avoid committing themselves on many thorny issues.

A favorite Communist theme in the early days of the Pathet Lao movement was that the Royal Government, by prosecuting an armed campaign against the guerrillas, was violating Article 15 of the Geneva cease-fire agreement. This had provided that "each party undertakes to refrain from any reprisals or discrimination against persons or organizations for their activities during the hostilities [of the Indochina War] and also undertakes to guarantee their democratic freedom." Because the Pathet Lao was organized before Geneva, its leadership could claim a valid grievance against Vientiane's efforts to reassert its authority over all the territory of Laos.

After the summer of 1959, the Communist portrayal of the Pathet Lao changed drastically. From being portrayed as one legitimate faction among many, the Pathet Lao became one of two opposing sides in a civil war. Gradually their views came to be represented as those of "the people of Laos" and the views of the Vientiane government as those of a minority. By then, the Pathet Lao was equipped with a powerful radio transmitter, which broadcast the views of the leadership on a station calling itself Radio Pathet Lao. This, too, was part of what Giap had called "people's war."

The Second National Congress of the Neo Lao Hak Sat, held in Sam Neua Province from April 6 to 11, 1964, elected a Central Committee of sixty-three members. This Central Committee then re-elected Souphanouvong as Chairman and elected other officers. They are: Vice Chairmen: Sithone Komadam, Phay Dang, and Kaysone Phomvihan; members of the Standing Committee: Nouhak Phoumsavan, Khamtay Siphandon, Phoun Sipraseuth, Sisomphou, Nhia Veu, and Kham Moun; and Secretary-General: Phoumi Vongvichit.[25]

Souphanouvong told the author, in December, 1962, that the day-to-day work of the NLHS is handled by about twenty subcommittees of the Central Committee, and that he was chairman of more than half of these committees and personally presided over them. This helps to explain Souphanouvong's lengthy absences at undisclosed locations in the mountains of Laos.

The actual distribution of decision-making authority within the movement, however, departs from this neat hierarchical structure. It is bound up with the ties with the Lao Dong Party.

Although Souphanouvong has been titular leader of the Pathet Lao movement since its founding, it is uncertain how much weight he carries in the inner councils of the NLHS, and more particularly in those of the Phak Pasason Lao.

The Vietnamese Communists have paid particular attention to securing absolute control over the Phak Pasason Lao. The fact that the titular leader of the front behind which the Party operates is a prince of the royal blood, and the fact that the program adopted by this front in 1964 failed to mention the incorporation of Laos in an eventual Communist-dominated federation with Vietnam and Cambodia, afford a glimpse of the distance that separates the word of the front and the intentions of the Party.

---

[25] Radio Pathet Lao, quoted by Radio Hanoi, April 11, 1964. For the action program adopted at this Congress, see Appendix VI.

6.

The First Coalition

The 1954 cease-fire agreements defined who held what in Indo-china. They established a *status quo* that the Conference partici-pants pledged themselves to honor by renouncing military conquest as a means of effecting territorial changes. The United States, in the tremendous striking power of the Seventh Fleet in the Western Pacific, held the key to enforcing this *status quo*.

The leaders of Laos saw clearly that their country's independence hinged on whether their larger neighbors and the big powers respected the pledge to renounce military expansion into Laos. Disturbances among neighboring countries had always had reper-cussions in Laos. In the centuries of wars waged by the princely states of Southeast Asia, the Kingdom of Luang Prabang had been swept this way and that, first the vassal of Annam and then of Siam. The French Protectorate, far from removing these destructive cur-rents, had brought them even more intimately into contact with the Kingdom.

In 1954, Laos benefited from a balance of interests that pre-vented any of its neighbors from launching a war of conquest on its soil. To avoid upsetting this balance, Laos sought to avoid aligning itself with either the Communist bloc or the non-Communist bloc.

The international situation looked favorable for this effort. The Chinese had embarked upon a policy of wooing Asian neutrals, and any pledge that Chou En-lai might have given at Geneva to respect the sovereignty of the Royal Government of Laos in return for exclusion of an American military presence in Indochina fitted in well with this policy. Communist China was not to take an active hand in Laos for more than six years. Peking had been anxious to extricate itself from the Korean War, and saw no need to become embroiled in another war with the United States in an area that, unlike Korea, did not contain American garrisons. And the Americans had no need of military positions in Laos, since their power was based on the ships of the Seventh Fleet, backed up by bases on Okinawa and in the Philippines.

The North Vietnamese position was less obvious than that of the Chinese, and it was here that the Royal Lao Government had to look for a threat to its sovereignty. However, North Vietnam, the newest and weakest member of the Communist bloc, was clearly under Chinese pressure to keep on good terms with Vientiane.

Scarcely a year after the Geneva Conference came the Bandung Conference of Afro-Asian states. This provided a good indication that the Chinese were pressuring the North Vietnamese to normalize their relations with the neutral, non-Communist government in Vientiane. A meeting of the Lao and North Vietnamese delegates to Bandung was brought about on April 23, 1955, in the presence of both Chou En-lai and Indian Prime Minister Jawaharlal Nehru.

At this meeting, Chou and Pham Van Dong, North Vietnam's Foreign Minister, gave verbal assurance of noninterference in Laos. Further, Pham Van Dong concluded a written agreement with the Lao delegation covering future relations between their two governments. The text of this agreement read:

> First, the Government of the Democratic Republic of Vietnam considers that the settlement which is due to take place between the Royal Government of Laos and the "Pathet Lao," by virtue of the Geneva agreements, is a question of internal order which the Royal Government of Laos and "Pathet Lao" are entirely free to solve in the best way possible in the higher interests of the country and people of Laos.
>
> Second, the Government of the Democratic Republic of Vietnam and the Royal Government of Laos will develop and harmonize the good neighborly relations which tie and should tie these countries to each other, within the framework of the Five Principles defined in the Sino-Indian Agreement of April 29, 1954.[1]

The North Vietnamese could well afford to make this statement; their principal preoccupation was the reunification of their own country, and the frustration of this objective had not yet made Laos of vital military importance to them.

The combination of correct relations with all its neighbors and

[1] Quoted in George McTurnan Kahin, *The Asian-African Conference* (Ithaca, N.Y.: Cornell University Press, 1956), p. 27.

the good will of the great powers was the *sine qua non* of peace in Laos. This the leaders in Vientiane energetically set out to achieve. In demonstration of its neutral posture vis-à-vis the Cold War, the Vientiane government permitted no embassy of either Communist China or Nationalist China, North Vietnam or South Vietnam, but strove to maintain friendly contacts with all of them. This was a variation of the Indian and Indonesian patterns of maintaining consuls in both Hanoi and Saigon.

Laos was walking a tightrope. The most vigorous proponent of this policy balance was Prince Souvanna Phouma. On becoming Prime Minister again at the beginning of 1956, he declared: "We will oppose any foreign interference in our own affairs. We will strive to maintain the best possible relations with our friends and our allies [i.e., France], and especially with our neighbors."[2]

Determined to keep Laos out of the Cold War, Souvanna Phouma visited Peking and Hanoi in August, 1956. In a joint statement with Chou En-lai, the Prince pledged his government to carry out a policy of "peace and neutrality," to subscribe to no new military alliance so long as Laos' security was not menaced, and to allow no foreign military bases other than as provided in the 1954 accords. Informally, Souvanna Phouma assured Mao Tse-tung that Laos desired friendly relations with Peking, although it could not permit diplomatic representation because of the continuing rivalry between Peking and Taipei. According to Souvanna Phouma's own account, Mao replied that his government was content with Laos' nonrecognition of both Peking and Taipei.

A few days later, Souvanna Phouma was received equally cordially in Hanoi. In a joint statement with North Vietnamese Government leaders, he gave assurances that Laos would not permit foreign powers to set up military bases on its territory. A short while later, Souvanna Phouma was received in the capital of South Vietnam with every display of good will.

Shortly after the establishment of the coalition in Vientiane, Chou En-lai voiced his satisfaction before the National People's Congress in Peking:

> The establishment of a coalition government in the kingdom of Laos and the settlement of the question of the provinces of Sam Neua and Phong Saly were signs that great progress had been made in the implementation of the Geneva Agreement on Laos. The Chinese Government welcomes the peaceful unification of the Kingdom of Laos on the basis of the Geneva Agreement, which provides a more favor-

[2] *Le Journal d'Extrême-Orient* (Saigon), February 29, 1956.

able condition for the independent development of Laos. Although the United States has not given up its attempt to drive Laos into the Manila Treaty [SEATO], Laos, like Cambodia, adheres to a policy of peace and neutrality.[3]

A few months after this Souvanna Phouma once again made his policy quite clear. Also, he gave one of his many indications that he was fully aware of the danger represented by Communist subversion and was determined not to allow it to endanger the course of neutrality:

> In the political field, the new government will strive to consolidate its prestige and maintain the Lao tradition to safeguard freedom and the complete independence of Laos. It will do all it can to check the Communists' sabotaging activities and the spread of Communist thoughts and ideas. Our neutral policy applies only to the military field. Politically speaking, we still adopt a system of constitutional monarchy and practice democracy. We have decided to maintain friendly relations with democratic nations.[4]

Security or Insecurity?

The preservation of the independence of Laos and Cambodia, and the support of non-Communist governments in those countries, had been the objective of Secretary of State John Foster Dulles since the Geneva Conference, as we have seen. In the aftermath of the cease-fire, Dulles had determined that these countries might be defended by a regional alliance guaranteeing collective action in case of aggression and the deterrent of over-all American nuclear striking power.

It became obvious immediately that aid programs would be required if the Royal Lao Government was to maintain its authority, even after the fighting on its soil had stopped and the Viet Minh had withdrawn. The aid that the United States had been furnishing under the 1950 agreements was continued, and a reinforced American aid mission, United States Operations Mission (USOM), began operations in Vientiane on January 1, 1955. In an exchange of notes the following July, the validity of the basic agreements was reaffirmed.[5]

French aid to Laos also continued in the forms of the military training mission permitted by the Geneva agreements and the provi-

[3] New China News Agency (Peking), February 11, 1958.

[4] Agence France-Presse, June 15, 1958.

[5] *Economic Cooperation. Agreement Between the United States of America and Laos* (Department of State, Treaties and Other International Acts Series, No. 3664 [Washington: Government Printing Office, 1956]).

sion of teachers and other assistance in the fields of education and cultural exchanges. Britain also undertook limited technical aid to Vientiane under the Colombo Plan.

Following the signing of the SEATO treaty in September, 1954, Secretary of Defense Charles E. Wilson requested the Joint Chiefs of Staff to set forth their views on the optimum size of the Lao armed forces that the United States should support to further the goals of the Mutual Security Program. The consensus of the Joint Chiefs was that, with the end of actual fighting in Indochina and with the inclusion of Laos under the "umbrella" provided by SEATO, it would be best to reduce the Lao Territorial army from its wartime strength of 15,000 men to the level needed for routine internal policing. In November, 1954, the Joint Chiefs advised the Secretary of Defense, "No force levels are recommended for this country."[6]

A key factor influencing the Joint Chiefs' decision was the prohibition inherent in the Geneva agreements against U.S. establishment of a Military Assistance Advisory Group (MAAG) in Laos to supervise the training of the armed forces. The State Department advised that the United States would respect this prohibition. The Defense Department thereupon concluded that in Laos it would be impossible to ensure effective training on the spot, unlike in South Vietnam, where a MAAG had been operating since 1950, and recommended against supporting a Lao army.

Within months after the Geneva cease-fire, it became apparent that the Pathet Lao were acting as a political force as well as a military force. In their two northern provinces, Pathet Lao cadres were not only recruiting young men but also drumming up popular support for the manifesto issued by Souphanouvong's "resistance government" in 1950, whose objectives included formation of a coalition government with Vientiane.

At this point, the Royal Government in Vientiane had no civic action program; it did not even have a Ministry of Rural Affairs. The army, which included many of the country's best-educated men, was now the only national organization that could enlist support for the central government. Thus the army, besides its policing function, would have the higher mission of awakening patriotism, unifying the nation, and lending substance to its independence.

Asked to reconsider their decision in January, 1955, the Joint Chiefs advised that their views on support of a Lao army had not changed. They stated that mutual-security support of a Lao army

[6] *Hearings,* II, p. 8.

could not be recommended "from the military point of view," but acquiesced in the provision of such support "should political considerations be overriding."[7] These views were communicated from Wilson to Dulles with the comment that Wilson would acquiesce in a program of support for a Lao army "for political reasons."

That same month, the State Department requested the American diplomatic mission in Vientiane to draw up its recommendation for the size of a Lao army. The mission in Vientiane, taking into account the potential political influence of such an army and the stimulus to the economy that army salaries would provide, came up with a recommendation for 23,600 men.

A year later, in January, 1956, the Joint Chiefs were asked to consider a small increase in the size of the Lao army. Again they acquiesced, this time on the basis that it seemed indicated "from a psychological, political, and morale aspect." Referring to the earlier correspondence, however, the Joint Chiefs stated that "their views . . . are still valid."[8] The Royal Army was increased to 25,000 men.

During 1955, it will be recalled, the Royal Army's probes into the Pathet Lao-occupied provinces of Sam Neua and Phong Saly had been forcibly rebuffed, with some casualties. By January, 1956, the Royal Government was encountering real difficulty in reasserting its authority there.

Now, by putting into the hands of the Royal Government a military weapon to meet a political threat, the United States had created the issue of "American imperialism" in Laos. Hanoi and Peking could not have done it better. The harassment of the Royal Army by the Pathet Lao was no military threat to the Royal Government; the objective of the Pathet Lao was political power. The weakness of the Royal Government was its political inefficacy in the countryside. The United States had done nothing to assist that government in asserting its authority. In areas of the country accessible to the Pathet Lao political cadres, the Royal Army became synonymous with repression.

A Congressional committee reported:

U.S. support of a 25,000-man army, of the entire military budget, and of segments of the civilian economy is, in fact, based on a political determination, made by the Department of State contrary to the recommendations of the Joint Chiefs of Staff. In Laos, the only coun-

[7] *Ibid.*
[8] *Ibid.*

try in the world where the United States supports the military budget 100 per cent, military judgments have been disregarded.[9]

As late as 1958, Defense Department documents continued to list the Lao army as being "not within force objectives." By 1959, executive-branch papers were speaking of an additional mission for the Royal Army, which originally had been intended only to maintain internal security. The army was then assigned the added mission of resisting outside aggression (against a regular North Vietnamese army of 300,000!). By 1960, executive-branch documents indicated that the military program in Laos had "just grown" on the Defense Department without military justification.[10]

On the basis of available documentation on the origin of United States support for the Royal Army, it seems farcical to argue, as did an official statement of the American Embassy in Vientiane, dated April 25, 1958, that Laos, with the advent of independence,

> inherited [sic] a 25,000-man army, which it desired to maintain in order to guard against potential Communist aggression originating in North Vietnam and the Pathet Lao provinces to the north. As it turned out, it was well that this army was maintained, for fighting soon broke out.

The thinking of the intelligent Lao leaders in Vientiane was more realistic. They saw the need for a small armed force to secure law and order on Lao territory, put down rebellion should it occur, and prevent lawless bands from marauding in the villages. This also had been the view of the Geneva powers when they agreed to permit Laos to retain a French military training mission and to procure arms for its own defense. In the event of an invasion, Laos would be compelled to seek international help. Prince Somsanith, for instance, one of the most intelligent of the Lao leaders, said categorically after his tenure as Prime Minister that what Laos needed was a police force, not an army.

The tendency of high-ranking State Department officials to assign to the U.S.-supported army in Laos functions far in excess of routine policing caused understandable uneasiness among the Vientiane leaders. They deplored the American habit of referring to the "containment" of Communist power by a string of national armies in the countries on China's periphery. To equate an army intended to maintain internal security in Laos with one ready to go to war against North Vietnam, and possibly even China, seemed sheer folly to these

[9] *Ibid.* Italics in original.
[10] *Ibid.*

men. Moreover, a "collective security" that provoked their neighbors by upsetting the delicate *status quo* of 1954 was, in their view, no security at all. It was the opposite—insecurity.

They recognized the extreme danger of being caught by a rebellion à la Giap, supported from North Vietnam, the guerrilla type of warfare that a conventional army could not deal with—just as the 450,000-man French Union Forces could not deal with the Viet Minh.

Nevertheless, with the United States equipping it and financing it to the last penny, the Royal Lao Army was built up, by 1959, to two paratroop battalions, one artillery battalion, one armored reconnaissance battalion, twelve infantry battalions, and twelve volunteer infantry battalions. This army was saddled with a Transportation Corps, an Ordnance Corps, a Quartermaster Corps, Military Police, and the other impedimenta of a fighting force in which jeeps have replaced elephants. The armed forces also included a "navy" of river patrol boats and an air force of six C-47 transports and a handful of light reconnaissance aircraft. These were officially described as "small by Western standards, but sufficient for the job at hand."[11]

The fact that Laos has few roads, most of which are unserviceable during the six months of the rainy season, appears not to have greatly influenced planning. The army's jeeps and trucks were hardly suited to ferreting out insurgents in remote villages accessible by little more than footpaths.

Even more serious, however, was the fact that the American-supported army was based on the lowland Lao, who inhabited the valleys, and ignored the mountain tribes, who inhabited the uplands that formed most of the country and, more particularly, its border regions. The Pathet Lao made a point of recruiting entire units of the ethnic minorities, but for years the Royal Army made no major effort to incorporate the Kha, Black Thai, or Meo. The situation changed in 1961, when their fighting qualities and strategic geographical distribution were finally recognized by the American Special Forces.

Also, there were serious deficiencies in the preparation given the officers of the Royal Army. During the first few years, little attention was paid to counterguerrilla training. Promising junior officers were sent off to staff school in the United States and France to study tactics for set-piece battles with neat front lines, thrusts, and flanking

[11] *Briefing Notes on the Royal Kingdom of Laos* (Vientiane: U.S. Information Service, May, 1959), p. E-2.

movements. Soon, Laos boasted five generals but possessed few officers or noncoms who could lead a squad of rangers on a week's jungle patrol.

Having justified American support for a Lao army on political grounds, the State Department went halfway toward meeting the Joint Chiefs' cautions that such support would be wasted if it was not coupled with on-the-spot training by Americans. The State Department set up an American military mission in disguise in Vientiane. This mission, known as the Programs Evaluation Office (PEO), was attached to the U.S. Operations Mission. All its members wore civilian clothes and were officially described as "technicians." Officially, their training activities were under the over-all responsibility of the French Military Mission.[12]

The head of the PEO was a U.S. Army general who had been removed from the roster of active officers. Because he wore civilian clothes, his presence in Laos became known only in 1961, when a *New York Times* reporter tracked down the whereabouts of Brigadier General John A. Heintges, a career officer who had distinguished himself in Europe in World War II and who had seemingly vanished into thin air after 1959, when, it became known, he had taken up his unpublicized duties in Laos.

The PEO's task was a monumental one. At the height of the Indochina War, the French had trained and equipped a Lao Territorial army of 15,000, with many French officers and noncoms acting as a cadre for the Lao troops. But the PEO had to form an army completely staffed and officered by the Lao.

The problems in administering this program were immense. It was necessary to station teams of PEO technicians at Luang Prabang, Paksane, Savannakhet, and Pakse as well as at Vientiane. Army recruitment was haphazard. Pay envelopes were mysteriously rerouted during their long journey from Vientiane to the soldiers in the field. Fully three years after the PEO was established, tables of organization and equipment were still being drawn up. Programming was based on sketchy Lao listings of troop units and unmethodical estimates of strength.

The American economic-aid program in Laos was built around the Royal Army. The existence of an army of this size in a country with virtually no productive capacity and little experience with a money economy created economic problems, and to deal with them, a program of considerable proportions had to be implemented.

[12] Department of State, *The Situation in Laos* (Washington: September, 1959), p. 23.

Without hard goods to soak up the salary payments to the army, a runaway inflation would have ensued. The solution was to finance a goods import program in order to maintain the value of the Lao currency, the kip.

Each month, the United States Government made a multimillion-dollar deposit in a New York bank account in the name of the Royal Lao Government. The latter then placed in circulation the equivalent value in kip, which was officially pegged at 35 to the dollar. The dollars were used to pay for hard goods that were then imported into Laos by commercial importers under a licensing system operated by the Lao government.

These funds came from Congressional appropriations under the Mutual Security Program. Although the PEO was attached to USOM, the PEO had sole jurisdiction of the spending of these funds. An official Embassy document stated:

> Most of this local currency generated by the dollar-aid program is not utilized by USOM in its own operations, nor has USOM the responsibility for the use to which these funds are put, since most of them go for the support of the Lao military establishment.[13]

The PEO also decided the military equipment supplied to the Royal Army. Funds for this also came out of the Mutual Security Program under the title Military Assistance Program. The amounts of the various categories of the American aid program can be seen from the figures in Table 1.

The PEO not only controlled the bulk of the aid funds spent in Laos, but also possessed its exclusive channel of communication to Washington, through the Commander in Chief, Pacific Forces (CINCPAC), whose headquarters were in Hawaii, and the Defense Department. At times this caused conflict with the authority of the Ambassador, who was the head of the "country team" of official Americans in Vientiane, and the State Department. In one instance, the PEO promised the Lao Defense Ministry a salary increase for the army. The move was approved by CINCPAC and sent back to the Defense Department in Washington. The State Department, fearing an inflationary effect on the Lao economy, cabled a protest. The increase, however, went through on schedule. The Central Intelligence Agency, whose functions extended from the field of intelligence gathering into actual operations, also maintained its own channels of communications to Washington.

The arrival in Vientiane of hundreds of Americans to implement

[13] *Briefing Notes on the Royal Kingdom of Laos,* p. D-5.

TABLE 1

U.S. FOREIGN AID TO LAOS, FISCAL YEARS 1955–63*
(*In Millions of Dollars*)

Fiscal Year	For Development Grants and Technical Cooperation	For Budget Support[a]	For Military Equipment[b]	Total
1955	$	$ 40.9	$	$ 40.9
1956	1.0	47.3	27.4	75.7
1957	1.5	42.9	4.3	48.7
1958	1.7	29.8	5.4	36.9
1959	1.7	23.4	7.5	32.6
1960	1.2	40.9	13.4	55.5
1961	1.4	29.1	33.4	63.9
1962	—.6	27.5	37.1	64.0
1963	....	38.5	24.0	62.5
	$7.9	$320.3	$152.5	$480.7

* *Source:* Agency for International Development.
[a] Principally to pay salaries of army and civil administration.
[b] Referred to in official publications as Military Assistance Program (MAP).
Note: Figures do not include funds for assistance under PL 480, which were minor, or expenditures of the CIA, which are secret. Military Equipment figures represent net deliveries, but other figures represent dollar obligations; in some years, actual expenditures were substantially lower.

this large program created a swarm of activity that caused no little astonishment in a country accustomed to thinking of foreigners in terms of the easygoing French. People who had always lived in wooden houses open to the ventilation of the breeze and with wide verandas on all sides looked on dubiously as Americans shut themselves up in air-conditioned cubicles. The Lao marveled at the Americans, who, in order to run the air conditioners, did not hesitate to set up a generating station, which required the transport of barrels of diesel fuel, which necessitated building a railway line to the Mekong. American know-how took care of everything.

The money fed into the economy of Laos to pay for the army—amounting to the highest per-capita influx of American aid into any Southeast Asian country, as can be seen from Table 2—went for importing an extraordinary variety of goods in order to soak up paper money and prevent a runaway inflation. Soon the shops along Vientiane's two paved thoroughfares began to look like the open-air market at the landing wharf of the Hong Kong–Macao ferry, with their shiny new aluminum pails, flashlights, cheap suitcases, and

TABLE 2

U.S. FOREIGN AID TO COUNTRIES OF SOUTHEAST ASIA, FISCAL YEARS 1946–63

Country	Population	Total[a] (In Millions of Dollars)	Per Capita
Laos[b]	2,500,000	$ 481	$192.3
South Vietnam[b]	14,617,000	2,656	181.7
Cambodia[b]	4,952,000	367	74.1
Philippines	30,200,000	1,851	61.3
Thailand	28,000,000	869	31.0
Indonesia	100,000,000	881	8.8
Burma	22,000,000	108	4.9
Malaysia	10,500,000	25	2.4

[a] *Source:* Agency for International Development, Statistics and Reports Division, *U.S. Foreign Assistance and Assistance from International Organizations—Obligations and Loan Authorizations* (Washington: 1964).

[b] Figures are for fiscal years 1955–63 only.

other bric-a-brac. Defending the range of goods allowed into Laos under the American commercial import program, the Embassy declared:

> Our [Economic Aid] Mission in Vientiane advises that there are only three Cadillacs in Laos, all models predating the aid program, and that only 30 Buicks, all lowest priced models, have been imported with funds derived from the aid program. It is known that licenses for a reasonable quantity of fishhooks and thermos jugs were issued. It is thought probably that festival decorations used in the celebration of the 2500th anniversary of Buddha were imported although not paid for with U.S. aid funds. There is no record of any automobile covers being included. It is known that feather dusters, sporting goods, fishing tackle, thermos jugs, decorations and musical instruments were included in the country's import plan, but insofar as the use of U.S. funds is concerned the Mission advises that quantities of these items imported were not significant.[14]

It is a matter of conjecture what a "reasonable quantity" of fishhooks is in a country where the people fish by dipping broad nets suspended on poles.

The import trade in Laos was concentrated in the hands of the Chinese merchants, who had access to the free-money markets outside the country and who had influence in the Lao Government. While the import program operated on the officially pegged rate of 35 kip to the dollar, free-market operators in Bangkok and Hong Kong gave up to 110 kip to the dollar. This great disparity led to

[14] Mimeographed statement dated April 25, 1958.

speculation in foreign exchange in which the hard goods themselves became merely the medium for defrauding the import program. This involved importing dollar-financed goods and then exporting them for resale for hard currencies, which in turn could be turned to importing more goods. In the later stages, the importers did not even bother to transport the goods to Laos, a costly business on the single railway from Bangkok, but merely bribed a customs official to issue a receipt for them, and resold them in Bangkok.

Under the weight of the commodity import program, the imbalance in Laos' trade increased dramatically, as shown in Table 3.

TABLE 3

LAO BALANCE OF TRADE, 1939–67*
(*In Millions of Kip*)

	Imports	Exports
1939	4.3	0.6
1949	65.4	7.3
1958	1,040.9	54.7
1962	1,929.6	62.0
1967	11,796.3	1,064.4

* *Source:* Joel M. Halpern, *Economic and Related Statistics Dealing with Laos* (Los Angeles: University of California, Department of Anthropology and Sociology, Laos Project Paper No. 11, 1961), extracted from Table 35, p. 39; *Far Eastern Economic Review* (Hong Kong), January 9, 1964, p. 52. Royaume du Laos, Ministère des Finances, Direction des Douanes et Régies, Bureau de Statistiques, *Statistiques Douanières du Commerce Extérieur* (Vientiane: 1967).

Despite American efforts to support the kip, its value on the free market declined steadily. In small market towns outside Vientiane, the price of 100 kilograms of polished rice rose from 450 kip in 1955, to 600 kip in 1956, to 950 kip in 1957; in the same period, the price of one can of kerosene rose from 110 to 260 kip; and that of one chicken from 20 to 80 kip. American Ambassador Parsons later attributed this inflationary trend to the Lao's loss of confidence in the stability of the kip following the initiation of negotiations between Souvanna Phouma and the Pathet Lao.[15] This explanation, however, appeared to be wide of the mark.

The profit to be reaped from discrepancies between the official and unofficial kip rate was so tempting that even Americans were implicated in malpractices in connection with the administration of the aid program. Subsequent disclosures made at Congressional hearings on the program in Washington compromised the reputations of

[15] *Hearings,* I, p. 232.

several Americans and undermined the confidence of those Lao who were more interested in preserving their country's independence than in lining their pockets.

The abuses of the import program had several other deleterious effects. The proliferating luxurious villas and large automobiles in the capital were in marked contrast to the rudimentary furnishings of the country at large. No traveler coming to Vientiane from the provinces could fail to be astonished by what he saw. The American aid program was obviously increasing the gap between the haves and the have-nots, and as a result it was creating grievances rather than eliminating them.

As pointed out by one observer:

> Corruption and extortion in the customs, banking, foreign trade, police, and other administrative departments were commonplace. Black market deals in American aid dollars reached such proportions that the Pathet Lao needed no propaganda to turn the rural population against the townspeople. The Chinese of Hong Kong and Bangkok and a few Lao officials profited from the American aid, while the poor Lao for whom it was intended stood by helplessly. Official Vientiane of course knew nothing about this prodigious fraud, although the entire city seemed to be involved.[16]

Enrichment of the small Lao elite in the capital undermined the Lao tradition of service, which counted the accumulation of wealth a perquisite of office but not a goal in itself. In an effort to counteract the corrupting effect of newfound wealth on public officials, especially younger ones, the government in 1959 issued an edict requiring civil servants to attend religious services.

With the sudden advent of the cash economy came new responsibilities of finance and taxation. The realization that the growing apparatus of ministerial offices depended upon the economic power of a foreign nation made many Lao feel that their country had less independence now than under the Protectorate.

The American program concentrated on financing the import of hard goods in order to prevent a runaway inflation, and neglected aid to the countryside, which would have had permanent effects. Of the $480.7 million obligated to Laos in fiscal years 1955–63, only $1.9 million was spent on improving agriculture—that is, less than 1 per cent of aid funds were spent in a field of activity that provided the livelihood of 96 per cent of the population. Of course, the agricultural economy of Laos indirectly benefited from the import program.

Except for emergency airdropping of rice to alleviate shortages in

16 Sisouk na Champassak, *op. cit.,* p. 64.

villages caused by the Indochina War, no village aid program was undertaken in earnest until the autumn of 1957, nearly two years after the USOM had been established. Prior to this, there had been experimental attempts to train young Lao to discover the basic needs of villages in terms of agriculture, education, health, and sanitation. Later, American specialists had been stationed in six provincial capitals to gather information and initiate some assistance on a limited scale. But in the 10,000 villages of Laos, the people had no intimation that a vast bureaucratic machine had arrived on the banks of the Mekong to help them overcome their age-old problems of malnutrition and illiteracy, disease and isolation.

Even where it did show up in the form of development projects instead of in sterile salary payments, American aid did little to improve the infrastructure of the country. American officials made a show of opening a newly surfaced road north of Vientiane in 1959, but in reality this was the completion of repair work on a stretch of the Royal Road, which had been ceremoniously inaugurated by the French Governor General on March 17, 1942.

The Lao administrators who, under the Protectorate, had gone around to the villages on bicycle and on foot, had graduated to the automobile, and paid fewer and fewer visits to the backwoods. In Vientiane, they moved serenely from diplomatic reception to diplomatic reception. Forfeiting their authority in the countryside, they retreated into the confines of the capital, where they played a political game of musical chairs for Cabinet posts.

From the neglected villages, officials in the provincial capitals began receiving reports that the Pathet Lao, who had already expanded their network of cells to cover virtually the whole country, were preparing to make a major issue of the widening gap between the haves and the have-nots in the coming elections.

It will be recalled that the agreements signed in November, 1957, by the Royal Government and the Pathet Lao had stipulated that supplementary elections would be held within four months with participation of the NLHS. Twenty additional seats in the National Assembly were to be contested, bringing its total membership to fifty-nine. (An extra contest would be held to elect a replacement for one member who had died.) The additional seats were to be contested in widely scattered parts of the country in accordance with a revised electoral map of Laos. Women would vote for the first time, satisfying a demand frequently advanced by the Pathet Lao. The elections were set for May 4, 1958.

The American Ambassador in Vientiane, aware that the NLHS

candidates would exploit any shortcomings of the aid program, initiated a crash program—dubbed "Operation Booster Shot"—to assist the villages. It was accurately described by a Congressional committee in 1959:

> Basically, this activity was a village aid program. The physical condition of the population in most remote areas was reported to be very bad. Few of the villages could be reached by road, and in most cases aid from Vientiane would have to be sent in primarily by air. In fact, most of it would have to be air-dropped due to a lack of airstrips usable by cargo-carrying planes. . . .
>
> The program took the form of more than 90 work projects, including well digging, erection of small irrigation and flood control dams, repair of schools and temples, repair of roads and airfields, and construction of hospitals; and the dropping of some 1,300 tons of food, medical and construction supplies and other useful commodities.
>
> The program did not overcome the Communist election slogans, related to the U.S. aid program, of "governmental corruption," "government indifference," or "U.S. domination."[17]

Operation Booster Shot did, however, for the first time bring meaningful aid to thousands of Lao besides the handful of officials and merchants in Vientiane who had been its principal beneficiaries up to then. But it was terribly late to attempt to undo the effective propaganda and coercion that the Pathet Lao cadres had been producing since 1954.

Thirteen NLHS candidates ran in the elections, and nine won. Another four seats went to the Santiphab (Peace) Party, formed in 1957 by Quinim Pholsena, a protégé of Souvanna Phouma, and which favored establishing contacts with Communist-bloc countries. Thus, "leftist" candidates had won a majority of the seats contested. Even more revealing, the NLHS candidates had won in widely scattered districts in both the north and the south. The progovernment forces had hopelessly weakened their cause by running eighty-five candidates for the twenty-one seats at stake.

Prince Souphanouvong, who showed up at the voting tent in Vientiane wearing patent-leather shoes and a dapper business suit with a kerchief tucked in his breast pocket, received 37,389 votes—more than any other candidate in the country. When the new members of the National Assembly convened a few days later, he was elected chairman.

Shaken by the success of the NLHS candidates in exploiting the issue of American aid, certain members of Souvanna Phouma's

[17] *Hearings,* II, pp. 45–46.

Cabinet began talking about Laos' neutral course in very different terms from those Souvanna Phouma had been using. Phoui Sanani-kone, the veteran of Geneva who was now Minister of Foreign Affairs, declared that Laos' neutrality "does not imply a neutrality on the ideological plane: We are anti-Communists." He further constricted his definition of neutrality by adding: "Today, since there is a balance of forces, to be neutral means not to take part in any military alliance."[18] Obviously, he referred to SEATO; Laos was still allied to France in her bilateral mutual-security arrangement.

Phoui was implying that neutrality in foreign relations did not preclude forceful measures at home against Communist agents. In September, 1958, after he had succeeded Souvanna Phouma as Prime Minister, he declared:

> Like all Buddhists, the Lao have the habit of practicing tolerance. . . . However, events have made it clear to us that what matters is no longer philosophic considerations, but the defense of our cultural heritage and our love of freedom, which are being endangered by a subversive proselytism.[19]

In Souvanna Phouma's mind, holding the elections marked the fulfillment of the obligations Laos had undertaken at Geneva. The Prince stated that his government regarded as "fully accomplished" the obligations that Phoui had announced four years previously. He declared that Laos pledged itself anew not to enter into military alliances and not to seek military aid from foreign sources "except for the purpose of its effective territorial defense."[20]

On July 20, 1958, the International Control Commission adjourned sine die over the objections of its Polish member and amid a chorus of protest from Hanoi and Peking. The adjournment coincided with a mounting crisis in the Lao Cabinet.

Souvanna Phouma's government had been under constant American pressure since he had entered negotiations with the Pathet Lao for a coalition. Following the electoral successes of the NLHS, the United States, using as a pretext the mounting evidence of corruption in the import program and the need for a monetary reform, held up the normal monthly deposit of dollars in the Lao Government's bank account in New York.

Souvanna Phouma soon had a full-scale parliamentary crisis on

18 *L'Indépendant* (Vientiane), June 17, 1958.
19 *Le Journal d'Extrême-Orient,* September 2, 1958.
20 Cmnd. 541, p. 121.

his hands—which was exploited by a group of would-be Young Turks, organized as the "Committee for the Defense of the National Interests" (CDNI). Describing themselves in their statutes and manifesto as a mass civic group, not a formal political party, the CDNI members favored reform in the civil service and, more importantly, a "hard" line in dealing with the Pathet Lao. Communist propaganda portrayed them as lackeys of American interests.

At all events, Souvanna Phouma was denied confidence by the National Assembly on the issue of monetary reform and resigned as Prime Minister on July 23.

Failure of the Experiment

The first coalition was at an end. It had been little more than an experiment, and its short life had been beset by turmoil and external pressures. A new Cabinet, formed by Phoui and voted into office by the National Assembly on August 18, excluded the NLHS ministers Souphanouvong and Phoumi Vongvichit and included four members of the CDNI who were not members of the Assembly. Souvanna Phouma became Ambassador to France.

One of Phoui's first official acts was to put an end to most of the abuses in the American aid program. Under American guidance, he instituted a monetary reform that revalued the kip at 80 to the dollar, and abolished the notorious system of import licenses.

In world affairs, Phoui made it clear, he favored keeping Laos on a neutral path. He warned that he would not brook the implantation on Lao soil of what he termed "Communist ideology." He was, he said, no less eager than Souvanna Phouma to integrate the Pathet Lao into the national community, but he was seriously worried by their links with a foreign country (i.e., North Vietnam).

Early in his tenure as Prime Minister, in the autumn of 1958, Phoui strayed from Souvanna Phouma's cautious avoidance of relations with the Communist or anti-Communist governments of the divided countries of Vietnam and China. Phoui established relations on a consular level with the anti-Communist governments.

Ngo Dinh Nhu, political counselor and brother of the South Vietnamese President, visited Vientiane in September, 1958, and was followed shortly by the South Vietnamese Foreign Minister. At the beginning of 1959, both South Vietnam and Nationalist China opened consulates in the Lao capital. On the other hand, Soviet overtures to open relations with Vientiane, which had been made as early as July, 1956, were not followed up.

All these developments, beginning with the adjournment of the ICC, were unfavorable to the North Vietnamese, who saw in them the prospect of a Vientiane government increasingly under American influence and therefore increasingly hostile to them. They had no representation in Vientiane, and had to depend on the Pathet Lao to influence developments in their favor and on the occasional direct contacts provided by visits such as Souvanna Phouma's in 1956.

North Vietnamese statements interpreted the ICC's adjournment as upsetting the *status quo* established at Geneva. Because their paramount objective was to reunify Vietnam under their direction, they could construe this upsetting of the Geneva arrangements only as a setback.

An official statement in Hanoi by the Vice Minister of Foreign Affairs, Ung Van Khiem, made it clear even before the ICC took the decisive vote to adjourn that North Vietnam regarded as "essential" the continued presence of the ICC in Laos.

> Peace in Indochina is indivisible: this was recognized during the discussions at the Geneva Conference and confirmed by the spirit of the final declaration, especially in Para. 4 and 5. In the light of Art. 39, 46 and 25 of the Geneva agreements concerning respectively Laos, Vietnam, and Cambodia, it is clear that the three international commissions should continue their activities as long as the political problems are not completely solved in the three countries [i.e., as long as Vietnam is not reunified]. In the present situation in Indochina, the winding up of the activities of the ICC in one country, Laos for instance, without taking into account the settlement of the political problems in the other two countries, would have dangerous repercussions on the effective implementation of the Geneva agreements and on the activities of the ICC as a whole. Such winding up runs counter to the spirit and letter of the Geneva agreements.[21]

This line on maintaining the ICC was faithfully echoed by Souphanouvong and other Pathet Lao spokesmen, the very men who had done the most to make the ICC's task impossible by preventing it from carrying out investigations in the border area. The NLHS newspaper declared:

> After the elections, the ICC will still have to continue its task . . . with a view to safeguarding peace in Laos at a time when peace in Indochina still is threatened, and the foreign reactionaries are still plotting to drag Laos into the Southeast Asian aggressive bloc. The

[21] Quoted by Vietnam News Agency (Hanoi), May 31, 1958.

presence of the ICC in Laos is therefore necessary, and conforms to the present practical situation.[22]

Significantly, Hanoi and Peking did not repeat two other themes that were taken up by the NLHS. The NLHS newspaper accused Souvanna Phouma's government, just a few weeks before its fall, of failure "to carry out a policy of neutrality in the real sense of the word," i.e., to establish relations with the Communist countries. The newspaper also protested the submission to the National Assembly of a draft decree providing for "the arrest, fining, and deprivation of political rights of those who had a tendency to favor a Communist system."[23]

The adjournment of the ICC in Laos coincided with renewed evidence of the Hanoi regime's concern about the refusal of the Ngo Dinh Diem regime to discuss reunification. Two years after the date for the scheduled Vietnam-wide elections had passed, there still appeared no possibility of this reunification. That the men in Hanoi were preoccupied with this problem is shown by an authoritative article written in May, 1958, by North Vietnam's Prime Minister, Pham Van Dong, who stated:

It is clear that the maneuvers of the American imperialists in South Vietnam are part of their over-all plan to sabotage peace and intervene in the domestic affairs of other countries. That is why the struggle of the Vietnamese people and the Government of the Democratic Republic of Vietnam against American intervention in the affairs of South Vietnam and for the country's reunification is inseparable from the general struggle of the peoples for peace and national independence.

The American invaders have insolently violated the Geneva agreements. They have prevented the calling of a consultative conference of representatives from North and South Vietnam to discuss the holding of free general elections. They have brought new war materials and military personnel into South Vietnam and built military bases; they have included South Vietnam in the "defense zone" of SEATO. They are now trying to compel it to join this aggressive bloc.

The Government of the Democratic Republic of Vietnam and the Vietnamese people are fully determined to resist the intrigues of the American imperialists, whose interference in the affairs of South Vietnam is the main cause of the present territorial division of the country and the chief obstacle to reunification. . . .[24]

[22] *Lao Hak Sat* (Vientiane), quoted by Vietnam News Agency, May 11, 1958.

[23] *Ibid.*, July 13, 1958.

[24] "The Foreign Policy of the Democratic Republic of Vietnam," *International Affairs* (Moscow), July, 1958, p. 20.

Whether or not free elections might have been held, as envisaged in the Geneva agreements, is not our concern here. What this article reveals is the charge by North Vietnam that the Americans were using South Vietnam as a "military base" and preventing reunification. Whatever understanding may have prevailed at the moment the agreements were signed, it was clear by the summer of 1958 that this understanding no longer existed. From this point, the actions on both sides, in both Vietnam and Laos, become a gradual escalation.

In late July and early August, the Vietnam News Agency, Hanoi's official mouthpiece, published a series of articles under the title "Imperialist Schemes in Vietnam Against Peace and Reunification." These amounted to a staff study of American military assistance to the Saigon regime, and they were obviously intended to alert the Lao Dong Party's cadres in the south to the possibility that a decision to mount an all-out guerrilla war against the Diem regime was imminent. The Party had had the foresight to leave caches of arms in the south when the bulk of the Viet Minh forces withdrew after the armistice. It had also pulled back into the north a large number of native southerners, who were subsequently indoctrinated and then infiltrated back into the south as guerrilla leaders.

Several approaches had been made on an official level to the Diem regime to initiate negotiations on the reunification issue, and on December 22, 1958, a final attempt was made when Pham Van Dong proposed in a letter the "normalization of relations" between North and South. No reply was received. Ho and Giap decided to take the reunification of their country into their own hands.

To maintain its contacts in the south, to infiltrate trained cadres from the north, and to receive back from the south couriers and recruits for indoctrination, the Lao Dong Party depended on trails through the mountains of eastern Laos, along which men and supplies could be moved with near-perfect concealment. The trails departed from points far north along the Laos-Vietnam border, and came to be known collectively as the Ho Chi Minh Trail. It was a two months' march through Laos into South Vietnam.

Phoui's government had come into office in Vientiane on a dual pledge of reform and firm measures against subversive agents at home. The breakup of the coalition had nullified the November, 1957, agreements between the Royal Government and the Pathet Lao. Phoui made it clear he regarded the Pathet Lao as agents of North Vietnam, and implied that he would have no compunction about using the Royal Army to clear out centers of Pathet Lao strength, on the pattern of the Katay Don Sasorith government in

1955. Such a move would mean that Royal Army troops would be patrolling right up to the borders of North Vietnam and interfering with North Vietnamese use of the trails in the eastern mountains of Laos.

Developments took an ominous turn when, in December, North Vietnam began accusing Phoui's government of perpetrating a series of air and ground violations of their common border, all of which Phoui stoutly denied, and between December 23 and 29, Hanoi dispatched across the border two companies of regular North Vietnamese soldiers. Some six miles inside Laos, the troops, estimated at 280 men, dug entrenchments and took up positions at the villages of Ban Taroua, Ban Tapang, and Ban Kapai, near the town of Tchepone in Savannakhet Province in the highly sensitive area just west of the demarcation line between North and South Vietnam.

The North Vietnamese lay claim to a frontier strip in that area, which they call the Canton of Huong Lap. However, the Royal Lao Government maintains that the map used at Geneva leaves no room for disputing its sovereignty over the area.

The accusations of ground violations are a characteristic tactic employed by Asian Communists when they are preparing their own military initiatives. Such accusations serve to confuse the proper location of blame for intrusions into another country. The accusations of air violations, however, are harder to explain. The air force at the disposal of the Lao Government included no fighter aircraft and appeared eminently unsuited to staging missions over North Vietnam. A clue may be had in accusations made by Chinese Communist organs toward the end of 1958 that American aircraft were flying over southern China, especially Yünnan Province. If the two sets of accusations are related, their explanation may lie in flights of American reconnaissance aircraft which the North Vietnamese identified as belonging to the Royal Lao Government.

The most logical explanation of the North Vietnamese dispatching of troops across the border near Tchepone seems to be that the North Vietnamese wished to emphasize, on the ground, their determination to keep Royal Government troops out of the area, and, in Vientiane, the desirability of adhering to the November, 1957, agreement, failing which, the North Vietnamese would support the Pathet Lao on the pattern of the precoalition period.

If the North Vietnamese action was intended as a warning, however, Phoui was not to be intimidated. Addressing the National Assembly in Vientiane, Phoui spoke of "a new and very grave, if not critical, situation" on the border and accused North Vietnam by name of interfering in the internal affairs of Laos. In addition, Phoui's government announced that it would bring the border violation to the attention of the United Nations.

On January 15, 1959, the National Assembly granted Phoui special powers to govern for one year without recourse to the votes of the deputies. A few days later, Phoui reshuffled his Cabinet, for the first time giving minor posts to three army officers. One of these was Colonel Phoumi Nosavan, who since his series of rapid promotions had associated himself closely with the Young Turks of the CDNI.

Phoui also declared that he was exploring means of dismembering the NLHS as a subversive organization. Several NLHS deputies in Vientiane, judging these indications not propitious and made uneasy by CDNI-inspired rumors of an imminent army coup, left town hastily in the direction of the North Vietnam frontier. In addition, according to Phoui, "in the provinces of Sam Neua and Xieng Khouang several important Neo Lao Hak Sat cadres and their families sought refuge in the Democratic Republic of Vietnam in order to get in touch with those Lao cadres who had refused to be integrated into the national community and are currently undergoing training from the North Vietnamese authorities."

In response to a vociferous campaign by Hanoi and Peking to have the ICC reconvened to deal with the charges and counter-charges of border violations, Phoui announced at a news conference on February 11: "The Royal Government considers that the agreement on the cessation of hostilities in Laos has been completely fulfilled." More specifically, he added that his government could not accept the view that Laos was bound by the terms of Geneva as long as a political settlement had not been reached in Vietnam. "No government worthy of the name," the Prime Minister said, "may mortgage the political future of its country on the basis of the situation existing in a neighboring country."

Phoui made it clear that he was accusing North Vietnam of activities that threatened his government's authority. "A neighboring country of the Kingdom," he charged, was waging a campaign against Laos "by acts of intimidation of all sorts, including the violation and occupation of its territory."[25]

Phoui's accusation was for the North Vietnamese the last in a long series of worsening developments in Laos. Gone was the ICC,

[25] Unclassified telegram from American Embassy, Vientiane, February 11, 1959.

whose presence in Laos had been turned into a greater disadvantage for the anti-Communists than for the Communists. A South Vietnamese consulate had been established in Vientiane. The coalition had broken up. Phoui's threat to move against the NLHS politically and against the Pathet Lao militarily heralded the scrapping of the November, 1957, agreement. Now Phoui's declaration that his government no longer considered itself bound by the terms of the Geneva cease-fire foreshadowed the possibility of unrestricted military aid from the West, and perhaps even alliances. The *status quo* established at Geneva was being scrapped. The United Nations, of which North Vietnam was not a member, was being brought into the picture as the potential arbiter of the conflict in Laos. All this jeopardized the favorable position of the Hanoi regime that had gradually developed with the increasing Pathet Lao strength and organization across the border.

The trump card remaining in North Vietnam's hand was the 1,500 Pathet Lao soldiers, forming two battalions, still awaiting assignment to the national army. Delays had been caused first by the Pathet Lao's demand for a preposterously high proportion of officers in the merged army, and second by a dispute over the rank to be awarded the senior Pathet Lao officer, Colonel Phoumi's old friend from Thakhek, Singkapo Chounlamany, who had also risen to colonel in the Pathet Lao army.

While negotiations between Vientiane and the Pathet Lao dragged on inconclusively, the Pathet Lao soldiers settled down to domestic life in the two camps in which they had been living since the signing of the November, 1957, agreement. One was in a valley south of Luang Prabang and the other was a former French Foreign Legion camp on the Plain of Jars, the Thong Mai Hin camp.

In mid-May, the Vientiane government adopted a firm attitude toward the two Pathet Lao battalions, and gave them an ultimatum: They must, within the next twenty-four hours, accept integration into the national army on the government's terms or else surrender and resign from the army. On May 17, the First Battalion south of Luang Prabang agreed to integration. A letter from Prince Souphanouvong, found on the person of the battalion commander and written some weeks earlier, instructed him to delay integration until after the next general elections. Evidently, Souphanouvong had intended the Pathet Lao troops to delay integrating as long as possible. But, in the face of the government's sudden ultimatum, he changed his instructions and ordered compliance with Phoui's integration ultimatum.

With the Second Battalion at the Plain of Jars, it was a different story. During eighteen months of living in camp, the Pathet Lao guerrillas and their families, largely Black Thai, Meo, and Kha, had been the object of increasingly lax surveillance. The Lao guards at the gates to the camp passed along food and water to the guerrillas and even, out of compassion, allowed some persons to slip in or out.

But on the morning of May 19 the guards were shocked out of their complacency. Overnight, the entire camp had been emptied. Its occupants—men, women, and children—had vanished, taking with them all their belongings.[26]

Upon learning of this colossal blunder, General Ouan Ratikon, who had been in charge of the government's efforts to negotiate the integration of the Pathet Lao troops, flew to the Plain of Jars and took command. He ordered the dropping of paratroopers along the battalion's presumed escape route and the scattering of leaflets bearing a reprint of Souphanouvong's last-minute message to the First Battalion ordering compliance with the integration demand.

In Vientiane, Souphanouvong and the other remaining NLHS members were placed under house arrest. There is evidence that the Second Battalion's escape was authorized not by Souphanouvong but by another, higher echelon in the Pathet Lao command, probably in Sam Neua or in Hanoi. The orders may very well have bypassed Souphanouvong completely, and it is possible he was not even aware of the battalion's intentior to escape into the forest.

In any case, the Second Battalion's commander, by alternating rear-guard skirmishes with bogus offers to negotiate, succeeded in getting his troops safely beyond the reach of General Ouan's paratroopers. The Second Battalion disappeared from view. By the standards of many another country, this overt treachery was sufficient cause for the Pathet Lao leaders still in Vientiane to be lined up against a wall and shot. But to the Buddhist Lao, such reprisals are unheard of. Souphanouvong was released from house arrest on June 6.

Phoui's government announced that the soldiers of the Second Battalion would henceforth be treated as deserters. It was now the beginning of the rainy season, and Vientiane observers predicted a temporary halt in military activity. But subsequent events demonstrated the folly of trying to forecast the future in Laos.

[26] Sisouk na Champassak, *op. cit.,* p. 80.

7.

The Failure of the "Hard" Policy

The escape of the crack fighters of the Second Pathet Lao Battalion under the noses of their guards in the spring of 1959 shattered, overnight, the accords worked out so patiently by Prince Souvanna Phouma with the Neo Lao Hak Sat. Once this became apparent, the Pathet Lao acted to reinstate their power in the provinces of Sam Neua and Phong Saly.

They did so with the active encouragement of the North Vietnamese, who had reason to be alarmed by the decisiveness exhibited by the anti-Communist Phoui Sananikone government. On June 8, Radio Hanoi reported: "The first number of a newspaper addressed to the people and published by the Pathet Lao battalion in flight has reached Hanoi. The newspaper explains that as the reintegration agreements have not been respected, the battalion is obliged to defend itself." The battalion completed its return to "its former revolutionary bases," according to the Hanoi newspaper *Nhan Dan* (*The People*), on June 10. On May 20, the North Vietnamese news agency had referred to the "civil war," portending further foreign assistance and the danger of escalating military shipments in Laos.

Ominously, beginning about mid-July, small detachments of guerrillas struck at isolated government outposts deep in the jungles of Sam Neua Province. The attackers were found to be Black Thai tribesmen who inhabit areas astride the Laos-North Vietnam border. It was uncertain whether they were members of the Second Battalion.

In accord with General Giap's precepts, each attack mounted a superior local force against a Royal Army garrison. Although, over-all, the Pathet Lao were numerically inferior, the Royal Army forces were scattered in companies and platoons across the length and breadth of Laos.

Nor was the morale of the Royal Army equal to that of the attackers. In Sam Neua Province, the troops garrisoning mud forts (the defenses of the towns consisted of mud forts and trenchworks; the soldiers lived in thatched huts, and sometimes wooden barracks) were supplemented by local "self-defense forces." These militia were considerably less reliable than the regular troops, and in the thick of an attack often went over to the Pathet Lao. This happened, for instance, in the village of Muong Son, thirty-five miles west of the town of Sam Neua, where the lieutenant in command of the Royal Army company defending the village was shot in the back by militiamen who deserted during a Pathet Lao attack on July 20.

As far back as the memories of the village elders go, combatants in the jungles of Laos had tricked the enemy by making him think he was about to be overwhelmed by a large, well-equipped army. Before launching an assault on a village, the attackers commonly sent messengers ahead into the villages, in the guise of travelers, to buy rice or opium in order to create rumors of a massive concentration of troops beyond the mountains. Usually the attacks were launched just before daybreak with a concentrated mortar barrage or volley of rifle fire. Often the attackers heightened the impression of massive numerical superiority by shouting at the top of their voice or by blowing bugles. The Pathet Lao guerrillas repeated this pattern in village after village. At the first blast of the bugles, the handful of terrorized defenders usually fled into the darkness of the surrounding jungle.

A further difficulty for the army garrisons was that they had little or no communication with their rear areas, since contact was limited largely to messengers or liaison planes. They were susceptible to the illusion that they were cut off, that they could not summon and receive reinforcements in time. Thus they frequently resorted to a standing order for garrisons under attack by superior forces to abandon posts and make their way through the jungle to the next post, there to regroup and prepare for a counterattack.

These conditions made the renewed guerrilla campaign in Laos a very fluid thing indeed. At the height of the monsoon season, when nine days out of ten were overcast and rain poured down, Vientiane went for weeks without definite word about the military situation along the North Vietnam border. Alarming rumors spread.

The situation looked threatening. Sop Nao, a village at the head of the traditional invasion route from Vietnam by way of the Dien

Bien Phu valley, was briefly occupied by guerrillas. The town of Sam Neua, a collection of shops and houses bordering a dirt road that led nowhere, with a population of about 3,000, was reported encircled by roving bands of guerrillas.

To the credit of the tiny Lao air force, its Beavers and C-47's succeeded in operating a hazardous airlift to the single grass airstrip a mile from Sam Neua. They brought troop reinforcements and ammunition, food and clothing, and above all reassurance for the panic-stricken population crowding the airstrip in the desperate fear that an entire North Vietnamese army was about to sweep down on the town.

On July 23, in response to a request from Prime Minister Phoui Sananikone, the United States announced it was furnishing additional technicians to conduct an emergency training program that would expand the Royal Army from 25,000 to 29,000 men. The technicians would remain in Laos for six months (the period was later extended in view of the continuing "crisis") and would wear civilian clothes. In the following two weeks, about a hundred of these technicians entered Laos, along with new equipment, including tanks and trucks, to replace worn-out Royal Army items.

In reply to a Soviet accusation that Phoui was handing over control of the Royal Army to the United States, a State Department spokesman declared, "The Lao army is controlled exclusively by the sovereign government of Laos." The American statement was only too true. The United States, despite its gifts of weapons and money, never controlled the Lao army. The tanks it gave the Lao army were to have far more effect in staging a *coup d'état* in Vientiane than in fighting the guerrillas in the roadless jungles of Sam Neua Province. This is the best evidence of how little control the United States exerted over the Lao army.

On July 29, a government communiqué stated that a grave situation had arisen in Sam Neua Province: "According to the latest reports reaching Vientiane, it seems established that the rebel bands operating in the Sam Neua sector do not belong to the rebel battalion from the Plain of Jars but represent new elements entirely equipped, armed, and stiffened [*encadrés*] by the Democratic Republic of Vietnam."

It had been decided, the communiqué stated, to charge certain NLHS leaders "whose collusion with the foreigner is established" with offenses against the security of the state. Prince Souphanouvong, under house arrest since the previous May, was removed from his comfortable single-story villa on the bank of the Mekong to the Phone Kheng police camp on the northern outskirts of town. Also detained in barracks were fifteen others, including Colonel Singkapo, Phoumi Vongvichit, Nouhak Phoumsavan, Sithone Komadam, Phoun Sipraseuth, and the editor of *Lao Hak Sat*.

Because of the threatening military situation, Phoui's government on August 4 proclaimed a state of emergency in five provinces—Phong Saly, Sam Neua, Xieng Khouang, Khammouane, and Savannakhet. On the same day it requested United Nations Secretary-General Dag Hammarskjöld to inform members of the situation and stressed the role of North Vietnam.

Hanoi and Peking propaganda immediately raised a barrage of objections to involving the United Nations, of which they were not members, in any peace-keeping role in Laos. This campaign was coupled with renewed calls for reactivation of the ICC and reference of the crisis to the Geneva Co-Chairmen, Britain and Russia. On August 8, a program was published in Peking and said to have been issued a week previously by the NLHS. It made nine points, including a demand for a coalition Lao government in which the NLHS would be represented.

Phoui's message to the United Nations was followed by a lull in guerrilla activity that lasted approximately a fortnight. But toward the end of August, the pinprick attacks began again in widely scattered areas of Laos adjoining the Vietnam border.

On September 4, Phoui sent a second message to the United Nations, stating categorically that North Vietnamese soldiers were fighting on Lao soil. He referred to the attacks of the previous month, and declared that "on August 30, a fresh attack, more violent than the previous ones, was launched against the posts of Muong Het and Xieng Kho. Elements from the Democratic Republic of Vietnam took part in the attack, which was supported by artillery fire from the other side of the frontier."

Muong Het and Xieng Kho are in the Ma River valley, approximately thirty miles north of the town of Sam Neua. The former was defended by 250 armed men, mostly militia. Xieng Kho's garrison was smaller. Simultaneous attacks had been mounted on two other posts in the same region, Sop Sai and Sop Bau, the latter defended by only 30 militiamen.

The clandestine nature of the military actions and the inaccessibility of the fighting area made it difficult to gauge the extent of the North Vietnamese involvement on the ground. The case against North Vietnam was seriously handicapped because Phoui's references to North Vietnamese "elements" were not substantiated by the capture of any foreign troops in these actions.

The scale of the fighting was considerably exaggerated by the Western press. The more than fifty newspaper correspondents who surged into Vientiane focused on the dramatic aspects of the situation, the minor armed clashes over a wide area that, when recounted in a coordinated story, made headlines. Their dispatches gave little or no description of the Communist infestation of northeastern Laos or of the years of insidious subversion of the Royal Government's authority there.

Reporters from Western countries, confronted with a guerrilla war, attempted to describe it with the standard military vocabulary. Terms like "advance," "front," "main line of defense," "move up," "fall back," and "storm" hopelessly distorted the picture for Western readers. One observer later drew up a glossary of military terms for Laos. A fortress was defined as a "mud fort in a clearing defended by at least six men," and a siege was a "concentrated attack lasting more than five minutes." Unfortunately, only a few correspondents got anywhere near Sam Neua during the rainy season and could appreciate the accuracy of these definitions.[1]

The Security Council met on September 7 to consider Phoui's charges against North Vietnam, and later that month dispatched an investigatory subcommittee to Laos. The subcommittee members flew to Sam Neua Province, where they interrogated a number of prisoners and refugees, several of whom were Black Thai. In its report, the subcommitte stated:

> Practically all witnesses (40 out of 41) stated that the hostile elements received support from the territory of the DRV [North Vietnam] consisting mainly of equipment, arms, ammunition, supplies, and the help of political cadres.[2]

On the question of whether there had been an actual invasion, the subcommittee reported that the evidence "did not clearly establish whether there were crossings of the frontier by regular troops

[1] One of these few was the late Bernard B. Fall, who has left us his firsthand observations and a damning indictment of some of the major newspapers and magazines in the United States, in his book *Anatomy of a Crisis: The Laos Crisis of 1961* (New York: Doubleday, 1969). Similar irresponsible reporting, however, was to be repeated in Laos in February, 1970.

[2] *Report of the Security Council Sub-Committee under Resolution of 7 September 1959* (United Nations Security Council s/4236, November 5, 1959), p. 31.

of the DRV." Subcommittee members talked, with the help of interpreters, to villagers who said they had seen strangers whom they identified as North Vietnamese soldiers passing through their villages. They also were shown damage caused by exploding shellfire. Aside from this slim evidence, and the absence of any North Vietnamese prisoners, the subcommittee members must have been impressed by the ease with which the inhabitants of both sides of the unmarked border could come and go in all innocence.

There may have been other reasons, however, for the subcommittee's failure to condemn North Vietnam for direct armed intervention. Phoui said later[3] that he felt the subcommittee had hesitated to substantiate his charges against North Vietnam because of international repercussions, particularly with respect to the Soviet Union. He felt nevertheless that the publicity given the subcommittee's investigation helped materially in damping down the crisis atmosphere that had been created. In the final analysis, the fact that the subcommittee did *not* report that there were no North Vietnamese troops in Laos is significant.

The subcommittee reported that the Lao government placed its casualties in the fighting between July 16 and October 11 at 99 killed, 96 wounded, and 125 missing.

At Phoui's request, a United Nations economic mission also visited Laos. Its report, while not exactly encouraging, was, in fact, the most objective survey of the country's economic needs ever made. As a result, the U.N. undertook some small-scale technical-assistance schemes, most of them in the field of public health, in order to fill some gaps in the American aid program. (As the mission report pointed out, only 8 per cent of American funds had gone to building roads, schools, and other developments.)

In the midst of these disturbing events in his Kingdom, Sisavang Vong died at Luang Prabang. At the time of his death, he was, at seventy-four, the oldest reigning monarch in the world. A beloved sovereign, Sisavang Vong had enjoyed the pleasures of royal life, receiving visitors to his palace on the bank of the Mekong or sailing off to France to take his cure at Vittel. During the dark days of 1953, when his capital was threatened by the Viet Minh, his stubbornly determined presence there in the face of French advice to retire to safety surely ranks among the splendid episodes of his Kingdom's history.

[3] In an interview with the author in Vientiane, April 6, 1970. The Security Council's decision to send an investigatory mission to Laos coincided with Premier Nikita Khrushchev's visit to the United States.

His successor, Savang Vatthana, was of a more austere, less flamboyant character. Educated at the Ecole de Science Politique in Paris, he had read widely and had traveled throughout the world. But from the first days of his reign, he was assailed by a host of troubles.

The disturbances of the summer of 1959 had demonstrated that the North Vietnamese, who were not members of the United Nations or any other significant international body and who possessed the most meager material resources, could nevertheless stir up a crisis in the neighboring kingdom when it suited their purposes, get all the capitals of the world stirred up, and then, with just as much control, tamp down the crisis. This exercise must have confirmed their judgment that the United States had learned nothing from the French experience.

An Abortive Putsch

Before the expiration of Phoui's one year of special powers, he announced his intention of reshuffling his Cabinet. The principal change he contemplated was the removal of ministers who belonged to the CDNI, the most important of whom were Khampan Panya, Minister of Foreign Affairs, and Phoumi Nosavan, Secretary of State for National Defense. When Phoui renounced his special powers, the National Assembly met in extraordinary session. On December 17, the deputies voted to prolong the Assembly's four-year mandate (which was to expire on December 25) until the new general elections, scheduled for the following April. The CDNI, whose main backers were high-ranking army officers, opposed Phoui and argued that an attempt to prolong the Assembly's mandate would be unconstitutional; they claimed that until the elections the country should be governed by a provisional Cabinet named by the King.

On December 30, Phoui submitted his resignation to King Savang Vatthana, in the belief that the National Assembly, which had closed its extraordinary session on December 25, would retain its mandate until the coming elections. However, during the early hours of December 31, soldiers acting on the orders of all five generals of the Royal Army occupied the principal public buildings in Vientiane. Four armored cars took up positions surrounding the residence of the King, who was in Vientiane for the extraordinary National Assembly session. Not a shot was fired.

Simultaneously, the radio station proclaimed that the King had accepted Phoui's resignation and that the army had taken over maintenance of public law and order until a new, legally constituted government could be named. The National Assembly, the communiqué said, was now considered dissolved, and all actions taken by this body after December 25 were considered null and void.

The King's presence in Vientiane enabled the generals to have frequent audiences with him, at which they protested their devotion to the throne and to the Constitution. None of the five was more energetic in these protestations than Brigadier General Phoumi Nosavan. Phoumi's four colleagues were Major General Sounthone Pathammavong, the chief of staff; Brigadier General Sing Ratanasamay, his adjutant; Brigadier General Ouan Ratikon, commandant of the armed forces; and Brigadier General Amkha Soukhavong, his adjutant.

The generals were careful to point out that they were acting to preserve constitutionality by preventing the National Assembly from illegally extending its mandate, and that they had no political ambitions. Their putsch was a natural consequence of their genuine disgust at the political situation. They wanted action. They were also disturbed that the elimination of CDNI influence from the Cabinet might lead to a reconciliation with the Pathet Lao, who had reacted to Phoui's reshuffle by stating their willingness to enter into "peaceful consultations" to settle their dispute "at any time." Had they, the generals of the Royal Army, not spent the last six months battling a rebellion whose leaders were sympathetic to the Communists? And here were these civilian politicians, many of them old-time masters at corruption and graft, arguing hotly about how long their terms should run. Was this not madness?

Besides frustration, another factor motivating the generals was their conviction that they alone could prepare the country to resist the Communist menace. The army has a peculiar status in Laos. It is the only organization that reaches every part of the territory and that involves the life of virtually every Lao family. It is the country's greatest unifier, a catalyst with the potential of making the diverse peoples of Laos feel as if they belonged to a single nation. The army may be slipshod and lazy, but without it there would be little to make the villages feel the existence of the monarchy, the flag, and the government.

Also, in economically underdeveloped Laos, the national army represents a reservoir of manual skills and practical training. Unlike a Western army, which puts to use skills acquired in civilian

life, the Lao army receives men with virtually no training whatsoever and is compelled to instruct them. This is another reason why
service in the army commands prestige in Laos.

Third, the army is the Lao economy's only sizable source of
circulating currency. In the army, many Lao are paid in cash for
the first time. In their native villages, they had usually worked for
remuneration in kind, such as rice, lodging, or a marriage into a
good family. The Lao soldier with his monthly pay, equivalent to
about $10, is a rich man compared to his peasant brothers who still
live in a barter economy.

For the inhabitants of Indochina, the military has long been a
remunerative way of life. Many of the top-ranking officers of the
Royal Army (and of the Pathet Lao, too) served as noncoms or
officers in the Lao Territorial army attached to the French Expeditionary Corps.

Phoumi Nosavan was among these. Commissioned as a lieutenant in 1950, he had taken part in the 1954 Geneva Conference
with the rank of major as military adviser to the Lao delegation.
He had spent a year at the French War College in 1957 and graduated with honors. He was soft-spoken, but his tenacity contributed
to his rapid advancement.

Like the other four generals involved in the attempted putsch
of December, 1959, General Phoumi was in deep sympathy with
the reforms advocated by the CDNI, a sympathy that appears to
have been encouraged by his contacts with the U.S. Central Intelligence Agency.

General Phoumi had a genuine desire to see Laos free itself from
the shackles of underdevelopment, and in this narrow sense he was
indeed a patriot, albeit a patriot who saw no objection to accepting,
under various guises, large amounts of money from a foreign
power.

The general was strongly influenced by Marshal Sarit Thanarat,
Thailand's Prime Minister, whom General Phoumi called uncle.
Under a benign army dictatorship instituted by Marshal Sarit, Thai-
land had achieved an economic stability and prosperity that was
the envy of Southeast Asia. Phoumi was also deeply impressed by
General de Gaulle.

The CIA chose to support General Phoumi because the army
was the only organization that could put through a program of development in a country where there were no effective political
parties, where basic education was still lacking, where malaria and

malnutrition were rampant, and where the most lucrative, if unofficial, export was opium. There was every indication that liberal democracy could not overcome such obstacles. The army, however, could provide a disciplined leadership for economic progress, even as the Communist parties professed themselves determineᵤ to provide in the underdeveloped countries.

If American policy required a strongman in Laos, General Phoumi was unquestionably the leading candidate. Of all the generals, he had the most drive. However, certain American officials did not share the CIA's optimistic evaluation of the capabilities of General Phoumi and the Lao army. After the putsch, Horace Smith, who had succeeded Parsons as Ambassador in Vientiane in 1958, bluntly told the author that General Phoumi was using anti-Communism, through the device of the CDNI, to further his own personal ambitions. A year later, when American policy found itself at a dead end and actually jeopardizing the whole Western position in Southeast Asia through a most unhealthy polarization in Laos, it was not for any lack of on-the-spot information.

Communist propaganda has pictured General Phoumi as an American puppet. That is quite wrong. Whatever encouragement he may have received at the outset from the CIA, General Phoumi later showed plainly that he was willing to resist pressures mounted by the entire apparatus of American diplomacy. In 1962, when even the CIA had been disabused of its high hopes for Phoumi and all U.S. agencies supported formation of a coalition government under Souvanna Phouma, the General proved to be a most stubborn and uncooperative man. Oddly enough, he grew in stature in Laos by this show of resistance against the Americans, and this played a not inconsiderable part in earning him a place in the troika under Souvanna Phouma.

The generals had badly underestimated adverse reaction outside their own country to their attempted putsch. Actually, they probably fully intended to hold the elections that were constitutionally due the following April and then to return power to a civilian Cabinet.

However, any such plans were abandoned when the British and French ambassadors, concerned lest a military dictatorship be interpreted as the final scrapping of the Geneva cease-fire, sought out Ambassador Smith, as well as the Australian chargé d'affaires, and went in a common front to the King. They told him that he had been misinformed if he believed that such a military dictatorship would receive the approbation of the countries with which Laos maintained relations. They advised him of their unanimous desire to see the constitutional process preserved. Immediately afterward, a telegram to the same effect arrived from the Secretary-General of the United Nations. The generals were constrained to pull back.

King Savang Vatthana thereupon named Kou Abhay, the aged and venerable head of the King's Council, as Prime Minister. On January 7, 1960, a new provisional civilian Cabinet entrusted with preparing general elections was formed. The only military man in the Cabinet was General Phoumi. As Minister of National Defense, Phoumi exercised considerable influence because his ministry controlled more than 80 per cent of the Lao budget. Although he had not come out top man, he had not done badly.

Electoral Rigging

The elections, set for the first Sunday in April, confronted Kou's government with the problem Souvanna Phouma's government had faced two years earlier: NLHS candidates, contesting the fifty-nine seats to be filled, might sweep to another victory on the strength of the undisrupted, ruthless guerrilla organization in the countryside. Yet, barring the NLHS candidates from the ballots would be a serious, open breach of the Lao government's pledge at Geneva to conciliate all factions. The government could take at least some comfort from the fact that the NLHS deputies who had been arrested the previous year were still awaiting trial in their police barracks outside Vientiane and thus would not be able to run.

In a blow aimed at other potential NLHS candidates, the government decreed higher educational standards and larger financial deposits for candidates. The educational requirement hit the NLHS particularly hard because, aside from its titular chief, very few of its cadres had any formal education at all; indeed, most of them were illiterate. Of the nine NLHS deputies elected in 1958, only three besides Souphanouvong met the new requirements.

Also, the electoral map of Laos was completely redrawn once again so as to gerrymander those districts, in the south especially, where it was thought the NLHS candidates stood a chance of winning a large vote, as they had done in 1958.

In the face of these obstacles, only nine NLHS candidates ran in the election. The government proudly announced that it had magnanimously permitted Souphanouvong to issue instructions, from his prison barracks, for the NLHS candidates to contest the election according to the rules and do the best they could.

Beneath the façade of contesting the elections against government-supported candidates, the tireless Pathet Lao political and guerrilla cadres went about their work at the village level. Even while guerrilla raids on government outposts decreased in frequency at the beginning of 1960, Vientiane's control over thousands of villages throughout the country was being systematically subverted.

The Pathet Lao technique was to turn to their own advantage the centuries-old system of local administration. From the capital, the established hierarchy of government radiated out to the provincial governors (*chao khoueng*) and thence to the district officers (*chao muong*). There it stopped. That was the extent of the centrally appointed officials.

To implement its measures, the government depended on the district officers to pass orders on to the village headman (*nai ban*). But the village headman was not appointed by the central government; he was elected by the village. So to prevent the central government's authority from reaching to the village, all the Pathet Lao had to do was to get their own agent elected village headman.

Conversely, the central government depended on the village headman to inform the district officer of local grievances. If it did not know what grievances the villages had, it could not respond to them. Tradition in Laos did not encourage the elevation to headman of a forward-looking young man. Although the village election was theoretically a democratic affair, with candidacy open to all, the post usually went to the village elder, the man who owned the most land and buffaloes, the man whose daughters were most sought in marriage because they guaranteed maximum advancement in the social scale.

If a village headman was not responsive to local grievances, the district officer had even less reason to concern himself with village demands. Secure in his government job, he was usually not even a native of the district he administered.

Nor were the deputies elected to the National Assembly a more effective channel of communications between village and capital. Most deputies were members of the Kingdom's leading families, elected as an honor. They were rarely schoolteachers or men who had made a reputation for honesty or efficiency in the district in which they were elected.

Just as the Chinese Communist Party had done in the 1930's and 1940's, the Pathet Lao now concentrated on placing their own agents on the village level. In China, the appointive authority had stopped at the *hsien,* or district. It was the township, or *hsiang,* that was all-important in the effort to substitute Communist authority for non-Communist.

In China, the intermediary between district and township had for centuries been the landed gentry, most of whom lived in the chief town of the district, gathering their rents from their surrounding lands. This class of people was lacking in Laos, however, where most of the peasants owned their own land and where they could increase their holdings merely by clearing a new patch of jungle. The absence of a landed gentry made it easier for the Pathet Lao to isolate the village from higher authority, but made it more difficult for them to incite peasant resentment over the alleged wrongs committed by the ruling class.

The Pathet Lao undertook a course of subversion that was a calculated combination of persuasion and coercion. Their cadres would live for six months in a village, observing its routine of everyday life and its channels of leadership. During this time, they would determine which man most suited their purposes. Usually he was a relatively young man. Next, the Pathet Lao cadres set about winning this man away from his allegiance to traditional authority. They impressed upon him that the Pathet Lao guerrilla network, which they portrayed as the defenders of "the people," operated in the countryside under the very noses of the government's troops, which they portrayed as molesters of "the people."

Another Pathet Lao technique was to incite dissatisfaction in the village with the traditional authority. Hard-core Pathet Lao guerrillas made the village unsafe for the district officer to visit, except under escort, and then the village cadres spread the word that the central government was neglecting the welfare of the village. Foreign aid, they said, was going to enrich a handful of well-placed men in Vientiane, while the village had no prospect of ever advancing itself under this government.

The Pathet Lao impressed on their agent-to-be the prospect of becoming the real chief of his village once the cause of "the people" had triumphed. If the incumbent chief was an exceptionally young or dynamic man, the Pathet Lao frequently concentrated on his deputy, fomenting a rivalry between the two men and trying to embroil the chief in unpopular measures that would work against him and in favor of his deputy. If a village was of special importance to the Pathet Lao, they sent their agent-to-be to Hanoi or even Peking free of charge for a year's "education." Also, they sent his children to North Vietnamese or Chinese schools, making them in effect hostages for the cooperation of their parents.

Working persistently and shrewdly, the Pathet Lao, through propaganda, split loyalties, and calculated intimidation, gradually arrived at the point where their words carried more weight than those of the central government. In all this, their minute knowledge of village life served them well.

Coercion was also put to effective use by the Pathet Lao. On occasion, the power of the guerrilla organization was impressed on the villagers by the assassination of a key anti-Pathet Lao figure well known to the inhabitants. Such acts persuaded the district officer of the inadvisability of cooperating too enthusiastically with the central government in its heavy-handed attempts to root out the Pathet Lao. On the very Sunday on which the 1960 elections were held, a Meo district officer accused by the guerrillas of meddling too much in the affairs of his villages was ambushed and killed while riding in his jeep between two villages near Nong Het in Xieng Khouang Province. One American observer called the Pathet Lao technique "a propaganda sentence punctuated by a terrorist period."

As the 1960 election campaign approached its climax, Royal Army units that had been concentrated in the north during the previous summer were dispatched to the south for mopping-up operations against Pathet Lao guerrillas, to make the countryside safe for balloting. In the course of these operations, the troops meted out discipline as a warning in villages suspected of harboring Pathet Lao cadres. Sometimes the discipline was imposed on an individual basis; not infrequently, however, a whole village was set afire. The Pathet Lao cadres in certain villages turned the mopping-up operation to their advantage by arranging anonymous denunciations of Communist complicity against villagers who had caused them particular trouble. The result of this countryside campaign was not the mopping up of the Pathet Lao but the alienation of the peasantry.

Meanwhile, the energies of the central government were monopolized by the election preparations. Satisfaction prevailed in Vientiane during those incredibly hot days of April when the sun melted the asphalt in the streets and the dry south wind lifted the loose sand from the Mekong's dry bed and whirled it, in tiny cyclones, into the baked city, foreshadowing the breaking of the monsoon. The country was once again quiet. Members of the interim Cabinet, having successfully arranged the electoral campaign, relaxed on veranda chairs in the evening twilight and concluded that perhaps

Laos was not condemned to perpetual chaos after all: The nation was in good hands; there was no National Assembly to raise embarrassing constitutional issues, and speculation about who would head the next government had not yet really begun.

The government's measures to ensure that no NLHS deputies were elected had been effective. On election day, it was clear from the first that there would be a landslide for the progovernment candidates, despite their habitual large number (almost three candidates for each seat) and their self-defeating family rivalries.

The results were incredible. In Sam Neua, the Pathet Lao base area, the NLHS candidate, a former governor of the province, was reported to have received a total of 13 votes to the successful candidate's 6,508.

In each of the six electoral districts of Champassak Province, progovernment candidates were reported to have received 90 per cent or more of the votes cast. In one of these districts, the leader of the Santiphab Party, Quinim Pholsena, was defeated by 17,175 votes to 721. In another, the NLHS candidate was credited with 4 votes to the opposition's 18,189, although there were at least 5 members of his immediate family eligible to vote for him.

The single NLHS candidate in Savannakhet Province was reported defeated by a margin of 7,414 to 881.

Plainly, the election had been rigged. Whether the soldiers guarding the polling places had exerted pressure or whether the vote totals had been falsified, the leaders of the minority Santiphab Party and the National Union Party were clearly justified in charging a fraud.

The real story of these elections emerged slowly. An observer who visited Sam Neua two days before the election saw Royal Army soldiers dropping progovernment campaign leaflets from planes. The NLHS candidate told him that he was fully aware that the legal opposition did not stand a chance but nonetheless was determined to go through with the election in accordance with Souphanouvong's instructions.

An example of the heavy-handed tactics was the telegram addressed by the Interior Ministry to civil servants in Pakse, capital of Champassak Province. It named the six progovernment candidates in the province and instructed civil servants to give them "financial, material, and moral support"—or face disciplinary sanctions.

CIA agents participated in the election rigging, with or without the authority of the American Ambassador. A Foreign Service officer flatly told an observer in Savannakhet that, prior to the voting, he had seen CIA agents distribute bagfuls of money to village headmen; the inescapable conclusion was that the United States had been buying votes.

For an intelligent opposition leader like Souphanouvong, the 1960 general election in Laos was more than a travesty of democracy. It was proof positive that the West can stage-manage an election just as efficiently as the Communists can.

Stiffer Attitudes in Hanoi and Peking

During the first few months of 1960, while overt guerrilla activity remained in a low key in Laos, the Vietnamese Communists sprang a major armed action in South Vietnam. To thousands of Viet Minh cadres who had been waiting out the years since 1954 in the villages of the south, this was the start of the violent phase of the struggle for reunification. The increasing risks to which the Lao Dong Party was willing to have its southern cadres expose themselves gave supreme importance to the possession of secure communications by means of trails through the mountains of Laos.

Hanoi's new line of increased force to achieve reunification with the south was formalized at the Third Congress of the Lao Dong Party in September, 1960. Le Duan, a high-ranking member of its Politburo and a native of the south himself, declared that the two strategic tasks for the party in the years ahead were the carrying out of a Socialist revolution in the north, on the one hand, and "the eradication of the colonial and semifeudal regime in South Vietnam and the realization of national reunification," on the other.

Three months later, a clandestine radio transmitter in South Vietnam broadcast news of the formation of the National Liberation Front of South Vietnam, which it described as a loose alliance of peasants, industrial workers, intellectuals, defectors from the Saigon regime's army and civil service, and representatives of all religious and ethnic minorities. At the end of 1961, in South Vietnam, a secret People's Revolutionary Party was formed. It was described as a Marxist-Leninist party with the mission of leading the National Front.

The relationship of these organs to Hanoi was later made clear in a document captured from local insurgents in May, 1962, that informed cadres that "The independent existence of the People's Revolutionary Party is only apparent. In reality, the party is the

Lao Dong Party of Vietnam, united in north and south, under the direction of the Party Central Committee whose chairman is President Ho."

Meanwhile, for reasons quite independent of North Vietnam's strategic interests in Laos, an ominous shift was taking place in Communist China's attitude toward the political situation in Laos. The Chinese had reacted quickly and unfavorably to the adjournment of the ICC, which came when the leaders in Peking were outraged at Soviet Premier Khrushchev's behavior over Lebanon and Jordan in July, 1958, particularly his eagerness to arrange negotiations with the Western powers and to invite India to a summit conference. The following month, the Chinese instigated the Quemoy crisis.

The events in Laos the following year found Peking in a more intransigent mood than Chou En-lai had expressed to the National People's Congress, in February, 1958. The crisis with India over the Tibetan revolt, and the U.S.S.R.'s tearing up of the two-year-old technical-assistance agreement in nuclear research, increased the Peking leaders' isolation in the Communist world and heightened their scornful determination to assert their influence.

The evolution of Peking's attitude toward Laos from hands-off-so-long-as-there-are-no-American-bases-there to a barely concealed concern for its own security was in accordance with the increasing doctrinal emphasis in Peking on support for "national liberation movements," which was becoming manifest in the period 1957–60.

It is particularly significant that the Chinese introduced the term "civil war" into the Laos situation in the spring of 1959, even before the North Vietnamese. In the disciplined and coordinated realm of Communist propaganda, the application of a term of such far-reaching implications as "civil war" to a situation in a neighboring country is unlikely to be haphazard or random.

"Civil war" was used for the first time on May 18 in a formal statement on the Laos situation by Peking's Ministry of Foreign Affairs. Barely two days later, Hanoi adopted the term, which thereafter was part of the North Vietnamese vocabulary in describing the summer's fighting.

To Peking, the developments unfolding in Laos increasingly assumed the pattern of an anticolonialist struggle, with growing American influence supplying the "colonialist" imprint. More and more, Peking had been supporting—verbally, only—the cause of anticolonialism. In the Middle East crisis of 1958, the walls of every

Chinese village had been plastered with huge posters proclaiming "The Chinese people support the Lebanese and the Jordanians in their anticolonial struggle!" and "Hands off Lebanon!" (Actually, few Chinese knew where Lebanon and Jordan were.) But this verbal support was backed up by the threat, more or less veiled, of help in the form of supplies or army "volunteers" on the Korea pattern. This loud championship of the anticolonial struggle, in furtherance of the Communist revolution, was of immense importance in Peking's growing quarrel with Moscow.

As early as May, 1958, at the 8th Party Congress, Chinese Communist Party Vice Chairman Liu Shao-chi spoke of the "uninterrupted revolution." A few months later it was disclosed that millions of Chinese peasants were being militantly organized into rural communes designed to raise the country by its own bootstraps and make the transition to a Communist society. And in the theoretical journal *Red Flag* in April, 1960, Peking warned that all "revolutionary" Leninists should support colonial revolutions "without the slightest reservations."

Peking had expressed its growing concern over what was happening in Laos:

> Disregarding the wishes of the people of Indochina for peace, the United States arbitrarily included these countries in the sphere of "defense" of SEATO. . . . The United States formally set up her foreign aid mission in Laos as an organization to carry out her military, political, and economic aggression. . . . A stream of arms and ammunition came into Laos from the United States and a large number of U.S. military personnel in the guise of "technical personnel" or "employees" arrived to control the armed forces and military bases of Laos. To completely wreck the Geneva agreements, the United States used all manner of base and underhand methods and indulged in open interference in Laos' political affairs. . . . The scrapping of the Geneva agreements by the Lao authorities at the insistence of the United States has now created a grave situation in Laos and menaced peace in the countries of Indochina and the Far East.[4]

The American military aid agreement with the Phoui Sananikone government, especially, was taken by the Chinese to be a violation of the conditions under which in 1954 they had accepted the status of Laos and Cambodia. The chief Chinese delegate to the second Geneva Conference was later to say in reference to the provision of military training to the Lao army, "Our agreement to this right for

[4] *Jenmin Jih Pao (People's Daily,* Peking), June 3, 1959.

France was an indication of confidence in France. If we then foresaw that France would arbitrarily transfer this right to the United States, we definitely would not have agreed to this right for France."[5]

On August 12, 1959, a spokesman of the Chinese Foreign Ministry took the Laos issue one step further than the Chinese had ever taken it before by implying that the security of China was involved. "The Chinese Government and people," the spokesman said, "are watching closely the daily deteriorating situation in Laos. All activities of the U.S. Government and the Laotian authorities violating the Geneva agreements and creating tension in Indochina, and further menacing the security of China, will certainly face the firm opposition of the Chinese Government and people. The U.S. Government and the Laotian authorities must bear full responsibility for the consequences of their activities."

Despite their hints of direct involvement in the Laos "civil war" in the summer of 1959, the Chinese Communists had taken no *action* toward involvement. Nevertheless, the statements from Peking raised once again in Washington the bogey of a massive invasion of Laos by Communist forces.

In the summer of 1959, the United States, despite the nuclear capability vested in the aircraft of the Seventh Fleet patrolling the western Pacific, began to envisage the possibility of having to engage in a ground campaign in Laos. With very little publicity, a stand-by force of American soldiers and their logistical support, known as Task Force 116, was set up on Okinawa, under the command of General Donald M. Weller. It would be assigned to intervene in Laos if the need arose.

In setting up this task force, the United States was moving dangerously near the very situation that, as Dulles had assured the Senate, American policy was designed to avoid—the unilateral commitment of American ground troops to Indochina.

Souphanouvong's Escape

Prince Souphanouvong and his NLHS colleagues, who had been arrested at the height of the "aggression" panic in 1959, had since been vegetating in the Phone Kheng police camp just outside Vientiane. Souphanouvong passed the time reading Greek classics. His colleagues in detention were seven other NLHS deputies—Phoumi Vongvichit, Nouhak Phoumsavan, Sithone Komadam, Phoun Sipraseuth, and three others—Colonel Singkapo, the military commander

[5] New China News Agency, Geneva, August 2, 1961.

who had been engaged in the abortive negotiations with Phoui's government for reintegration into the Royal Army, and seven lesser personalities suspected of carrying on activities on behalf of the NLHS.

After the government's announcement that the suspects would be charged with offenses against the security of the state, defense lawyers had been appointed, and a trial date set. However, it soon became apparent that the detention of the NLHS deputies was acutely embarrassing to the government. The trial date came and went. It was not even certain whether prosecution of these NLHS deputies would serve the government's purpose of dismembering the NLHS. Despite the government's announcement that four other NLHS leaders—Kaysone Phomvihan, Phay Dang, Khamtay Siphandon, and Souk Vongsak (a deputy from Luang Prabang who had fled Vientiane before the "aggression" crisis)—would be tried in absentia, all of them were still at large and in a position to call upon North Vietnam for aid. In this light, Souphanouvong represented a "moderate" among the NLHS leaders.

Moreover, the trial, if held, would be certain to produce statements for the defense that would prove exceedingly embarrassing to the Vientiane government. The main defense attorney was the leader of the Santiphab Party, Quinim Pholsena, a humorless man who had been a member of the Constituent Assembly in 1947. He would relish the opportunity to further his inordinate ambitions by a successful defense of the "Red Prince"—Souphanouvong.

Souphanouvong, the defense argument would run, had spent ten years in the jungle fighting to free Laos from the fetters of colonialism, while General Phoumi had been living in luxury on a fat salary paid by the Americans. Who, then, was patriot and who traitor?

Several foreign embassies advised Vientiane strongly against holding the trial, and three successive governments had been only too glad to demur. Souphanouvong had passed these ten months conducting a long-range attempt to win the loyalty of his prison guards, an attempt that he described as successful in an account published in the Hanoi newspaper *Nhan Dan* in May, 1961.

Before the politicians of Vientiane could find a solution to their dilemma over the trial, the NLHS "traitors" found one for them. In the early morning hours of May 24, 1960, amid the raging of a violent tropical thunderstorm that flung almost solid sheets of water across the jungles, Souphanouvong and his co-prisoners escaped from Phone Kheng, taking their guards with them. When the day guards arrived on duty at 6 A.M., they found the barracks deserted.

While in prison, Souphanouvong had maintained contact with the rest of the Pathet Lao leadership by means of smuggled messages. We have already seen that, by means of such messages, he ordered NLHS candidates throughout Laos to engage in the 1960 electoral campaign despite indications they could not win. How much actual authority Souphanouvong exercised during his captivity remains unclear, but it is fairly clear that the influence of the "Vietnamese faction" in the Pathet Lao, represented by people like Kaysone, grew during this period.

Once free, Souphanouvong did not hurry to rejoin the top command in Sam Neua or to travel to Hanoi. During the next five months, according to his own account, he traveled 300 miles on foot, visiting Pathet Lao strongholds in each province. He says he finally arrived in Sam Neua on November 7, 1960. By that time he was tired out from his long trek and noticeably weakened by illness.

Coup d'État

The matter of deciding upon the composition of the Cabinet had dragged on for weeks since the April election. It was obvious that General Phoumi, while not a member of the National Assembly, would have the largest say in any Cabinet formed during CDNI control over the deputies' votes. The general exuded optimism about the political course the country was taking; he called the election results "better than expected."

The Cabinet list presented to the National Assembly included General Phoumi as Minister of National Defense. The Prime Minister was Prince Somsanith, who had been elected a deputy unopposed and who had acquired a reputation for honesty during his tenure as Governor of Nam Tha Province, when he claimed to have visited all the province's 200 villages—not once, but twice or more —on foot.

Nevertheless, the situation in Laos was not good, especially in the military. The great vacuum left by the French between the Mekong and the Annamite Mountains still had not been filled. Confusion, corruption, and an acute lack of soldierly qualities inherent in the Lao had conspired to frustrate American efforts to create an effective fighting force, in the Western sense of the term. PEO instructors complained that the Lao seemed unable to master the techniques of modern warfare. Lao officers sent for training to Thailand did not even bother to show up for classes.

On the Lao side, serious questions were being raised about the value of the American military-aid program and the lack of economic development resulting from concentration on military objectives. The principal newspaper in Vientiane, the organ of Phoui Sananikone's political party, described the trucks and jeeps which the Americans had given the Lao, many of which lay rusting in vacant lots, as *"un tas de ferraille"* ("a heap of scrap metal").

Among the officers of the Royal Army, the generals' attempted putsch had set a dangerous precedent, whetting appetites for political power. Phoumi's adoption of civilian dress and of the other prerogatives of ministerial position in Vientiane was alienating a growing number of middle-rank Lao officers. This was especially so after the renewal of fighting against the Pathet Lao, when many of these officers recalled that they had never seen General Phoumi anywhere near a battlefield. Although the generals and a small coterie of staff officers in Vientiane associated themselves with the self-styled Young Turks of the CDNI, by no means the entire Lao army lent its support to these professed reformists in their comfortable villas by the Mekong.

Discontent among the 600 men and officers of the Second Paratroop Battalion attained such proportions that news of it reached King Savang Vatthana. This battalion, the best unit in the Royal Army, had borne the brunt of the fighting against the guerrillas. During the crisis of 1959, its young commander, Captain Kong Le, had led the battalion into action in Sam Neua Province. After that, his battalion had undertaken a series of mopping-up operations in southern Laos in preparation for the elections.

Kong Le and his three companies of devoted soldiers had then been posted to Vientiane, where they expected to have a brief respite from fighting. There they were housed in ramshackle buildings on some outlying mud flats. Kong Le protested to the Ministry of National Defense about the conditions in which his battle-weary men were compelled to live; he demanded that a large and relatively lavish mansion that had just been completed to house the family of Chief of Staff General Sounthone Pathammavong be turned over to the Second Battalion.

In response to these remonstrations by Kong Le, the Ministry informed the battalion on Friday, August 5, that a work order had been approved for construction of new barracks for the men. On Monday, the men expected to begin work on the new site of their camp. Instead, they were abruptly ordered on operations the following morning to clean up a suspected pocket of Pathet Lao guerrillas thirty miles west of Vientiane. On Monday, also, General Phoumi and the entire Cabinet emplaned for Luang Prabang to discuss with

King Savang Vatthana plans for the state funeral of King Sisavang Vong, whose body had remained embalmed in a large sandalwood bier since October, 1959. While at the Royal Palace, General Phoumi assured the monarch that the rumored dissension in the army had been taken care of.

Only hours later, Kong Le's battle-dressed paratroopers climbed in jeeps and, at three the following morning, rolled out of their encampment, presumably bound for the airport. Instead, the paratroopers fanned out across the town and occupied all strategic points: the offices of the Prime Minister and all other government Ministers, the electric power station, the radio station, and the telegraph office. They parked jeeps on the airport runways to prevent any aircraft from landing, and set up roadblocks along all approaches to the capital. They took over the large Chinaimo army camp downstream from Vientiane, and commandeered its armored cars and tanks.

The whole operation went off like clockwork. Few shots were fired, and except for two resisting guards at General Sounthone's house, there were no casualties.

Vientiane Radio began announcing a series of terse communiques formulated in perfect French. Their import was that the Second Paratroop Battalion had assumed full civil and military powers in Laos. When Vientiane's population turned out on the streets at daybreak, they were confronted all over town by squads of paratroopers in green-and-brown camouflage uniforms and red berets.

8.

Return to Neutrality

Vientiane, under the paratroopers, came alive with activity. Squads of determined-looking men, bearing rifles almost too big for them, guarded all public buildings. Jeeps and trucks loaded with cheering soldiers hurtled through the streets. At some corners, armored cars were parked in the shade of serene flame trees, the crews lounging on the turrets reading newspapers or mimeographed pamphlets. Some drank beer from their canteens (they were under orders to pay full price for their beer and to refuse even a free cigarette from a civilian). On the fifteen-mile drive into the capital from the Mekong ferry crossing downstream, the author's taxi was stopped at two roadblocks manned by paratroopers, who made the passengers, including three bonzes, get out so the car could be searched.

Until now, the Lao army had never been rated very highly. Even the deployment of four armored cars in the generals' putsch attempted the previous January had had a faintly ludicrous air to it. But there was nothing ludicrous about the control Kong Le's Second Paratroop Battalion now exercised over Vientiane. These men possessed an efficiency and, above all, an enthusiasm that had been almost unknown before.

Ironically, the boxes of ammunition toted by Kong Le's hustling soldiers and the trucks they rode in were emblazoned with the Stars and Stripes and clasped hands, the insignia of the American aid program. Nevertheless, they proclaimed their determination to put an end to "foreign interference" in Laos, an expression they obviously directed against the United States and its activities in the little Kingdom over the past six years.

The Little Captain

The man behind this transformation was tiny in stature (5 feet 1 inch tall), shy in speaking, innocent of politics, and naïve to the point of being credulous. A more unlikely strongman could hardly be imagined.

Kong Le, the son of a Phou-Thai tribesman from southern Laos, was born in Muong Phalane in central Savannakhet Province. He claims to have one older brother, two younger brothers, and a sister, who has remained in Savannakhet. He has been married at least three times. His first wife was a Black Thai, who bore him five children. Nothing is known about his second wife. In 1959, he took for his third wife the niece of General Ouan Ratikon.

Kong Le's military career began in 1948 or 1949, when, after one year of formal schooling in the Savannakhet *lycée,* he was recruited by the French to fight the Viet Minh. He rose through the ranks and was promoted to captain in the Territorial army on January 8, 1952. He became an adept field officer, probably the best in the Lao army. The British military attaché shortly after the coup described him as "having an instinct possessed by all great captains, but in need of more formal training in matters of tactics."

In 1954, he was in command of a detachment of thirty men in Luang Prabang. In October, 1957, he was sent to the Ranger School for field-grade officers in the Philippines, under the American training program for officers in the Royal Lao Army. There he met Kamlon Thongpant, a Lao officer who shared his growing misgivings about the mounting American influence in their homeland. The two officers soon decided to attempt a coup against the Lao government, and they used their remaining few months in the Philippines to work out their plans. In January, 1958, they returned home, and the Second Paratroop Battalion was formed under Kong Le's command. "From that moment on, I chose the men," Kong Le recalled later. Carefully keeping his motives secret, Kong Le sounded out a number of fellow officers on their attitudes toward the war against the Pathet Lao. Those officers he judged would be in sympathy with a coup to restore national unity, he had placed in his unit. He chose seventeen such officers, and confided to them his plan to overthrow the government. At the same time, he worked to mold his battalion into a functioning unit whose efficiency and loyalty he could count upon implicitly.

In Vientiane, the commander positioned his co-conspirators at strategic locations: Kamlon, also a captain, commanded a small group of men from the battalion at a point on the road to Paksane, north of the town; Ketsana Vongsouvan, a loyal lieutenant, had charge of another such group near the Chinaimo army camp, on the eastern outskirts of Vientiane. Two other lieutenants, Soulivan Sihavara and Deuan Sunnalath, were also assigned to strategic points. Kong Le, with the main body of the battalion, made his headquarters at the Sikhay military camp, near the Vientiane airport.

Thoughout that June and July, a Coup d'État Committee conducted regular meetings to plan the details of the uprising against the Somsanith government.

The objective of the plotters was simple: They wanted to rid the country of a regime that they believed was leading Laos into a new form of colonization, this time under the United States. The fact that Kong Le had never attracted much attention from the Vientiane politicians and their American advisers was of considerable help to him in keeping his plans secret. While he and his paratroopers had been hacking through dense jungles to locate Pathet Lao guerrillas, men like General Ouan Ratikon had sat in their offices amid wall maps covered with red and blue arrows and explained the anti-Communist campaign. It was a General Ouan, not a Captain Kong Le, who had the privilege of conferring with the Commander in Chief of American Pacific Forces in Hawaii.

Quinim Pholsena, the Santiphab Party leader, perhaps the only civilian to be taken into the confidence of the Coup d'État Committee, warned Kong Le that his military skills could not solve the political problems that would arise following the coup. Quinim advised him to consult Souvanna Phouma. The Prince was again in Vientiane, having returned from his ambassadorship in Paris. He had run unopposed in Luang Prabang for the National Assembly in April, 1960, and had been elected chairman. However, the Prince was not made privy to the coup plot.

The success of the coup brought an abrupt end to the obscurity in which Kong Le had lived. Overnight, he became a magnetic public figure, as the people responded enthusiastically to his simplicity and earnestness. For virtually the first time, the Royal Lao Army had a hero. Vientiane students organized themselves in support of the paratrooper junta, and Lao students left schools in France and the United States to return home and join the small group around Kong Le. It was an extraordinary episode in a country traditionally apathetic about politics.

A number of rumors circulated about the new hero. His good

luck in the thick of fighting was said to be uncanny, and inspired the widespread notion that he wore an amulet. As proof of his amazing luck, an actual incident was cited: At the battle of the Ca Dinh River against superior forces of General Phoumi Nosavan in November, 1960, Kong Le's personal bodyguard had been seriously wounded but Kong Le himself had escaped untouched. Various rumors that he had died also received wide circulation. When he was enduring great hardship on the Plain of Jars, it was rumored that he had been killed in a mutiny of his men; another time he was reported to have been caught in a fatal ambush by Meo guerrillas.

Kong Le, plucked from the familiar milieu of his trusted soldiers and thrust in the public limelight, acted with a strange mixture of humility and flamboyance. He delighted in pleasing the people; while in Vientiane he passed out hundreds of photographs of himself in his captain's uniform.

Inexperienced in political oratory, he addressed the crowds in simple, homespun terms, reducing the most complex international situations to easily grasped ideas.

At a public rally at the Vientiane sports stadium on August 11, two days after the coup, he expressed in broad terms his goals: an end to the government's military campaign against the Pathet Lao ("I am tired of seeing Lao fight Lao") and an end to corruption in the army, the bureaucracy, and the National Assembly ("I am willing to die for Laos, but not to cover up incompetence and corruption"). He told the people:

> During my period of military service, all Lao governments and the Royal Army have informed us that there were enemies outside Laos ready to enter and cause agitation within our country. But I and my friends, in our work together, have never seen such enemies coming to make trouble. We have only seen Lao killing Lao without cause.
>
> In my experience, many past Lao governments have told us they wished to follow a neutral course, but they never did so. My group and I decided to sacrifice everything, even our lives, in order to bring neutrality and peace to our nation.

A mimeographed leaflet he ordered distributed at this time defended the course taken by the military: "If we did nothing, our country would have become prey to others, just as in former times we were a prey to the French." One wonders if Kong Le comprehended even dimly the dangerous precedent he had set for Laos. Never before had the power of the army been so dramatically demonstrated.

Kong Le expressed a rarely voiced indignation at the worst abuses of the American aid program, again the subject of rumors about corruption. "I like honesty," Kong Le told the stadium audience. Then he charged that the members of the Somsanith government had been "bought as slaves," and that this government, which had "foolishly led the people" to become involved with the American dollar, had to be destroyed.

Kong Le ended the rally with a strong plea that Souvanna Phouma, whom he described as a man who "can restore control" and "return the country to normal," be named by the King as Prime Minister. It was Souvanna Phouma's government that had stood for reconciliation among all the Lao in 1956 and 1957 and had resisted the American Ambassador to achieve this.

Communiqués attributed to Kong Le and broadcast on the radio defined the aims of the *coup d'état* as the protection of nation, religion, monarchy, and Constitution. In order to achieve these goals, the communiqués declared, the Coup d'État Committee intended to recognize human rights; revamp the internal affairs of the National Assembly; eliminate corruption in government and reorganize the administration; abolish all foreign military intervention and remove foreign bases; strictly adhere to the United Nations Charter, maintain a neutral policy, and promote friendly relations with neighboring countries; and accept from all countries aid without strings attached.[1] At first, Kong Le signed his name as "Chief of the Revolutionary Party," then as "Chief of the Revolutionary Committee," and finally as "Chief of the Coup d'État." Despite the free use of the word revolutionary, there was no intention of opposing the monarchy.

Within hours after seizing control of Vientiane, Kong Le demanded that Somsanith and his fellow Cabinet ministers return to Vientiane from Luang Prabang. Ensconced with his band of faithful officers in the colonial-style yellow stucco building that housed the Prime Minister's office, Kong Le declared over a loudspeaker outside the office that Somsanith's failure to appear would be interpreted as a "hostile act."

On August 13, with no repentant Cabinet ministers yet in sight, a small crowd assembled outside the Prime Minister's office to demand action to force the removal of the Somsanith government. Students and *fonctionnaires* mingled in front of the building, where they were joined by a long line of saffron-robed bonzes. Then the crowd, led by a number of paratroopers, marched in some disorder and merriment out of the yard and up the street toward the National

[1] See texts in Appendix IV.

Assembly, picking up adherents along the way. By the time it reached the Assembly building, the mob numbered more than 1,000. Some carried crudely painted banners proclaiming "Down with U.S. Imperialism!" and showing Uncle Sam passing out bagfuls of money. But there were no acts of hostility toward American residents in Vientiane.

At the entrance to the Assembly building, the demonstrators were met by Souvanna Phouma, dressed impeccably and puffing on his pipe, making his first public appearance since the coup. He addressed the crowd briefly, urging moderation, and was loudly cheered. Then he withdrew and, behind closed doors, presided over a National Assembly meeting. As the hours dragged on, the crowd outside became restive. Egged on by paratroopers who had been posted around the building, ostensibly to safeguard the deputies, some demonstrators brought up sound trucks and threatened to storm the building. However, the only damage inflicted was a broken pane of glass in the front door. When the session ended, it was announced that the deputies had passed a vote of censure against the Somsanith government.

Meanwhile, a series of radio communications had been transmitted between Vientiane and Luang Prabang. The result was that on the afternoon of the demonstration, an Air Laos airliner—a 1939, four-engine Boeing Stratoliner, a make of plane curiously suited for short hops over the country's precipitous mountains— roared over the capital. When it rolled to a stop on the airfield, General Ouan Ratikon alighted. He surveyed the battle-ready paratroopers encircling the airfield, and announced he had been commissioned to determine the coup leaders' "true intentions" and report them back to Luang Prabang. Apparently, General Ouan on his return convinced Somsanith that the coup was a serious undertaking, for the latter resigned the following day. He then returned to Vientiane, accompanied only by Ngon Sananikone, the Minister of Economy.

General Phoumi, the Defense Minister, however, was having none of this mutiny. Upon learning of the coup, he had flown from Luang Prabang to Bangkok for hasty consultations with Prime Minister Marshal Sarit Thanarat, and thence to the town of Savannakhet. There, he was joined by twenty-one Cabinet members and National Assembly deputies. Under General Phoumi's leadership, they formed a Counter Coup d'État Committee, and on August 16, they sent a C-47 over Vientiane to drop leaflets announcing the new group. Two days later, a transmitter in Savannakhet began making regular broadcasts denouncing the Second Paratroop Battalion as traitors and saying there would be a march on Vientiane by loyalist soldiers.

Neutrality Again

In the meantime, however, the thirty-four remaining members of the National Assembly removed from the Cabinet the CDNI leaders (to whom they owed their seats won in the rigged elections of the previous April). A new Cabinet, formed exclusively of men who had not held posts under Somsanith and headed by Souvanna Phouma as Prime Minister, was unanimously approved by the Assembly.

The new government, said Souvanna Phouma, was committed to a policy of "true and wise neutrality." He pledged himself to "respect all Laos' obligations, including the Geneva agreements." This reversed his 1958 declaration that he regarded Laos' commitments at Geneva as "fully accomplished." His change in position reflected the unsettled nature of the Pathet Lao rebellion.

In its nine days under military administration, Vientiane had functioned smoothly and efficiently. The post and telegraph services, closed down in the predawn hours of August 9, had reopened four days later. A paratrooper had moved into the Immigration Office, long a chief source of the corruption associated with "squeeze" and "key money," and had begun issuing residence and travel permits. The Vietnamese population of the town, who had been lying low because of the high price of keeping their papers in order, had flocked to the Immigration Office in large numbers as soon as word had got around that permits were being issued with dispatch and for nothing more than the legal fee.

On August 17, the paratroopers handed over their administrative functions to the newly formed Cabinet and vacated the Prime Minister's office. The civil servants resumed their shuffling of dossiers in a dozen different ministries and the administrative life of the capital returned to the sleepy inefficiency to which it was accustomed.

If Souvanna Phouma had not been in the capital, Kong Le's coup might well have led up a blind alley. It was probably because of Souvanna Phouma's insistence that Kong Le respected legal procedures once he had seized power.

Kong Le had had another stroke of luck. New PEO deliveries had filled Vientiane warehouses with new and reconditioned weapons, and the paratroopers immediately put these depots under guard. In addition, there was plenty of ready cash in Vientiane's National Bank, which dispensed the pay for the whole army. Thus, Kong Le's troops were in an excellent position to ward off any opposition movement from the provinces.

Souvanna Phouma, however, was determined to effect a reconciliation with the ousted Cabinet members. This necessitated a settlement with General Phoumi, whose independent position in Savannakhet carried the dangerous overtones of a civil war between two factions of the Royal Army. Souvanna Phouma was also eager to obtain the King's approval of the new Cabinet.

With these objectives in mind, Souvanna Phouma flew in a borrowed U.S. Army liaison plane on August 23 to the French air base at Séno, and proceeded by car to Savannakhet. He was accompanied by General Ouan and Captain Kamlon. The Prince spent the entire day talking with General Phoumi, to whom he proposed that a meeting of both factions of the National Assembly be held in Luang Prabang, considered neutral ground, with the objective of reconciling policy differences and forming a coalition government. General Phoumi supported his plan and agreed to attend such a meeting.

Six days later, the proposed meeting opened in Luang Prabang, attended by thirty-four deputies who had accompanied Souvanna Phouma from Vientiane and twenty-one who had flown north from Savannakhet with General Phoumi. The setting was the spacious house of the Governor of Luang Prabang Province. Both men addressed a united session of the National Assembly.

Souvanna Phouma and General Phoumi then embarked on a series of tête-à-têtes in the office of the Provincial Governor. These lasted for almost two days, at the end of which Prince Somsanith appeared at the Royal Palace to tender his resignation to the King. This was accepted forthwith, and the King named Souvanna Phouma as Prime Minister, empowered to form a new Cabinet.

In the resulting Cabinet, General Phoumi had a major role as Deputy Prime Minister and Interior Minister, and several posts were restored to members of the old Somsanith government. Quinim Pholsena, who at Kong Le's insistence had been included in the August 17 Cabinet, was given the minor post of Information Minister, whose official duties consisted mainly of censoring press cables, but who was to play a much more important role after Souvanna Phouma initiated dealings with the Pathet Lao.

General Phoumi, emerging from the session clad in a crisp new green fatigue uniform without any insignia of rank, announced that the new government would grant amnesty to Kong Le and his battalion.

He and Souvanna Phouma announced in a two-paragraph communiqué that they were agreed on the need to re-establish peace and concord among all Lao and to preserve constitutional legality. It was the first of many such communiqués. Whatever the differences among the Lao leaders, they were never so great as to prevent the declaration of agreements "in principle" among all factions.

By the afternoon of August 31, everything appeared settled. The new government seemed to have the blessing of the Western powers, whose embassies had dispatched their first secretaries to witness the National Assembly deputies' unanimous ratification of the Cabinet. Most important, Souvanna Phouma had the obvious sympathy of the new United States Ambassador, Winthrop G. Brown, a New Englander who had arrived in Vientiane just the week before the coup. On his return to Vientiane, Souvanna Phouma reported his evaluation of the American position: "The Ambassador assures me that the United States remains absolutely neutral in this matter."

On that fateful afternoon, General Phoumi clambered aboard his mud-splattered C-47 to fly back to Savannakhet "to clear up remaining business" there, he explained. Speaking in his usual soft French, which reporters had to lean forward to hear, he said, "I hope that with the authority commanded by Prince Souvanna Phouma everything will be arranged. Otherwise, there is nothing."

Yet General Phoumi never showed up in Vientiane. Instead, as if indicating passive disapproval, he shut himself up in Savannakhet.

Perhaps the deciding factor was a rash broadcast by Kong Le on the last afternoon of the negotiations in Luang Prabang. On learning of the composition of the new Cabinet, he had rushed to the radio station and, in an emotion-filled voice, declared that his men were determined to oppose the return to power of "corrupt officials" who wished to pursue the civil war. He said his men would rather "die to the last one." Later, Kong Le was severely reprimanded for this outburst by Souvanna Phouma.

Many members of the defunct Somsanith government were genuinely fearful of returning to a Vientiane controlled by paratroopers. This was made clear by a remark made to the author by Education Minister Nhouy Abhay. As he boarded Souvanna Phouma's plane to return home (he had been in Paris when the coup occurred and had flown directly to Luang Prabang), he smiled and said, only half joking, "You see, I am the only one who has nothing to fear!" Indeed, most of the former ministers who decently could stayed away from Vientiane.

In Vientiane, it was no longer fashionable to be living in the largest house or driving the largest car. The author was startled to see a Lao businessman friend driving around the capital in a battered Morris Minor. He had put his shiny black Mercedes in his garage for safekeeping, he explained with a twinkle in his eye. *"C'est plus prudent!"*

The probable reason for General Phoumi's remaining in Savannakhet was that he was advised by members of his entourage there that his compromise with Souvanna Phouma, which granted him a Cabinet post but not control over the vital Defense Ministry, was not to his advantage. It would be smarter, he was likely told, to gamble his future on opposing Kong Le in Vientiane by force of arms.

It would take time to mobilize an army to march against the 600 paratroopers and other less reliable units defending Vientiane. But Prince Boun Oum na Champassak, the venerated southern leader, was loyal to the Counter Coup d'État Committee, and so the Phoumists could count on the support of the army units stationed in the lower Mekong Valley. The provincial governors were another matter. Most of those in the north had sent telegrams of support to Souvanna Phouma. Even so, the Phoumists might gain allies in northern Laos, because Souvanna Phouma's contacts with the provincial governors there were more formal than personal.

Colonel Khammouane Boupha, the Governor of Phong Saly, equivocated between expressing his loyalty to either Souvanna Phouma or General Phoumi, and at the same time arranged to remain on good terms with the Pathet Lao.

General Phoumi, of course aware of Kong Le's superiority in matériel, saw a possibility of overcoming this. If he undertook a struggle against the *coup d'état,* he was certain to receive support from Thailand, which had been alarmed by the overthrow of Somsanith, and from powerful interests within the agencies of American diplomacy. Marshal Sarit held the belief that a coalition government in Laos would open the door to the Communists on his border, and some American officials shared this belief. The Phoumists' capture on August 22 of the town of Paksane, on the banks of the Mekong, only ninety miles east of Vientiane, undoubtedly served to reassure the General's backers that an armed expedition against Vientiane was worth the gamble.

There remained the Pathet Lao.

Voice from the Jungle

Prince Souphanouvong learned of Kong Le's *coup d'état* while on his trek from Vientiane to Sam Neua. A statement attributed to him was broadcast by the clandestine Radio Pathet Lao in one of its first transmissions, on August 24. It applauded the coup and pledged "full support" to the policy of neutrality and reconciliation enunciated by the new government in Vientiane. Also, it urged that diplomatic relations be established with neighboring countries as soon as possible. However, it demanded that no concessions be made to the Phoumists. Once again, as when Phoui eliminated the CDNI from his Cabinet in December, 1959, the Pathet Lao had quickly opened the door to a new coalition.

Souvanna Phouma, when he returned from the Luang Prabang meeting, had issued an appeal to the Pathet Lao to place their confidence in him and send representatives to Vientiane to resume negotiations to end the civil war. This struggle had not been decided in fifteen months of campaigning across the length and breadth of Laos. In his statement, he assured the Pathet Lao: "I shall turn all my efforts toward ending this fraticidal struggle and re-establishing the union we formed in 1957."

Undoubtedly, the Pathet Lao were banking on the failure of the Prime Minister's attempt to come to terms with the Phoumists. The Pathet Lao reaction to the appeal for a resumption of negotiations was speedy. However, it came in a New China News Agency dispatch datelined Hanoi and quoting the "minimum conditions" that the Central Committee of the NLHS had decided upon for again entering into negotiations. These conditions were: immediate dismissal of the Phoumists from the government; termination of the civil war and a halt to mopping-up operations; release of prisoners detained for pro-Pathet Lao activities and restoration of their democratic rights; pursuit of a policy of "real peace and neutrality"; establishment of diplomatic relations with all countries; and acceptance of aid from "all countries willing to extend assistance to Laos with no political and military strings attached."

As was their custom, the Pathet Lao immediately set about strengthening their hand for these negotiations by a series of military initiatives.

In the first few days in September, Black Thai guerrillas began infiltrating across the Ma River to re-establish Pathet Lao control in the villages of northern San Neua Province, and again took over Sop Nao in the Dien Bien Phu valley after brief skirmishes with Royal

Army troops. Pathet Lao guerrillas also reoccupied vantage points in the limestone mountains east of Thakhek, where thousands of natural caves had afforded the Viet Minh an impregnable hideout during the Indochina War. Other bands blew up a number of bridges south of Pakse on the road linking Laos and Cambodia.

In Sam Neua town, the garrison commander, Colonel Khamkong Vongnarath, was under pressure from both Vientiane and Savannakhet for the allegiance of his two infantry battalions, numbering some 1,500 men. He resolved the dilemma by taking an ambivalent position: He proclaimed his determination to take orders only from Savannakhet but welcomed aid in any form from any quarter for the defense of the town. On September 28, the Pathet Lao attacked in force. Colonel Khamkong's soldiers put up a hopeless siege defense against the attackers, who held the mountain heights overlooking the valley, and then broke out of the town after sabotaging its landing strip. They retreated southwestward toward the Plain of Jars over the same rugged trails that the French garrison troops had taken seven years previously. In possession of the town, the Pathet Lao established their usual administrative committee and began the patient process of educating the inhabitants to the benefits of "liberation." They reinstated Thao Ma, a former private secretary of Souphanouvong and once the highest-ranking Pathet Lao official in the province (by virtue of the 1957 reintegration agreement), as Acting Governor.

On October 2, Pathet Lao pursuers overtook Colonel Khamkong's retreating troops at Muong Peun, twenty miles southwest of Sam Neua town. Khamkong's men surrendered, handing over their American weapons and ammunition. (Six Catholic missionaries—three Frenchmen, two Canadians, and an American, Father Lucien Bouchard of South Attleboro, Massachusetts—managed to avoid capture and made their way back to Vientiane in five days of walking.)

On receiving news of these Pathet Lao victories, Souvanna Phouma dispatched Quinim to make contact with the Pathet Lao commanders in the area and to attempt to reassert Vientiane's authority there. He bitterly blamed the fighting at Sam Neua and Muong Peun on the Phoumists, and contemptuously advised the military to "go back to their tents instead of seeking high positions for the advancement of their personal ambitions," a remark directed against General Phoumi. After a final unsuccessful attempt to arrange a meeting with General Phoumi, he formally dropped the latter from his Cabinet.

Arms and Money for General Phoumi

Meanwhile, on September 10, General Phoumi broadcast from Savannakhet that a Revolutionary Committee, headed by Prince Boun Oum, had been set up to succeed the Counter Coup d'État Committee. The Prince, in the same broadcast, declared: "In order to restore peace and tranquillity in the country, to protect the King and religion and the freedom of the people, we revolutionaries, in the name of the citizens of Laos, hereby declare that we seize power and abrogate all constitutional rights of the present government from this date." This unilateral suspension of the Constitution was later to embarrass Boun Oum's government when it wanted to take office by legal process in Vientiane.

On September 19, Radio Pathet Lao announced that guerrilla forces loyal to Prince Souphanouvong had been ordered to avoid clashes with troops loyal to Souvanna Phouma, and suggested that soldiers of the two factions should, wherever possible, join in fighting Phoumist troops.

General Ouan Ratikon, who had returned to Vientiane, offered his services to Souvanna Phouma's government, and been placed over Kong Le as commander of all troops loyal to Vientiane, formally warned Phoumist commanders that they faced prosecution as mutineers unless they disassociated themselves from the Revolutionary Committee. In mid-September, Kong Le's paratroopers, outnumbered 4 to 1, routed the Phoumist occupiers of Paksane, under Colonel Bounleuth Sanichan. Later that month, they pushed them down the Mekong Valley to the south bank of the Ca Dinh River, where a front stabilized temporarily.

It was plain that General Phoumi was rapidly building up his matériel and manpower for a march on Vientiane. From mid-September, Savannakhet was the scene of an increased number of landings and takeoffs by unmarked C-46 and C-47 transports, manned by American crews. These planes belonged to Air America, Inc., a civilian charter company with U.S. Air Force organizational support and under contract to the U.S. Government. The aircraft, giving the Phoumist forces a badly needed logistical supply system, ferried military supplies from Bangkok to Savannakhet, the headquarters of the Revolutionary Committee, and shuttled between Savannakhet and outlying garrisons loyal to General Phoumi.

The Phoumist forces were substantially augmented by 200 paratroopers, originally intended to form a First Paratroop Battalion, who had newly completed training in Thailand. They had been returned by the PEO to southern Laos despite the Prime Minister's request that they be sent to the Plain of Jars, where a tug of war was under way for the allegiance of Colonel Khamhou Bhoutsarath, commander of the Second Military Region with headquarters at Xieng Khouang.

The Xieng Khouang garrison had proclaimed its loyalty to Souvanna Phouma after the fall of Sam Neua to the Pathet Lao. But in mid-October the garrison switched to General Phoumi, largely due to the influence of the Meo leader Toubhy Lyfong. He opposed Vientiane's prospective negotiations with the Pathet Lao, and had flown from Vientiane to Xieng Khouang a few days before they were to begin. (Despite heavy fortification by the Phoumists, Xieng Khouang was recaptured by Kong Le with Pathet Lao assistance in January, 1961.)

Souvanna Phouma's difficulties were measurably increased by Thailand's imposition of an unofficial blockade on Vientiane. This was a product of Marshal Sarit's opposition to Souvanna Phouma's government, which he feared would make a deal with the Communists and outflank him. By far the greater portion of Vientiane's supplies came across the Mekong from Thailand, so that cutting off this traffic soon had a drastic effect on the capital's economy. The railhead in the Thailand town of Nong Khai was particularly important in the supplying of petroleum products, which accounted for 26 per cent of the value of Laos' total imports. After the flow of these had been cut off, Souvanna Phouma resorted to obtaining petroleum products elsewhere, first from Burma and then from the Soviet Union, which had responded favorably to feelers to open an embassy in Vientiane. In this way, the blockade, inspired by Marshal Sarit's fear of Communism, actually played into the hands of the Communist powers. Their best interests were served by a Souvanna Phouma so weakened and isolated that he would turn to them in desperation. Insofar as it affected the movement of rice and vegetables, the blockade was not completely effective: The Thai peasants had traditionally ferried their produce across the Mekong in sampans, and they were not going to let a bureaucratic edict interfere with their small profit. Although rice prices on the Vientiane market nearly doubled during the blockade, no serious shortages ever developed.

A feeling of nervousness pervaded Vientiane, heightened by sporadic shooting incidents and isolated acts of sabotage perpetrated by night raiding parties. In one such incident, a half-dozen mortar shells were lobbed into the vicinity of the power station, and the United Nations representative in Vientiane, Édouard Zellweger, said that he had seen flashes of firing coming from the Thailand bank of the river opposite his house. However, the mortar fire might have come from a boat in midstream. Thailand formally denied implication in the affair.

In these circumstances, Souvanna Phouma was less and less inclined to enter into any bargain with General Phoumi. When King Savang Vatthana requested the two men to meet in Luang Prabang and General Phoumi suggested formation of a three-cornered coalition by Prince Boun Oum, Prince Souvanna Phouma, and Prince Souphanouvong, these moves were politely rejected by Souvanna Phouma.

The announcement at the end of September that a Soviet Embassy would be established in Vientiane produced near panic in the State Department. A rapid series of maneuvers and announcements ensued, one effect of which was to alert the Soviet Union to the possibilities opened up by the lack of control exercised by the United States over a delicate foreign-policy situation in an election campaign.

Negotiations with the Pathet Lao

These developments in the military, economic, and political fields moved toward a climax about the middle of October. At this moment, the Pathet Lao, having buttressed their bargaining position by once more consolidating their control over their base area in northern Laos, opened the way for the negotiations with Vientiane. The trio of Pathet Lao negotiators, Nouhak Phoumsavan, Phoumi Vongvichit, and Singkapo Chounlamany,[2] had slipped back into the capital. On October 11, in the starkly furnished conference room of the Prime Minister's office, decorated only with a portrait of the King, Souvanna Phouma and the Pathet Lao emissaries exchanged the customary Buddhist greeting of clasped hands and a slight bow of the head, and sat down at a makeshift wooden table.

[2] An intriguing sidelight is provided by remarks attributed to Singkapo by Wilfred G. Burchett in a later interview. Singkapo said that Souphanouvong, on learning of Kong Le's coup, detached Singkapo from the walking party. " 'It was decided I should go back and re-establish contact. I was to travel light and fast. What had taken us three months to cover I did in seven days and nights of travel, stopping only for snatches of sleep. I got back to a point close enough to Vientiane to establish contact with Kong Le and he sent a helicopter to pick me up.' " (*The Furtive War: The United States in Vietnam and Laos* [New York: International Publishers, 1963], p. 188.) But Kong Le, in August, 1960, had no helicopters. Interestingly, four months later, in December, the Thai border police photographed a wrecked Soviet-built helicopter that had been abandoned only a few hours earlier, in Loei Province, upstream and across the Mekong from Vientiane.

The resumption of negotiations between the Royal Government and the Pathet Lao appeared in Washington to confirm the worst fears of a number of high-ranking State Department officials who were less convinced of Souvanna Phouma's trustworthiness than was Ambassador Brown. The coup had come as a complete surprise, and therefore the State Department had no prepared policy on how to deal with its aftermath. The American Embassy in Vientiane had no biography of Kong Le (whether or not the CIA had such a document is uncertain). On the defensive because of its lack of preparation, the State Department devoted itself to denying French assertions that the coup had fundamentally transformed the situation in Laos by shattering the illusion that the Royal Army would defeat the Pathet Lao rebels. Attention at the State Department was also focused on protesting to the Thais that the United States was still as resolved as ever to support the anti-Communist struggle. How exactly this was to be done when the Royal Government was in the process of negotiating with the pro-Communists was, however, problematical.

Messages from the State Department in the days following the coup advised Ambassador Brown to take such action as would remove Kong Le from the scene as expeditiously as possible. The messages, however, gave no specific orders as to how Brown should effect this. In any case, it became impossible to eliminate Kong Le and restore the *status quo* after Prince Somsanith resigned. Some suitable accommodation, then, had to be worked out with Kong Le. However, Brown made no overtures to Kong Le, feeling that he was too swept up in his immediate administrative problems to be accessible and that he would be cool to any American proposals.

As the days went on, the State Department messages to Brown became less and less coherent. Conflicting suggestions would appear within the same telegram. The State Department felt that Kong Le should be gotten rid of, but it had no means to achieve this; there was no over-all policy directive permitting speedy, deliberate action against Kong Le, who was not a Communist.

With Souvanna Phouma, on the other hand, Brown early established cordial relations. He felt that the calm, self-assured Prince was the best hope for keeping Laos from being swept by a Communist revolution manufactured by the Kingdom's more powerful militant neighbors. He proposed to the State Department that the United States throw its support to the new government. But Brown was unable to muster the backing in Washington necessary if the Prince's leadership was to assert itself in the face of the growing challenge from the Pathet Lao and the expanding influence of the Soviet Union, China, and North Vietnam.

Displaying more decisiveness than the State Department (possibly these agencies were less subject to the disruptive effects of the Presidential election campaign then in full swing), the Pentagon and the Central Intelligence Agency in Washington set in motion actions consistent with their past efforts in Laos and with their interpretation of the current situation—they immediately began building up General Phoumi.

The Pentagon's support for General Phoumi was motivated by the conviction that the entire American defense posture in Southeast Asia, and more particularly in South Vietnam and Thailand, depended on unconditional support to anti-Communists in Laos (and, conversely, the conviction that U.S. support for a government that was negotiating with Communist insurgents and preparing to take them in would provoke disastrous repercussions in these countries). But there was a flaw in this logic. The American military was acutely aware that the Royal Lao Army was not a first-class fighting force, that it was up against a cunning and patient enemy, and that its chances of victory were remote. Even so, the deleterious effects of abandoning General Phoumi appeared to the Pentagon considerably more nightmarish than those of continuing to back his forces in a heretofore fruitless war.

The CIA was in a position to size up the situation with considerable accuracy. For years, its field agents had been submitting precise, first-hand reports about the balance of forces. Of all the agencies represented in Laos, the CIA had the closest contact with the villages in the hinterland; its men spent more time in the field than the Embassy or the PEO personnel and they had excellent sources of information among both the Lao and the mountain people. They could not be deluded about the factual weaknesses and strengths of the American position in Laos. The CIA recognized that General Phoumi was no paragon of virtue. But he and his fellow generals represented the army, and the army was still the only cohesive country-wide organization comparable to the Pathet Lao and the NLHS.

Ambassador Brown gave the various American agencies in Vientiane relatively free play in forming their opinions about the situation and recommending actions. At the same time, however, he made it clear that he wished to be kept informed about dissenting recommendations.

American support for the factions in Laos was implemented by the aid program. Unexpectedly, the first statement that the aid program had been affected by these developments came from General Williston B. Palmer, the Pentagon's Director of Military Assistance. During a brief stopover at the Saigon airport on October 1, he announced that aid to Laos was being stopped because of the three-way split in Laos.

This statement was denied two days later in Vientiane on Brown's order. General Palmer's statement, an Embassy spokesman declared, had been made "without instructions from or knowledge of the Washington agencies concerned." The spokesman added, "In fact, United States military aid to Laos has not been suspended," but acknowledged that delivery of supplies to Kong Le's paratroopers had virtually ceased since the coup. This was understandable; the United States had been reluctant to make deliveries to what appeared to be a mutinous band of soldiers.

On October 7, Souvanna Phouma declared that the United States had suspended its cash-grant aid to his government. On the same day, a State Department spokesman in Washington confirmed that payment of funds for the September army salaries had not been made to the Vientiane government. Souvanna Phouma's government was immediately in jeopardy.

Simultaneously, Washington announced that former Ambassador J. Graham Parsons, now Assistant Secretary of State for Far Eastern Affairs, was being dispatched in haste for consultations with Souvanna Phouma. Upon disembarking at the Vientiane airport on October 12, Parsons made it unmistakably clear that resumption of American cash-grant aid to Souvanna Phouma's government depended on the attitude Souvanna Phouma took toward pending political questions, most urgent of which was the negotiations with the Pathet Lao that had commenced the previous day.

Parsons entered the talks with Souvanna Phouma with three principal objectives: (1) He wanted to get the Prime Minister to break off his negotiations with the Pathet Lao forthwith; the discussion on this was delicate, since Souvanna Phouma attributed the breakup of the first coalition in 1958 largely to Parsons' reports to Washington that the coalition would open the way to Communist control. (2) Parsons wanted Souvanna Phouma to guarantee that he would enter into negotiations with General Phoumi. The Prime Minister replied that if resuming talks with the Phoumists was so urgent, it was up to General Phoumi to come to Vientiane. (3) Parsons wanted Souvanna Phouma to move the capital from Vientiane to Luang Prabang, presumably because Washington felt that there the King would exert a conservative influence on the government.

On none of these points would Souvanna Phouma make concessions. Next day, Parsons flew to Luang Prabang for an audience with King Savang Vatthana. Souvanna Phouma angrily interpreted this as an effort to go over his head. Now any agreement with the Americans was unthinkable. Yielding to any U.S. request at this juncture would finish his political career.

Souvanna Phouma's bargaining position was bolstered by the arrival in Vientiane on October 13 of a burly Russian named Aleksandr N. Abramov. He was the first ambassador of a Communist country to enter Laos. After his initial meeting with Souvanna Phouma, Abramov emerged smiling broadly. Asked for the Soviet position on Parsons' trip, Abramov replied, still smiling: "I would have liked to meet Mr. Parsons, but he left in such a hurry."

Parsons had now gone on to Bangkok, accompanied by Ambassador Brown, and the two diplomats spent the next few days looking for some way out of the impasse. Souvanna Phouma's position in relation to the Pathet Lao was reviewed. General Phoumi was weighed against Souvanna Phouma. Finally, they worked out a course of action that was a compromise between all-out support for General Phoumi and all-out toleration of Souvanna Phouma's predilection for coexistence with the Pathet Lao.

On his return to Vientiane, the sympathetic Brown suggested to Souvanna Phouma that the Prince would not want the Pathet Lao guerrillas to take over the country while the non-Communist forces were squabbling among themselves. Brown then pointed out that General Phoumi shared this wish. Next, Brown proposed that the Prime Minister agree to deliveries of American military equipment to General Phoumi at Savannakhet. In return, the cash-grant aid to Vientiane would be resumed.

Souvanna Phouma assented to this gentlemen's agreement with Brown on one condition—none of the military equipment delivered to General Phoumi must be used against Souvanna Phouma's commander, Kong Le; it must be used against the Pathet Lao only. Souvanna Phouma, in agreeing to this proposition, full of risks to himself, did so to demonstrate to Parsons and the rest of the State Department that he was a patriot. Indeed, after this there was no more talk by American officials about Souvanna Phouma's neglect of his country's best interests.

On October 17, the State Department announced the resumption of cash-grant aid to Souvanna Phouma's government. Eleven days later an agreement "in principle" was announced between Souvanna Phouma and Abramov for Soviet aid to his government, but there was no evidence that the Soviets could establish a large-scale aid program on short order. In fact, the first shipment of petroleum supplies from the Soviet Union did not arrive in Vientiane until December 3. The Soviet aid program, moreover, did not include cash grants. Up to the day Kong Le's troops left Vientiane, he paid them with funds from American aid.

The promised aid to General Phoumi began arriving in large quantities. Included were funds, logistical support, and technical aid. Besides the Savannakhet transmitter, American technical aid provided for the operation of clandestine radio stations that were used by the Phoumists to encourage defections from Kong Le's troops and other forces loyal to Souvanna Phouma, without attacking the Prince by name. The main fault with the gentlemen's agreement between Souvanna Phouma and Brown was that making American aid available to General Phoumi also indicated that he had official American support. From there, he hypothesized that he could use this support to oust Souvanna Phouma; after all, he himself had made no promises. The United States was thus in the position of furnishing assistance to a rebel movement against a government with which it maintained diplomatic relations.

General Ouan Ratikon, who had flown to Luang Prabang with Souvanna Phouma, had remained there after the Prince returned to Vientiane. Weeks went by, and still General Ouan did not return. Finally, Souvanna Phouma confirmed rumors that were circulating in Vientiane. General Ouan had defected to the Phoumists. To succeed him, Souvanna Phouma named Sounthone Pathammavong, the only general left in Vientiane.

General Sing Ratanasamay, Lao military attaché in Paris, returned to Laos and went to Savannakhet to join General Phoumi. By mid-November, the Phoumists had three of Laos' five generals. A fourth, General Amkha Soukhavong, the only Christian general in the Royal Army, was kidnaped by Phoumist agents while on a mission for Souvanna Phouma in Xieng Khouang. He was flown to prison in Savannakhet, and was not released until May, 1963.

On November 11 came the hardest blow of all. In Luang Prabang, the Third Infantry Battalion mutinied against Souvanna Phouma's authority and declared for General Phoumi. A detachment of three companies of militia commanded by Captain Southep, a protégé of General Ouan, was dispatched to join forces with two Pathet Lao columns, whereupon the combined units were to encircle Luang Prabang and force the surrender of the Third Battalion. But halfway on the march to Luang Prabang, the militia detachment set up camp at Muong Kassy and waited. Kong Le's queries to Captain Southep were met with silence. The reason was that Southep, too, was a Phoumist. He was secretly monitoring Kong Le's radio messages to Phong Saly and other provincial capitals, and passing the information to Phoumist agents. He had had the foresight to take with him from Vientiane a stolen set of codebooks.

General Phoumi, meanwhile, was building up his main force in the Mekong Valley. Advance units, when sufficiently trained and indoctrinated, probed Kong Le's defense line on the Ca Dinh River on the left bank of the Mekong. In one such action, Phoumist patrols crossed the Ca Dinh and a pitched battle developed, during which the Phoumists brought artillery batteries into play for the first time. Kong Le's two companies of troops, without artillery support, fell back in confusion.

Souvanna Phouma was in dire straits. His relations with the Royal Palace had been edgy since the Phoumist coup of November 11 in Luang Prabang, following which Souvanna Phouma had publicly warned that he would not be bound by the King's decisions if the monarch was not a free agent. He divided his time among harried Cabinet meetings, consultations with loyal officers, and trips to villages in northern Vientiane Province, an area known to be heavily under the influence of the Pathet Lao "administrative committee" network. When he exhorted a crowd of villagers to grow more vegetables to defeat the blockade instead of attending Pathet Lao meetings, he was loudly cheered, and even Pathet Lao soldiers in their mustard-colored fatigues drifted into the villages to listen to him. On more than one occasion, he turned a hostile crowd, obviously cued by Pathet Lao agents, into a cheering mob of sympathizers calling out his own slogans of "Peace and Neutrality!" and "Reconciliation!" Nevertheless, his political position in Vientiane became increasingly isolated, while in the countryside his authority was eroded from both left and right.

There were reports that thousands of rifles and carbines from the warehouses in Vientiane had been distributed, on Kong Le's orders, in the Vientiane region to a "people's militia," of which a large proportion were Pathet Lao agents. Phoumi Vongvichit, still carrying on negotiations with Souvanna Phouma's government, told the author on November 30 that "as armed forces of the people, the Pathet Lao fighting units have up to the present made use only of arms and matériel which they have received from the people, or else seized from the hands of their enemy, the rebel lackeys of the American imperialists." He also indicated that the Pathet Lao command regarded its position as much more advantageous now than it had been in 1957. Any new coalition agreement "would have to be based on the agreements signed in the past and at the same time," he stressed, "be adapted to the present situation in the country."

The inroads that the Pathet Lao had made since the coup into the village organization of even Vientiane Province is well illustrated by detailed accusations broadcast by Radio Savannakhet on November 30, 1960:

> Village headmen in Phone Hong district [about forty miles north of Vientiane] were informed of the creation of village committees in their areas. This was directed by Thao Chan together with five armed men to supervise the organization. The newly created committees will have full authority to deal with affairs of their villages. At Ban Nasai and Na Phoh, the Neo Lao Hak Sat village committees take no recognition of the officially elected headmen despite the respect paid them by the local residents.
>
> On November 19, the *Chao Muong* [District Officer] of Phone Hong sent a messenger to the NLHS [in a nearby village completely dominated by the Pathet Lao] asking them to come to discuss the situation. They came in. He asked them not to spread false rumors or incite the people. The leader of the NLHS replied that they did so in compliance with the popular will.
>
> At Ban Liang San, more than two hundred soldiers have been training the villagers for the "people's militia." These soldiers are being fed by the village headmen [of the area]. No one could refuse, since the soldiers always say, "We must all be united."

The Pathet Lao had greatly strengthened their ground position under their unofficial cease-fire agreement with Souvanna Phouma. At the beginning of November, they had captured Ban Ban as part of the process of re-establishing their control over the whole tier of districts along the North Vietnam border. Moreover, as early as October, intelligence reports had disclosed the infiltration of North Vietnamese Army elements into the ranks of Pathet Lao units, to serve as "stiffeners." The number of these "stiffeners" was to increase steadily throughout the winter and into the spring of 1961. In Hanoi, Ho Chi Minh was reported to have approached Gopala Menon, the Indian chairman of the ICC in Vietnam, and urged the reactivation of the commission in Laos.

Leaving behind the Pathet Lao emissaries, with whom he had been making little progress in negotiating a solution, Souvanna Phouma left Vientiane on November 18 and flew to Sam Neua for talks with his brother, who had on several occasions refused to make a trip to Vientiane. The two men embraced each other warmly on the balcony of Souphanouvong's villa.

In two days of talks in Sam Neua, Souvanna Phouma obtained his brother's agreement to take part in a coalition that would include representatives of the Vientiane government, the Pathet Lao, and the Phoumists. The only limitation on this suggested coalition Cabinet was that it would exclude military officers as ministers, a stipulation that reflected the Pathet Lao's refusal to deal with General Phoumi. There appeared little probability that General Phoumi, who had previously declined an offer to participate in a coalition on much more favorable terms, would now accept this one. Nevertheless, Souvanna Phouma sent a delegation of National Assembly deputies to Savannakhet a few days later in an effort to persuade the General to call off his plan to seize Vientiane by force.

On December 2, the National Assembly delegation came back from their unsuccessful mission to Savannakhet. Their return led to the ugliest pro-Communist demonstration yet staged in Vientiane. A small core of agitators, mainly students, incited a crowd to bottle up inside the parliament building the thirty National Assembly deputies remaining in Vientiane and to chant slogans denouncing negotiations with General Phoumi.

Soviet Airlift

The next day, Abramov, at the ceremonial inauguration of Soviet flights transporting oil from Hanoi to Vientiane, used the occasion to cite Khrushchev on "the need for abolishing colonialism and foreign intervention." But his words elicited only a perfunctory round of applause from the small group of spectators, who saw irony in them. A row of saffron-robed bonzes chanted *sotto voce,* and the portly Abramov awkwardly squatted down on his haunches and joined his palms in Buddhist greeting. The Russian civilian pilots, in their heavy clothing, looked singularly uncomfortable as they peered at the corrugated-iron shacks and the jungle beyond, shimmering in the midday heat.

The Russians, in undertaking to supply one of the belligerents in Laos, were simply following the precedent set by the United States. Appropriately, the World War II-vintage planes they put on the Laos–North Vietnam run had just come from an airlift operation in the Congo.

With Vientiane apparently in imminent danger of attack from the Phoumists, whose forces were reported to be approaching up the Mekong Valley, Souvanna Phouma for the first time made a flat request to Ambassador Brown that aid to General Phoumi be stopped. The American Embassy, realizing that General Phoumi fully intended to violate the American guarantees given Souvanna Phouma in mid-October, obtained assurances from the Defense Department that technical, logistical, and material assistance to the Revolutionary Committee would be stopped. Brown was able to report to the Prime Minister after a delay of two days that no such assistance had been furnished since November 30.

"The Lao Won't Fight"

It had long been an axiom that the Buddhist Lao would not fight. Their religion forbade them to kill even animals. Their way of life was serene rather than belligerent. Their nature was peaceable, and they had a knack for compromise that always came to their rescue and avoided conflict.

The French in Vientiane had adopted this axiom as a favorite explanation for the failure of the American effort to equip and train the Royal Lao Army to put down the Pathet Lao revolt. But French officers who fought in the Indochina War declared that small units of Lao soldiers, properly trained and under skilled leadership, fought well on the offensive. That the axiom contained a certain amount of truth was accepted by the American military advisers of the PEO although many agreed that the explanation might be more complex than a Buddhist aversion to killing.

The fact remains that the Lao capital, in the next few days of December, was to witness a battle that would kill an estimated 600 people and injure another 1,000. What is the explanation?

It is that the soldiers of both Kong Le's battalion and General Phoumi's forces were armed to the teeth with modern rifles, machine guns, mortars, and artillery. When fired in the confined quarters of the streets of Vientiane, with their thin, wooden houses and shops, these weapons could not but spread death and destruction.

The author saw soldiers repeatedly change sides in the course of the battle. Squads of frightened-looking infantry made a hasty retreat along the side of a deserted street although no one was advancing against them. In fact, throughout much of the battle the combatant forces were separated by a no man's land more than four city blocks wide, which shifted back and forth in the general direction of where the enemy's positions were reported to be.

Both sides poured out a deafening volume of fire across this area, and made up for any lack of bravery by keeping fingers pressed on triggers. Indeed, the attitude on both sides was that the enemy had to be repelled at all costs but the individual soldiers wanted no responsibility for any bloodshed. This explains the wide distances between opposing forces, the heavy dependence on mortar and artillery fire, and the absence of hand-to-hand fighting.

The battle was preceded by an abortive countercoup led by the commander of the Vientiane Military Region, Colonel Kouprasith Abhay. Taking advantage of the approach of the Phoumist troops, he and his men on the morning of December 8 effected a sortie from their Chinaimo camp, where they had been more or less confined since August. They forced Kong Le and his red-armbanded men to withdraw westward, and seized control of the capital with little resistance. In leaflets distributed to the populace, the colonel's soldiers, who wore white armbands, claimed that their countercoup was aimed at forestalling a Pathet Lao takeover rather than against Souvanna Phouma, for whom Kouprasith declared his full support.

Kong Le and his men established a temporary headquarters at the airfield, where the Prime Minister visited just before nightfall. He had already paid a call on Kouprasith and now had the pledge of both men to hold their respective positions until daybreak. But in the morning, red armbands were everywhere. Under cover of night, Kong Le's men had moved in and had occupied the town once again, without so much as firing a shot. Whether Kouprasith's men had merely abandoned their untenable positions voluntarily or had been driven from them by the threat of serious fighting is not clear. They returned to the Chinaimo army camp, where they awaited a more opportune moment to strike against Kong Le.

For Souvanna Phouma, the situation had deteriorated so badly that he despaired of a solution. His last shred of hope that the Pathet Lao and Savannakhet factions might still come to terms, with him as a conciliator, disappeared on December 9.

Several planeloads of Savannakhet troops dropped on the eastern outskirts of the town had rendezvoused with Kouprasith, giving rise to wild rumors, all untrue, that General Phoumi might launch his impending offensive that very night.

In the empty hallways of the building that housed his office, Souvanna Phouma found a typist to peck out a final communiqué declaring in effect that the end had come: "By reason of the situation created by the misunderstanding that has arisen between military factions in the Vientiane region, the Government is obliged to delegate all its civil and military powers to the High Command of the Army effective at 9 A.M. today, December 9, 1960, in order to preserve security and the functioning of public services." This was not a resignation from office; it was simply a delegation of powers to General Sounthone Pathammavong, the senior army officer in Vientiane.

After a last-minute effort to bring about a meeting near Vientiane of Colonel Kouprasith and General Sounthone, Prince Souvanna Phouma turned his black Peugeot sedan toward the airport for the last time. Without making any further statement, he left Vientiane shortly before six in the evening and landed in the Cambodian capital of Phnom Penh about two hours later, a voluntary exile.

The Die Is Cast

Quinim Pholsena, Souvanna Phouma's senior remaining Cabinet minister, slipped out of Vientiane on the morning of December 10 aboard a Soviet Ilyushin transport bound for Hanoi. In twenty-four hours in the North Vietnamese capital, he made a firm deal with the Russians: In exchange for a formal alliance between Kong Le's troops and the Pathet Lao, the Russians would airlift into Laos arms and supplies for the resistance against General Phoumi's American-supplied troops.

The Russians, seeing the opportunity afforded them by the possibility of supporting Souvanna Phouma and his able military commander, Kong Le, against the imminent attack of the Phoumist rebels, apparently arrived at their decision in a week of urgent consultations in Moscow at the beginning of December. Quinim's signature merely formalized the bargain.

The alliance with the Pathet Lao would permit Kong Le to withdraw his men, with their jeeps, trucks, and armored cars, safely into the hinterland should the Phoumists capture Vientiane. The airlift of Soviet supplies, especially food and gasoline, would permit Kong Le's men to continue operating as a fighting force even though they were cut off from American supplies, and the provision of heavy weapons would give them a capability equal to that of the Phoumists. For the Pathet Lao, the airlift meant a share in Soviet weapons and ammunition, enabling Prince Souphanouvong to re-equip his guerrillas for regular combat operations. The entire complexion of the Laos confrontation had changed.

On the runway at the Vientiane airport by the afternoon of December 11, in full view of American observers, olive-drab Ilyushins were unloading six 105-mm. howitzers complete with ammunition and North Vietnamese gun crews to man them (neither Kong Le nor the Pathet Lao had any cannoneers).

General Sounthone, finding himself incapable of steering the ship of state through such perilous waters, abruptly announced that he was turning back full powers to what remained of the civilian government, namely Quinim.

Kong Le, again headquartered in the Prime Minister's office, was making final preparations for the defense of the capital. On the eve of the battle, he walked quietly about the tree-shaded yard of the stucco building, talking to small groups of paratroopers who sat in their jeeps beside boxes of ammunition and supplies. In his left hand, the diminutive captain twirled a grenade.

The first fighting in the town broke out shortly after one in the afternoon on Tuesday, December 13, on the eastern outskirts near the Chinaimo camp. It was the siesta hour. Houses were shuttered and the people inside as the din of crackling rifle fire, machine guns, and mortar explosions increased in intensity.

Outside the bookshop where Quinim Pholsena, the Acting Prime Minister, lived, a jeep pulled up and tooted its horn. Quinim appeared, flustered and in great haste. The soldiers in their bulky field jackets took him aboard. But the jeep would not start. The soldiers pushed it for about 100 yards, then abandoned it. Another jeep was commandeered to take Quinim to the airport. There he boarded an Ilyushin transport for Hanoi. With him, he took 25 million kip (about $312,500) in cash, for which he left a signed receipt at the National Bank.

From Chinaimo, Colonel Kouprasith sent tanks and armored cars along the road into the town. He also dispatched three river boats upstream to an island opposite the center of the town, from the cover of which they could train fire on defenders retreating slowly down the main streets, which paralleled the river.

The entire length of the left bank, a thoroughfare where the Lao were accustomed to take leisurely Sunday walks, suddenly became a dusty line of firing troops. Lao soldiers fired blindly and incessantly in the general area where an enemy might be hiding; there was ammunition aplenty. An occasional tank rumbled up to take a position on the embankment and fire a round or two, either downstream or directly across the mile-wide Mekong into the Thai village on the other side, causing some casualties, mostly civilians.

Carefully located machine-gun nests manned by Kong Le's soldiers stubbornly held up advances by whole companies of Kouprasith's troops. On the afternoon of the first day, the Colonel's troops occupied the entire twenty-block center of the town, but they failed to search the surrounding houses for pockets of resistance. That night they were driven back, almost to the eastern town limits, by the paratroopers, who had a far better knowledge of night fighting, and whose jeeps circulated freely in the reoccupied center on December 14.

From the fierce resistance put up by the paratroopers, it was apparent that the battle was going to be a long one. During brief lulls in the firing in daytime, the civilian population cautiously opened their doors to steal a look outside. They saw streets littered with fallen telephone wires and tree branches. Heaps of empty mortar shells cluttered street intersections, along with ammunition boxes bearing the clasped-hands emblem of the American aid mission. Almost every building in Vientiane bore scars from small-arms fire and mortar fragments.

One of the first buildings to go was the Immigration Office; it had served as a riflemen's nest and was the target for a direct mortar hit. The army headquarters was also destroyed. Diagonally across the street from it, the American Embassy lost its old building, containing the Ambassador's office, when the eaves caught fire from a neighboring flaming shed. However, a newly added wing escaped destruction.

At night, no civilians ventured out, because any moving thing was likely to draw fire. Tracer bullets painted great red arcs in the sky, and an occasional jeep whined frantically by in the deserted streets.

The proprietor of the Constellation Hotel, Maurice Cavalerie, a Frenchman who had seen much turmoil in China and Indochina, explained that the reason he had firmly locked the front doors during the battle was to keep his staff of waiters and houseboys inside rather than to keep soldiers outside. "I opened the doors just now and lost five boys," he complained during a brief lull in the firing.

By the afternoon of December 14, when it looked as if Kouprasith lacked sufficient strength to gain control of the city, General Phoumi's forces had reached the city and were able to join battle. The Phoumists emplaced their artillery pieces on a slight rise near the National Assembly building on the northeastern fringe of the town, and began shelling the airport at a range of approximately three miles. Kong Le's artillery pieces, manned by the North Vietnamese, retaliated by shelling the Chinaimo army camp, in an artillery duel that lasted until the battle ended. At night, when small-arms fire subsided and the stillness was punctuated by only occasional machine-gun bursts, the distant pounding of artillery fire and the whistling of shells overhead continued.

The Vientiane radio station had gone off the air, and the cable office had shut down as soon as the fighting began. Now the only links with the outside world were the American, British, and French embassies. Ambassador Brown remained in the U.S. Embassy throughout the fighting. Several streets away at the Settha Palace Hotel, Soviet Ambassador Abramov had taken shelter, and he, too, remained throughout the battle. (Afterward he flew to Bangkok aboard a British military aircraft and thence to Phnom Penh.) A mile-high column of black smoke rose into the cloud-studded, blue tropical sky over the crippled town.

On December 16, Kong Le's troops, inferior in numbers and armament despite the Soviet deliveries, began an orderly withdrawal from the western end of the town, taking all their military equipment with them. Seventy-six hours after the first shot had been fired, the last Kong Le paratrooper trudged out of the town.

A strange quiet settled over the littered streets of the capital. Not until forty-eight hours after the end of the fighting did the leaders of the Revolutionary Committee, General Phoumi and Prince Boun Oum, make their appearance. While still in Savannakhet, the headquarters of the Revolutionary Committee, they had laid the groundwork for forming their own government.

Forty deputies out of the total fifty-nine in the National Assembly had arrived in Savannakhet by December 11. Next day, this majority met in session to pass a vote of censure against the Souvanna Phouma Cabinet. This was followed shortly by a royal proclamation from Luang Prabang entrusting the Revolutionary Committee with the "temporary conduct" of the Kingdom's affairs.

At his refuge in Cambodia, Souvanna Phouma spoke bitterly against the United States. In an interview, he said of Ambassador Parsons, a man with whom he had never had good personal relations:

He understood nothing about Asia and nothing about Laos. The Assistant Secretary of State is the most nefarious and reprehensible of men. He is the ignominious architect of disastrous American policy toward Laos. He and others like him are responsible for the recent shedding of Lao blood.[3]

The next day in Washington, a new Administration was inaugurated. Soon it would face the same agonizing decision— whether or not to send American troops to Indochina—that had been faced by the Eisenhower Administration in 1954.

[3] *The New York Times,* January 20, 1961.

9.

Two Prime Ministers

It was an ironic twist of fate that Eisenhower, whose immediate objective on assuming the Presidency in 1953 had been to extricate the United States from the Korean War, spent his last days in office wrestling with another critical situation in Asia.

In late December, 1960, the President's top diplomatic, military, and intelligence advisers began a series of White House meetings to review the situation in Laos after six years of consistent United States support of anti-Communists. This was the picture that confronted them:

The Pathet Lao forces, which had numbered a few hundred poorly armed guerrillas at the 1954 cease-fire, had increased to several thousand; moreover, they had gained as allies the crack paratroopers of Captain Kong Le, who had been driven out of Vientiane but not defeated and who possessed brand-new American weapons taken from the capital's warehouses. The Soviet Union had posted an ambassador to Laos and was openly running an airlift from North Vietnam to supply weapons, ammunition, and food to Kong Le and the Pathet Lao. The United States had alienated Souvanna Phouma and committed itself to support a largely military government that was avowedly anti-Communist and thus had no claim to the magic mantle of "neutrality." Meanwhile, Souvanna Phouma, clinging to that mantle and claiming still to be the legal Prime Minister, had been befriended by the Communist powers. Effective authority was being exercised in his name by Quinim Pholsena, who was much less favorably disposed to the West and frankly anti-American.

In short, the American policy of attempting to contain Communist expansion in Laos by inadequate ground action (supporting the efforts of the Royal Lao Army) and strategic deterrence (the threat to commit American troops) had failed; while there had been no invasion by Communist forces, seven years of subversion had achieved virtually the effect of an invasion.

Soviet Support of Souvanna Phouma

The Soviets were apparently taken aback by Souvanna Phouma's departure from Vientiane on December 9. Now their claim that their actions were in support of the legitimate government was being jeopardized by the distinct possibility that Souvanna Phouma, who was tentatively staying in Phnom Penh, might resign, which he could do with a simple message to the King. The Prince was bitter at the United States for following what he considered a short-sighted, hopeless policy, and he was especially angry at his own military commanders for pursuing, hell-bent, a course of action that made street fighting and its heavy toll of civilian lives inevitable. Disgusted with the whole tragic episode, he probably would not tarry long in Phnom Penh but would fly to Paris to rejoin his wife and children in a comfortable retirement from political life.

A reliable American source affirms that the Prince dispatched a telegram to the Royal Palace on December 11, informing the King of his reasons for leaving Laos and placing himself "at the disposition" of the monarch. But because of the fighting, the telegram was not delivered in Luang Prabang until weeks later, on January 9. By that time he had made up his mind to stick it out.

The Soviets, aware that their best interests lay in persuading Souvanna Phouma to remain as Prime Minister despite the loss of Vientiane to the Phoumist rebels, acted with dispatch. A Soviet note on December 13 assailed the United States for backing General Phoumi, declaring that:

> if two or three months ago the Government of the United States made some effort to camouflage its unlawful actions in Laos, lately the United States has in effect become a party to military operations on the side of the rebels against the lawful government of Laos and the Laotian people.
>
> Flouting the sovereign rights of the Laotian Government headed by Prince Souvanna Phouma, the United States now openly supports the rebel group of Nosavan, supplying it with arms, military equipment, ammunition and money. . . .
>
> United States military advisers and instructors not only train the rebels but also directly supervise their military operations against the troops of the legitimate Laotian Government. The United States

Government also makes extensive use of Thailand, its ally in the military SEATO pact, which makes the territory of its country available for active military operations against the Government units and effects a brutal economic blockade of Laos. . . .

All this is a glaring violation by the Government of the United States of Article 12 of the Final Declaration of the 1954 Geneva Conference on Indochina, which contains an undertaking by every participant in the aforesaid Conference, including the United States, to respect the sovereignty, independence, unity, and territorial integrity of Laos and to refrain from any interference in its internal affairs.

On December 17, the State Department categorically rejected these charges and declared that "the responsibility for the present fratricidal war in Laos . . . rests squarely and solely upon the Soviet Government and its partners." It further stated:

The United States has repeatedly made clear its consistent policy of supporting the Kingdom of Laos in its determination to maintain its independence and integrity. Such support will continue. The United States has warned against efforts to seize control of or to subvert that free nation.

The note defended the supplying of American weapons to the Royal Lao Army, and declared that "such American advisers as have been in the country either administering the American military aid program or in the Franco-American training program are located at various training sites and supply depots and have not led any military actions."

Two days later, the State Department announced immediate resumption of military assistance to the Revolutionary Committee headed by General Phoumi and Prince Boun Oum, which had been entrusted by the King with the temporary conduct of the Kingdom's affairs.

During this interchange of notes, Ambassador Abramov, who was now also in Phnom Penh, gave Souvanna Phouma the Soviets' assurances that they would continue to regard him as the legal Prime Minister unless he resigned. Quinim Pholsena and Phoumi Vongvichit flew to Phnom Penh aboard a Soviet Ilyushin transport and pleaded with the Prince to stay on. Quinim brought word that he was maintaining a skeleton Cabinet in northern Laos in expectation of the Prince's return.

On December 22, in Moscow, following reports from Vientiane that Boun Oum had formed a Cabinet, First Deputy Foreign Minister V. V. Kuznetsov handed the British Ambassador a second Soviet note on Laos. It contained these two important paragraphs:

In conformity with universally recognized international standards, only the legitimate Lao Government is entitled to request any assistance from other states and to receive such assistance from them. In the light of this, the actions of the U.S. Government in rendering active military, material-technical and financial assistance to the rebels —actions which go to the length of the actual participation of servicemen of the United States and its allies in the military operations of the rebels against the legitimate Lao Government—are nothing but a flagrant violation of international law and the Geneva agreements on Laos under which the participants of the Geneva Conference of 1954 pledged themselves not to interfere in the internal affairs of Laos.

The Soviet Government believes that the Government of Great Britain is aware of the fact that the national Lao Government headed by Prince Souvanna Phouma has announced that it is continuing to function, that it is the legitimate government of Laos and that it regards the formation of a "government" led by Boun Oum as an act against the constitution.

Nine days after this Soviet note was delivered, the author interviewed Souvanna Phouma. The Prince immediately declared that the National Assembly's censure of him, on December 12, was not valid because it had been voted during an extraordinary session held in neither the royal capital nor the administrative capital, but in Savannakhet. He regarded the King's dealing with the Revolutionary Committee as maladroit and beyond the royal authority. An underlying factor here was the long-standing personal rivalry between the vice-regal branch of the royal family and the royal family itself, which had lain barely beneath the surface since formation of the Lao Issara in 1945.

The Prince said that he had not submitted his resignation to the King and made no mention of sending to Luang Prabang a telegram indicating his willingness to resign. He contended that he was still Prime Minister. The 1947 Constitution offered no guideposts. It did not indicate how soon a Prime Minister must resign after losing the confidence of the National Assembly, but merely stated, in Article 22, that the "vote of a motion of censure involves the resignation of the entire Government."

In Vientiane on that same day, December 31, a Lao source reported that "five battalions" of North Vietnamese troops had crossed the border into Laos near Route Coloniale 7 and were attacking Nong Het. The newly formed Cabinet of Prince Boun Oum distributed the information in a press communiqué, and Delegate Sisouk na Champassak relayed it to United Nations Secretary-General Dag Hammärskjold in an interview arranged by the U.S.

Simultaneously, the State Department announced it had turned down an appeal from India to support the reactivation of the International Control Commission in Laos. The U.S. was also unresponsive to a proposal, on January 1, from Prince Sihanouk of Cambodia for an international conference on Laos, to be attended by all the countries that had participated in the 1954 Conference, plus the three ICC countries and Laos' neighbors Burma and Thailand.

The National Assembly deputies returned to Vientiane and vainly awaited news from Phnom Penh that Souvanna Phouma had resigned. Finally, they decided to overlook Boun Oum's suspension of the Constitution on September 10, and unanimously endorsed the Prince's Cabinet on January 4. It consisted entirely of Phoumist politicians, whom Souvanna Phouma labeled a "bunch of clowns." General Phoumi was the new Deputy Prime Minister and Minister of Defense. Six ministers, including those of Finance and Interior, were relatives of Boun Oum, who now installed himself and his retinue of relatives, servants, and hangers-on in the spacious suburban villa formerly occupied by General Sounthone Pathammavong.

Once again, the United States threw its support to the most feudal elements of the country, extending recognition to the Boun Oum government. Britain, France, and Canada also acknowledged it. The Soviet Union and India continued to recognize Souvanna Phouma; Communist China, North Vietnam, and Poland, which had no formal diplomatic relations with Laos, supported Souvanna Phouma.

Shift of Course

It was clear that Laos was not a bastion of the Free World. The United States was confronted by the prospect of having tied itself to a minority government whose constitutionality was in doubt and whose only source of internal support was an army incapable of victory. The time for sitting tight was past. Action had to be taken at once.

John F. Kennedy, in the first few days of January, declined to be associated with the departing Administration's handling of the deteriorating situation in Laos. On January 7, the Eisenhower Administration published a White Paper on Laos, setting forth a sharply revised line of thinking:

The United States believes that it can best contribute to a solution of the Laos problem:

First, by attempting to further international recognition and understanding of the true nature of Communist intentions and actions in Laos;

Second, by the United States itself continuing clearly to show that it has no intention and no desire to establish a Western military position in Laos;

Third, by joining with other free nations to support and maintain the independence of Laos through whatever measures seem most promising.[1]

Translated from diplomatic parlance, this statement meant three things:

First, the United States wanted to make known how much aid the Kong Le–Pathet Lao alliance was getting from the Soviet airlift and the encadrement of North Vietnamese regulars. However, the U.S. had to stop short of calling this aid a violation of international agreements, since many countries felt that the United States itself had violated such agreements. This outside aid consisted of supplies transported in unarmed aircraft, unmarked except for serial numbers, belonging to the Soviet Union and piloted by Soviet crews in civilian clothes; this set-up closely resembled that of General Phoumi, who since September had received aid delivered by Air America aircraft under contract to the United States Government and piloted by American crews. The outside Communist personnel were North Vietnamese instructors and technicians; the American equivalents were PEO advisers and technicians, who had been training the Royal Army since 1955. United States condemnation of the Communist bloc for intervention in Laos would find little, if any, international support. Moreover, the Communist position on the ground was stronger than could be accounted for by the receipt of outside aid. Both Eisenhower and Kennedy appreciated this fact.

Second, the United States wanted to avoid an escalation of the commitment in Laos. Despite the Communist gains in the previous six years, it did not want to "establish a Western military position in Laos"—i.e., to garrison Laos with American troops.

Third, "whatever measures seem most promising" to maintain the independence of Laos prepared the ground for American support of a Vientiane coalition government including the Pathet Lao. Though purposely vague, this paragraph was by far the most significant of the three. It represented, at long last, a step forward

---

[1] Department of State Press Release No. 9, January 7, 1961.

out of the bog in which American policy toward post-1954 Indochina had been mired.

The Eisenhower Administration policy-makers, meeting in Washington in the last days of December and early January, agreed that Laos could not be forfeited to the North Vietnamese without serious consequences for the American position throughout Asia. They also agreed that direct American intervention was as unpalatable in 1960 as it had been in 1954, the last time the situation in Indochina had reached such a critical point. A coalition was the one remaining alternative that, it was hoped, would neither turn Laos over to the North Vietnamese Communists nor involve American troops in action in Indochina.

What were the facts on the ground that had to be considered? Militarily, American power in the Pacific—i.e., the Seventh Fleet—was as preponderant as always, and the gap between this power and that of North Vietnam was as wide as in 1954, if not even wider. However, American power had to be brought to bear effectively (as it had not been from 1954 to 1960). The war under way in Laos was still General Giap's textbook "people's war" (as it had been in 1954), and this warfare must be understood (as it had not been from 1954 to 1960). Lastly, the West continued to hold many political advantages, the chief one being that, basically, Souvanna Phouma still faced to the West.

These realities on the ground, it is obvious in retrospect, had been lost sight of by Eisenhower's policy-makers. The North Vietnamese-stimulated crisis atmosphere of 1959 had led to the American involvement with General Phoumi. This in turn limited the Administration's freedom of action and when in the autumn of 1960 the more serious crisis arose, bringing direct Communist intervention into the picture, the United States was boxed in a corner. The new men of the Kennedy Administration had a clearer perspective on the realities previously referred to, and they proceeded to make them once again the basis of American actions in Laos.

Kong Le's Daring Stroke

General Phoumi's troops, after taking Vientiane, were slow to pursue Kong Le's paratroopers, who had staged an orderly withdrawal from the smoking capital along the Royal Road. Where normally only ox carts, bicycles, and an occasional bus traveled, now the paratroopers' U.S.-supplied jeeps and 2½-ton trucks churned northward.

At the outset, an altercation took place between Kong Le and a subordinate, Lieutenant Deuan Sunnalath. Deuan, who had had no troops under his command, had left Kong Le's ranks to join Colonel Kouprasith at the Chinaimo army camp before the Colonel's abortive countercoup of December 8. After its failure, Deuan had rejoined Kong Le, who had accepted him back without asking questions. Deuan was in sharp disagreement with Kong Le, pressing strongly for a counterattack against Vientiane after December 16, but he was overruled.

Rear-guard paratroopers protected the retreating column from any advance patrols of General Phoumi's forces. However, the General made no serious effort to attack from the rear or to cut off the paratroopers' retreat by dropping paratroopers into the hills ahead. Kong Le, after he had moved his trucks and five remaining 105-mm. artillery pieces (one of the original six had been knocked out in Vientiane) across the Lik River, destroyed the bridge to prevent pursuit.

Soviet Ilyushin transports, no longer able to land supplies for Kong Le at the Vientiane airport, now parachuted weapons, ammunition, and food rations onto a whitewashed drop-zone in the rice paddies near Phone Hong, a village 40 miles north of the capital. When Kong Le's column was in the foothills, the Soviet planes landed and made parachute drops at the small field at Vang Vieng. American intelligence estimated that Soviet aircraft flew 184 missions into Laos between December 15 and January 2.[2] Light Czech-made liaison planes ferried officers and advisers back and forth at will between Vang Vieng, Sam Neua town, and Hanoi.

As Kong Le moved northward, the mountainous terrain increasingly favored him. Each day it became more unlikely that General Phoumi's column, which had laboriously ferried its armored cars across the Lik, could strike a telling blow; confined to the road, unable to maneuver, the Phoumist column was vulnerable to land mines, which Kong Le's troops used with effect, and to guerrilla harassment from the Pathet Lao.

At Sala Phou Khoun, the Royal Road reaches a fork; to the left lies Luang Prabang, to the right the Plain of Jars. Kong Le's objective was the latter, with its all-weather landing field, heavily fortified by the Phoumist troops. With lightning rapidity, he trucked an advance striking force past Sala Phou Khoun and onto the western rim of the rolling plain. Closely coordinated attacks by Pathet Lao guerrillas created the necessary diversion from the opposite direction, along the northeastern periphery. A concen-

2 Department of State Press Release No. 2, January 4, 1961.

trated bombardment by Kong Le's artillery against the Phoumists sent them fleeing from their exposed positions and into the surrounding hills, leaving most of their supplies to the attackers. Several planeloads of Phoumist paratroopers, flown in to retrieve the situation, were dropped over the rugged area, but becoming scattered, joined the general panic. U.S. military advisers with the Phoumists were evacuated by Air America transports. As the last C-46 banked away from the airfield, the first of the airlift Ilyushins skimmed over the green hills.

Xieng Khouang town, twenty miles southeast of the Plain of Jars airfield, soon fell to the Pathet Lao. However, its military commander, Lieutenant Colonel Vang Pao, a Meo, conducted an orderly evacuation of his troops into the surrounding mountains.

Kong Le's daring stroke had gained control of the most important military complex in northern Laos. He and his Pathet Lao allies now possessed a base area linked by airlift and the old Route Coloniale (called, since 1950, Route Nationale) 7 with North Vietnam. (See Map 3.)

Soviet Motives

The Plain of Jars was transformed into a vast armed camp. A British observer on a visit there in February reported that "the overwhelming impression . . . is that of massive military assistance" from the Communist bloc.

What were the reasons behind the Soviet Union's sudden commitment to supply, openly and directly, the Kong Le–Pathet Lao alliance with aid in such immense quantities as to enable the Pathet Lao forces to make the basic transformation from guerrillas to regular forces? Why did the Soviet Union involve itself in such a distant battle, an action that gave the lie to simultaneous Soviet professions of peaceful coexistence and concern over the possibility that the Laos crisis might escalate into a larger war? Why did the Soviets undertake to rescue Souvanna Phouma from the dire straits in which U.S. pressure had placed him?

There is one answer to these multiple questions: The Soviet Union was acting out of the imperative need to retain the allegiance of North Vietnam in the developing quarrel with China.

The position of the North Vietnamese leadership in Communist-bloc affairs in the autumn of 1960 resembled that of the Viet Minh leadership vis-à-vis the Chinese, French, and nationalists when these four factions were contending for power in Hanoi in 1945 and 1946. Although relatively weak at the start, the Vietnamese Communists, in both cases, had gained strength by adroitly shifting their deciding weight in disputes.

Ho Chi Minh's position had been precarious, but not necessarily disadvantageous, ever since Mao Tse-tung had come to power in Peking in 1949. A common background in revolutionary activity had created a strong bond between the two Asian Communist leaders, and thousands of North Vietnamese cadres had been trained by the Chinese Communists during the eight-year war against the French. Chinese aid to the Viet Minh had been considerable (American-made artillery supplied by the Chinese had been crucial in the Viet Minh's successful siege of Dien Bien Phu), although the Vietnamese had repaid at least a part of this wartime aid in rice and salt, and sought to preserve the distinction between their regime and the Chinese.

The Soviet Union, on the other hand, had shown little concern about North Vietnam. It had lagged behind China in recognizing Ho's government, in 1950. Stalin was deeply involved in European political maneuvers, and these sometimes worked to the detriment of the Viet Minh struggle against the French. Such maladroit Soviet moves as its proposal, on January 24, 1957, to seat both North and South Vietnam in the United Nations prolonged the coolness between Hanoi and Moscow and, conversely, strengthened the solidarity between Ho and Mao, both rulers of divided countries with rival regimes supported by the "imperialists."

This rapport between the two countries continued into 1956, when Hanoi carried out a Chinese-style land reform, which was directly supervised by Chinese cadres. This was a disastrous economic failure, and marked a turning point in Hanoi-Peking relations. The Vietnamese did not follow in 1958 when the Chinese initiated their "Great Leap Forward" and the communes. As Chinese influence decreased, Moscow's increased, amid promises of Soviet largesse for North Vietnam's industrial rebuilding program.

These shifting influences were reflected in the emergence within the Lao Dong Party of pro-Soviet and pro-Chinese factions, which subtly competed for predominance under Ho's watchful eye. The rivalry between these two factions grew increasingly violent, until by the end of 1960, it shook the Lao Dong Party to its foundations

In November of that year, Ho flew to Moscow for a meeting of eighty-one Communist parties from all over the world. While there, he apparently attempted to mediate the dispute between

China and Russia. But the differences that separated Khrushchev and Mao had become so great that they were no longer susceptible to mediation, even by such a veteran Comintern hand as Ho.

During this period, the Chinese viewpoint was exerting a renewed attraction in Hanoi. The North Vietnamese, by 1960 embarked on an armed struggle to topple the Ngo Dinh Diem regime in the south and reunify their country, had more sympathy for Mao's militant arguments for Communist guerrilla warfare against the American presence in Asia, Africa, and Latin America than they had for Khrushchev's efforts to reach a *détente* with the West.

The Soviet Union, aware of this advantage held by the Red Chinese, acted to offset it by granting North Vietnam, in August, 1960, large credits to finance an ambitious expansion of industry. In December, the U.S.S.R. capped its persuasive efforts by initiating the airlift from North Vietnam to the pro-Communist forces fighting the "imperialists" in Laos. The Soviet Union had calculated that this move would preclude accusations by Lao Dong Party militants that the U.S.S.R.'s conciliatory policy was betraying the Communist cause, and would prevent the Lao Dong Party from throwing its entire support to the Chinese Communist Party.

Souvanna Phouma in the Center

Still in Phnom Penh, Souvanna Phouma watched with sardonic satisfaction the State Department's ineffectual attempts to persuade the Soviet Union to call off the airlift. He remained bitter at the flagrant failure of the U.S. to back up its assurances that American military supplies turned over to the Phoumists would not be used against Kong Le's forces. Speaking to James Wilde, a Canadian working for *The New York Times,* he said in an interview published by that newspaper on January 20, 1961, "What I shall never forgive the United States for, however, is the fact that it betrayed me, that it double-crossed me and my government." He felt it was up to the big powers to find a solution, because the Lao had lost control of the situation.

Two weeks later, Souvanna Phouma told Takashi Oka of the *Christian Science Monitor* of his desire to complete the task of forming a coalition government, which had been interrupted by General Phoumi's seizure of Vientiane. This would require patience, however. He expressed hesitancy about returning to Laos; as an exile, he compelled others to come to him, since he was certain the present opposition of the Boun Oum regime and the Pathet

Lao would lead only to continued strife and greater foreign interference in Laos. If he returned to Vientiane, he would appear to
lend his support to the Boun Oum government, which he considered illegal. If he went to northern Laos, he would be placing
himself as a hostage in the eager hands of the Pathet Lao. The best
solution was an exploratory trip, and he spoke hopefully of visiting
Kong Le on the Plain of Jars, and Colonel Khammouane Boupha,
the Phong Saly warlord, who claimed his forces were loyal to Souvanna Phouma. "As with Kong Le, there is a certain accommodation with the Pathet Lao, but the royal troops stay royal troops,"
the Prince remarked.

He said that in any genuine plebiscite, 95 per cent of the vote
would be for nationalist candidates, and the remainder for the
Pathet Lao and the pro-Americans. He called for an international
conference to frame a big-power guarantee of Laos' neutrality, with
the three Lao factions forming a united delegation. His own centrist
position would pull together the two extremist wings, the Pathet
Lao and the Phoumists.

"The Americans say I am a Communist," the Prince observed.
"All this is heartbreaking. How can they think I am a Communist?
I am looking for a way to keep Laos non-Communist." His remarks
became more pointed: "To be pro-West, on the other hand, does
not necessarily mean to be pro-American. To be anti-American
does not mean to be pro-Communist. When we say we are anti-
American, we are against the American policies of the moment. We
are anti-American because these Americans don't understand Laos,
they have regard only for their own interests."

To refute the American charge that he was blind to the danger
from the north, he cited the ancient, deep-seated Lao fear of the
Chinese. In 1945, he recalled, after the Potsdam Agreement had
stipulated that Chinese Nationalists would occupy northern Laos,
inhabitants of Luang Prabang started building canoes and rafts to
flee downstream when the Chinese army of occupation was still
200 miles away.

On February 20, Souvanna Phouma flew to the Plain of Jars,
where he was greeted by the skeletal Cabinet that Quinim Pholsena
had informed him would await his return. It was made up of three
men: Khamsouk Keola, Acting Prime Minister; Quinim Pholsena,
Minister of Foreign Affairs, Defense, and Finance; and Prince
Sisoumang, who held the portfolios of Interior, Economy, and
Social Welfare, and the remaining minor portfolios. These men had
established themselves in the limited accommodations available in

Khang Khay, a village of about 1,000 souls. Not far from the Prime Minister's office, a full Soviet Embassy had been set up.

At Phong Savan, a great opium-trading center on the road between Khang Khay and the Plain of Jars airfield, lived a dozen Russian aircraft technicians, who serviced the airlift planes. They were lodged in what had been the Snow Leopard Inn but was now the Friendship Hotel. At opposite ends of Phong Savan's main street, Czech and North Vietnamese information offices had been established. And in near-by Xieng Khouang town were billeted an "economic and cultural delegation" from Peking.

At the Plain of Jars airfield, North Vietnamese technicians proudly manned the old French control tower to direct the Soviet airlift planes. Near Phong Savan, the North Vietnamese had set up a tent hospital to care for Pathet Lao wounded. The Plain of Jars was becoming a mirror image of the PEO compound in Vientiane.

Among those who greeted Souvanna Phouma was his army commander, Kong Le. His troops wore American uniforms, distinguishing them from the Pathet Lao, who wore mustard-colored uniforms. Kong Le's American weapons and vehicles were supplemented by generous quantities of Soviet-type small arms and Molotova trucks and armored cars.

Soviet 37-mm. radar-directed antiaircraft guns were set up around the Plain of Jars, and Vietnamese instructors were training Kong Le's troops in their use. Their crews meant business: They shot down a reconnaissance American C-47 attached to the air attaché's office in Saigon, killing seven and capturing the one survivor. The American Embassy in Saigon falsely claimed that the plane had been on a routine liaison flight between Vientiane and Saigon.

Harvard Fighters and Special Forces

With the political and military initiative wholly in the hands of the Communists, the Kennedy Administration sought as best it could to limit the damage in Laos to consolidation by the Kong Le–Pathet Lao alliance of control over the entire eastern half of the country. In early January, the U.S. sent the Phoumist forces six AT-6 Harvard trainer aircraft armed with machine guns and equipped to fire rockets and drop bombs. These were manned by Lao pilots trained in Thailand. The introduction of these six planes effected a small but noticeable escalation of the conflict, and the Soviet Union protested to the United States when the planes strafed the Kong Le–Pathet Lao forces along the Royal Road. The AT-6's were not used against the airlift's Ilyushin-14's. A tacit agreement between Washington and Moscow required airlift planes to be unarmed.

More significantly, the U.S. replaced General Heintges' PEO infantrymen with a contingent of about 400 Special Forces personnel from Okinawa, to act as cadres for the Phoumist troops. Called White Star Mobile Training Teams, they were under the command of a tough American of Finnish extraction, Lieutenant Colonel Aito Keravuri. They were particularly effective in working with Colonel Vang Pao's Meo fighters, who had reorganized themselves into guerrilla bands in the mountains surrounding the Plain of Jars. The White Star detachments lived and fought for long periods in the field under miserable conditions, and showed that the Meo added a new dimension to the protracted Laos conflict.

However, these efforts by Washington no longer had the previous objective of *militarily defeating* the Pathet Lao, an objective that had been rendered infinitely more difficult than before because of the massive Soviet assistance to the Pathet Lao. Now the American objective was to keep the Mekong Valley out of Pathet Lao control, thus easing the pressure on the Thai government, and consolidating a bargaining position vis-à-vis the Communist bloc in the increasingly likely event of a new international conference.

Despite its limited objective, the U.S. endowed its efforts with an ever-greater urgency because of the rapid build-up in Communist strength and the State Department's failure to get the Soviets to halt the airlift. Reports reached Vientiane of well-armed Pathet Lao columns on the march over much of northern Laos, particularly in Luang Prabang and Phong Saly provinces. Barely twenty miles north of Vientiane, there occurred clashes involving guerrillas permanently based in a mountain resort called Phou Khao Khouei.

General Phoumi's armored column was moving northward from Vientiane at a distressingly slow pace, balked by land mines and trees felled across the narrow road, sometimes for hundreds of yards at a stretch. Correspondents who visited the "front" found the Phoumist troops catching fish in mountain streams by exploding grenades underwater. They had neither the dedication of Kong Le's paratroopers nor the merciless discipline of the Pathet Lao. Sentries were posted here and there; whenever they heard a burst of small-arms fire in the near-by forest, they would fire several random shots and then flee back to the main camp.

Vietnamese Cadres

The Phoumist soldiers' disinclination to engage the enemy was due partly to rumors that the opposing forces included regular North Vietnamese troop units. Soldiers from the North Vietnamese 335th Division had been reported present in northern Laos since the previous October. After January, an increasing number and variety were reported. Also reported were elements of the 316th Division, 120th Independent Regiment, and 359th Frontier Guard Regiment.[3] Both the 316th and the 335th divisions were veteran units formed largely of mountain tribesmen. The 316th had captured Sam Neua from the French in the spring of 1953, and had fought in the battle of Dien Bien Phu.

Further evidence of North Vietnamese soldiers in Laos came from diaries kept in Vietnamese that were captured by the Phoumist troops. One carried the bearer's oath "to respect the people, to aid the people, and to defend the people," and described the "soldier of the People's Army" as he who "defends the sovereignty, national territory and security of the Democratic Republic of Vietnam"—an indication that North Vietnamese soldiers sent into Laos were told that they were defending their homeland from possible attack by the Americans.

In the midst of this foreign involvement, King Savang Vatthana on February 19 addressed a message to his people. He harked back to King Sisavang Vong's stubborn refusal to be intimidated by the Viet Minh invasions of 1953 and 1954:

> Lao people, our country is the most peaceful country in the world. . . . the people of our country have always strictly applied the teachings of Buddha concerning forgiveness, gentleness and charity. At no time has there ever arisen in the minds of the Lao people the idea of coveting another's wealth, of quarreling with their neighbors, much less of fighting them. And yet, during the past twenty years, our country has known neither peace nor security.
>
> Our august father, a magnanimous sovereign, witnessed several foreign invasions. He faced them with courage. Since our accession to the throne, enemies of all sorts have tried to cross our frontiers,

[3] Department of State, *A Threat to the Peace: North Viet-Nam's Effort to Conquer South Viet-Nam* (Washington: Government Printing Office, 1961), Part 1, p. 39. See also Government of the Republic of Vietnam, *Violations of the Geneva Agreements by the Viet-Minh Communists* (Saigon: Ministry of Foreign Affairs, 1961), p. 35. The latter source mentions two other independent regiments, the 270th and the 148th; and states that from the 335th Division, the 83rd Regiment operates in northern Laos, the 280th Regiment in central Laos, and the 673rd Regiment in southern Laos.

to destroy our people and to destroy our religion and our nation's aura of peace and concord.

Lao people, the misfortunes which have befallen us have been the result of disunity among the Lao on the one hand and of foreign interference on the other. Foreign countries do not care either about our interests or peace; they are concerned only with their own interests.

The King coupled this exhortation with a declaration of Laos' neutrality. Speaking before the Boun Oum Cabinet and assembled foreign diplomats, he proposed that Burma, Cambodia, and Malaya form a commission to visit Laos "to establish that this country threatens no one and aspires solely to peace." He said: "This commission would have as its mission the denouncing of all foreign intervention, direct or indirect, open or camouflaged, which would result in the imperiling of the Kingdom's independence, integrity, and neutrality." This proposal, according to a diplomatic informant, was drafted behind the scenes by the State Department, which was perturbed by the sparse international recognition accorded the Boun Oum government and by the continued insistence of Cambodia on the convening of an international conference to discuss the situation in Laos.

The initiative for a new commission was almost immediately rejected by the Communist countries and by two of the proposed members, Cambodia and Burma, on the grounds that acceptance would imply taking a position for Boun Oum against Souvanna Phouma, in other words in an internal state matter. The Cambodian reply made it clear that foreign intervention on behalf of the one Lao government was no less reprehensible than intervention on behalf of the other. But the King had raised his voice in favor of reconciliation and he had not specifically condemned Souvanna Phouma (there had been, after all, an explosive reaction in 1945 to his father's condemnation of Souvanna Phouma's elder brother). It was the King's message more than any other factor that decided Souvanna Phouma to leave Phnom Penh the following day in an Ilyushin transport and begin his exploratory visit to Khang Khay.

After this visit, the Prince established contact with Vientiane through emissaries, and at the beginning of March, he and General Phoumi confounded foreign observers by meeting in Phnom Penh. Their exchange was cordial. In a joint communiqué issued on March 10, they stated that they "strongly oppose foreign interference and refuse to allow the Kingdom and its people to bear the cost of a deadly struggle for influence in which they have no part."

Washington reacted with tentative approval, of particular significance because the communiqué called for an international conference to untangle the complicated situation in Laos.

For three days, neither Radio Hanoi nor Radio Peking mentioned the March 10 communiqué. Then, apparently because of the American endorsement, both North Vietnam and China sharply denounced the communiqué as evidence of an imperialist plot to hoodwink Souvanna Phouma. Perhaps as a result of their unfavorable response, Souvanna Phouma issued a more cautious statement when the meetings with General Phoumi ended on March 15.

An international conference became the Prince's watchword. In Hong Kong the following day, about to set off on a world tour, he called it "the only solution." On March 22, Moscow Radio broadcast an interview in which Souvanna Phouma called for a cease-fire in Laos to precede the conference, apparently to mollify the United States, which refused to participate in any conference so long as the Pathet Lao were still making gains on the ground in Laos.

The North Vietnamese flatly opposed any cease-fire that would limit the military gains they were making, but voiced support for the proposed conference. Peking took the same line.

The Pathet Lao, encadred by the North Vietnamese, struck sharply in the first days of March, spreading terror and confusion down the Royal Road. On March 9, the Vientiane government announced that Sala Phou Khoun, the vital road junction between Luang Prabang and Vientiane, had fallen. Within the next twenty-four hours, the entire road as far as Muong Kassy had been taken by the Pathet Lao. Entire companies of Phoumist troops panicked, throwing away their arms and fleeing for safety to the surrounding mountains. All idea of a Phoumist offensive against the Plain of Jars was abandoned. The new situation was more threatening than the 1959 "crisis" had ever been.

Bitter fighting developed at the head of the valley north of Vang Vieng, where Phoumist troops made a stand. Among those captured by the Pathet Lao was the son of Phoumist General Sing Ratanasamay. A shrapnel-wounded soldier taken prisoner by the Phoumists, who called himself Private Boun Kong, a common enough name in Laos, turned out to be Vi Van Sang, a member of the 925th Independent Regiment of the North Vietnamese Army. He said he belonged to one of two 42-man sections of mortar and machine-gun specialists who had been ordered into Laos on February 19. They had marched for four days along Route Coloniale 7 to the area of Nong Het, and thence traveled by truck convoy to the Plain of Jars, where they had been attached to the 6th Pathet Lao Battalion.

The Phoumists' situation worsened from day to day. The Ilyushins parachuted some of Kong Le's paratroopers into attack positions to help the Pathet Lao break through the disorganized Phoumist lines. On March 23, North Vietnamese assault troops led a successful Pathet Lao attack on Kam Keut in Khammouane Province. By the end of the month, the pro-Communist forces controlled portions of six provinces: Phong Saly, Sam Neua, Luang Prabang, Xieng Khouang, Vientiane, and Khammouane.

The Pathet Lao–North Vietnamese initiatives, undertaken without any Soviet assurance of unconditional support for North Vietnam in the event of American retaliation (in this period, not a single Soviet statement promised such support to North Vietnam), had strengthened the Soviet bargaining position vis-à-vis the West.

American Intervention Weighed

The critical deterioration of the Western position in Laos confronted President Kennedy during his first hundred days in office with a dilemma that had confronted the White House in the dark spring of 1954: whether or not to send American troops to the jungles of Indochina, and if so, in what numbers, and how, and where. Dulles had been tragically correct in his thesis, enunciated at the height of the Dien Bien Phu crisis, that if the United States took a firm stand to resist the Communists with force, American intervention would be increasingly costly as time went on. The decision lay with the United States, but its effects would be felt not only in Laos, but in the rest of Asia and Europe where the United States had alliances. The Communist powers were watching Kennedy for the slightest hint of weakness in the Laos situation. Irresolution carried with it the penalty of forfeiting the Western position in Laos and perhaps Indochina and the rest of Southeast Asia.

Kennedy met with his top advisers to consider the alternatives to continued reliance on the Phoumist troops. The prospects were not good. Admiral Harry D. Felt, Commander in Chief of U.S. forces in the Pacific, dispelled any illusions about the complexity of the logistics problems. In the event of large-scale movement of North Vietnamese troops into Laos in response to the commitment of American troops there, the enemy supply line would be short, the American line long. An official calculation disclosed that the

United States had hardly enough conventional equipment and ammunition at hand, in the spring of 1961, to fight a limited war in Indochina. Kennedy knew—having learned "with stunned amazement" a few weeks after taking office—that if he sent 10,000 men to Southeast Asia, his own country would have practically no strategic Army reserve left for other contingencies.[4]

After deliberation, seventeen steps to progressive commitment were reportedly decided on. The number of steps actually taken would depend on how hard the United States was pressed.

A Marine helicopter repair base was set up in northeastern Thailand at the all-weather airfield at Udorn, and an initial flight of helicopters was posted there from the vast deployment of the Seventh Fleet. Gasoline, ammunition, and weapons were stocked in advance bases along the Mekong. Lieutenant General Thomas J. Trapnell, commander of the 18th Airborne Corps, part of the Strategic Army Command at Fort Bragg, North Carolina, was sent to Laos to reconnoiter the fighting conditions in the field.

On Okinawa, Task Force 116 was placed on alert. Troops included two regiments and headquarters of the Third Marine Division with Marine Air Group 16 (between 15,000 and 20,000 men), the Second Airborne Battle Group of the 503rd Infantry Combat Team (1,900 men), and the First Special Forces Group (300 men). These could be airlifted rapidly to Laos aboard C-130 turboprop transports, which were capable of landing on relatively rough fields.

If Task Force 116 was put in action, its mission would be to seize the key points of Mahaxay and Tchepone, with its vital airfield, and these would become the cleats for a line between the Laos-Vietnam border at the Seventeenth Parallel on the east and the Thai border at just about Thakhek on the west. Below that line, American forces would protect the southern "panhandle" of Laos, including Route Nationale 9, against Communist control.

If this plan was implemented, a large area would require garrisoning by American troops. The troops would be vulnerable to guerrilla action. In combat against the North Vietnamese, they would be fighting on the defensive against an enemy highly skilled in attritional warfare and intimately familiar with the terrain.

Yet the commitment of American forces to Laos would be the logical outcome of the polarization of forces within Laos. U.S. policy in Laos since 1954 had put up a bold front to the Commu-

4 Major General Chester V. Clifton, *Hail to the Chief* (Association of the United States Army, January, 1964).

nists. Now that front was being probed. And the will to carry that policy to its conclusion was tempered by the sober calculation that, in the event of fighting, there was no reason to think that the Americans would be any better off than the French had been when compelled to withdraw their men, tanks, and planes from the Red River Delta.

The grave consequences of an open American commitment in Indochina weighed heavily on President Kennedy. Having assessed the dangers and worked out with his advisers the contingency plans, he went before the television cameras on March 23 to enlist the support of the American people and to notify the Soviet Premier that the United States was leaving an honorable way out of the crisis that confronted them both. The way out was embodied in an American declaration of support for a British proposal, made in Moscow that very day, for a joint British-Soviet appeal to both sides in Laos for a cease-fire, reactivation of the ICC in Laos, and an international conference on Laos after the cease-fire had become effective.

In his television address, the President said:

First, we strongly and unreservedly support the goal of a neutral and independent Laos, tied to no outside power or group of powers, threatening no one, and free from any domination. Our support for the present duly constituted government is aimed entirely and exclusively at that result. And if in the past there has been any possible ground for misunderstanding of our desire for a truly neutral Laos, there should be none now.

Secondly, if there is to be a peaceful solution, there must be a cessation of the present armed attacks by externally supported Communists. If these attacks do not stop, those who support a truly neutral Laos will have to consider their response. . . .

No one should doubt our resolution on this point. We are faced with a clear and one-sided threat of a change in the internationally agreed position of Laos. This threat runs counter to the will of the Laotian people, who wish only to be independent and neutral. It is posed rather by the military operations of internal dissident elements directed from outside the country. This is what must end if peace is to be achieved in Southeast Asia.

Thirdly, we are earnestly in favor of constructive negotiation among the nations concerned and among the leaders of Laos which can help Laos back to the pathway of independence and genuine neutrality. We strongly support the present British proposal of a prompt end of hostilities and prompt negotiation.

My fellow Americans, Laos is far away from America, but the world is small. Its two million people live in a country three times the size of Austria. The security of all Southeast Asia will be endangered if Laos loses its neutral independence. Its own safety runs with the safety of us all—in real neutrality observed by all.

I want to make it clear to the American people and to all the world that all we want in Laos is peace, not war; a truly neutral government, not a cold war pawn; a settlement concluded at the conference table and not on the battlefield.[5]

The situation was handled with remarkable skill. No crisis of tension was created in the American electorate. The pros and cons of American intervention were not brought into public debate, as in 1954. There were no public threatening statements by military officers such as Admiral Radford. Instead, preparations were made quietly and deliberately; ships put to sea and troops were alerted. The Soviets were informed of these moves, but without any hysterical warnings from Washington. The domino theory still applied to Indochina; the stakes were just as high. And many underlying hesitancies were still there, as in 1954. Admiral Arleigh Burke, Navy Chief of Staff, sent by the President to brief a bipartisan group of Congressional leaders, found them opposed to intervention but, in the interest of national security, prepared to back the President in any decision.

Kennedy, with his intuitive awareness of the country's mood, paced his actions to the needs of the crisis without exacerbating matters by stimulating public debate, and therefore public uncertainty, over the Administration's course. This was no mean accomplishment.

As Kennedy put it, there were contradictions in American feeling—an extreme desire to stand up to the Communists but a strong reluctance to become involved in any military action. He was acutely aware of the political consequences of either action or inaction, and especially of the old Republican charge of "Democratic wars." But he had no doubt that the nation would follow the President if he ordered men into combat.[6]

It was of the utmost importance that North Vietnam, especially, understand the firmness of the American resolve to prevent a Communist takeover in Laos. But the United States unfortunately had no diplomats in Hanoi or in Peking. In this situation, Kennedy had to depend upon Moscow's channels of communication with Hanoi

[5] *Public Papers of the Presidents, 1961* (Washington: Government Printing Office, 1962), p. 214.

[6] Conversation with Chalmers M. Roberts, reported in *The Washington Post*, November 30, 1963.

and Peking. The President and Secretary of State Dean Rusk met constantly with Soviet Foreign Minister Gromyko in Washington, and Kennedy sent his Ambassador in the Soviet Union halfway across Siberia to deliver a personal message to Khrushchev, who was visiting Novosibirsk.

Khrushchev's Dilemma

Kennedy's course of action had put Khrushchev on tenterhooks. Like Kennedy, he faced the very real prospect of being dragged willy-nilly into a most unprofitable confrontation far from home. Supporting his Asian allies in a war against the United States would produce serious risks and would limit his ability to exploit issues much closer to home and of much greater interest, such as Berlin.

Khrushchev had to explain to the North Vietnamese the precise degree of American firmness as he understood it from Kennedy himself. Moreover, he had to do this without appearing as an appeaser to the North Vietnamese. While details of the exchanges between Moscow and Hanoi and between Peking and Hanoi are not yet known, the available evidence indicates the outlines of the arguments on all sides. Khrushchev was compelled to weigh his moves against his American policy and against his Communist-bloc policy. Khrushchev could agree to a cease-fire in Laos with little sacrifice to himself. His reasoning with the North Vietnamese probably ran like this: In order to prevent the Americans from intervening in Laos, it is necessary to agree to a cease-fire; we are supporting Souvanna Phouma, who is the legal Prime Minister of Laos, and in the long run this policy will achieve the same ends as a military victory by the Pathet Lao.

For the North Vietnamese, however, a cease-fire meant considerable sacrifice. Their men, fighting with the Pathet Lao, were on the way to "liberating" Laos from foreign domination, a task at which they had been working patiently for fifteen years. Giap's analysis of "imperialist" behavior in his theory of "people's war" foresaw that the risk of retaliatory action against the base area (in this case, North Vietnam) would increase as the struggle became more acute; the most dangerous time was at the brink of victory. Therefore, the North Vietnamese were in no mood to follow Khrushchev's advice blindly. Also, the Vietnamese Communists harbored a deep-rooted suspicion of the Russians, the origin of which went back to Ho Chi Minh's days in the Comintern. Stalin had been dead wrong, in the 1920's, in advising the Chinese Communists to cooperate with Chiang Kai-shek. Ho had been there. *He knew*. Why should he now place any greater stock in Khrushchev's advice?

The Politburo of the Lao Dong Party probably calculated that the Americans, despite their threatening moves, would not actually intervene in Laos unless the Mekong Valley fell to the Pathet Lao. By a shrewd projection of the well-known official American reluctance to commit garrison troops to mainland Southeast Asia and the primary American preoccupation with the security of Thailand, the Vietnamese Communists probably judged that they could carry on their covert activities in the uplands of Laos with relatively little fear of provoking American intervention.

Peking was holding up to Hanoi, by public statements and no doubt by secret communications, developments in Laos as proof positive of the correctness of the militant line in advancing Communist control over the revolutionary movements in the underdeveloped countries. In this view, the American military preparations were the latest confirmation of "U.S. imperialism" as the "international gendarme" that rushed troops here, there, and everywhere in a vain effort to police the world.

The Peking government had another concern in Laos. Remnants of the defeated Kuomintang armies, forced out of China by the Communist takeover in 1949, had since subsisted in the mountains of northern Burma and reportedly had been supplied with arms by aircraft from Taipei. When in 1961, the Burmese Government used force to dislodge them, several thousand of these armed men drifted eastward into Thailand and Laos. No one knew exactly how many there were or what their movements were. On March 14, 1961, however, Lucien Coudoux, a journalist, saw approximately 1,200 of these irregulars at Ban Houei Sai, on the Laos side of the Mekong, crossing the river into Thailand; they carried American rifles, machine guns, mortars, and bazookas. A month later, an official of the Chinese Nationalist Consulate in Vientiane reported that Nationalist aircraft had airlifted 4,000 Kuomintang troops from Nam Tha to Ban Houei Sai.[7] The reasons for this move may be disclosed in future publications of diplomatic correspondence; now it appears extremely likely that it was closely tied to American efforts to persuade the Soviets to cooperate in reaching a settlement in Laos.

Even at the height of the military crisis in the spring of 1961, Peking refrained from hinting at committing its own troops in Laos

[7] United Press International dispatch, April 12, 1961.

except for one statement. That was made by Foreign Minister Chen Yi at the Djakarta airport on April 2. He said that if SEATO forces intervened in Laos, China would send troops if requested to do so by Souvanna Phouma. There was little risk in this statement, since neither proviso was likely.

Caught between considerations of Communist solidarity and the desire to avoid entanglement in a thoroughly unprofitable situation, Khrushchev temporized. Days went by, and Moscow made no response to the British proposal for a joint British-Soviet appeal for a cease-fire and the convening of a conference. Khrushchev was careful not to identify himself too closely with the drive forward of the Communist-supported forces in Laos; the Soviet press did not accord prominent attention to the Pathet Lao advances and made no mention of the Soviet airlift.

At long last, on March 27, *Pravda* dropped a hint that the Soviet Union would agree to call for a cease-fire in Laos *before* an international conference. "It is quite evident," *Pravda* commented, "that the realistic way to the solution of the Laos problem lies not in aggravating the situation in the area of Laos, not in preparing military intervention, but in peace talks and in the calling of an international conference and the renewal of the work of the ICC." The foreign ministers of the SEATO powers, who had opened their annual meeting that very day in Bangkok, breathed a sigh of relief. It was obvious that if there were to be "peace talks" between the factions in Laos, someone had to order the pro-Communists to stop shooting.

Then the Soviets did a remarkable thing. On April 4, they beamed a program in the Vietnamese language *only*—declaring that the Soviet Union did not demand a cease-fire in Laos as a "precondition" to an international conference and that the conference was the "main point" of the Soviet plan. However, the broadcast added, "a cease-fire in Laos will help to create a favorable atmosphere for negotiations." This was tantamount to a direct appeal to North Vietnam, and to an admission that the Soviets recognized that only the North Vietnamese had the power to control the ground fighting in Laos and thus to call a cease-fire. The North Vietnamese, however, were being advised by the Chinese not to sacrifice their gains in Laos by agreeing to a cease-fire.

A long commentary in the official Peking *People's Daily* on April 1 had expressed serious concern about American military bases near its own southern border, and made it clear that the Chinese opposed a cease-fire in Laos, whether it was proposed by the United States *or* by the Soviet Union:

According to what has been disclosed by U.S. press reports alone, scores of U.S. warships, several hundred aircraft, and thousands of troops have completed redeployment and entered into a state of war readiness. . . . With a view to rescuing the rebel clique and expanding the civil war in Laos, the United States has built an air force base capable of handling large aircraft at Udorn in Thailand, only 50 miles away from Vientiane across the Mekong River . . .

Can it be said that all these deployments made by the U.S. government are aimed at promoting a cease-fire in Laos? Is it not more true to the fact to say that it is adding fuel to the fire and ready to expand the civil war in Laos?

The paper went on to issue forceful verbal support: The fight that was being waged in Laos was a just one. The fight that the North Vietnamese were engaged in was just.

The SEATO Paper Tiger

The annual meeting of the SEATO Council of Ministers, in Bangkok, came on March 27, just at the peak of Pathet Lao fortunes, and so was widely viewed as a forum in which to iron out differences in views on collective action in Laos. In fact, nothing of the sort occurred. There was no decision to act.

The meeting acquainted Secretary of State Dean Rusk with the extent of SEATO opposition to collective action. French Foreign Minister Maurice Couve de Murville, whose intelligence corroborated American estimates of North Vietnamese backing of the Pathet Lao, made clear France's unwillingness to embark on a second Indochina War. British Foreign Secretary Lord Home, still awaiting a reply from Moscow on the cease-fire proposal, was of course unable to support SEATO intervention.

Clearly, there would be no joint intervention. If Laos required outside help, the United States alone would have to shoulder the burden. SEATO had shown itself to be a paper tiger.

Radio Hanoi and Radio Peking had been busily laying down preconditions for a cease-fire, notably including the withdrawal of American military advisers from Laos. Yet it was to be another month before Moscow had gained enough freedom of action from its Vietnamese and Chinese allies to join London in an appeal to the rival Lao factions to cease fire.

The Pathet Lao continued their military offensive. On March 31, they captured Tha Thom, in southern Xieng Khouang Province, in an attack mounted by paratroopers dropped by Soviet transports and ground troops believed to include regular North Vietnamese cadres. The defenders were routed, and some of them fled almost as far as Paksane on the Mekong before regrouping.

Again, on April 3 and 7, the Ilyushins dropped several companies of Kong Le's paratroopers near Vang Vieng, an act that prompted the State Department to announce it was considering a "strong statement" to Moscow. The paratroopers rendezvoused with Pathet Lao partisans, and on April 22 the combined force surged out of the mountains above Vang Vieng. By this maneuver, they cut off the Phoumist forces, whose company included four American advisers, and scattered the remainder as far south as the Lik River.

The conversations between the State Department and the Russians were stymied by the Soviet demand for withdrawal of American military personnel from Laos and the American demand for a halt to the Russian airlift. Early in April, the State Department depicted the extent of this airlift in alarming terms. On April 19, the United States transformed its military advisory personnel in Laos from civilian PEO status to uniformed MAAG status. The State Department defended this move by again holding that the U.S. was not bound by the 1954 Geneva agreements, which it had not signed.

The middle of April brought the disastrous Bay of Pigs invasion in Cuba. Kennedy, who took "full responsibility" for it, henceforth adopted a new approach to the Laos problem. Previously, he had taken a vital interest in every detail of the contingency planning; afterward, according to a reliable source who observed his behavior during this critical time, the President showed less interest in the military map work of positioning potential American troop strongpoints in Laos.

Pathet Lao columns on the march in northern Laos, especially in Luang Prabang Province, were helping consolidate the pro-Communists' political control over large regions inhabited by sparse populations, mostly mountain tribesmen. Typically, the village of Ban Nam Bac on the Hou River, about halfway down the old invasion route from Dien Bien Phu to Luang Prabang, went under Pathet Lao control with barely a skirmish. Emissaries then set out for the valleys farther west in order to spread the word that "liberation" was near.

Toward the end of April, the garrison at the mountain village of Muong Sai, a great opium-trading center, came under a "rolling" mortar barrage—that is, rounds aimed on successive lines that moved horizontally across the town, from one end to the other. Most of the houses were set afire, but the civilian population had already fled into the hills. From the accuracy of the fire, it was obvious that it was the work of expert gunners; from its volume, the garrison at Muong Sai realized that it was heavily outnumbered and outgunned.

After the mortar barrage came concentrated fire from small arms, machine guns, recoilless rifles, and everything else that could fire a bullet. Once again the insurgents attacked at daybreak with telling effect. By evening, the smoking ruins of Muong Sai were in their hands, and the Pathet Lao infantry was mopping up resistance to make the place safe for the political officers attached to the attacking units.

Meanwhile, diplomatic interchanges had resulted in a compromise formula that would preserve "face" for Khrushchev among his Asian allies and that would ensure a cease-fire before the conference met, as the Western powers insisted. The international conference had been agreed to *before* a cease-fire prevailed in Laos, but would not meet until *after* the cease-fire took effect. The withdrawal of American troops and cessation of the Russian airlift operations were temporarily left unsettled.

On April 24, three separate messages went out from London and Moscow. The first informed the "military authorities, parties and organizations in Laos" that an international conference would convene at Geneva on May 12, and called upon them to cease firing before then and to send "appropriate representatives" to negotiate a cease-fire agreement. The second invited to the conference the governments of the thirteen nations originally suggested by Prince Sihanouk—all the countries that had participated in the 1954 Conference, plus the three ICC countries and Laos' neighbors Burma and Thailand—in addition to Laos (if and when the two rival governments led by Souvanna Phouma and General Phoumi once again merged). The third, addressed to India, with copies to Canada and Poland, sought reactivation of the ICC in Laos.

Predictably, these moves won immediate backing from Hanoi and Peking.

> The government of the Democratic Republic of Vietnam hopes that the measures put forward by the Co-Chairmen will bring about peace in Laos and create conditions for the Lao people to build for themselves a peaceful, neutral, independent and unified Laos.[8]

An official Chinese government statement declared:

> The Chinese government fully supports the appeals of the Co-Chairmen of the Geneva Conference to the parties concerned in Laos to

[8] Radio Hanoi, April 25, 1961.

cease fire before the convocation of the international conference and their appeal to the representatives of the parties concerned in Laos to enter into negotiations for concluding an agreement on questions connected with the cease-fire.[9]

Military commanders on both sides in Laos issued cease-fire orders to take effect May 3 at 8 A.M. For the Pathet Lao, the cease-fire order was issued by radio from Sam Neua and was signed by General Khamtay Siphandon, "Commander in Chief of the Neo Lao Hak Sat Armed Forces." The cease-fire was vague in the extreme, making no stipulations to halt troop movements or to specify territorial controls. While soldiers of both factions remained stationary along the Royal Road, the Pathet Lao on the morning of May 3 attacked and captured the village of Muong Phalane in Savannakhet Province, enabling them later to seize the vital airfield at Tchepone. General Phoumi's troops reoccupied the village of Ban Hat Bo in the valley above Paksane after the cease-fire had gone into effect.

The first contingent of ICC personnel was soon on its way to Laos. The delicate question of which government the commission should be accredited to had been resolved by assigning a separate group to each capital. The Indian chairman, Samar Sen, established his headquarters in Vientiane on May 8, but the ICC group traveling to Souvanna Phouma's capital of Khang Khay on the Plain of Jars was subjected to several days' delay.

An ICC message was sent to Souvanna Phouma from Saigon, where the ICC plane had stopped over. Because there were no direct communications between Saigon and Khang Khay, the message was dispatched to Hanoi for forwarding. Surprisingly, the North Vietnamese telegraphers reported that they could not deliver the message because no one in Hanoi knew where to find the Prince. An effort to reach the Prince through Pathet Lao liaison officers on the stabilized "front" at the Lik River was similarly frustrated.

Hanoi's ignorance of Souvanna Phouma's whereabouts was all the more extraordinary inasmuch as he had passed through the North Vietnamese capital only a few days previously on his return home from his world tour.

When the planeload of ICC personnel finally arrived at the Plain of Jars, they were taken in hand by the Communist-appointed provincial governor and lodged in the town of Xieng Khouang, far away from Khang Khay, where they might stumble on some of

[9] New China News Agency, Peking, April 26, 1961. Marshal Chen Yi later asserted at Geneva that a cease-fire had never been a precondition to the holding of the conference.

the Vietnamese military advisers who were shuttling around the countryside with such telling effect. When the author visited Xieng Khouang at the beginning of June, an ICC officer told him that the commission members were not allowed to deal directly with Souvanna Phouma.

An ironic scene occurred at the Vientiane airport when arriving ICC personnel were debarking from their plane. Right next to them landed a helicopter carrying evacuated Lao soldiers wounded in fighting six days after the cease-fire deadline. The American helicopter pilots employed by Air America still reported being shot at regularly. When four AT-6's took off with rockets slung under their wings and returned without rockets, only one reasonable conclusion could be drawn.

Not until several days after the May 3 broadcast of the cease-fire order did the opposing sides actually establish liaison with each other. The initial, wary contact between the opposing military forces occurred on the banks of the Lik River, where the "front" had stabilized with the Pathet Lao and Kong Le forces in control of the north bank and the Phoumists dug in on the south bank. On May 5, after an exchange of messenger-borne letters, a Phoumist officer, Lieutenant Colonel Siho Lamphouthacoul, crossed the makeshift foot bridge, alongside the blown-up road bridge, and met a junior-grade Pathet Lao officer in the shade of a candy-striped tent fashioned out of parachutes. Next day, they met in an abandoned house by the roadside (the civilian population had fled into the hills). Two Lao flags fluttered from a pole in the breeze.

As in Korea, the Communists demanded that the truce talks be held in territory they controlled. This demand and others of a similar nature were to lend to these talks an uncomfortable Cold War chill.

10.

Negotiations: Ban Namone and Geneva

The cease-fire proclaimed on May 3, 1961, marked a definite transition of Western policy from a military to a political orientation. Six weeks earlier, at the end of March, the United States had come within a hairsbreadth of deciding to commit American ground and air forces to Laos. If the Pathet Lao had exploited their military and psychological advantage in the spring of 1961 and compelled the Phoumist government to relinquish its control over any of the Mekong Valley towns, the United States almost certainly would have intervened. Instead, the Pathet Lao spun out their advantage by consolidating their control over much of the upcountry and heightening the general impression of their formidable strength.

American intervention would have scrapped, overnight, the 1954 agreements, and with them the hope of an unallied Laos forming a demilitarized zone between the Sino-Soviet bloc and the main Southeast Asian position of Western influence (in Thailand), and the possibility of preserving Laos' independence without committing a single American soldier. Scrapping these agreements would have shifted the basis of American policy from the concept of an "umbrella" provided by superior reserve striking power to one of forward commitment and possibly limited warfare on the pattern of Korea.

Even though both sides had flouted the Geneva agreements by clandestinely pouring military hardware and "advisers" into Laos, the concept of an unallied Laos was still salvageable. The task was to avoid intervention, not to run headlong into it. In order to transform the cease-fire into a situation advantageous to the U.S., American thinking about Laos had to be readjusted.

This readjustment, first indicated in January by the State Department White Paper on Laos, was provoked by the Soviet airlift, which of course had been a predictable response to American aid to the Phoumists by airlift and other means.

Just as American aid to the Phoumist government in Vientiane gave the United States a measure of influence over that government, so Russian aid to the Souvanna Phouma government in Khang Khay gave the Soviet Union leverage on the pro-Communist forces. The Soviet airlift had enabled the Pathet Lao to upgrade themselves from a motley guerrilla band to a regular armed force of considerable weight. But after this transformation, the Pathet Lao could no longer function on the crude matériel from home workshops and village factories. Their sophisticated Soviet weaponry required resupply from the arsenals of Kiev and Minsk. In short, the Pathet Lao were now dependent on the Soviet airlift. Therein lay the key to transforming the cease-fire into a political settlement acceptable to the United States.

Soviet military supplies were being flown into Laos under an agreement with the Khang Khay government. If the Pathet Lao received a large share of these supplies, it was because of their alliance with Kong Le, which permitted them to claim that they supported this government. Officially, Soviet aid was helping the Royal Lao Army commanded by Kong Le, not the Pathet Lao, and the Royal Government headed by Souvanna Phouma, not the NLHS headed by Souphanouvong. There was no indication that if the United States abandoned the Phoumists and threw its support to Souvanna Phouma, the Soviet Union would hold out for more than a government headed by Souvanna Phouma in which the NLHS had representation. Pathet Lao military gains that threatened to embroil the Soviets in a confrontation with the United States were viewed by the U.S.S.R. as counterproductive, even if made under the guise of revolutionary warfare. The Soviet Union had other interests that weighed more heavily than Laos. At this point, Soviet motivations diverged from North Vietnamese and Chinese motivations, opening up the possibility of a political settlement.

Soviet reluctance to become embroiled with the United States in a revolutionary war in small, faraway Laos had become, by 1961, a major point of contention between Khrushchev and Mao Tse-tung. Soviet feelers for a *détente* with the incoming Kennedy Administration had seriously displeased Peking. This was made plain by the

Chinese response to Kennedy's accession to the Presidency. The Soviets welcomed the new Administration, saying that the change in American leadership held out the promise of a new era in relations between the socialist and capitalist worlds. But the Chinese greeted the advent of Kennedy with an outpouring of vitriolic propaganda pegged to the theme that "Kennedy is more dangerous than Eisenhower," not less so, as Khrushchev supposed. As 1961 opened, Peking and Moscow were poles apart on how to deal with the Americans, and this question was set forth with particular clarity in Laos.

In a speech on January 6, Khrushchev specified his interpretation of the obligation to aid revolutions in the underdeveloped countries. He argued that the Communist bloc must provide aid to "national liberation movements" fighting "wars of liberation," which originate as popular insurrections, not wars between states. However, Communist-bloc countries should not internationalize "wars of liberation," for this would lead to dangerous escalation. Instead, they should prevent the foreign "imperialist" powers from intervening by *threatening* to intervene in turn. In this way, they would ensure the victory of "the people." In terms of Laos, this meant that the Soviets favored supporting the Pathet Lao in a "war of liberation," but did not favor support so extensive as that of North Vietnam, a Communist-bloc country that was taking the initiative in driving the "imperialists" out of Laos.

This was an important distinction. It explained how the Soviet Union could maintain good relations with nationalists like Souvanna Phouma and Prince Sihanouk of Cambodia. Eventually, their countries might become "people's democracies," but for the time being the first objective of the Communist bloc should be to hasten the elimination of foreign "imperialists" from these countries.

Cambodia had best fulfilled expectations of the 1954 Conference that the Indochina states would adopt neutral positions in the Cold War. Sihanouk had become an ardent advocate of this course. His country was more prosperous than Laos, but much weaker than its two other neighbors: Cambodia's army had about 30,000 men, South Vietnam's 150,000, and Thailand's 90,000. Although Cambodia did not border a Communist country, it was relatively easy for Communist agents to infiltrate, especially across its mountainous northeastern provinces adjoining Pathet Lao-held areas of southern Laos. Cambodia had less than 5 million people, including large Vietnamese and Chinese minorities numbering approximately 300,000 each.

Sihanouk kept his country peaceful by maintaining friendly relations with major foreign powers. The Cambodian capital had embassies of the United States, Britain, France, the Soviet Union, and Communist China. The presence of these embassies served to guarantee Cambodia's security from Thai irredentism and from Vietnamese imperialism.

From the American point of view, Cambodia was the Indochinese state that had received the least aid—far less than either of the pro-Western regimes of Laos and South Vietnam[1]—and the only one completely free of warfare. No Communist insurgents were leading a "people's war" to overthrow Sihanouk's popular government, and an American felt secure traveling in any part of the country.

The word "neutralist" is commonly used to refer to the happy position achieved by Sihanouk, in which a small, weak country cautiously walks a tightrope between two opposing powerful blocs. The author, however, prefers to avoid applying the word to Laos. "Neutralism" is a word coined by certain French newspapers in the dark, Cold War period of 1949–50. It designated a political tendency to extricate oneself from a definite alignment with one bloc of countries against another bloc of countries. However, neutralism did not become a serious policy until General de Gaulle had restored France to a respected place in the council of nations. Then, with a sound economic base and a military no longer tied down in colonial wars, France could advocate neutralism because it was at last strong enough to determine its own future, no longer to be dictated to by either Cold War bloc.

The situation of Laos is obviously different and will remain so. A small country in an economically and militarily precarious position vis-à-vis more powerful neighbors, Laos must depend on an *external* balance of forces. It is not strong enough to compel its neighbors to recognize its right to pursue any foreign policy it chooses, as De Gaulle can do in Europe. To convey the concept of a Laos that is not aligned with one bloc or the other, the author has chosen to refer to Laos as *neutralized* by international agreement rather than as *neutralist* by its own volition and power. The author has also avoided using the term "neutralist" to identify one faction in Laos that has sought to steer a middle course between two others, which are loosely referred to as "leftist" and "rightist" in allusion to the foreign powers supporting them.

The suggestion that Laos be neutralized by international agree-

[1] See Table 2, p. 105.

ment was made as early as September 29, 1960, when in a speech before the General Assembly of the United Nations Prince Sihanouk declared:

> While this situation owes its origin undeniably to foreign interference from the two blocs, it is obvious that to avoid the risk of a show of strength, the only reasonable and valid solution to eliminate this new and dangerous trouble-spot is the neutralization of Laos backed by international guarantees of its unity and territorial integrity.

The American-launched trial balloon in favor of the Boun Oum government and an inspection commission composed of Burma, Malaya, and Cambodia had come down without positive result. In its wake, American policy began to adjust itself to the need to neutralize Laos. But to achieve this, it was necessary to deal with Prince Souvanna Phouma.

Kennedy delegated Averell Harriman to explore the possibility of joint Soviet-American support for a Lao Government, headed by Souvanna Phouma, that would be neither Communist nor anti-Communist. Harriman had gained some experience in dealing with the Russians as American Ambassador to the Soviet Union. On March 29, he reported to the President on conversations he had had with Souvanna Phouma in New Delhi and Paris. Harriman felt it was encouraging for the United States that the Prince continued to regard himself as the central wheel in a three-wheeled mechanism. Souvanna Phouma, Harriman commented, "is a factor that has to be dealt with, and I think he should be in any government. He thinks he ought to be Prime Minister. Whether that should be or not, I don't know, but he certainly should be in any government."

Harriman felt that the best hope for preserving Laos' independence from North Vietnam lay in American support for a neutralized Laos under a coalition government guaranteed by both the Soviet Union and the Western powers. He thought that a coalition government could be formed in Laos without leading to a Communist takeover. Despite Soviet probing for weak spots, Harriman said, "I think Mr. Khrushchev doesn't want war. He's made that very plain."

Actually, Washington had no alternative to a coalition including the Pathet Lao except intervention with American troops, if it was not to see Laos become a North Vietnamese satellite and U.S. influence in Southeast Asia wane and perhaps disappear. Britain and France would oppose SEATO intervention in Laos, as the Bangkok meeting had shown all too clearly, and for the United States, a military venture in Southeast Asia was not worth the risk of jeopardizing European partnerships. The "decision" to accept a coalition in Laos was virtually thrust upon the Kennedy Administration.

The Soviet Union, unwilling to risk war over Laos, was agreeable to a coalition in Laos. But it remained to be seen how the Pathet Lao could be made to accept the coalition government. They were under the direction of Hanoi. Their troops were dependent on the Soviet airlift for supplies, but this was a temporary dependence, and Hanoi was to make it as brief as possible.

Truce Talks

Ban Namone, the village finally agreed upon as the site of the cease-fire talks, consists of some seventy wooden houses built on stilts, and is situated on the Royal Road about thirty-five miles north of the Lik River. It is a peaceful spot. In early May, just at the beginning of the rainy season, the air between showers is cooler than in the plain of Vientiane and has a bright, clear quality. Towering white cumulus clouds appear over the green hills at about noon, and by late afternoon turn a menacing gray that heralds the daily rainstorm. From the surrounding forests, columns of blue smoke evidence the slash-and-burn agriculture of the mountain tribesmen. A few small paddy fields afforded landing space for helicopters, and a mud-floored bamboo schoolhouse, decorated with Lao flags, became the meeting room.

The Pathet Lao, by their own description, were the fighting units of a political party whose program supported Souvanna Phouma but that held no membership in his government. Since the cease-fire was to be signed by the forces of the two rival "governments" of Laos, there was little legal justification for Pathet Lao participation in framing the cease-fire. However, no objection was made to the Pathet Lao demand for an equal role in the talks.

Souvanna Phouma's delegation was headed by Pheng Phongsavan, a close associate who had been a member of the Prince's 1953 Cabinet. The Pathet Lao delegation was led by Nouhak Phoumsavan, the Lao who had traveled to Geneva in 1954 on a Vietnamese passport. The Phoumist delegation, led by General Sing Ratanasamay, comprised only military officers, because Vientiane had assumed that the talks would deal solely with implementing the cease-fire.

The close coordination between the centrist and Pathet Lao delegations became evident when, in a statement issued from Souvanna Phouma's capital on May 8, Pheng and Nouhak declared that "military talks must be held [and] at the same time political talks should be held in order to broaden the Royal Government and reorganize it into a coalition government and form a unified Government delegation to the forthcoming international conference at Geneva."[2]

Despite this last-minute surprise, the three delegations convened in the schoolhouse at Ban Namone for their first meeting on May 11, with the centrists occupying the head of a U-shaped table. In attendance were the ICC military observers. No records were kept, except for notes made by Western journalists after the meeting. (Correspondents from the Soviet Union, North Vietnam, and China arrived a few days later.) The meeting was cordial and lasted one hour. At its conclusion, the ICC felt sufficiently encouraged to telegraph Geneva that a cease-fire was in effect, which overstated the case. This gave the Western delegations the green light to open the international conference on Laos.

At the second meeting two days later, the representatives of the three factions signed a typed statement confirming that military commanders all around had ordered their troops to cease fire. However, there was no pinpointing of troop locations, specifying of ground controlled by the various forces, or indicating of whether the cease-fire prohibited troop movements behind the points of contact or the airlifting of supplies that was going on at Vientiane and the Plain of Jars.

The cease-fire thus disposed of, the meeting broke up amid considerable conviviality. The Pathet Lao delegates, seemingly forgetting their vitriolic propaganda against the "Phoumi–Boun Oum clique," fraternized jovially with the Phoumists, and Nouhak clapped his arm around the shoulders of General Sing. Members of the three delegations toasted each other in glasses of hot tea poured from thermos flasks, exchanging news about their families and trading letters for delivery.

At a two-hour meeting the following day, the Vientiane delegates agreed to the introduction of political matters, and were roundly cheered by Pheng and Nouhak. The latter declared that "the most urgent question is to form a provisional coalition government." The meeting broke up with the appearance of a cold chicken buffet lunch.

In a united front, Pheng and Nouhak now insisted that the talks take up the formation of a coalition government, the abrogation of agreements by the Boun Oum government (the target was the American MAAG), and the rewriting of electoral regulations restricting NLHS activities. Nouhak expressed the hope that a coali-

---

[2] New China News Agency, Xieng Khouang, May 8, 1961.

tion might be formed shortly so that it could determine the responsibilities of the ICC, which had yet to travel outside either of the two "capitals" to verify the cease-fire. Obviously, the objective was to keep the ICC—which could act only on instructions from the Co-Chairmen or by unanimous request of the three Lao factions—in a state of prolonged inactivity.

On May 17, the negotiators announced they had agreed to form a provisional coalition government that would organize elections for the National Assembly. Two days later, however, in the face of flagrant cease-fire violations, the Vientiane delegation insisted that the delegates drop the political negotiations and concentrate immediately on enforcing the cease-fire.

Their concern had been aroused by continued Pathet Lao pressure on a Meo entrenchment on a mountaintop at Padong, only a few miles south of the Plain of Jars. Since April, increasing numbers of Pathet Lao had been committed to action in this sector. Several artillery bombardments had succeeded each other, one heavier than the last. On May 15, the defenders estimated, 100 shells fell on Padong, in the forty-eight hours of May 26–27, some 400 shells. Lulls between these bombardments suggested that the Pathet Lao, aided by North Vietnamese, were using coolie labor to move their 75-mm. mountain guns up rugged slopes to closer positions, as at Dien Bien Phu.

On May 30, an Air America helicopter maneuvering in mist to land at Padong crashed, killing the two American crew members and critically injuring an American attached to MAAG. A few days earlier, another Air America helicopter had made a forced landing because of engine failure and its two crew members and an American journalist on board, Grant Wolfkill, had been rounded up by local partisans and turned over to the Pathet Lao.

Pathet Lao pressure was also being felt elsewhere. Guerrilla activity north of Luang Prabang and against boats on the Mekong had served to blockade food supplies to the royal capital, and in a month prices in the local market had doubled.

The delegates agreed on May 26 to setting up three military subdelegations, which would meet at the same time as the main delegations but in a small woodshed near the schoolhouse, in order to work out implementation of the cease-fire. The Pathet Lao continued to refuse to permit the ICC to do any verifying. ICC requests to travel into areas where there had been complaints of cease-fire violations were refused, on the ground that transport facilities were inadequate. An ICC suggestion for joint efforts to draw up a map clearly indicating troop positions was also turned down by the Pathet Lao.

The Pathet Lao recommended that the ICC send field teams to verify the cease-fire at Ban Hin Heup and at Kiu Ka Cham, farther north on the Luang Prabang road, places where there had been virtually no firing since May 3. However, ICC suggestions of visits to Padong and other Meo strong points in Sam Neua Province, as well as southern Laos, were rejected by the Pathet Lao. They saw no need for ICC inspection of areas wholly "liberated by the patriotic forces," where "bandits" were being mopped up. Later, when the Phoumists unexpectedly insisted that Pathet Lao actions at Padong violated the cease-fire, the Pathet Lao charged that the Meo and their American advisers had been parachuted into their positions after the cease-fire had gone into effect. This claim was obviously spurious, because correspondents had visited the Meo and their hardy commander, Vang Pao, as early as March.

The Meo outposts in Xieng Khouang and Sam Neua provinces were sustained by supplies ferried in by Air America C-46's and C-47's, whose courageous crews risked death almost daily in these hazardous missions to Laos' most rugged terrain.

Meanwhile, the main body of delegates in the schoolhouse listened for hours as Nouhak declared that he favored discussion of restoration of democratic rights in Laos, equality for all minority groups, unification of the armed forces, and other such generalities.

On June 7, the Vientiane delegation formally requested the other two delegations to permit the ICC to send a field team to Padong to investigate the situation. Nouhak agreed "in principle."

After the meeting, the Phoumists flew by helicopter back to Vientiane, where they were met with shocking news: Padong had been abandoned the previous evening. The Phoumists charged that eight companies of mixed Lao and Vietnamese troops had been engaged in the siege of Padong.

At Ban Namone on June 14, the Indian observer at the military talks, Major General Shiv Dayal Singh, rose from a wooden bench and, over Pathet Lao opposition, read a letter addressed by the commission to the three factions. The letter reminded the delegates that "at the meeting held at Ban Namone on 7 June 1961 all parties agreed in principle that the Commission should go and examine the situation in some sensitive areas," and requested the delegates to suggest sites for investigation and provide necessary facilities, in what was by now a familiar ICC plea. Angered by this active participation by the ICC, the Pathet Lao successfully demanded that the ICC remove its observers permanently from the sessions at Ban Namone.

The Ban Namone talks revealed the perspective in which the Pathet Lao viewed the situation in Laos. The Pathet Lao talked of themselves and the followers of Souvanna Phouma as the supporters of "the people." They did not refer to their armed forces in the language of soldiers, as the Phoumists did, but called them the "people's patriotic defense forces." These forces never launched an offensive; they cleared up "bandits" dropped in the "liberated areas" by U.S. "imperialists." The "small minority" represented by the "Phoumi-Boun Oum clique" were preventing peace from being restored in the Kingdom. Whenever the Phoumist delegates requested a recess to consider some new Pathet Lao demand, they were accused of obstructing the peace talks in order to give the Americans time to ready their final plans for aggressive intervention in Laos. The Pathet Lao made the loudest outcries against breaches of the cease-fire, but blocked any on-the-spot inspection by the ICC; they vigorously protested Phoumist attacks, but flagrantly mounted offensive operations against the Meo around the Plain of Jars; and they decried foreign intervention, but depended on massive outside aid.

Counting Swans at Geneva

The relative ground positions in Laos were reflected in the attitudes of the various delegations who gathered at Geneva on May 16 for the Conference of foreign ministers on Laos. The North Vietnamese and Chinese delegations, bolstered by the military advantage gained by the Pathet Lao, anticipated squeezing the maximum political concessions from the frustrated supporters of General Phoumi. The United States was prepared to engage in a long holding operation.

The Conference opened in the familiar atmosphere of mutual suspicion. The United States strenuously but unsuccessfully objected to the seating of a Pathet Lao delegation as a full participant. However, these objections were seriously weakened by the precedent set at Ban Namone. The first session was attended by Quinim Pholsena and Phoumi Vongvichit representing the centrists and the Pathet Lao, respectively, and boycotted by Phoui Sananikone, representing the Phoumists, in protest against the seating of the Pathet Lao. At a subsequent meeting, Phoui came up with the mischievous suggestion that leaders of the fifteen other political parties in Laos should also be seated. His idea was not adopted.

The delegates recessed for the summit meeting of Kennedy and Khrushchev at Vienna. The joint statement issued by the two leaders on June 4 showed how close their interests were in Laos:

> The President and the Chairman reaffirmed their support of a neutral and independent Laos under a government chosen by the Laotians themselves, and of international agreements for insuring that neutrality and independence, and in this connection they have recognized the importance of an effective cease-fire.[3]

The aura of optimism emanating from this statement was short-lived, however. News of the fall of Padong, reaching Geneva almost immediately after the Conference had resumed, threw the meetings into deadlock. The United States let it be known that it was considering pulling out of the Conference in view of the flagrance of the Pathet Lao violation of the cease-fire. The Chinese thereupon accused the United States of delaying, even sabotaging, the Conference. The Chinese were prepared for a long stay in Geneva: They had taken six-month leases on a villa and limousines. For a while, the delegates were uncertain whether plenary sessions would be resumed. Soviet Foreign Minister Andrei Gromyko gave vent to the general impatience: "One cannot sit indefinitely on the shores of Lake Geneva counting swans."

The atmosphere improved toward the end of June, as the result of a princely summit meeting in Zurich. There, Souvanna Phouma, Souphanouvong, and Boun Oum reached agreement in principle on forming a coalition including all three factions. The princes also decided that the ICC observers should be readmitted to the Ban Namone talks and that the Phoumists should end their boycott of the Geneva sessions.

The Geneva delegates resumed their meetings, and proceeded by fits and starts toward a common declaration of the neutrality of Laos. A major reason for the slow pace was that the delegations were working under no fixed deadline, as they had in 1954. Consequently, there was less bargaining *en coulisse*. This suited the Chinese particularly. They exploited every possible angle inside the Conference in order to maintain a steady propaganda barrage against the United States.

By the end of the year, the Chinese had withdrawn their objections to majority vote within the ICC and had softened their recalcitrant stand on clauses governing the withdrawal of foreign troops and military personnel, banning the introduction of fresh

---

[3] *Public Papers of the Presidents, 1961*, p. 438.

troops, eliminating military bases in Laos, and ruling out the use of Lao territory as a corridor or staging area for direct or indirect aggression against unspecified countries.

The ICC mandate was perhaps the biggest stumbling block. Debate on the exact relationship between the ICC and the future Lao government continued, on and off, for several months.

The United States believed that it could enlist Russian influence on the Chinese and Vietnamese in support of a practicable *modus vivendi* in Laos if only the U.S. gave full backing to Souvanna Phouma's political program. Acting on this premise, the U.S. took initial cautious steps to give assurances to the Prince. By making its sentiments clearly understood without actually committing itself to any promises, the State Department attempted to gain his confidence without losing that of General Phoumi. Following the initial approach in March, an invitation to Washington had been extended to Souvanna Phouma on April 9, but this had not been taken up.

General Phoumi's Obstinacy

The delicate task proved more difficult than the State Department had expected. General Phoumi, seeing that his position was being cut away from under him, reacted with displeasure to the maneuver and lapsed into an obstinate silence. Since the State Department's actions were largely predicated on considerations of Sino-Soviet rivalries that he could not fathom, the General's reluctance to be removed as Vice Prime Minister, and perhaps from the Cabinet entirely, is understandable.

Moreover, General Phoumi undoubtedly harbored the illusion that the CIA, with which he had had close contacts in the past and which he had always known to have the last word, would once again outweigh the counsels of the Ambassador. A meeting of himself, Admiral Harry D. Felt, and Brigadier General Andrew Jackson Boyle, the MAAG commander, in early October perhaps strengthened his feeling that not all the agencies of the United States government wholeheartedly supported the State Department.

Nevertheless, it was clear that the State Department was having none of General Phoumi and his annoying reluctance to enter a coalition with the centrists and the Pathet Lao. Harriman, now Assistant Secretary of State for Far Eastern Affairs, held two days of talks with Souvanna Phouma in Rangoon in mid-September, after which he stated that the State Department wanted to get the three princes into a coalition Cabinet. "But it's up to Prince Boun Oum to make his own decision," he added.

Harriman then flew to Luang Prabang for an audience with the King, who had privately expressed his fears that Laos would be judged by the Geneva Conference as by an international tribunal. In Vientiane, the following day, Harriman held a two-hour interview with Prince Boun Oum and General Phoumi. He listened with ill-concealed impatience to their reasons for refusing to cooperate at this late hour with Souvanna Phouma.

It was increasingly urgent to form some kind of stable coalition. Souvanna Phouma was under ever-greater pressure to give a freer hand to the North Vietnamese and Chinese through "aid agreements," which threatened to undermine all remaining Western pretensions to influence in Laos.

Souvanna Phouma in Khang Khay was certainly aware of the role of North Vietnamese military personnel in the Pathet Lao and in Kong Le's forces. He was in a singularly poor position to protest the presence of these "advisers and technicians" to North Vietnamese representatives, who would remind him that he had once tolerated American advisers and technicians in Vientiane.

Beginning with his ·visit to Hanoi in April, 1961, Souvanna Phouma had signed a series of agreements with North Vietnam. These dealt with economic and cultural cooperation (April 28), exchange of press correspondents and photographs (June 7), cooperation in broadcasting (June 7), exchange of specialists and foreign training grants (July 13), commercial relations (July 13), exchange of payments (July 13), and town planning for Khang Khay (September 13).

These agreements permitted the North Vietnamese to run trucks in and out of Lao territory controlled by the merged Pathet Lao and Kong Le forces. The trucks could be on an official mission, bringing construction workers and materials in conjunction with the town planning for Khang Khay. There was no control over whether they carried military personnel and supplies as well. The Soviet airlift was soon extended to Tchepone, which was in "liberated" territory and had to be defended against the threat of Phoumist attacks.

By August, 1961, the United States estimated the North Vietnamese forces in Laos to include 1,000 combat troops and support personnel in Sam Neua; between 1,200 and 1,500 troops at Ban Liang, two miles northeast of Khang Khay, available for combat missions; up to 300 advisers to Pathet Lao battalions and 100 combat-tactics instructors on the Plain of Jars; 300 security personnel and antiaircraft gunners on the Plain of Jars and at Ban Liang;

and 50 tank and armored-car crew members. These figures were indicated in a mimeographed statement circulated at Geneva by the American delegation.

No public mention of these troops was made by Hanoi, of course. Even in the closed-door sessions of the Conference, Hanoi refused to acknowledge their presence in Laos.

In Laos, the ripening of the upland rice crop in September would afford the Pathet Lao the fresh food stocks they needed in the villages to resume fighting on a broad scale. Also, the onset of the dry season would again make the trails passable.

Commenting on the still fluid situation at the end of September, the Peking *People's Daily* on September 25, 1961, said that "a resumption of the war in Laos is poised like an arrow on a drawn bow."

Just before the Ban Namone talks ended in September, the delegates arranged for a meeting of the three princes in Vientiane. At this gathering, the princes decided that Souvanna Phouma would seek the King's authority to form a new government, and worked out the Cabinet representation for the three factions. But General Phoumi became dissatisfied with the distribution of Cabinet posts and prevented any further progress toward formation of a coalition.

Despite American efforts to bring the sides together, the meeting in Vientiane broke up without result. On the last day of the year, the Vientiane radio broadcast a lengthy diatribe against Souphanouvong, thus deepening the prevalent gloom.

Siege at Nam Tha

From the beginning of January, 1962, there were indications that the North Vietnamese were hoping to mount a set-piece battle that would humiliate General Phoumi's army and crush Vientiane's opposition to a three-way coalition. Intelligence reports mentioned the finding of telltale caches of rice and other supplies all over northern Laos. By the middle of January, a battalion of North Vietnamese foot soldiers were known to be operating in the region of the Beng River valley; they probably used Pathet Lao-occupied Muong Sai as a base.

Northern Laos appeared to be the logical setting for the decisive Pathet Lao victory wanted by the Vietnamese. A Phoumist defeat there would exclude Vientiane troops from a band of territory along the border of China, which was then building the first road into Laos from Yünnan Province under an agreement announced by the New China News Agency on January 13. Also, a triumph could be achieved there with the maximum shock but without throwing pro-Communist forces into the Mekong Valley and risking American (or Thai) retaliation.

Suspicions of a forthcoming attack received further confirmation when a mixed force of Vietnamese and Pathet Lao attacked and reoccupied the village of Ban Na Mo, thirty miles northwest of Muong Sai, displaying such vigor that the defending garrison retreated in haste a full ten miles south.

Twenty miles west along a rugged trail lay the provincial capital of Nam Tha, a town of 1,800 that had always remained free of Pathet Lao influences. Lying in a wide bowl-like valley at the junction of four rivers pointing in the four directions of the compass, Nam Tha surely reminded the North Vietnamese of Dien Bien Phu. Indeed, a private who had been at Ban Na Mo and who kept a diary in Vietnamese, observed, "Our troops, following the instructions of Uncle Ho, have come here to bring our contribution to the construction of a Dien Bien [Phu]."

From the latter part of January on, the indefatigable Vietnamese dug a network of trenches on the heights just east of Nam Tha. It was excellent field training for the Pathet Lao. On January 25, under cover of mortar fire, their patrols overran one or two leading Phoumist outposts, enabling them to advance their trench network to within twelve miles of Nam Tha. Town officials formed a militia and armed it with old rifles from whatever stocks were available.

General Phoumi decided to reinforce the garrison with Lao troops, a tactic about which American military advisers expressed private reservations. This was a region where no Lao lived; the local inhabitants belonged to the Thai tribes or the smaller Pu Noi tribe. On January 27, General Phoumi flew in a first group of reinforcements to Nam Tha, who landed on the single tiny airstrip. The garrison swelled to 5,000 men. General Phoumi's commander in the Nam Tha sector, Major General Bounleuth Sanichan, watching additional reinforcements arrive, told correspondents confidently, "Nam Tha has never been captured by the Pathet Lao before. We will bring up as many reinforcements as required to stop them."

Pilots winging low over the mountain heights dominating the wide valley reported seeing the Vietnamese trundle into position three 120-mm. mortars (these would be used later to interdict the airstrip). On January 30, for the first time, an American supply plane was hit by ground fire while taking off. The Phoumists flew in four 105-mm. howitzers and twelve 75-mm. mountain guns.

The Pathet Lao released the text of a letter they had sent to the Geneva Co-Chairmen in which they accused the Vientiane regime of "spreading rumors" that they were violating the cease-fire. The Pathet Lao "cannot stand idly by," the letter warned. "When necessary, they will take appropriate measures in self-defense and hit back at the invaders," it said, without specifying Nam Tha, which had never been in Pathet Lao territory. [4]

The Pathet Lao and their Vietnamese supporters began the siege in earnest in February. On the first day of the month, the airstrip was hit by mortar shells for the first time. On the third, the shelling reached the town itself, causing panic among those who had not already fled into the hills.

"The enemy is in a precarious position. Our troops are above him and dominate him," the Vietnamese platoon soldier recorded in his diary. "Today we celebrated the Tet [Vietnamese New Year, which fell at the beginning of February] with a bombardment of the airstrip, which is burning and enveloping the countryside in thick black smoke."

He recorded two bombardments on New Year's Day, three the day before, and four the day before that. "The airstrip is finished. The planes which have already landed there cannot take off."

The Vietnamese had managed to set up a mortar on a mountain slope nearer than the others to Nam Tha on the southeast. Despite repeated swoops by General Phoumi's AT-6's against this position, the mortar continued to shell the airstrip with deadly accuracy. Meanwhile, the Vietnamese had been extending their network of trenches on the heights to the northeast and southeast, so that they were gradually forming a ring around the town.

The shelling of the town by mortar increased noticeably on February 12, and in the following three days General Phoumi rushed in several hundred fresh paratroopers. These landed in a drop zone on the western outskirts of the town. Only 4,500 yards away was the Vietnamese trenchwork. Sporadic shelling continued throughout the month, but on March 1, an on-the-spot MAAG unit reported that the Vietnamese eased off and even moved back some of their mortars.

[4] A book published in Hanoi in 1961 contains a map giving the positions occupied by the Pathet Lao at the time of the ceasefire of May 3, 1961. See Quang Minh, *Au Pays du Million d'Eléphants* (Hanoi: Editions en Langues Etrangères, 1961), map opposite p. 145. This is the only document from a Communist source known to the author showing the 1961 positions. All subsequent maps show the positions at the June 24, 1962, ceasefire, with Nam Tha, of course, included within the Pathet Lao area. (See Map 4, p. 243.)

On March 13, Phoumi Vongvichit, who had returned to the Plain of Jars from Geneva, issued a statement saying that Souvanna Phouma, as the Prime Minister-designate of the coalition government, is "entitled to reserve the important portfolios for his own party of neutrals." This surprisingly conciliatory statement appeared aimed at General Phoumi himself. General Phoumi continued in his obstinate unwillingness to cooperate on the proposed coalition and in his refusal to concede to Souvanna Phouma the important ministries of Defense and Interior. In an effort to force an accommodation, the U.S. shut off its cash grants to the General at the beginning of February.

The deadlock persisted. The Pathet Lao gained ground. Alarmed by the increasingly suicidal character of General Phoumi's stubbornness, Harriman hurried off to Bangkok, where Marshal Sarit, who had reluctantly accepted American determination on a coalition including the Pathet Lao, was prevailed upon to meet with General Phoumi and Harriman. The Thais, while they looked upon the coalition proposal as a risky bet, had no alternative to offer, short of garrisoning Laos with American troops—something they were not in a position to order.

The meeting took place at the town of Nong Khai on the Thai side of the Mekong, on March 24. Amid considerable diplomatic trepidation, Marshal Sarit talked in low tones in Thai for about twenty minutes, explaining patiently why it was advisable for General Phoumi to accede to the coalition. He did not look at Phoumi. When he had finished, the General replied in French, enumerating the reasons for his reluctance. After several minutes of this, Harriman, apparently not realizing that the General's speech was the necessary prelude to his acceptance without loss of face of Marshal Sarit's advice, lost patience and interrupted him. He said flatly that the General was wrong and intimated that the Phoumist forces were finished in Laos if they did not agree to the coalition.

Back in Vientiane, Harriman had further conversations with General Phoumi in what one of the General's aides termed an "animated and occasionally venomous" atmosphere. Shortly after this, a State Department official who had accompanied Harriman to Laos, William H. Sullivan, showed up in Khang Khay, Souvanna Phouma's "capital." There, he gave reassurances to Souvanna Phouma that the United States was doing everything possible to expedite the formation of a coalition.

Sullivan's trip to Khang Khay, when it was disclosed in Vientiane, did little to improve the atmosphere. Harriman termed General Phoumi a soldier who was out of step and said he was leading his country to destruction. The agencies of the United States Government were now in a peculiar reversal of the positions they had occupied in 1960. The State Department was refusing economic aid to a regime that the Defense Department was supporting with arms and advisers. In 1960, the State Department had supported a regime in Vientiane with economic aid while the Defense Department had actively worked against it by providing military aid to a rebel faction.

On May 2, with the rainy season already imminent, the Vietnamese launched a major probe against Nam Tha's defenses from the southeastern quarter of the perimeter. It was repulsed by the defenders, who by now were cut off from any means of supply except parachute drops.

The following day, the first anniversary of the cease-fire among the three factions, a combined Pathet Lao and Vietnamese force surprised the garrison of Muong Sing, some twenty-five miles west of Nam Tha, a two days' march by trail. They captured it after only slight resistance from one company of Phoumist troops. This effectively interdicted General Phoumi's last usable airfield of any size in northern Laos.

On May 4, the Vietnamese captured a defense outpost only 2,500 yards east of Nam Tha. At 3 A.M. on May 6, a concerted mortar barrage opened on Nam Tha. Using flares to coordinate their movements in the predawn darkness, four battalions opened an attack on the lightly defended northwest quarter of the perimeter. Meanwhile, other forces swarmed down on the town from their trenches on the heights to the east, southeast, and northeast, pouring a hail of small-arms fire into the mud breastworks in which General Bounleuth's defenders had been pinned during the three-month siege.

First one sector caved in, then another. The twelve-man American White Star team was evacuated by helicopter at 7:30 A.M. Six hours after the start of the Vietnamese attack, the 5,000 defenders were withdrawing in panic-stricken disorder.

A Phoumist picked up the diary from the lifeless body of the Vietnamese soldier who had written of his platoon's New Year's celebration and his implicit loyalty to Uncle Ho. On the next to last page was the following entry:

OUR ARMY

We are the men who, years ago, vanquished the enemy at Dien Bien [Phu], fighters who for years have struggled and overcome every obstacle and every danger without discouragement.

On every front we are the first-line troops.
With every day that passes, we are proud of our Army.

The disorganized crowd of General Bounleuth's soldiers streamed southward to the Mekong, 100 miles away. Some did not stop there, but hired boatmen to take them across, where they were interned by the Thai Border Police.

The violation of the cease-fire by the Pathet Lao was patent. The rout of the Phoumist troops was complete. Expressing concern for Thailand's security, President Kennedy announced that, at the invitation of the Thai Government, he had ordered American ground and air units to take up positions at Udorn and elsewhere in northeastern Thailand. As he phrased it later:

> The dispatch of United States forces to Thailand was considered desirable because of recent attacks in Laos by Communist forces, and the subsequent movement of Communist military units toward the border of Thailand.[5]

A White Star patrol back up the trail to Nam Tha found only scattered bands of Pathet Lao guerrillas and no North Vietnamese. So far as the author was able to determine, there was no movement of "Communist military units" toward the Mekong. The significant thing about the Nam Tha debacle was that it was the first instance in which it was credible that Communist forces *were* intent on moving into the Mekong Valley. In the confusion surrounding the whereabouts of the Pathet Lao forces and the question of North Vietnamese and even Chinese presence in the area, the swift American reaction cheered the Thais. They were reassured of the validity of the American commitment to go to Thailand's aid in a crisis even without SEATO. It was safe to assume that the American reaction to a genuine Communist move would be similar to that of May, 1962. While this understanding between Washington and Bangkok stood, the Thai government might not turn to "neutralism," no matter what happened in the upcountry of Laos.

President Kennedy, discussing the reasons for the dispatch of troops to Thailand at his news conference on May 17, showed the Administration's uncertainty about Communist intentions when he gave the following answer:

> We're concerned about the breach of the cease-fire, the sign of deterioration in Laos, which brought Communist forces to the border of Thailand up in the—near the Mekong River section of—not too

[5] *Public Papers of the Presidents, 1962* (Washington: Government Printing Office, 1963), p. 396.

far from Nam Tha, and we did not know whether this was an indication of a general breach of the cease-fire which, of course, would immediately imperil Thailand.[6]

The New China News Agency, on May 12, actually distributed a report to the effect that Ban Houei Sai itself had been "liberated." The alleged liberation was subsequently forgotten by the Chinese.

In Vientiane six months later, Souphanouvong revealed that a difference of opinion had existed within the NLHS Central Committee as to whether the Pathet Lao should press all the way to the Mekong after the collapse of Phoumist resistance. Presumably, this course of action was urged by Kaysone and the "Vietnamese faction."

In Vientiane, the Phoumists sent a telegram to Souvanna Phouma in Paris, informing him that they agreed that he could appoint his own followers to the key ministries of Defense and Interior. The Prince made plans to return to Laos immediately. So did Prince Boun Oum and General Phoumi, who were in the middle of a trip to a number of Asian capitals in quest of financial aid for the Royal Lao Government. They had received short shrift in Bangkok, as General Phoumi's conduct of the Nam Tha defense had left the Thai leaders thoroughly alarmed at the prospect that they might be dragged into a war in Laos with such allies. None of the other so-called anti-Communist governments in Asia, except South Korea, was willing to make any substantial offer of assistance to them.

Boun Oum's government had reacted to the cut-off of American cash grants by ordering the National Bank to place in circulation its considerable stock of printed banknotes. The result was that the dollar backing of the Lao currency dropped from 90 per cent in January to about 60 per cent in June, a change that produced a 20-per-cent increase in the price of food.

The Troika Under Way

The most important of a long series of princely summit meetings convened on the Plain of Jars at the beginning of June. Souvanna Phouma, borrowing a trick from Mendès-France, said that whether or not there was agreement, on June 15 he intended to return to Paris, where his daughter, Princess Moune, was to be married to a French nobleman.

Under this deadline, agreement was reached on June 11 on the division of powers in the coalition, which had been the main stum-

[6] *Ibid.,* p. 403.

bling block. The three princes affixed their signatures to the document almost exactly thirteen months after the Ban Namone talks.

Souvanna Phouma was to be Prime Minister. General Phoumi retained one of two posts of Deputy Prime Minister, and Souphanouvong held the other. Boun Oum, who had intimated his desire to return to the relative peace of southern Laos, announced his retirement from politics.

Under the key Paragraph 5 of the agreement, either Deputy Prime Minister was empowered to veto a decision in Cabinet session. This arrangement, which soon became known as a troika, after the Russian three-horse sleigh, required unanimity among the three factions for important proposals.

Other portfolios were divided up among the three factions by mutual agreement. Phoumi Vongvichit joined Souphanouvong in the Cabinet, as he had done in 1957. He assumed the portfolio of Information, Propaganda, and Tourism. The Pathet Lao were also represented by two secretaries of state, who had lesser power than full ministers. Souvanna Phouma retained the key portfolio of Defense, and his associate Pheng Phongsavan became Interior Minister.

On June 23, Boun Oum formally presented his resignation, and the following day Souvanna Phouma, who had been officially charged by the King with forming the new government, took the oath of office in Vientiane. There still remained to be decided the role to be played by the National Assembly in relation to the new Cabinet, which was provisional and had the main task of working for reunification of the country. Reintegration of the separate administrations and armies of the three factions was the troika's main challenge. After that, it was expected that national elections would be organized to elect a new National Assembly and in turn permit the formation of a permanent Cabinet.

At the first meeting of the provisional troika Cabinet, Phoumi Vongvichit jarred the proceedings by unilaterally announcing to the press that it had been decided to protest the presence of American troops across the Mekong in Thailand. The troops were, in any case, shortly to be withdrawn, having served their function. But amid all the doubts and rude shocks, there was more good will than ill will at the launching of the venture in troika government; Souphanouvong showed up at the American Embassy on the Fourth of July to drink a toast to President Kennedy and the friendship of the American people.

Meanwhile in Geneva, Foreign Minister Quinim Pholsena had

presented to the Conference delegates a statement outlining Laos' neutrality. This was incorporated into a Declaration signed by the thirteen other foreign ministers present.

On July 23, after fourteen months of plenary and restricted sessions, all the foreign ministers signed the Protocol, which established a new *status quo* in the strife-ridden little kingdom.[7] Souvanna Phouma was present for the ceremony.

The signing of the agreements was interpreted differently in Moscow and Peking. The official Soviet reaction was that this conclusion of so many months' ardent bargaining proved once again that negotiations could settle even the thorniest international issues dividing the socialist world and the capitalist world. The Peking *People's Daily,* on the other hand, described them as "a major victory of the people of Laos in their struggle for independence, unity, peace, and neutrality of their homeland."

> The agreements reached at the international Geneva Conference on Laos show once again that international disputes can be settled through negotiations. But these agreements have by no means been won easily. The conference was convened only after a struggle. And these agreements were reached only after a serious and complex principled struggle.[8]

Few of the signatories harbored many illusions as to the durability of the settlement at Geneva. Looking ahead beyond the agreement, the Chinese foresaw the complete "liberation" of Laos, that is, the final elimination from Laos of all Western influence.

Chinese verbal support for the activities of North Vietnam's agents in Laos was to be repaid handsomely within the coming year in the ever-sharpening Sino-Soviet quarrel. Ho Chi Minh, for his part, had indebted himself to his powerful neighbor without having had occasion to see his neighbor's mettle tested. The impression that the Chinese had come out of the episode on top of the heap was strengthened by a revealing incident inside a closed session at Geneva. In the midst of a Chinese tirade against the activities of the United States in Laos, the acting chief American delegate, William H. Sullivan, arose to object strenuously. If China believed that the Americans and the Russians were going to fight China's wars for it in Laos, so that the Chinese could effect a costless takeover, Sullivan declared, then the Chinese were making a major miscalculation. At this, the Soviet delegate interrupted to suggest

[7] Texts of Declaration and Protocol in Appendix V.
[8] *People's Daily,* July 24, 1962.

that it was Sullivan who was committing the major miscalculation in underestimating the solidarity between the Soviet Union and the Chinese People's Republic.

It was a strange new world in which the ship of American diplomacy was navigating.

11.

The Second Coalition

The Laos civil war had become far more than that because each side had become closely identified with the interests of one or more foreign powers. It was the purpose of the 1961–62 Geneva Conference to neutralize Laos by providing the coalition government with certain international guarantees that would minimize foreign intervention.

The effective neutralization of Laos did not go against the interests of any of the Conference participants; nevertheless, there was considerable doubt all around that effective neutralization could be achieved. There was continuing bitter hostility in United States relations with Communist China and North Vietnam. There was rivalry between Communist China and the Soviet Union involving the question of the risks to be taken in expanding Communist control in the underdeveloped countries.

Communist China and North Vietnam were insistent on the theme of American "aggression" against Laos. The Chinese Communists pressed for an international condemnation of American actions in Laos, arguing that the conflict in Laos was a matter basically to be settled by the Lao themselves. In this context, the seating of the Pathet Lao faction at the Conference was a major victory for the Chinese Communists. The West, never able to produce convincing proof of either Chinese Communist or North Vietnamese intervention in Laos, was compelled to match accusation for accusation. The West sought the adoption of effective controls on future intervention, an effort that met stiff opposition and was not altogether successful.

Thus, the Declaration and Protocol on the Neutrality of Laos, signed in Geneva on July 23, 1962, was viewed negatively by the

United States and positively by North Vietnam and Communist China. For all the big powers, the agreement was more a face-saving device to freeze the *status quo* than a foundation for stability in the area. For the North Vietnamese, it was a device for hamstringing American policy in Southeast Asia and a useful precedent for an agreement to freeze the *status quo* in South Vietnam. Ho judged that the Declaration and Protocol on the Neutrality of Laos would not constitute a serious obstacle to pursuit of his long-term objectives in Indochina.

The Geneva Agreements of 1962

The 1954 Conference had produced a cease-fire agreement between the commander of the French Union forces, including Lao Territorial units, and the commander of the Viet Minh forces, acting on behalf of the Pathet Lao. In addition, the Conference had produced two unilateral declarations by the Royal Lao Government promising that Laos would follow a strictly neutral course in foreign affairs, and a declaration binding all the participants to respect this neutral course.

The 1962 documents, signed by all the Conference participants, pledged the signatories not to impair the sovereignty, independence, neutrality, unity, or territorial integrity of .Laos. They agreed to refrain from interfering in the internal affairs of the Kingdom. They would not attach political strings to aid to the coalition government. They would not entice Laos into any military alliance, specifically SEATO, or establish military bases on Lao territory. They would not introduce foreign troops or military personnel into Laos. And within seventy-five days, they would withdraw those present under the guise of advisers and technicians.

In view of the specificness of the 1962 documents, and of the commitments made by the participants in the second Conference, it might appear at first sight that the 1962 agreement held out a better prospect of removing Laos from the currents of big-power manipulation and neighborly spoliation than had the 1954 agreement. As we have seen, the 1954 agreement had not been observed in its spirit by either Communists or non-Communists.

Unfortunately, the second agreement was no more effective than the first, partly because the ICC's mandate had been diluted at the insistence of the Communist powers, and partly because the ICC was now dealing with a coalition of three separate factions, each of which possessed its own territorial administration and armed forces. The 1962 provisions for neutralizing Laos were full of loopholes.

As in 1954, the ICC, again composed of India, Canada, and Poland, was entrusted with supervising the implementation of the provisions. Its work, however, could be sabotaged at the whim of either the Communists or the non-Communists.

Unlike 1954, there was no provision for stationing fixed ICC inspection teams in the countryside to keep track of foreign troops and arms, although the Western delegates had fought hard to have such a provision included in the Protocol. A Franco-American proposal would have allowed the ICC to set up both fixed and mobile inspection teams with "free and unrestricted access" to all parts of Laos and "full freedom to inspect, at any time, all aerodromes, installations or establishments and all units, organizations and activities which are or might be of a military nature." In contrast, a Soviet draft would have had the ICC, "in agreement with the Government of Laos, set up suitable groups" to control the withdrawal of foreign military personnel, but made no mention of subsequent introductions of foreign soldiers.

Since the ICC inspection teams set up in 1954 had been effectively blocked by Pathet Lao subversion, the Protocol's failure to provide for fixed teams did not appear to be an irretrievable loss for the West. The Protocol did specify that ICC teams could be dispatched by helicopter for a "length of stay . . . determined in relation to the requirements of the particular investigation."

A concerted Western effort eliminated the word "agreement" to designate the relationship between the ICC and the Lao government. It was argued that "agreement" might be interpreted to mean that the ICC could not take any step without government permission. In the final version, the Protocol stated that the ICC was to act with the "concurrence" of the government. Since the troika Cabinet gave the Pathet Lao an effective veto over government decisions, the Communists still could obstruct ICC operations. However, some legalists pointed out that the clauses were so worded as to make it appear that the Lao government had given its "concurrence" when it signed the Protocol.

The ICC was further weakened by limitations on its authority to make decisions. Once the ICC, on Royal Government request or concurrence, had undertaken an investigation, questions relating to initiating and carrying it out could be adopted by majority vote of the Commission. But the conclusions and recommendations resulting from such an investigation had to be adopted unanimously.

Unanimous ICC decisions were also required on questions relating to violations of the cease-fire or of provisions for withdrawal of foreign troops or prohibition of foreign troops, military personnel, and armaments. Under the 1954 agreements, the ICC had needed only a majority vote in making any recommendation except those concerning violations believed to threaten a resumption of hostilities between the French and the Viet Minh (or Pathet Lao).

These difficulties were somewhat mitigated by the Protocol's creating a closer liaison between the ICC and the Co-Chairmen than had been provided in 1954. The ICC was charged with immediately reporting to the Co-Chairmen any Protocol violations, in addition to preparing its periodic reports on the general situation.

Diplomatic Implications of Neutrality

In keeping with the international nature of its sponsorship, the newly established troika government in Vientiane declared that it was prepared to exchange diplomatic representation with all friendly countries. In Souvanna Phouma's view, this meant that if both Communist China and Nationalist China wished to maintain embassies in Vientiane, they would be free to do so. The same applied to both North Vietnam and South Vietnam. However, each of the rival Chinese governments felt that maintaining its ambassador accredited to a state to which its rival was likewise accredited would be tantamount to acknowledging that there were two Chinas, one governed from Peking and the other from Taipei. Therefore, each would refuse to accept the existence of two Chinese embassies in Vientiane. The two rival Vietnamese governments (which had followed a slightly modified version of the Chinese tactic, both maintaining consulates in India, for instance), refused to permit the establishment of dual diplomatic representation in Vientiane at ambassadorial level, and the South Vietnamese Ambassador withdrew.

Exactly a month before the 1962 Geneva agreement was signed, Peking had announced, on June 23, that it had arranged with Souvanna Phouma to exchange ambassadors following installation of the coalition. Not surprisingly, Liu Chun, the head of Communist China's cultural and economic mission on the Plain of Jars, an expert on ethnic-minority questions, was named Peking's first ambassador to Vientiane.

In August, when Souvanna Phouma returned from his trip to Geneva and Washington, where he conferred with President Kennedy, the presence in Vientiane of the Communist Chinese Liu Chun and of Dr. Han Lih-wu, long the Nationalist Chinese Ambassador to Thailand and accredited to Laos since the days of the Boun Oum government, created a minor diplomatic crisis. Liu

Chun, although he had not yet presented his credentials to King Savang Vatthana, appeared at the airport to greet the returning Prime Minister. Over the protests of a Lao protocol officer, Liu Chun joined the diplomatic queue at the side of the Soviet Ambassador. When Souvanna Phouma, moving slowly up the line and shaking hands, approached Dr. Han of Nationalist China, Liu Chun thrust himself forward between the two, claiming loudly that he, and not Dr. Han, was the representative of the 650 million Chinese. Souvanna Phouma took this calmly, but the Phoumist security officer at the airport refused to allow Liu Chun to drive back into the town flying his yellow-starred red flag, and a heated two-hour dispute ensued. Prince Souphanouvong intervened to suggest that the Communist Chinese ambassador remove the flag for the sake of expediency. Eventually Souvanna Phouma prohibited the flying of the flag until Liu Chun had presented his credentials, but allowed him to proceed home with his flag flying.

Subsequently Taipei announced that it was severing relations with Laos. South Vietnam followed a similar course after the arrival in Vientiane of the new North Vietnamese Ambassador, Le Van Hien, a minister in Ho Chi Minh's original 1945 government.

Hanoi hailed the establishment of its embassy in Vientiane as a great triumph for North Vietnamese diplomacy. Its press and radio told the North Vietnamese that this was a hard-earned victory, coming after eight years of imperialist machinations had frustrated their efforts to gain representation in the neighboring kingdom.

As time went on, the diplomacy of both Peking and Hanoi increasingly took on the aspects of a double game. While their ambassadors maintained correct relations with Souvanna Phouma in the Lao capital, their military advisers played a more ominous role at Khang Khay, the Pathet Lao headquarters. These agents enjoyed a complete monopoly, since there were no Russians with the Pathet Lao.

Souvanna Phouma established diplomatic relations with a number of East European countries, including Czechoslovakia and Yugoslavia. In this, he was following the example of Prince Sihanouk, who believed that having as many embassies as possible in his capital furthered his country's neutrality.

The restored confidence between Souvanna Phouma and the United States was manifest after he had had a series of meetings with President Kennedy and the new men in the State Department. When asked later how he viewed American intentions, the Prince replied with a wave of his arm, "Oh, with these people, it's entirely different."

Much of the Prince's optimism could be attributed to the new American Ambassador who had reached Vientiane in July. Leonard Unger, a forty-four-year-old career diplomat, had spent the previous four years in Bangkok, part of the time as deputy chief of mission, and could speak enough Thai to make a speech understood by the Lao. Unger possessed another advantage: His superior officer in Washington—Averell Harriman—was receptive to his ideas. Unger's predecessor had had to manage without this advantage.

The economic situation facing Souvanna Phouma was not good. The spread between the official kip rate of 80 to the dollar and the black-market rate was steadily growing. At the end of 1961, the black-market rate stood at 120 to the dollar. Then, following the cut-off of U.S. cash grants, Boun Oum placed in circulation large quantities of paper money not backed by dollar deposits in the United States. By the summer of 1963, the progressive reduction in dollar backing of the kip notes in circulation (which had increased in the same period from 2.7 billion kip to 6.1 billion kip) had pushed the black-market rate to 360 to the dollar.

Inflation hit particularly hard in Vientiane and the other Mekong Valley towns, which were dependent upon Thailand for rice and vegetables. In Vientiane, the consumer price index for a Lao family rose from 115 (with 1959 representing a base of 100) in 1961, to 268 in mid-1963. The countryside, which lived largely by a barter economy and in isolation from the Mekong Valley towns, was not affected by the inflation. The fighting was only an indirect cause of the inflation in that it led to uncertainty about continued American backing for the currency of the Royal Government.

On January 1, 1964, the coalition government, compelled to effect the first devaluation since 1958, pegged the kip at 240 to the dollar. A smooth transition to the new official value was made possible by public assurances from the United States, Britain, France, and Australia of their backing for a $7.8-million stabilization fund (the United States provided $4.0 million, Britain $1.7 million, France $1.7 million, and Australia $0.4 million) separate from the month-to-month budget support, which the United States promised to continue.

The extent of the government's deficit can be judged from the figures presented by Souvanna Phouma in the autumn of 1963, when conditions had returned to relatively average norms, for the fiscal year 1964. Expenditures were estimated at 6.386 billion kip (of which 3.469 billion kip were for military expenditures and 2.917 billion kip for civilian), and receipts at only 1.480 billion kip. The difference represented the amount of foreign aid on which Laos was dependent for its continued day-to-day existence.

The deficit was met by the continuation of the U.S. budget-support program. However, U.S. cash-grant aid, which had been in effect since the 1958 monetary reform, was scrapped. A commercial import program was inaugurated, designed to bring into Laos strictly controlled types and quantities of hard goods to soak up the paper money circulated by salaries. This program was to provide budget support of roughly $10 million per year. Mindful of the corruption under the previous import program, the United States tied the new program to a strict licensing system, coupled with enforced customs checks on goods entering the country. But these safeguards produced a mass of red tape that subjected imports to considerable delays. In a period of continuing inflation, such a licensing system was unworkable, especially since even the closest watch on the long river border could not prevent some re-exporting of goods brought in. The new system was abandoned and another devised.

The economic situation was complicated by the peculiar fact that the country had two sets of currency in circulation. There was, first of all, the Vientiane-issued kip-note currency, which was backed, in varying degrees, by the dollar. There was also a whole series of kip currency with no hard-currency backing that Souvanna Phouma's regime in Khang Khay had paid out to administration officials and troops on the Plain of Jars. These notes, rough imitations of the Vientiane notes printed by the American Banknote Company and the English firm of Thomas De La Rue, Ltd., had been printed in Czechoslovakia. The government had the problem of removing from circulation these notes, whose value on the free market was a good deal less than the Vientiane notes.

The coalition had to decide what to do about the aid agreements entered into with foreign governments by the two separate regimes of Souvanna Phouma at Khang Khay and Boun Oum at Vientiane. This was one of the first matters to be discussed in the Cabinet meetings. It was decided to honor all previous aid agreements that were not prohibited by the Geneva Protocol because of their military nature. The decision was announced by Souphanouvong on August 6: "The coalition Government will continue to maintain commitments with the Soviet Union, China, and North Vietnam, as it will with the United States."

The Chinese were pushing ahead with construction of roads linking Yünnan Province with Phong Saly and Nam Tha. The first indication that the Chinese had offered to construct the roads had come during Souvanna Phouma's visit to Peking in April, 1961, and actual work had begun late that year. Later, details of this vast construction project, involving several thousand Chinese laborers, were given by a New China News Agency dispatch from Peking on January 13, 1962.

The North Vietnamese had concluded a number of similar assistance agreements with Souvanna Phouma during his tenure as Prime Minister on the Plain of Jars. Besides those already referred to, these included: an agreement for aid during 1962 (signed on December 15, 1961); a protocol for reconstruction and construction of roads over the Annamite Mountains; a protocol on general conditions for delivery of goods; a protocol on general conditions of North Vietnamese "technical specialists" in Laos; a protocol on general conditions of Lao students and trainees in North Vietnam (all signed on March 10, 1962); and a protocol on aid for public health in 1962 (signed on June 9, 1962).

The official Lao Presse news agency reported on December 10, 1962, the completion of construction and repair work on four roads over the Annamite Mountains: one over the historic northern passage from the Dien Bien Phu valley as far as Sop Nao; one from the Vietnam border to Sam Neua town; one from the pass at Nape to the town of Kam Keut; and the fourth from the Mu Gia Pass to Nhommarath. The report made no mention of Route Nationale 7, which linked the Plain of Jars and the Vietnamese seaport of Vinh and which American air reconnaissance showed had also been repaired for heavy-duty traffic by the end of 1962. "The Vietnamese technicians and laborers who have been working on the repair of these roads are returning and will continue to return until they are all back in Vietnam," the agency reported.

These agreements were confirmed by dispatching General Phoumi to Peking and Hanoi, in his capacity as Finance Minister of the coalition, to countersign the documents previously signed by Souvanna Phouma. The road construction provided for in these agreements was so obviously of permanent strategic advantage to China and North Vietnam that it raises the question of why the General consented to validate these accords. Actually, he had little choice in the matter; he could not afford to scrap the principle of honoring previous bilateral agreements. Agreements signed by the Boun Oum government, one in particular, were of equal strategic significance to his own faction.

MAP 3. Land Communications in Laos

(The General, however, reportedly balked at countersigning additional agreements that would have permitted free trade across the Laos-North Vietnam border, thus allowing the North Vietnamese to send agents across the border at their pleasure, and the arming of North Vietnamese convoys into Laos against attacks by Meo guerrillas.)

The coalition government also received promises of aid for economic development from other quarters. The Soviet Union proposed to build a new hospital in Vientiane and a 50-kilowatt radio transmitting station to supplement the existing American-supplied 5-kilowatt station. France set about installing a modern telephone system in Vientiane. Japan sent technicians to supervise construction of a water-distribution system in the capital.

The advent of the first Communist-bloc aid in Vientiane led to the usual unanticipated results. Souvanna Phouma agreed to furnish fuel for the Soviet-built transport planes that the Soviets placed at his disposal, and housing for the Russian pilots who were training the Lao to fly the planes (there was no room for the Russians at the Soviet embassy). Since the money for the petroleum supplies and the rent for the house occupied by the Russians came from the Lao government budget, this meant that in effect the United States was paying to house Russians and fuel Russian planes.

Floating Partition

The single most important reality of the troika coalition period was that the three separate factions continued to control the administration and military security of their own areas. These areas were not fixed. There were no front lines. Patrols of Phoumist soldiers often brushed with Pathet Lao patrols, and these brushes meant continued skirmishing in the countryside. A village in Pathet Lao hands one week might well be occupied the following week by Phoumist troops, whose stay was bound to be just as brief.

The *de facto* partition of the kingdom gave rise to seemingly insoluble differences. There was, for instance, the matter of authorizing armed guards from each faction to enter Vientiane to ensure the security of their political leaders. Since the days of the Boun Oum government, law and order in Vientiane had been preserved by the National Police Force of 3,000 men and an independent paramilitary organization known as the Department of National Coordination, which possessed its own force of 1,800 men organized into three battalions. When the coalition was formed, the centrists insisted on bringing back to Vientiane a certain number of their own security forces, and the Pathet Lao demanded an equal force of their own that would have immunity to arrest and reprisal.

Allocating the strength for each faction required considerable time and bargaining. General Phoumi assured Souvanna Phouma of the good behavior of the men of the Department of National Co-ordination (which also had responsibility for checking immigration papers). The Pathet Lao ministers were permitted a guard force of 100 men, who settled down in a row of houses near the American Embassy compound, where, encouraged by Souphanouvong, they began planting gardens and growing their own vegetables.

The task of maintaining liaison with the ICC was initially farmed out to a tripartite cease-fire commission, but it became apparent that this body, which operated on the same troika principle as the Cabinet, could reach no major decisions. Soon, all decision-making was back in the hands of the Cabinet, and the ICC tended to deal more and more with Souvanna Phouma himself.

The ICC spurred the three factions to take steps toward unifying the administration and the armies. Although agreement in principle was reached on the three factions' contributions to a unified army, the shooting incidents in the countryside, where the cease-fire was frayed in the extreme, gave a truer impression of the state of affairs. The question of preparing general elections for a new National Assembly had not even been broached.

In the *de facto* partition, General Phoumi's trump card was the continued legality of Air America, whose airlift permitted thousands of Meo tribesmen to remain outside the clutches of the Pathet Lao. By the summer of 1963, this airlift was dropping forty tons of supplies a day in flights all over Laos, including Pathet Lao-controlled areas. Air America's contract was with the American economic-aid mission in Vientiane. The mission, in turn, operated under an agreement with the Royal Government.

The Pathet Lao continually accused the United States of intervention in Laos and of obstructing the implementation of the Geneva Protocol, and charged the Phoumist faction with violating the cease-fire. At a meeting in Sam Neua Province of the NLHS Central Committee in the last week of September, Kaysone Phomvihan demanded the withdrawal from Laos of both the American economic-aid mission and the U.S. Information Service, which he claimed were a cover for military advisers in civilian clothes. His demand did not elicit any action, however, from the Soviet government, Co-Chairman of the Geneva Conference. The reason was that the

Soviets were finding their own involvement in Laos a source of increasing embarrassment.

In the first week of October, Souvanna Phouma sent identical letters to Soviet Ambassador Afanasseyev and American Ambassador Unger asking for logistical support in flying supplies to isolated pockets of centrist troops, who heretofore had received all their supplies by means of the Soviet airlift. This of course referred to Kong Le's troops.

The Prime Minister's request surprised Western observers, who had assumed that the arrangements between Kong Le and his Pathet Lao counterparts for sharing airlifted supplies had been working smoothly. For many months, Kong Le's troops had been armed exclusively with Soviet-type weapons and depended on resupply from Communist-bloc stocks to keep in combat preparedness.

Soon there were other hints of trouble in the Kong Le–Pathet Lao alliance. Reports were received of dissatisfaction among Kong Le's soldiers, who claimed they were running short of food and clothing. In some cases, it was reported, the discontent had been stimulated by Pathet Lao agents who had infiltrated the centrist army during its vigorous recruiting on the Plain of Jars. Finally, Kong Le discovered signs of treachery by his Pathet Lao allies: Two centrist soldiers stationed at the quartermaster depot in Vinh, North Vietnam, to supervise distribution of Communist-bloc supplies to the centrist and Pathet Lao forces in Laos had been subverted by the North Vietnamese and had falsified records to divert to the Pathet Lao thousands of tons of ammunition, parachutes, and other matériel earmarked for Kong Le. In a rage, Kong Le ordered the two back to the Plain of Jars and had them placed under arrest. The Soviet Union, which had been the source of most of the matériel, knew nothing of the misallocation of supplies until the process had been going on for some time.

When Souvanna Phouma appealed for help in getting badly needed supplies to his troops on the Plain of Jars, the Soviet Embassy immediately promised him the use of transport planes that had been flying the airlift from Hanoi to the Plain of Jars. The North Vietnamese, for reasons of their own, backed the Pathet Lao policy of subverting Kong Le's centrist troops. This policy depended on isolation of the centrists. Therefore, the promised Soviet aircraft did not show up in Vientiane for several weeks.

The American Embassy realized that subversion of Kong Le's forces would reduce the centrist faction to impotence (Souvanna Phouma had little enough backing in the country as it was, without losing his army on the Plain of Jars) and a return to the disastrous bipolar situation of the previous two years. Taking into calculation the dilemma in which the Soviets had been placed by their contradictory needs to support Souvanna Phouma and to retain the good will of the North Vietnamese, and the paramount American interest in preserving the three-sided coalition, Unger immediately authorized Air America aircraft to ship supplies to Kong Le in accordance with Souvanna Phouma's request.

The Pathet Lao, who still retained their headquarters on the Plain of Jars together with Kong Le, had reason to be displeased by the abrupt termination of the Soviet airlift, revealed by General Singkapo Chounlamany in an interview on November 6.[1] They had even more reason to be displeased by the new role of Air America, which had upset their calculations. While their agents commandeered a portion of the blankets and medicines flown to Kong Le by Air America, their military spokesmen claimed the airlift was illegal and threatened to shoot down the Air America aircraft with the antiaircraft batteries that ringed the Plain. By this time, however, the North Vietnamese had completed repair work on Route Nationale 7 and could truck military supplies overland to the Pathet Lao. Souvanna Phouma, for the time being, protested against neither the use of the North Vietnam road for import of military supplies nor the Pathet Lao threat to fire on airlift planes, believing that such protests might well lead to the complete breakdown of the coalition, a development he wished to avoid at all costs.

Prisoners captured by each side in the fighting in 1961 and 1962 were exchanged within the time limit set by the Geneva Protocol. The Pathet Lao turned this exchange to their advantage by unloading at Vientiane airport three Vietnamese whom they claimed had infiltrated into Laos from South Vietnam and been captured near Tchepone. The trio were in an unhappy position because the South Vietnamese Embassy refused to have anything to do with them, claiming that they were North Vietnamese agents in disguise. Even if they were from the South, intense "re-education" during their captivity had obviously ended their usefulness to Saigon.

Stepped-Up Commitments

Since their Party Congress in September, 1960, the Vietnamese Communists, using guerrilla pressure, had been making slow but steady progress toward reunifying their country by overthrowing the Saigon regime of President Ngo Dinh Diem. The insurgency in

[1] With Ray Herndon of United Press International.

the South, fed by widespread popular resentment against a narrow and dictatorial government backed by the United States (i.e., foreigners), was given new impetus.

Ho Chi Minh's strategy in the South was following closely the pattern set by the Viet Minh in the Indochina War and by Ho's use of the Pathet Lao to achieve his long-term objectives in Laos. He realized that, given sufficient international concern over the explosiveness of the situation in South Vietnam, a "neutralist" government might take power in Saigon, either by a coup, as in Laos, or by a cease-fire and an international conference. Such a conference would open up the prospect of resumption of contacts between the two halves of the country, including trade that would give the North access once again to the rich rice surpluses of the Mekong Delta.

The United States realized the dangers of an unsuccessful involvement in the South Vietnam fighting. Coming on the heels of the experience in Laos, a withdrawal of the American presence in South Vietnam under guerrilla pressure would just about put the seal of infallibility on General Giap's method of "people's war." The United States was just becoming aware of the implications of this type of conflict, in an age where nuclear weapons were canceled out as suicidal, for the underdeveloped nations of Asia, Africa, and Latin America. In April, 1961, Truong Chinh, an important member of the Central Committee of the Lao Dong Party, wrote in the Hanoi journal *Hoc Tap* (*Studies*) that "socialist North Vietnam is providing good support for the South Vietnamese revolution, and is serving as a strong base for the struggle for reunification." In May, President Kennedy dispatched Vice President Lyndon B. Johnson to Saigon to reassure Diem that withdrawal of American support from the Phoumists in Laos did not imply immediate American withdrawal of support from his own regime.

The following month, an American mission headed by Dr. Eugene Staley visited South Vietnam. Its members inspected the situation on the ground and gathered information for a report to the President. They discovered that the American MAAG detachments that had been training the South Vietnamese army since 1955 had rarely ventured outside the large towns where their training camps were located and knew virtually nothing of the extent of the insurgents' hold on the countryside.

In many cases, the Diem government had deliberately sought to keep the Americans ignorant of the deterioration of its authority. By the end of 1961, the insurgents were reported to have drawn up plans to set up a liberated area in the highlands near the Laos border, and to have created a shadow administration over all South Vietnam on the village level.

Finally, the crisis provoked in May, 1963, by the Diem regime's repressions against Buddhist priests revealed its isolation from the country at large. But the full extent to which the Americans had been deceived about the gravity of the situation did not become apparent until Diem was overthrown in a military *coup d'état* on November 1 of that year.

The situation had so deteriorated that the insurgents no longer depended upon the funneling of supplies from North Vietnam along the Ho Chi Minh Trail in Laos (although the use of this network of trails would again become essential in case of an escalation of the commitment of North Vietnamese men and material in South Vietnam). The estimate that the rebellion against the Saigon government had reached the "take-off point" explains North Vietnam's readiness to agree to negotiate for a neutralized Laos at Geneva in the spring of 1961.

At about the time of the Staley mission, Hanoi appears to have made a reappraisal of U.S. intentions and of its own prospects for "liberating" South Vietnam. June, 1961, saw the first (unsuccessful) U.S.-sponsored guerrilla raids from South Vietnam into the north. The new outburst of American activity in South Vietnam accorded with the North Vietnamese leaders' doctrine that the imperialists grow more desperate as the liberation struggle approaches its climax. American officers were now leading South Vietnamese troops into combat, and some were being killed. American pilots were flying combat missions in planes bearing the markings of the South Vietnamese air force. American helicopters piloted by American crews were ferrying troops into battle.

However, the use of massed formations of helicopters in South Vietnam threw the Viet Cong off balance and held them off balance during the first half of 1962 before they developed successful defensive tactics (unlike the Pathet Lao, the Viet Cong possessed no anti-aircraft guns). The American pressure on the Phoumists in Laos during these six months to agree to a coalition may have been regarded by Hanoi as a cover for a planned action against North Vietnam from both South Vietnam and the Meo-held areas of Laos. Taking into account the arrival of American troops in Thailand in May, 1962, in reaction to the Phoumist debacle at Nam Tha, Hanoi very probably concluded that North Vietnam was being threatened by hostile action, and possibly by full-scale invasion. Hanoi's nervousness at this prospect may well be imagined, given the state of tension between Peking and Moscow, which existed already, and Moscow's apparent reluctance to be drawn into an Asian adventure leading to a confrontation with the United States.

During the first week in August, 1962, photographic reconnaissance flights by RF-101 Voodoo jets, which had been making regular aerial surveillance of northern Laos in connection with contingency planning related to the deployment of American troops in Thailand, revealed a convoy of several hundred vehicles moving over the newly improved Route Nationale 7 from North Vietnam into Laos. Close inspection of the photographs (which were so sharp that the license plates on the trucks were legible) showed that the convoy, consisting of two main sections and a third smaller section, contained truckloads of North Vietnamese troops, tanks, armored cars, and a small number of towed artillery pieces. The force moved overland into Pathet Lao encampments on the Plain of Jars, where they constructed large camouflaged tank parks, seemingly indicating the arrival of further forces. (American aerial reconnaissance continued. On August 13, 1962, one of these RF-101 aircraft was hit by antiaircraft fire while over the Plain of Jars. Although badly damaged, the plane managed to return to its base at Bangkok. The existence of the aerial reconnaissance was made public by the State Department on May 21, 1964.)

These North Vietnamese combat troops were quite distinct from the technical experts and cadres that North Vietnam had maintained in Laos since the end of 1960, and by 1962 were fully integrated into Pathet Lao units as instructors and stiffeners. In the ensuing weeks, the new arrivals split up into battalion strength and moved southward to take up stationary positions along the entire length of the Laos-Vietnam border. Their presence there was screened by Pathet Lao control of the contiguous areas, and by the continued refusal of the Pathet Lao to permit officials on mission from Vientiane to enter these areas.

Just inside Laos, on the crests of the passes across the mountains, the North Vietnamese sat quietly. It is many times more difficult to defend a downward-sloping road than it is to hold the crown of a mountain pass. By the end of August, there were an estimated 10,000 North Vietnamese military personnel in Laos, including both the frontier-guard troops and the cadres integrated into the Pathet Lao units.

The stepping up of commitments in South Vietnam and Laos in 1961 and 1962 by the Americans and the North Vietnamese had complicated the working of the neutralization formula codified at Geneva in July, 1962. In very much the same way, the 1954 neutralization attempt had been corrupted by North Vietnam's increased commitment in South Vietnam after 1958. The link between Vietnam and Laos was clear.

The Vietnamese Who Weren't

The United States had set the tone for compliance with the Geneva Protocol provisions relating to withdrawal of foreign troops by starting as early as June 23 to pull out the White Star teams of military advisers who had been working with the Meo since 1961. Thereafter, the number of American military advisers in Laos, which had reached a peak of about 800 men, steadily decreased. The number of MAAG personnel processed at exit points by the ICC between the signing of the Protocol on July 23 and the October 7 deadline was 666. One of the last to leave, MAAG Commander Major General Reuben H. Tucker, referred to the situation in Laos as "a can of worms." Not a single American military man was left in Laos in uniform, except for the Embassy's military attaché and his small staff.

This strict compliance with the Geneva Protocol must have dumfounded the North Vietnamese. The American behavior was inexplicable, if not downright unimperialist.

Intelligence reports from the tightly sealed border areas during September indicated that here and there a few hundred troops had been pulled back into North Vietnam. As a *pro forma* gesture, Hanoi agreed to public withdrawal of a token number of North Vietnamese "advisers" and "technicians" whose presence in Laos had never before been officially admitted. The ICC was permitted to establish inspection teams at the Plain of Jars and at the village of Nom Ping in Khammouane Province, to check out the withdrawing personnel. Following an initial departure of five officers and twelve noncoms, another planeload of eight officers, five noncoms, and five "experts" left the Plain of Jars airfield for Hanoi on September 29 aboard an Ilyushin transport. On October 23, the ICC recorded the departure from Nom Ping of five men dressed in green fatigues without caps or insignia of rank. Their leader made a brief speech of farewell for the benefit of some 150 inhabitants of the surrounding region who had come to see them off. Officials of the Pathet Lao-appointed administration in the region thanked the five Vietnamese for their selfless services rendered to Laos during the past year. Then five village girls stepped forward and handed each of them a gift of pillows and bed sheets, whereupon the Vietnamese climbed aboard their single-engine Russian biplane and took off for Hanoi.

On October 7, the official North Vietnamese news agency carried this report: "The Vietnamese military personnel which were previously sent to Laos at the request of the Royal Lao Government have all been withdrawn from Laos." No such request had ever been made.

That same evening in Vientiane, Souvanna Phouma, puffing on his pipe and exuding optimism at a party in honor of his birthday, told his guests that he had reason to believe that the countries that had sent troops into Laos "will ensure with diligence that the last stragglers will leave with a minimum possible delay."[2]

The State Department estimated that "several thousand" Vietnamese troops had left Laos by the deadline, but this left several other thousands still within the country. U.S.S.R. Deputy Foreign Minister Georgi Pushkin, who had handled most of the Soviet negotiations at Geneva, had told State Department officials privately that the North Vietnamese troops would merely "fade into the jungle."[3]

This is, in effect, what happened. On November 10, when London released the text of the ICC's report on compliance with the troop-withdrawal provisions, a Foreign Office spokesman commented: "We know that at the time of the Laos cease-fire there were about 10,000 North Vietnamese troops in Laos. A number of those chose to withdraw secretly and only forty passed through the ICC check points. It is not at all clear what happened to the remainder and how many may have remained."

There was considerable debate in American diplomatic circles over whether to file a protest on the violation of the troop-withdrawal provision of the Geneva Protocol. Those who favored doing so argued that failure to act would set a dangerous precedent for violation of the provisions dealing with arms shipments and use of Lao territory for aggressive purposes. The opposing argument was that filing a protest would quite possibly dash any hopes of political unification of the country, which was far more important than checking out Vietnamese troops. Besides, the United States had the means of keeping track of these troops and thus determining whether they intended to follow up with any aggressive action against the Mekong Valley. Either the Communist signatories were

[2] Reuter dispatch, Vientiane, October 7, 1962.
[3] United Press International dispatch, Washington, October 4, 1962.

willing to support the tacit "no conquest" understanding among the Geneva signatories, in which case it was senseless to force a split over the first violation, or else they had no interest in such an understanding, in which case sending the ICC into the jungle to look for Vietnamese foot soldiers would prove nothing that was not already known, and the United States had better start thinking about an entirely different approach to the problem.

Despite ICC assurances that it was fully aware of the charges and countercharges about the presence of troops and that if and when it had reasonable evidence of a violation, it would "immediately take appropriate action about it as laid down in the Geneva Protocol," a combination of Pathet Lao secretiveness and Polish obstruction was to prevent the ICC from registering any formal violation of the provisions for troop withdrawals. The United States, while continuing to draw attention to the North Vietnamese presence and to pressure the ICC to undertake field investigations, did not make the issue a *casus belli*. The acceptance of the presence of these forces was part of the price to be paid for neutralizing Laos without committing American troops.

Internal Problems

All the agreements for the division of powers that had been so laboriously negotiated at Ban Namone, Ban Hin Heup, Zurich, the Plain of Jars, and Geneva remained to be implemented. The coalition principle had yet to be tested in practice.

There was, to begin with, the problem posed by the National Assembly. Its members, elected in the rigged elections of 1960 and still reflecting the anti-Communist complexion of that period, continued to sit in Vientiane and would indeed sit until 1965 by virtue of a Constitutional amendment extending their mandate from four to five years. Although the three princes had agreed that the coalition government would be set up by the direct appointment and investiture of the King, no one had given any serious thought to dissolving the Assembly, for that would have meant holding fresh elections within ninety days, and not even the Pathet Lao were prepared for that.

When the Assembly met for its regular session in October, therefore, Souvanna Phouma chose what appeared to him to be the logical way out of the dilemma. He went before the Assembly and requested a vote of full powers. The Pathet Lao reacted immediately and angrily to this initiative, calling it an "illegal and treacherous act" and accusing the Prince of throwing overboard the principle of unanimity decided upon in the Plain of Jars agreement of June 11.

The task of implementing the internal agreements among the three factions had been entrusted to a Commission in Charge of Applying the Geneva Agreements. Rightist, centrist, and Pathet Lao factions had representatives on this commission, headed respectively by Ngon Sananikone, Quinim Pholsena, and Phoumi Vongvichit. The three factions settled on the rule of unanimity. Since one of the main functions of the commission was to act as liaison with the ICC in investigating charges of ceasefire violations from any faction, the commission soon fell into disagreement and consequent paralysis.

Under the commission, there were three tripartite committees: the Ceasefire Committee, the Committee for Integration of the Armed Forces, and the Committee for Integration of the Civil Administrations. The meetings of the Ceasefire Committee, on which the work of the other two committees obviously depended, showed the intractable nature of the problem. In fifty-eight official and fourteen informal meetings held between July, 1962, and April, 1963, when it finally broke up with the departure from Vientiane of the Pathet Lao members, the committee was able to reach agreement on only three agenda items. These were agreement to consider the effective date of the ceasefire among the three factions to be June 24, 1962, agreement on abstaining from provocative propaganda, and agreement on abstaining from provocative military activity.[4]

The absence of any agreed map showing the disposition of opposing armed forces had been a fact of life from the earliest truce negotiations.[5] In this situation, each side was able to charge the other at will with violations of the ceasefire. The North Vietnamese published a map shortly after the May 3, 1961, ceasefire showing their version of who controlled what as of that date.[6] Padong, located well behind the line of control claimed by the North Vietnamese for their Pathet Lao allies and where sharp fighting had

[4] I am indebted to General Bounthieng Venevongsos for information about the workings of the committee, on which he was the senior representative of the rightist faction. Although a portion of the minutes kept by General Bounthieng was lost when the Mekong River flooded his home in 1966, most of his records were saved.

[5] See above, pages 207–8.

[6] In Quang Minh, *Au Pays du Million d'Eléphants* (Hanoi: Editions en Langues Etrangères, 1961), map facing p. 145.

flared after the ceasefire between rightist and Pathet Lao troops, was not shown. Moreover, the Pathet Lao did not hesitate to move the line of control several hundred square miles in their favor after the battle of Nam Tha in May, 1962.[7]

It was natural that production of an agreed map became one of the first items of business before the Ceasefire Committee when it met in Vientiane. The rightists and centrists were generally amenable to producing a map attempting some approximation of reality. Although it might prove to be a map-maker's nightmare, it would show the emplacement of every group of soldiers in Laos. In this respect, the rightists were even prepared to allow the Pathet Lao to claim control over areas whose actual control depended on the continued presence of North Vietnamese troops, and also to allow the Pathet Lao to claim islets of control well inside the rightists' area, as for example in Sayaboury Province on the west bank of the Mekong. Movement would be allowed outside these islets, but only on condition that persons travel unarmed.

The senior Pathet Lao representative, Phoun Sipraseuth, rejected this proposal, however. He countered with a proposal that the committee produce a map showing little more than a single line extending from one end of Laos to the other. This scheme would take almost no account of islets of control within each other's general area of control. Moreover, "violations" of the air space over each other's area of control would be prohibited, a stipulation that would automatically deprive the scattered bands of rightist troops holding out deep inside Pathet Lao territory of their supplies and would compel them to evacuate their strongholds.

In the end, no map could be agreed upon. The Pathet Lao were in effect demanding the formalized partitioning of Laos, and the feeling that no government possessed the authority to divide the territory of the kingdom helped unite the rightists and Prince Souvanna Phouma in opposition to the proposal. This did not prevent the Pathet Lao from pursuing their aim of consolidating their control over the portion of Laos in their hands by other means.

The jigsaw puzzle of control of territory by the three factions was inherently unstable, and as soon as one of the factions decided to disrupt it, it could not survive for long. This was particularly true of the Plain of Jars, where Kong Le estimated the size of the forces in confrontation as: for the centrists, 4,500 soldiers under his direct command; for the Pathet Lao, 6,000

[7] See *Une Année pour l'Application des Accords de Genève de 1962 sur le Laos* (Le Comité Central du Neo Lao Hak Sat, 1963), map p. 22.

MAP 4. Approximate Ceasefire Line of May 3, 1961

men controlling irregular areas interspersed among the centrists and another 1,200 men controlling various high points on the Plain's perimeter. Outside the Plain, Kong Le had another 5,500 men, mostly scattered in small garrisons in central Laos and along the Royal Road. The Pathet Lao forces elsewhere in Laos, according to American estimates at the time, were 12,000 men, fairly evenly distributed all the way from Phong Saly and Sam Neua provinces to the Cambodian border. The 2,000-man army of General Khammouane Boupha in Phong Saly Province, nominally loyal to Souvanna Phouma, was regarded as strongly anti-Phoumist, due in part to the fact that the General found it advisable to remain on good terms with the Chinese, who had established a consulate in the capital of his province.

The largest military force in Laos was the Phoumist army, which had swelled to an estimated 48,000 men by the end of 1962. Most of them were in the Mekong Valley, but they included detachments of Meo guerrillas scattered all over northern Laos. Thus, the jigsaw puzzle of centrist and Pathet Lao forces on the Plain of Jars was surrounded by areas occupied by tribal forces loyal to the Phoumists. Thus, a centrist company in a stream bottom might be overlooked by a Pathet Lao mortar position that was overlooked by a Meo mortar position farther away.

Control of the larger towns—Khang Khay, Xieng Khouang, Phong Savan, and Ban Ban—and the vital Plain of Jars airfield was shared by the centrists and the Pathet Lao. However, as Kong Le realized, in a showdown his limited forces could not hope to defend any of the town positions against the Pathet Lao. The airfield had virtually no value, since its use by either side could be interdicted by artillery and mortar fire.

Treachery on the Plain of Jars

Souvanna Phouma had never publicly announced his position on the airlifting of supplies to Kong Le's troops by Air America aircraft. On November 27, an Air America C-123 transport plane on such a mission was shot down as it landed at the Plain of Jars airfield, killing the two American crew members. The Pathet Lao charged that the United States was intervening in Laos in flagrant disregard of the Geneva Protocol. The clandestine Voice of the Lao Kingdom radio station crowed that the American plane had been "shot down by local air defense units of the Lao patriotic forces."[8]

[8] Quoted by New China News Agency, November 29, 1962.

The incident revealed in a flash the degree to which Pathet Lao agents had infiltrated the centrist forces. The antiaircraft unit that downed the plane was the Phetsarath Artillery Group (after Prince Phetsarath), commanded by Colonel Deuan Sunnalath, the paratroop officer with whom Kong Le had quarreled in Vientiane. Of the group's 270 men, 60 were former members of the Pathet Lao who had been demobilized in 1957 and who had joined the centrist units on the Plain of Jars during 1961.

The destruction of an aircraft belonging to the strongest capitalist power in the world imbued the gunners with the *élan* of winning that is so vital to Communist revolutionary warfare. The Vietnamese political commissars who shepherded Colonel Deuan's dissidents celebrated the event in countless meetings. Kong Le's deputy commander on the Plain of Jars, Colonel Ketsana Vongsouvan, was outraged by the act. But his attempt to arrest Colonel Deuan's gunners was frustrated by the Pathet Lao.

In Vientiane, Souvanna Phouma dejectedly announced that the plane had been shot down by centrist, not Pathet Lao forces, and weakly promised an investigation. The centrist delegate to the tripartite cease-fire commission, Colonel Somboun Vongphrachanh, threatened to order centrist forces to retaliate by shooting down any aircraft flying supplies to the Pathet Lao.

The Pathet Lao launched an attack on Air America, charging that they had never been consulted on its operations, which included liaison flights as well as cargo flights. Souvanna Phouma was in the middle: He had neither endorsed the Air America airlift (the contract was a carryover from the Boun Oum government, and had merely been initialed for the coalition by Keo Viphakone, Secretary of State for Social Welfare, a Phoumist) nor prohibited it.

In order to ease the problem, the American Embassy arranged that Air America turn a number of cargo planes over to Souvanna Phouma for exclusive use as supply transports to Kong Le's headquarters. These planes were marked with the Lao three-headed elephant, but had American crews because no Lao crews had been trained to fly them.

At this point, the Soviets stepped into the picture. On December 2, the first of a consignment of nine LI-2 twin-engine transports were delivered at the Vientiane airport. The Soviets, stressing their observance of the Geneva Protocol, stipulated that three of the planes were for the centrist faction, three for the Pathet Lao, and three for the Phoumists. It would be several weeks before Lao crews could be trained to operate the aircraft.

The Soviets, still seeking to cultivate their North Vietnamese comrades, turned over to Hanoi all the Ilyushin-14 aircraft that had been operated by Soviet crews on the airlift between Hanoi and Laos since December, 1960. In this way, the Soviets withdrew from the airlift picture in Laos, thereby forfeiting an important bargaining lever in the delicate balance of pressures. It was up to the North Vietnamese to keep the Pathet Lao in food and ammunition, a task made a great deal easier by the repair of the roads across the Annamite Mountains. Nonetheless, the Ilyushins, with Vietnamese crews, were almost immediately assigned to specialized missions, dropping military supplies and carrying personnel on liaison flights.

In January, a second incident showed how paper-thin was the peace prevailing in Laos under the troika government. An ICC helicopter, one of four painted white and used for liaison flights, made a forced landing between Vientiane and Luang Prabang, in an area under Pathet Lao control. For weeks, Souvanna Phouma was refused permission to send technicians to repair the helicopter. After permission finally was granted, the repair team found the craft had been completely stripped by the Pathet Lao.

On February 11, Souvanna Phouma left Laos to accompany the King on a tour of signatory countries of the Geneva Protocol. The following evening, Colonel Ketsana was assassinated at his home in Phong Savan on the Plain of Jars. Ketsana had been one of the original seventeen officers who had joined Kong Le in planning and executing the August 9, 1960, *coup d'état,* and his loss by Pathet Lao treachery was deeply felt by the centrist military. Ketsana had resisted the growth of Communist sympathies among the centrists. Perhaps more immediately connected with his assassination were his statements urging the ICC to investigate reports of North Vietnamese troops in the border areas.

Kong Le issued orders that all Pathet Lao personnel and defectors to the ranks of Colonel Deuan were henceforth to be forbidden entry into zones controlled by his own troops. The tension between Kong Le and the Pathet Lao was increasing daily, despite efforts at mediation by Pheng Phongsavan, the Acting Prime Minister.

If the centrist soldiers were compelled to defend themselves, they would soon exhaust their ammunition. The intentions of the North Vietnamese among the Pathet Lao was another uncertain element in any engagement between the two factions. Several of Kong Le's officers and men reported recognizing their former Vietnamese instructors still in Laos in early 1963.

King Savang Vatthana and Souvanna Phouma concluded their

tour abroad at the end of March. In Vientiane, on the evening of April 1, the King gave a reception for Cabinet ministers and foreign diplomats. One of those present was Foreign Minister Quinim Pholsena, who had busied himself ever since formation of the coalition with making sure that the Chinese Communist and North Vietnamese ambassadors felt at home in Vientiane. In December, he had unilaterally dispatched a message of felicitations to the National Liberation Front of South Vietnam on its second anniversary. He had then set about compiling regulations whereby foreign diplomats would have to obtain his ministry's authorization before requesting appointments with the Prime Minister.

After the reception, Quinim Pholsena and his wife returned to their home in his large black Mercedes-Benz convertible shortly after 9 P.M. As he descended from the car, a corporal on guard at the front entrance squeezed the trigger on his Russian submachine gun, instantly killing Quinim, one of the most complex and least loved Lao leaders.

The assassination of the avowedly anti-American Foreign Minister was the last straw for the Pathet Lao. In the last week in March, centrist positions in Khang Khay and Xieng Khouang came under fire from Colonel Deuan's dissidents. Simultaneously, the propaganda outlets of the Communist powers began a campaign charging the centrists with "provocations," a familiar gambit that usually signaled the start of a major Pathet Lao military effort to shift the balance of power in their favor.

On March 31, a series of shootings occurred, leading to full-scale fighting. The Pathet Lao may have underestimated Kong Le's willingness to resist the pressure put on him to withdraw from the positions his troops shared with theirs and with those of Colonel Deuan. Kong Le resisted bravely, and reported the situation back to Souvanna Phouma, who ordered him to defend himself but to take no action that could be interpreted as offensive.

Before April was many days old, Kong Le had suffered about thirty casualties and had been compelled to abandon the "hostage" positions his outnumbered garrisons held at Khang Khay, Xieng Khouang, and Ban Ban. Nevertheless, he was able to withdraw to safety in relatively good order, and deftly maneuvered to retrieve all his Russian armored cars from Xieng Khouang. He thereupon set about manning a more restricted defense perimeter. Establishing a new command post at Muong Phanh, three miles west of the Plain of Jars airfield, he deployed his troops so as to control the extreme western third of the Plain.

The three delegation heads of the ICC, in an effort to determine the facts of the fighting on the Plain of Jars, made a series of helicopter trips from Vientiane to Khang Khay, beginning on April 6. They returned from these trips with reports that cease-fire agreements were being negotiated, but each day their reports carried less conviction.

Souvanna Phouma convened an emergency Cabinet meeting in the capital on April 8, and, over his own signature, wrote a request to the ICC to dispatch an ICC team to the Plain of Jars for the purpose of controlling the cease-fire. Souphanouvong, aware that there was a split in the ICC over assigning responsibility for the fighting, opposed sending an ICC team to the Plain of Jars, claiming that the fighting was an internal dispute among the centrists, between the Kong Le forces and the forces loyal to Colonel Deuan; in this contention, he was to be supported by Dr. Marek Thee, the chief Polish delegate.

Within hours of Souvanna Phouma's request to the ICC, Souphanouvong departed from Vientiane for Khang Khay, now controlled exclusively by the Pathet Lao. He said that security precautions in the capital had been inadequate since Quinim's assassination. He was followed on April 19 by Phoumi Vongvichit, whose Ilyushin-14 was struck en route to Sam Neua by ground fire, presumably by Meo guerrillas, an incident indicating that peace was precarious in other areas of Laos besides the Plain of Jars. The departure of the two Pathet Lao ministers left two junior Pathet Lao officials—Prince Souk Vongsak, Secretary of State for Public Works and Transport, and Kampheuane Tounalom, Secretary of State for Planning—to attend Cabinet meetings in Vientiane. Souphanouvong had learned from his experience during the break-up of the first coalition not to be caught off guard in Vientiane.

The North Vietnamese may well have begun asking themselves at this point what they had gained by the second conference at Geneva that they could not have gained by pushing the Pathet Lao forward in the nibbling process that had preceded the cease-fire. They had allowed themselves to be persuaded by Khrushchev to settle for something less than the complete exclusion of the Americans from Laos, much as in 1954 they had deferred to Molotov's desire to liquidate the Indochina question and had left the southern half of their country in the hands of the French-supported Bao Dai puppet government. Now, the Americans had been invited to join in support of the Souvanna Phouma government, and the neutralization that the North Vietnamese had hoped would work to their advantage was working against them. If these were the fruits of the second Geneva Conference, they were bitter indeed. Their efforts to place pressure on Kong Le's forces by pinching off his supplies had been frustrated by the Americans. And in the ICC, the Indian chairman was no longer favorably disposed toward the Pathet Lao, as he had been before 1958; that radical reversal could be chalked up to the Chinese attack in the Himalayas.

Failure of the ICC to Control the Conflict

The Indian Chairman of the ICC, Avtar Singh, had been under U.S. pressure to continue the on-the-spot investigations based on allegations of foreign troops in Laos. Two ICC investigations at the end of December had failed to substantiate these charges, although American intelligence had reported that large numbers of North Vietnamese troops were present in Laos. The ICC finally decided on trips to Tchepone (to check for North Vietnamese troops) and Phou Ka Te (to check for American troops), in the South, and to the Plain of Jars (to check for North Vietnamese and American troops in various sectors), after months of haggling over such details as how far from their landing point the ICC teams would be allowed to walk. The trips to Tchepone and Phou Ka Te were made on April 13; the trip to the Plain of Jars was delayed by the outbreak of fighting and the submergence of the troop-investigation issue by the more urgent need to police the cease-fire.

Avtar Singh's position became more difficult as the ICC delegates met to determine the content of their report to the Co-Chairmen on the Plain of Jars fighting. The Polish delegate, Dr. Thee, at first insisted that the Plain of Jars situation was less urgent than the Indian and Canadian delegates contended, since the opposing sides were reportedly negotiating a renewal of the cease-fire agreement, which had been broken barely hours after its conclusion. When pressed to submit a draft report, Dr. Thee produced an account of the fighting that fully supported the Pathet Lao position and sharply differed from the views of his two colleagues. Clearly, it would take days, if not weeks, of arguing for the ICC to get unanimity on the report, as required by the Protocol.

During this time, the three ICC delegates, accompanied by the British and Soviet ambassadors representing the Co-Chairmen, continued making their helicopter trips to Khang Khay, where they were hospitably received by Prince Souphanouvong, exuding good will and optimism. On one of these trips, when the Indian and

Canadian delegates attempted to convey to the Prince the urgency with which they viewed the situation, Souphanouvong remarked that certainly the Pathet Lao were not attacking anyone, and all was calm around Khang Khay, as the distinguished foreign guests could see for themselves. British Ambassador Donald Hopson picked up this remark and declared that if this were the case, then Souphanouvong could have no objection to the dispatch to Khang Khay of an ICC inspection team. Souphanouvong expressed his agreement. Realizing that Souphanouvong had committed a most damaging *faux pas* in full hearing of the three ICC delegates and the British and Soviet ambassadors, Dr. Thee inserted himself in the conversation. Shortly after this incident, Souphanouvong communicated a radically different view to the ICC: On no condition, Souphanouvong now declared, would the Pathet Lao permit an ICC team at Khang Khay.

Meanwhile, the Pathet Lao and dissident centrists were steadily gaining ground against the Kong Le forces. Simultaneously, Communist propaganda adopted an ominous new slant on the fighting. On April 10, a New China News Agency dispatch accused the United States of sending agents to the Plain of Jars to provoke trouble between Colonel Deuan and Kong Le. The NCNA dispatch laid the groundwork for linking Kong Le's efforts to defend himself with American intervention, and for portraying Deuan as the true centrist commander. Deuan had remained with about 150 men at the Pathet Lao armed camp at Khang Khay, thus compounding his treachery to his former commander.

Two days later, the NCNA reported a statement from General Singkapo, the Pathet Lao commander, who took up the theme of U.S. intervention:

> They have dispatched large numbers of bandits disguised as neutral [centrist] troops to attack the Pathet Lao fighting units at Khang Khay, and to attack progressive-minded units of the neutral [centrist dissident] forces at both Khang Khay and Xieng Khouang. . . . U.S. imperialism and its lackeys have recklessly violated the Geneva agreements and the cease-fire order and are pushing a wicked plan aimed at undermining the neutral [centrist] forces under Prince Souvanna Phouma, splitting the Lao national front, and whipping up greater confusion and tension in Laos.

The American Embassy in Vientiane soon disclosed that, for the first time since 1960, the U.S. was once again supplying arms and ammunition to Kong Le. Souvanna Phouma remained silent on this subject.

Souvanna Phouma was in despair over the failure of the international machinery established to deal with precisely such crises, and alarmed by a fresh Pathet Lao advance that had dislodged Kong Le's meager forces from the village of Phong Savan, thereby shattering the illusion that a cease-fire agreement was being negotiated. On April 19, he addressed a message directly to the Co-Chairmen asking them to "intervene with a view to ending the violations of the cease-fire." He also addressed an appeal to Souphanouvong to bring the Pathet Lao to heel. Privately, he denounced in exasperated tones the Pathet Lao for using Deuan's dissidents as a *"paravent"* ("screen") for their actions against Kong Le so they could claim that the fighting did not involve them but was a dispute within the centrist ranks.

The message from Souvanna Phouma forced the Russians' hand. On April 22, an editorial in *Pravda* confirmed the ominous turn in developments, echoing the Chinese line sounded twelve days previously; the Russians blamed the U.S. for the tension in Laos and virtually accused the U.S. of violating the 1962 Geneva agreements.

The ICC acted on Souvanna Phouma's request for a team on the Plain of Jars despite Polish objections that all factions of the coalition had not consented. Avtar Singh pointedly asked Dr. Thee whether he, who professed such concern for respecting the sovereignty of Laos, was proposing to challenge the Prime Minister's authority to make governmental decisions. Did the Polish representative mean to imply that Poland no longer regarded Souvanna Phouma as Prime Minister of the Royal Government of Laos? When confronted with this argument, Dr. Thee gave in.

However, the Polish delegation refused to permit participation of its members on the team, although Article 15 of the Protocol stipulated that only a majority vote was required to implement a Royal Government request. The team finally dispatched to the Plain of Jars, called a "temporary team on a continuing basis" in order to avoid the charge that it was a fixed team, comprised only Indian and Canadian personnel. As the British pointed out in a note to Moscow on May 7, the Polish delegate had directly violated Article 16, which stated:

> Each member-state of the Commission shall ensure the presence of its own representatives both on the Commission and on the inspection teams, and shall promptly replace them in the event of their being unable to perform their duties.

The ICC debate over the report to the Co-Chairmen on the

fighting reached its climax at a stormy meeting in which Dr. Thee refused to modify his views, which were contrary to those drawn up in draft form by his colleagues. He finally declared that he intended to submit a minority report. This would go against Article 14 of the Protocol, which required unanimity on ICC decisions relating to cease-fire violations. Matters came to a head when Avtar Singh flatly rejected Dr. Thee's minority report. Dr. Thee rose from the table and walked out, a tactic he had employed, unsuccessfully, on at least one previous occasion. He sent his minority report directly to the Co-Chairmen.

Avtar Singh was resolved to have the ICC inspection functions reaffirmed; he felt that backing down on this provision of the Geneva Protocol would imply the Commission's abdication of any further responsibility for what transpired in Laos. The Indian and Canadian delegations debated, but did not act on, a suggestion to station teams to police the cease-fire not only on the Plain of Jars but also at other sensitive points such as Vang Vieng, where centrist, Pathet Lao, and Phoumist garrisons were in proximity, and Attopeu in the South.

North Vietnam's Unasked Aid

Kong Le's arsenal of Soviet-type weapons would soon be useless for lack of bullets. He had not received any matériel through Communist-bloc channels since the previous October, and he was still awaiting delivery of 6,000 tons of petroleum and other supplies that the Soviet Union had placed at his disposal but that were said to be blocked at Hanoi. In this situation, the American Embassy in Vientiane let it be known that the United States, acting at the request of the Royal Lao Government and within the limits allowed by Article 6 of the Geneva Protocol, had resumed shipments of American arms and ammunition to Kong Le. Again, as the previous November, Souvanna Phouma remained silent; it was not even known whether he had been consulted, or whether the request from the Royal Lao Government had been signed by a Phoumist minister. Souvanna Phouma, attempting to keep the coalition together, was reluctant to commit himself on such inflammatory matters. The Phoumist ministers could act in the name of the government *on matters to which Souvanna Phouma did not raise objections.* The Pathet Lao, for the moment, raised objections to decisions reached in this manner; they retained for the future their option to act also in the name of the Royal Lao Government.

The American arms and ammunition were parachuted from Air America aircraft onto the Plain of Jars. Also, Air America planes landed at Muong Phanh, where Kong Le had opened up a new dirt landing strip. For the time being, the Pathet Lao had failed in their attempt to expel him from the Plain of Jars.

By June, it had become so obvious that North Vietnam was providing the Pathet Lao with supplies and cadres that Souvanna Phouma no longer bothered with the politeness of avoiding reference to it. He openly decried the Pathet Lao dependence on foreign arms, but the denunciation had a hollow ring.

On the road between Khang Khay and Xieng Khouang, members of the French Military Mission had seen truckloads of Vietnamese soldiers wearing the uniforms and caps of the Pathet Lao. The French, unlike most Westerners, can easily tell a Lao from a Vietnamese. When they addressed these soldiers in Lao, the latter were unable to reply.

During the fighting on the Plain of Jars in the summer of 1963, Kong Le's radio officers almost daily monitored two-way conversations in Vietnamese, and heard firing orders given in Vietnamese. A detachment of Kong Le's forces reported the capture of eighteen Vietnamese soldiers on April 12 in fighting along the road to Xieng Khouang, but said their prisoners escaped two days later when the detachment was attacked. On April 21, documents taken from the bodies of three reportedly Vietnamese soldiers who were killed in an exchange of gunfire along the same road were sent to Vientiane by Kong Le's chief of intelligence, Colonel Soulivan Sihavara.

A significant incident revealed the extent of North Vietnamese duplicity concerning its personnel in Laos. The North Vietnamese Embassy claimed that between 300 and 350 Vietnamese "construction workers" had been in Laos making improvements in the town of Khang Khay under North Vietnam's aid program to Laos. After the Pathet Lao forced Kong Le to evacuate his troops from Khang Khay, Souvanna Phouma sought to effect the withdrawal of these "construction workers." He pointed out to North Vietnamese Ambassador Le Van Hien in Vientiane that the work called for under the aid program had long since been completed. The Ambassador protested that arrangements for evacuating the "construction workers" were proceeding with all possible speed. However, unaccountable and repeated delays seemed to befuddle the issue of whether, from the official point of view, there were any North Vietnamese in the Pathet Lao-held areas of Laos.

The issue, coupled with the fighting on the Plain, grew to such proportions that the official Vietnam News Agency announced that all Vietnamese personnel had left Khang Khay in accordance with the agreements between the Democratic Republic of Vietnam and the Royal Lao Government. But on June 6, Souvanna Phouma declared that he had received reports of a convoy of trucks moving behind the Pathet Lao lines on the Plain. On June 8, in an interview with a British correspondent, the North Vietnamese Ambassador stated that the "construction workers" were still at Khang Khay and that "more than fifty" trucks had arrived to transport them back to North Vietnam. Hours later, however, the North Vietnamese embassy distributed a mimeographed communiqué to Western correspondents in Vientiane claiming that the Ambassador had been misquoted and that he had actually said that all Vietnamese at Khang Khay had departed four days previously. It was clear that the borderline between legal aid to the coalition government and illegal aid to one faction thereof had grown murky.

Close liaison between London and Moscow, repeated trips by both British and Soviet ambassadors to Khang Khay, and another high-level mission by Harriman to Khrushchev all elicited Soviet expressions of cooperation in preserving the *status quo* in Laos. But they produced neither a less truculent attitude on the part of the Pathet Lao nor a noticeable moderation in the line followed by Radio Hanoi and Radio Peking. "I fear that Soviet influence on Hanoi is not totally effective," Souvanna Phouma said on December 16, 1963.[9] Clearly, the Russians were still caught between wanting no further entanglement in Laos, a motivation reflected in their support for Souvanna Phouma's government, and wanting the support of the men in Hanoi, a motivation reflected in their reluctance to exert restrictive pressure upon the Pathet Lao.

The machinery set up at Geneva proved unable to control the ground situation in Laos, which had no agreed cease-fire line and hundreds of miles of unpatrolled borders. This was well illustrated by the diplomatic interchanges made in the name of the Geneva Conference during that summer of 1963. The Soviet Government, as one of the two Co-Chairmen of the Geneva Conference, based its messages to the Lao Government on minority reports by the Polish member of the ICC and on irregular communications from Souphanouvong at Khang Khay. The Soviets unilaterally published a number of these drafts, which placed the blame for violations of the Geneva Protocol on the United States and its Asian allies. The

[9] *The New York Times,* December 17, 1963.

British Government, the other Co-Chairman, found these accusations objectionable and responded by publishing and circulating to signatory governments sets of documents presenting both sides of the question.

The Soviet behavior, coupled with the Poles' simultaneous obstruction of the ICC (which did not go so far as to break up that body), indicates that the Soviets were willing to go along with the North Vietnamese presence in Laos on condition that Hanoi did not provoke a showdown leading to the collapse of the coalition government in Vientiane. In other words, the Soviets were prepared to guarantee, within reasonable limits, that North Vietnamese infractions of the Geneva Protocol would not be censured by the ICC so long as the North Vietnamese themselves did not give their game away.

The experience of the centrists during their alliance with the Pathet Lao between December, 1960, and the final break in April, 1963—when the extent of North Vietnamese direction was revealed for the first time—had been one of shock and disillusionment. This disillusionment was expressed in many ways. Nowhere had it set in so deeply as among the loyal officers and noncoms around Kong Le. These men, many of whom had returned to Laos from studies abroad in the autumn of 1960 to offer their services to the paratrooper captain, had genuinely believed that the best chance of extricating their country from the eddies of the Cold War lay in declaring peace with the Pathet Lao, whom the Americans had encouraged them to look upon as enemies for six years.

A major in Kong Le's army told the author, and his sentiments were typical, that he had first understood what a foothold the North Vietnamese had when he had been dispatched to pick up a jeep at Sop Nao in northern Laos in the autumn of 1961. There he found that the jeep was being held in a large camp that the North Vietnamese had established near the village. His efforts to obtain the jeep were rebuffed by the Vietnamese, who treated him like a stranger in his own country.

Widespread disgust with the Pathet Lao who had opened the door to the Vietnamese was reflected by Kong Le's soldiers during the tricky withdrawal from Xieng Khouang and Khang Khay in 1963. Kong Le's soldiers called the Pathet Lao *"kap kap,"* the Lao expression for toads, apparently because of their propensity for digging trenchworks, a technique they had learned from the victors of Dien Bien Phu.

The insecurity resulting from the fighting on the Plain of Jars led to the reinforcement of the North Vietnamese border-patrol in the first half of May by two battalions, which moved into the area around Nong Het. This raised to eleven the number of battalions on the Laos side of the border. They were located as follows: two in Sam Neua Province; two near Nong Het in Xieng Khouang Province; three in Khammouane Province near the passes over the central spine of the Annamite Mountains; two in Savannakhet Province north and south of Route Nationale 9; and two in Attopeu Province, well south of the Seventeenth Parallel. The evenness with which they were distributed from north to south indicated that their mission was to guard the whole border, keeping cross-border trails open.

Each battalion numbered about 450 men, and rotated back and forth across the border to well-provisioned camps. In these camps, each battalion's support troops remained in readiness to march up to the crest line if its front-line troops engaged in action. In the North Vietnamese view, these troops were under a chain of command entirely separate from that of the cadres who had been integrated into Pathet Lao battalions. The ratio of encadrement was about forty per battalion for specific purposes (political teams, artillery teams, communications teams, and vehicle-maintenance teams).

A North Vietnamese villager, in an interview published in the West at about this time, reported that among the tasks assigned to the people of his village to fulfill their thirty days' *corvée* labor for the central government was the transport of provisions to North Vietnamese troops serving in Laos. This work was placed in the same category as building roads, strengthening dikes, and constructing bridges, houses, supply stations, and provision depots, so it may be judged what importance Hanoi attached to the maintenance of these border-patrol troops.[10]

The airfield at Tchepone was the second point in Laos at which the North Vietnamese set up antiaircraft installations. When the Soviet airlift stopped and the Ilyushins were turned over to the North Vietnamese, Tchepone became an important landing field. The members of an ICC inspection mission arriving at Tchepone on April 13, 1963, were politely but firmly detained on the field; the local Pathet Lao commander refused to let them investigate the installations in the vicinity.

[10] P. J. Honey, "Village Life in North Vietnam," *China News Analysis* (Hong Kong), No. 486, September 20, 1963, p. 5.

Intelligence reports reaching Royal Army commanders testified to the seriousness of the Vietnamese foothold in southern Laos. During the dry season from September, 1962, to May, 1963, the Pathet Lao and their Vietnamese mentors completed work on two airstrips along the Vietnamese border south of Tchepone. A field at Chavane once used by the French and suitable for handling aircraft of the C-47 or Ilyushin-14 type, was rehabilitated, and a new field was constructed in a mountainous area of northern Saravane Province, near Ban Phaloung.

The Pathet Lao also made improvements in ground transportation in southern Laos by opening to truck traffic in the dry season a rough trail extending southward from Nhommarath to Muong Phine to Saravane. This strategic route through the mountains parallel to Route Nationale 13—envisaged but never completed by the Vichy administration—permitted the North Vietnamese to haul to South Vietnam loads too heavy to be carried by porters.

During April and May, 1963, Pathet Lao agents began appearing in villages on the left bank of the Kong River north of Attopeu to recruit coolie labor to carry supplies. Some 300 of them, interrogated by Phoumist agents upon their return to their home villages, revealed that they had carried wooden cases containing unknown goods from Chavane to a Pathet Lao supply depot at Sam Luang. Later, another 500 villagers were employed to carry similar cases from Sam Luang farther to the southeast, that is, toward the South Vietnamese border.

Installations used by the North Vietnamese in Attopeu Province were reported to include a rest camp at Vang Tat near the South Vietnam border for the use of Viet Cong insurgents, an infirmary at Pok Bay about six miles from the Cambodian border, a depot for food and arms at Phou Katom, a mountain also about six miles from the Cambodian border, and a small-plane airstrip at Hatha on the Cambodian border southeast of Attopeu town, on the Ho Chi Minh Trail.

During the spring of 1963, an unprecedented rice shortage developed in the southern reaches of the Mekong Valley around the island of Khong. This was attributed to Pathet Lao requisitioning of rice for transport eastward to supply the depots along the Vietnamese border. As a consequence, rice had to be flown in from Thailand by Air America aircraft to the populous Mekong Valley towns.

The privileged nature of this Vietnamese sanctuary in southern Laos was placed in question when, during a visit to South Vietnam in March, 1964, General Phoumi reached an agreement with

Premier Nguyen Khanh allowing South Vietnamese forces to pursue insurgents across the border into Laos. In view of the consolidation of the North Vietnamese security network in the Pathet Lao-held border region of southern Laos, however, the agreement between the two governments was likely to be more theoretical than real.

At the Edge of the Precipice

On December 20, 1963, representatives of the three factions met again on the Plain of Jars, where an uneasy temporary truce arranged by Kong Le and Singkapo prevailed. They issued a communiqué calling for a new meeting of the princes as soon as possible.

With the help of the ICC and the British and Soviet ambassadors, Souvanna Phouma and Souphanouvong met in Sam Neua from January 17 to 20, 1964, and reaffirmed their support for the principles previously negotiated. Further, reflecting the disquiet produced by the assassination of Quinim and other incidents in Vientiane, which was under the total control of rightist paramilitary police, the two princes announced they planned to move the coalition government to Luang Prabang, which would be demilitarized.

But the continued fighting, accompanied by the usual contradictory charges of foreign intervention, made a genuine reconciliation impossible. The Pathet Lao and North Vietnamese opened their dry season campaign at the end of January with attacks in central Laos and reopened attack against Kong Le's remaining positions on the Plain in February.

A pessimistic Souvanna Phouma left for official visits to Hanoi and Peking in early April with the question of North Vietnamese troops uppermost in his mind. He found the atmosphere in Hanoi grim. The North Vietnamese kept one of his trusted aides a virtual prisoner in his quarters for the duration of the visit, and allowed him barely a half-hour in which to read over their draft of the joint communiqué and make such changes as he deemed necessary. It was in the course of this visit that Souvanna Phouma became fully aware for the first time of the serious intent of the leaders in Hanoi to acquire the hegemony over Indochina that the French had possessed, regardless of the cost to themselves and to the native peoples. General Giap told Souvanna Phouma bluntly they could not tolerate the presence of troops on the Plain of Jars other than those of the Pathet Lao.[11]

[11] Interview of the author with Souvanna Phouma, Vientiane, April 8, 1970.

While Souvanna Phouma was in Hanoi and Peking, preparations had been going on for a new summit meeting on the Plain. On April 17, Souvanna Phouma, Souphanouvong, and Phoumi Nosavan met amid elaborate security precautions. They failed to reach any agreement. When the Prime Minister returned to Vientiane, he was in a mood of deep dejection, and he announced his decision to resign, since he had failed in his objective of restoring national unity.

In the early hours of April 19, the Phoumist commander of the Vientiane military region, Kouprasith Abhay, and the head of the paramilitary police, Siho Lamphouthacoul, both now risen to the rank of general, seized the moment to lead forces under their command in a putsch attempt. Ambassador Unger was absent from Vientiane. The generals arrested Souvanna Phouma.

12.

Unfulfilled Expectations

The events in Vientiane on the morning of April 19, 1964, marked a milestone in recent Lao history. Their importance was comparable to that of the events of August 8, 1960. The attempt by rightist officers to take matters into their own hands, although it failed almost from the start, shook the foundations of the coalition government more violently than had the departure of Prince Souphanouvong from the capital the previous year. In the tripartite structure of the National Union Government, Souphanouvong could claim that his decision to leave had been dictated by reasons of personal insecurity in rightist-controlled Vientiane and that his absence was temporary. How, on the other hand, could one believe that there was still good will when supporters of one of the three parties were declaring flatly that they had replaced the tripartite government? In the days that followed, as the war elsewhere in Indochina escalated, the various professions of support for the coalition government in Laos took on a hollow ring.

Firing broke out at 3 A.M., as troops acting under the orders of Generals Kouprasith and Siho moved to relieve centrist guards at various locations. The houses of both Prince Souvanna Phouma and Interior Minister Pheng Phongsavan were hit, and both men narrowly escaped injury. They were placed under arrest. Some 200 officers of the Centrist army and their families sought refuge in foreign missions. The radio, broadcasting in the name of a Revolutionary Committee, carried alarming and untruthful reports that Souvanna Phouma had resigned and Kong Le had associated himself with the coup, along with a series of charges about the coalition government and the ICC's failure to supervise the ceasefire.

General Phoumi's name was not included in the list of the members of the Revolutionary Committee.

The coup had arisen out of a complex combination of circumstances involving the relations among the armed forces and between the armed forces and the Cabinet, as well as the withdrawal of the NLHS ministers from Vientiane and the renewed fighting on the Plain of Jars. More than anything else, it was the failure of the National Union Government to function under the provisions of the agreements of 1961 and 1962 that created the conditions for the coup attempt.

Prince Souvanna Phouma's first action after the signature of the Declaration on the Neutrality of Laos and its Protocol was to go to Washington, where he met President Kennedy on July 27, 1962. The visit made up for the planned 1961 visit to Washington, cancelled when Souvanna Phouma thought he was being snubbed by Dean Rusk, and marked in the Prince's mind the American acceptance of him as Prime Minister at long last. Kennedy's Laos policy, indeed, hinged on strong support for the Prince by all agencies of the American Government and in conjunction with the Soviet Union. When Souvanna Phouma returned to Laos, where the tripartite commissions were holding their meetings, he used the assurances of support given him by Kennedy to request a resumption of deliveries of American military supplies to the rightist army, which had been cut off since the previous February.

The Positions of the Three Armies

The Prime Minister's request was supported by General Phoumi, who, while he held the post of Deputy Prime Minister, was no longer Defense Minister and no longer had troops under his direct command. Ambassador Unger recommended to Washington that deliveries of military supplies to the rightist army be resumed.[1] The supplies in question were described by Souvanna Phouma as "necessary supplies and repair parts to properly maintain U.S. furnished equipment, i.e., vehicles, aircraft, signal equipment, weapons," training ammunition, and "consumable supplies such as petroleum, oils and lubricants (POL), lumber, cement, and bulk clothing textiles."[2] Although he had retained the sensitive portfolio

[1] Message from Unger to State Department dated September 10, 1962, reproduced in *Hearings, IV,* p. 441.

[2] Letter from Souvanna Phouma to Unger dated September 10, 1962, in *Hearings, IV,* pp. 441–42.

of Defense Minister in the coalition, Souvanna Phouma was not a military man and in fact possessed a well-bred contempt for the military. His ignorance of military affairs was reflected in the statement in his letter that "the amount of supplies furnished" was to be based on the requirements for "operations under peacetime conditions." Laos was either at peace, in which case there could be no rationale for continuing to supply the huge rightist army, or it was at war, in which case there could be little hope of maintaining in being the new coalition government.

The centrist army under General Kong Le on the Plain of Jars was, for its part, dependent on the Soviet airlift for supplies for its Soviet-bloc weapons. The termination of this airlift was announced in November, 1962, however. From that time on, with the exception of the few transport planes furnished to all three factions in response to Souvanna Phouma's plea in October, the Soviet Union ceased to deliver any military equipment to any faction in Laos. A portion of the military supplies delivered by both the Soviet Union and China to North Vietnam, however, found their way to the Pathet Lao. By the spring of 1963, the supply position of the centrist army had become critical, and Kong Le himself commented to a Yugoslav journalist, "The Russians have betrayed us." In these circumstances, the resumption of delivery of American military supplies to Kong Le was announced by the State Department on May 12, 1963.

The NLHS, finally, proposed in the Committee for Integration of the Armed Forces that the pledge of a unified national army contained in the Zurich communiqué be implemented by taking 10,000 men and officers from each of the armies of the three factions. Tripartite agreement on this proposal was reached on November 27, but further discussion was stalled by the leader of the rightist delegation, Kouprasith Abhay.[3] The committee thus never really came to grips with the problem of procedures for integration, which had proved to be the undoing of the 1957 agreement. As the National Union Government did not succeed in forming a national army, there was obviously no agreement on military supplies for such an army, and the statement by Prince Souphanouvong that the government "did not once discuss the question of the needs of national

[3] See the communiqué of November 27, 1962, in Notes et Études Documentaires, No. 3189, May 10, 1965, *L'Evolution de la Situation au Laos; Chronologie (Juin 1962–Avril 1963)*, p. 26. The text of the Zurich communiqué is in Appendix VII.

defense, not to speak of taking any decision concerning the introduction of foreign arms into Laos" is substantially correct.[4]

With a renewed flow of military aid from the United States, the rightist army was bolstered just when Souvanna Phouma, as Prime Minister of the National Union Government, should have been pushing for tripartite agreement on demobilization and integration of the armed forces as one of the essential steps toward neutralization. Instead, rightist units were dispatched to reinforce centrist garrisons in certain areas, notably on the Plain of Jars, where Kong Le's troops faced heavily equipped Pathet Lao and dissident centrist forces backed by the North Vietnamese. At the end of April, 1963, rightist troops recaptured Tha Thom and Tha Vieng.

Kouprasith, who was commander of the Vientiane Military Region, was pressing to gain control over the centrist forces stationed at Vang Vieng, which fell under his territorial area of responsibility. These centrists received their orders and supplies from a *cabinet spécial* set up in Vientiane under Souvanna Phouma's immediate authority, and their ranks included a number of Kouprasith's soldiers who had deserted in the heat of battle in 1960 and joined Kong Le in his retreat from Vientiane.

Simultaneously with this increase in tension among the still separate armies, a newly created paramilitary police force appeared on the scene. Effective police control in Vientiane remained in the hands of the rightist faction after formation of the National Union Government, although relatively small detachments of centrist and NLHS security forces were posted in the city for the personal protection of members of the government. In this situation, the De-

---

[4] Message dated May 18, 1963, from Prince Souphanouvong to the Co-Chairmen protesting the State Department's announcement of delivery of military supplies to the centrists, reproduced in *Une Année pour l'Application des Accords de Genève de 1962 sur le Laos* (Le Comité Central du Neo Lao Hak Sat, 1963), pp. 57–58. Ambassador Sullivan claimed in 1969 that he did not know whether Souphanouvong had endorsed the earlier request by Phoumi and Souvanna Phouma for American military supplies for the rightist army. (See *Hearings, IV*, p. 443.) In a conversation with the author on September 11, 1970, Ambassador Unger maintained that Souvanna Phouma had informed him that Souphanouvong had agreed to request aid from the United States and the Soviet Union. This last assertion seems to come closest to the truth: The American Embassy was not anxious to question the assurance given by Souvanna Phouma, while the NLHS undoubtedly maintained silence, giving the impression of assent, until it felt that its protest against U.S. military aid would bolster the legitimacy of its withdrawal from Vientiane. The rightist army continued to call itself the Royal Lao Army as before.

partment of National Coordination under General Siho, with three battalions of what were euphemistically known as border police, armed with heavy weapons, increasingly enforced their own law. Siho's police swaggered about town looking for ways in which to provoke incidents with the centrists and NLHS and did not hesitate to come to blows with rightist army men. They attempted to intimidate the NLHS ministers by surrounding their houses. Their actions broke up negotiations for the return of NLHS ministers to Vientiane in September, 1963, when a Pathet Lao guard was found shot dead. And when the April 19, 1964, coup broke out, their actions in stopping and searching the Indian and Polish members of the ICC at roadblocks, cutting off electricity and water to their houses, and harassing the French effectively blocked a return to neutrality in Vientiane.[5]

General Phoumi, as leader of the rightist faction in the National Union Government, theoretically had command over both Kouprasith and Siho, and on more than one occasion, at risk to himself, he admonished them to use restraint.[6] In one incident, Siho's police surrounded Phoumi's house on the pretext of ensuring his security; on the day of the coup attempt, Phoumi's son, who was a pilot in the Royal Lao Air Force, took off from his base in southern Laos intending to bomb Vientiane in the belief that the coup leaders had arrested his father but was turned away by a message saying that his father was safe. Phoumi himself, in an interview at the time, said that the coup attempt had "made things difficult" for him and his political future was obscure.[7] That there were personal grievances, as well as doubts of Phoumi's anti-Communist position, among Kouprasith's subordinate; (fighting had broken out briefly at one point at Vang Vieng between rightist and centrist soldiers) was made clear by Kouprasith in an interview in which, after allowing that he respected Phoumi, he went on to add that "some things he has done with the economy of the nation are wrong, including the introduction of gambling and the monopolies. Some things he has done have helped to support and strengthen the Communists in their attack on us."[8] There can be no doubt that these

[5] The turbulent events of this period provided the inspiration for Jean Lartéguy's novel *Les Tambours de Bronze* (Paris: Presses de la Cité, 1965), in whose pages many of the persons involved can easily be recognized.

[6] Conversation of the author with General Phoumi in Bangkok, June 11, 1970.

[7] *Bangkok Post*, May 6, 1964.

[8] *Bangkok Post*, May 7, 1964.

conflicts on several levels led finally to the climactic confrontation a few months later in which Phoumi lost his position.

Rumors that trouble was brewing had been circulating in Vientiane for several days before the April 19, 1964, coup attempt. The generals may have received forewarnings of a renewed offensive on the Plain of Jars. There had been some fighting earlier in the year in Khammouane Province, mainly directed against the centrists, and it was not unnatural to suppose that Pathet Lao forces would try to drive Kong Le from the Plain; they had been well supplied with Russian equipment, and, although it was too late in the year to envisage an extended push, they were quite capable of securing the western portion of the Plain before the rains.

It seems unlikely that the generals would have acted without at least tacit encouragement from South Vietnam and Thailand, both of which harbored reservations about the 1962 agreement and shared the rightists' ill will toward the coalition experiment. It will be recalled that Phoumi had visited Dalat in March for talks with General Nguyen Khanh, who had been given the green light by the Americans only a few weeks previously for his successful coup overthrowing the regime of General Duong Van Minh, whom Khanh accused of adopting a neutralist policy influenced by French thinking. Khanh, who at this time was an advocate of bombing attacks against North Vietnam,[9] was being demonstratively backed by Defense Secretary Robert S. McNamara. The Thai Government, for its part, was aware of American contingency planning for a bombing campaign against the North requiring the use of air bases in Thailand and would naturally have assumed that the United States, in the event of such a contingency, planned to extend the hard-line policy to Laos as well.[10]

[9] Conversations of the author with General Khanh in Paris during 1968 and 1969. On June 25 and 30, more than 30 men belonging to the South Vietnamese Special Forces were reported to have parachuted into the Tchepone region. (Letter from Phoumi Vongvichit to ICC Chairman Ashok B. Bhadkamkar dated September 28, 1964, reproduced in *Message No. 35 of 16 September 1965 from the International Commission for Supervision and Control in Laos to the Co-Chairmen of the Geneva Conference,* pp. 33–36.)

[10] "By mid-1964, the situation in both Laos and Vietnam was increasingly threatening. In mid-1964, we and the Thai agreed to engage in bilateral contingency planning so that we would be better prepared to meet an emergency if it should arise and if both Governments should decide to act." (Statement by Ambassador Unger on security relations between the United States and Thailand in *Hearings,* V, p. 615.) In March, 1964, the United States moved the first six F-100's to the Royal Thai Air Force Base at Takhli. (*Ibid.*)

The final push that set the coup attempt in motion was supplied by Souvanna Phouma himself when he announced his readiness to resign, following the failure of the long-awaited tripartite summit meeting on the Plain of Jars on April 17. The generals then moved.

But if Kouprasith and Siho were hoping that President Johnson's approach to the conflict in Laos would differ from Kennedy's, they were disappointed. They shortly discovered, in one of those turnabouts that Laos produces, that the United States was determined that Souvanna Phouma should survive, while Hanoi and Peking wanted to see him discredited. Ambassador Unger hurried back to Vientiane from Saigon and assured the Prince (in a conversation between a second-floor balcony where the latter was being held prisoner and the roadside beyond the garden fence) that the United States still supported the National Union Government. Unger and the other Western ambassadors also called on Phoumi and asked him to do what he could to restore order in the government and armed forces. The King, after a meeting at Luang Prabang with Souvanna Phouma, Phoumi, and the generals, also made known his opposition.

Balked in their bid for power, the members of the Revolutionary Committee issued a communiqué on April 23 stating that the coalition would continue in office, although a "committee of national defense" would preside. The next day, a communiqué was issued, following a Cabinet meeting presided over by Souvanna Phouma, saying that there was continuity of the National Union Government. General Phoumi was to take over the Defense Ministry, and the *cabinet spécial* of the centrist army was to be removed from Vientiane (it went to Vang Vieng).

In an attempt to untangle the lines of command and supply of the rightist and centrist armies, on May 2 Souvanna Phouma announced an agreement between the rightists and centrists, as a result of which the former were dissolved and henceforth accepted his leadership. He also said that he had taken back control of the Defense Ministry from General Phoumi and that the rightist and centrist armies would be merged. This merger did not in fact take place, although new arrangements were made whereby General Ouan Ratikon, the senior general in length of service, became Commander-in-Chief, and other generals were given new staff jobs or regional commands or retained their previous posts. From this time on, the commanders of Laos's five military regions acquired power and influence resembling in their absoluteness the power of ancient warlords; they stayed on indefinitely in their fiefs, unless disgraced, and they refused to allow any of their troops to be transferred, even temporarily, to the command of another region, a fact that considerably hampered effective planning against the Pathet Lao.

As had happened before, the United States was caught up in a train of events it had failed to foresee. The rationale for resuming the delivery of American supplies to the rightist army in 1962 was that North Vietnamese forces remained in Laos after the signing of the Geneva agreement, and they were backing Pathet Lao forces equipped with a large quantity of Soviet arms.[11] The resumption of American deliveries was actually recommended by Unger on September 10, 1962, that is to say almost a month before the October 7 deadline for the withdrawal of all foreign troops from Laos, including the North Vietnamese, and was justified by him on the basis of the exception contained in Article 6 of the Geneva Protocol:

> The introduction into Laos of armaments, munitions, and war material generally, except such quantities of conventional armaments as the Royal Government of Laos may consider necessary for the national defense of Laos, is prohibited.

The "national defense of Laos" was the same mirage that had led John Foster Dulles to equip a 25,000-man army with tanks and artillery in the 1950's; it is surprising that President Kennedy did not perceive that new shipments of arms to the Royal Lao Government would undermine his Laos policy of neutralization, because it provoked the very danger it was meant to prevent—a civil war that invited foreign intervention. The similarity between 1962 and the 1950's extends even to the resurrection of the old Programs Evaluation Office (PEO) under the new name of Requirements Office.[12] Later, this disguised military aid mission supplied whole aircraft, as well as repair parts, and ammunition for purposes other than training.

---

[11] As Sullivan later testified, "There was a great deal of artillery, a great deal of other items of equipment that made Souvanna fear that these were being turned or could be turned against his government and he, therefore, needed equipment to provide forces for defense against that." (*Hearings, IV*, p. 443.)

[12] The existence of this office as early as October 12, 1962, is confirmed by the letter from Unger to Souvanna Phouma of that date in *Hearings, IV*, p. 442. Like the old PEO, this office was staffed by retired military personnel in civilian clothes working under the cover of the economic aid mission in Vientiane but actually placed under the direct authority of the American military aid mission in Thailand (see *Ibid.*, pp. 527–28).

The Kennedy Administration's action in supplying military equipment to Prince Souvanna Phouma for use by the rightist army was taken without the unanimous approval of the tripartite Lao Government as required by the Plain of Jars Agreement. This clear flouting of the spirit of the Geneva Protocol contributed in large measure to the NLHS decision to withdraw its ministers from Vientiane in 1963. Inasmuch as this withdrawal by the NLHS encouraged the rightist opportunists in their uncooperative behavior, the American actions in the autumn of 1962, no less than the North Vietnamese actions, led directly to the attempted coup of April 19, 1964, and to the Pathet Lao and North Vietnamese retaliatory advance on the Plain of Jars, which in turn precipitated hostilities between the United States and North Vietnam several weeks prior to the famed Gulf of Tonkin incident, on a front that was for both countries far removed from the main focus of interest.

It is difficult to avoid the impression that a Prime Minister of the National Union Government who conceived of his position in a less exalted manner and an American President with a little more foresight might yet have succeeded in tamping down the flames of war in northern Laos. President Kennedy's "strategy" of supplying arms to the centrists was successful in that it halted the dependence of the centrists on Communist arms and "ended the alliance between the neutralists [centrists] and the Pathet Lao."[13] Why he failed to apply the same "strategy" to ending the alliance between the Pathet Lao and the North Vietnamese remains a mystery. In any event, the expectations that had been raised by the Geneva agreement and the launching of the second coalition in 1962 went unfulfilled. By 1964, it seemed that none of the countries involved in Laos possessed the influence or the will to arrest the slide toward a resumption of the fighting.

Kong Le Is Driven from the Plain of Jars

On April 27, 1964, after a lull of two months, fighting broke out in the Phou San Massif northeast of the Plain of Jars. The Pathet Lao radio claimed the fighting had been initiated by rightist troops. Souvanna Phouma, apparently reversing the earlier decision gradually to reinforce Kong Le's positions in that strategic place, declared that, in his capacity as Defense Minister, he had ordered that the rightist troops in the sector be replaced by centrists; the fighting, he said, had broken out while this replacement was in

[13] Arthur M. Schlesinger, Jr., *A Thousand Days* (Boston: Houghton Mifflin, 1965), p. 517.

process, and he warned the Pathet Lao that, unless it was brought to a halt, the rightists could not be taken out.

At the same time, on the political front, Souvanna Phouma gave two absent Cabinet ministers belonging to his own Neutralist Party, the Phak Pen Kang, eight days to return to Vientiane and, when they failed to do so, announced their replacement. They were Khamsouk Keola, Minister of Public Health, and General Heuan Mongkhonvilay, Secretary of State for Veterans Affairs. Both had left Vientiane in 1963 because of the tension created by Siho's police. Khamsouk, after being expelled from the Central Committee of the Neutralist Party, had gone to the Soviet Union and China without authorization and had eventually gone to Cambodia, where he learned of his dismissal from the Cabinet. Since both men belonged to Souvanna Phouma's party, the latter was entitled to replace them in the Cabinet, but the NLHS reacted by charging that the Prime Minister had violated the 1962 Plain of Jars agreement. Souvanna Phouma was now left with only Prince Sisoumang Sisaleumsak at his side from the tiny band of centrists who had rallied to him on the Plain of Jars in the equally dark days of February, 1961.[14]

The ICC had informed the Co-Chairmen three days after the coup attempt of the danger that the coalition might break up. On May 1, a joint message from Britain and the Soviet Union was sent through the Prime Minister to the three factions and to the other signatories of the Geneva Protocol. It condemned the attempted coup, confirmed the Co-Chairmen's full support for the tripartite government under Prince Souvanna Phouma, and expressed the hope that the three leaders, as well as the governments of all the states concerned, would adhere strictly to the Geneva Protocol.

In an effort to unruffle Prince Souphanouvong's feathers, Souvanna Phouma met Souphanouvong at the Plain of Jars on May 4. Souphanouvong claimed that Souvanna Phouma had become a prisoner of the rightists and that the government in Vientiane no longer conformed to previous agreements. He said that, as the 1962 Plain of Jars agreement provided for unanimity on important decisions taken by the National Union Government, any decisions taken by the government in Vientiane in his absence were void. Souvanna Phouma retorted that the government would not allow

14 See p. 182, above. Prince Sisoumang was related both to Souvanna Phouma and to the reigning branch of the royal family of Luang Prabang. His mother, Princess Sangakham, was Souvanna Phouma's sister, and his father, Prince Sisaleumsak, was the eldest son of King Zakarine.

itself to be paralyzed by the absence of ministers from the capital. Unfortunately for the Prime Minister's case, Kong Le had just been compelled to cable the rightist generals in Vientiane his pledge to support them so long as they continued to keep Souvanna Phouma in his post of Prime Minister.

As Kong Le had expected, the adversary launched a new attack on May 13 against his positions in the center of the Plain, with the intention of cutting off his garrison at Xieng Khouang town. Fierce artillery barrages three days later compelled him to abandon his command post at Muong Phanh. The NLHS claimed that some of Kong Le's soldiers had mutinied. By the end of May, these "patriotic neutralists" under Colonel Deuan Sunnalath, together with the Pathet Lao, occupied virtually all that portion of the Plain that had been held jointly by Kong Le and the Pathet Lao two years previously and had also moved southeastward from Xieng Khouang as far as Tha Thom. Incensed at evidence provided from the Plain of direct North Vietnamese intervention on the side of the Pathet Lao, Souvanna Phouma exhibited North Vietnamese identification cards and other documents recovered in the fighting. When he had been at Khang Khay and had seen the North Vietnamese troops there, Souvanna Phouma had declared in his talks with North Vietnamese diplomats that he would never allude to the presence of these troops in Laos so long as they left promptly after the ceasefire. Now, that hope had vanished.

It was only natural that the North Vietnamese should have attached so much importance to the destruction of Kong Le and his small army on the Plain of Jars. Kong Le was, after all, the very symbol of genuine neutralism in Laos, and genuine neutralism worked to the detriment of the North Vietnamese, with their ulterior motives. His competence in military tactics, often in the face of superior odds, his popularity with men, and the obvious sincerity, even naïveté, of his personality all lent particular weight to his statements to the ICC observers on the Plain about the extent of the North Vietnamese intervention. Hanoi had not admitted in 1962, as it had in 1954, the presence of "Vietnamese People's Volunteer Forces" in Laos, and so the reports of a witness of Kong Le's stature, one who did not feel himself impeded by diplomatic considerations, were doubly embarrassing to Hanoi. Kong Le represented a bone in the throat of the leaders in Hanoi, and an intolerable rival to the opportunist Deuan, should they decide to put forward the "patriotic neutralists" as a replacement for Souvanna Phouma's centrists.

On May 13, the day of the fresh attacks against Kong Le, Souvanna Phouma wrote to the Chairman of the ICC asking that the ICC "organize one or more mobile observer teams to go on the spot" to investigate the situation in the vicinity of Tha Thom, on the ICC's authority under Article 8 of the Geneva Protocol.[15] The ICC had maintained an observer team on the Plain since April, 1963. On May 16 and 17, its position near Muong Phanh was struck in the artillery shelling, and its three members were evacuated. Souvanna Phouma convoked the ICC members and British and Russian ambassadors on May 17 and strongly protested the actions on the Plain that had forced the withdrawal of the only ICC team anywhere in Laos outside Vientiane.[16]

In its last report, which was published only on June 20 and from which the signature of the Polish representative was missing, the ICC team on the Plain reported that the size, direction, and scale of the attacks of May 16 and 17 warranted the assumption that they were the work of far more than a small number of defected neutralists, as claimed by the NLHS. "The consequences that could flow from the changes in military postures of the opposing forces in Laos" were disturbing, the ICC reported. "These are of two kinds. Those who have successfully acquired terrain may be encouraged thereby to seek further military gains; those who have lost territory could be led to embark on retaliatory action."[17]

With the Co-Chairmen unable to exert concerted influence to stop the fighting, or even to agree on its origin, and with Prince Norodom Sihanouk's proposal to reconvene the fourteen-nation conference to deal with Laos and also prepare for an international meeting "to deal with . . . the whole of the former Indochina" going unheeded, Souvanna Phouma on May 19 sent letters to the British and Russian ambassadors in Vientiane requesting that they arrange consultations on the spot.

The Poles now found themselves in an awkward position, as Souvanna Phouma appeared determined to expose the North Vietnamese role in the fighting. The Polish delegate solved his em-

---

[15] Ministère des Affaires Étrangères, *L'Ingérence Nord-Vietnamienne au Laos* (Vientiane: 1964), pp. 25–26.

[16] *Ibid.*, p. 34. The Indian colonel commanding the observer team on the Plain was so shaken by the artillery shelling of May 16 and 17 that during tea with the British military attaché (representing the Co-chairman) before the team's evacuation, his teacup and saucer clattered. Kong Le, as usual, was unruffled.

[17] *Ibid.*, p. 38.

barrassment by claiming that he was being held practically under house arrest by Phoumist guards, among whom feeling was running high because of the events on the Plain, and departed for Warsaw, leaving instructions that his alternate was not authorized to stand in for him at ICC meetings.

On May 21, the United States announced that American jets were making reconnaissance flights over Laos at the request of Prince Souvanna Phouma's government to help gather information on the intentions and dispositions of the Communist forces. Such information would be handed over immediately to the ICC. While these flights were technically a breach of the Geneva agreement, the American statement said, they were justified by the repeated Communist violations of the agreement and by the Pathet Lao's refusal to allow the ICC access to territory under its control.

When Souphanouvong cabled on May 30 requesting the return of the remaining NLHS Cabinet ministers, Prince Souk Vongsak and Kampheuane Tounalom, and the 100 Pathet Lao guards who had been living in Vientiane, Souvanna Phouma replied that they would be sent, in the care of the ICC, to Hanoi, where Souphanouvong would no doubt arrange to contact them. Subsequent arrangements were made to keep a junior NLHS representative in Vientiane, as well as the Pathet Lao guards.

Souvanna Phouma also announced that the current business of the absent NLHS ministers would henceforth be handled by other members of the Cabinet. Souphanouvong construed this as a further departure from the Plain of Jars agreement and, in letters to the Co-Chairmen on June 3, stated that he no longer recognized Souvanna Phouma as Prime Minister of the tripartite coalition government.[18] He was supported by the Poles, who contended that the signatories of the Geneva agreement had an obligation to maintain in being the tripartite structure of the Lao Government. This again revealed the Poles' contradictory attitude, as they had been the loudest to defend the "sovereignty" of Laos at Geneva. William Sullivan, who arrived in Vientiane in late 1964 to replace Ambassador Unger, challenged them on this point by pointing out that the Geneva agreement contained no mention of the Plain of Jars agreement. Perhaps this was an unwise position to take, however, because the revision of the strict interpretation of tripartism it implied was to produce other, equally dangerous, complications, of which the April 19 coup attempt had provided a foretaste.

[18] For the evolution of the NLHS position on the legality of the Vientiane government, see below, p. 279.

American Air Strikes

The American reconnaissance flights had been acknowledged by the State Department only after their existence had been reported by the New China News Agency. They were then acknowledged by Souvanna Phouma in response to reporters' questions. On June 6, the Pathet Lao downed one of the planes and captured its pilot, broadcasting his name and serial number. The following day a second jet was downed, and the State Department disclosed that it was an armed escort for a reconnaissance flight that had originated from aircraft carriers in the South China Sea. In retaliation, six F-100 jet fighter-bombers, flying from South Vietnam, rocketed Pathet Lao installations, including an anti-aircraft position. Now Souvanna Phouma became alarmed by the growing chorus of denunciation from Hanoi and Peking. He threatened to resign unless the United States ceased the attacks, about which he said he had not been informed in advance. He later announced to the press that all flights had been stopped. Two days later, however, following a conference with Unger, he said that the suspension had been only temporary, to bring about a "calm in the operation zones." New information, he declared, "shows that important movements of Pathet Lao and Viet Minh [North Vietnamese] troops are taking place." The American reconnaissance flights with escorts resumed.

As Souvanna Phouma later explained his assent to the flights, the verbal agreement that he had reached with Unger to permit escorted American reconnaissance flights over Communist-occupied portions of Laos was a direct result of the lie Souphanouvong had had the gall to tell him about the origin of the fighting.[19] Since

---

[19] As of April 17, 1970, when the author was able to verify this fact with an American official in Vientiane in a position to know, the verbal agreement with Unger was the only bilateral agreement in existence that provided authority for American air action over Laos. The author does not consider this unusual, however, given the Prime Minister's strong personal feelings, expressed on numerous occasions, about what he interpreted as Hanoi's betrayal, and the view shared by himself and Unger that the measures undertaken by the United States had been made necessary by the other side's violations of the Geneva agreement and were strictly temporary. It has been officially stated that these measures never figured prominently in discussions between Souvanna Phouma and Presidents Kennedy, Johnson, and Nixon: "In these meetings over the years, there has been extremely little discussion of U.S. military activities in Laos." (*Hearings, IV,* p. 441.)

Souphanouvong had told him that the Pathet Lao[20] and North Vietnamese were not involved, Souvanna Phouma decided to take matters into his own hands and ask the United States to fly reconnaissance missions along the roads leading from North Vietnam into Laos. Under cover of a letter dated June 16, Souvanna Phouma sent three aerial photographs of a convoy of North Vietnamese troops in the Mu Gia Pass heading for Laos to the Chairman of the ICC for forwarding to the Co-Chairmen.

On June 11, while the temporary suspension of American flights was still in effect, an attack by T-28 propeller fighter-bombers, which had recently been furnished to the Royal Lao Air Force, on the Chinese Economic and Cultural Mission at Khang Khay killed one Chinese, Kao Yun-peng, and wounded five others. The United States disclaimed responsibility. *The New York Times,* however, revealed that some of the T-28 pilots were nationals of Thailand. A journalist who inspected one of the planes close up found that its markings were painted on reversible panels—Lao on one side and Thai on the other. Bombing operations on the Plain of Jars continued heavy into July.[21]

The attack on the Chinese mission at Khang Khay came on the heels of the most severe warning statements from Peking on the situation in Laos so far. On May 26, Foreign Minister Marshal Chen Yi declared:

> The Chinese Government believes that Prince Phouma fully understands that, by working for the cooperation of the three Lao groups as the leader of the neutralist [centrist] group, he is respected by the Lao people, and that otherwise, if he becomes the leader of the Rightist Phoumist group, which is alleged to have incorporated both the neutralist [centrist] and Rightist [Phoumist] groups, he will completely forfeit his political standing. The neutralist [centrist] group represents a social force that objectively exists in Laos. People are bound to come forward to raise the banner of the neutralist [centrist] group.[22]

[20] This part of Souphanouvong's lie was exposed when the New China News Agency reported on October 24, 1964, that the Pathet Lao unit responsible for the capture of Phou Kout on the western fringe of the Plain of Jars was among fifteen such units awarded medals for valiant action.

[21] See the diary of a North Vietnamese soldier who was on the Plain at that time, reproduced in *Message No. 35, op. cit.,* pp. 120–28.

[22] New China News Agency, May 26, 1964; *People's Daily* (Peking), May 27, 1964.

And in a lengthy statement on the situation on June 9, the Chinese Government concluded:

> Owing to the intervention and aggression by the United States and its followers, the Government in Vientiane is no longer the original Laotian Government of National Union, Prince Souvanna Phouma has descended from the position of Premier of the Government of National Union to that of a government controlled by the rightist group, the Geneva agreements are in danger of being completely wrecked, and Laos has been pushed to the brink of a total split and a general civil war.[23]

"Civil war" had been the term the Chinese used to describe the ominous situation in Laos in the spring of 1959.[24]

The consultations Souvanna Phouma had requested in May finally began in Vientiane in June, 1964, with the ambassadors of Britain, France, the United States, Canada, South Vietnam, Thailand, and India taking part. With India abstaining, the consultants on June 29 "condemned the recent Pathet Lao attacks on the neutralist [centrist] forces of General Kong Le, attacks clearly made with North Vietnamese assistance, as being in flagrant violation of the Geneva agreements. In the course of this study, evidence was produced concerning the use by North Vietnam of Lao territory to interfere in the internal affairs of the Republic of Vietnam." The evidence included aerial photographs of trucks making their way southward through Laos toward the long, open border of South Vietnam. Whereas up to now the American Government had followed the practice of compartmentalizing Laos and South Vietnam as separate problems, this first public condemnation of North Vietnam for having violated Article 2(i) of the Geneva agreement[25] indicated that a new practice was emerging. This practice was formalized a few months later when the first of a series of periodic meetings among the ambassadors in Laos, South Vietnam, and Thailand, together with the American military commander in Saigon, was held to discuss matters of a secret nature connected with the war.[26]

The initial acceptance by the United States of the presence of North Vietnamese troops in Laos after the deadline for withdrawal

---

[23] New China News Agency, June 9, 1964; *People's Daily* (Peking), June 10, 1964.

[24] See p. 135, above.

[25] See Appendix V.

[26] *Hearings, IV,* pp. 479–80. The date was November, 1964.

came now to be regarded in Washington as a mistake. When the acceptance of the removal of the token ICC observation team from the area of Communist control was demanded in addition, the United States reacted by publicly justifying reconnaissance missions over Laos. These developments strengthened the hand of those in Washington who felt that the leaders in Hanoi should be taught a lesson and that North Vietnam should be made to pay for its unacknowledged military involvement in Laos and South Vietnam. The combination of Hanoi's demonstrated intention to make use of the trails through Laos (the actual use was still small) in disregard of the provisions of the 1962 Geneva agreement and the deteriorating military and political situation of the Saigon government was worrisome. When an American destroyer and three North Vietnamese torpedo boats exchanged gunfire off the Red River delta on August 2, U.S. Navy aircraft were diverted from their missions over Laos in order to attack bases inside North Vietnam itself. At the same time, the State Department announced that a formal protest was being directed to Hanoi through the ICC. The U.S. Congress voted a resolution, the "Tonkin Gulf" resolution, granting President Johnson extraordinary powers to resist Communist actions in Southeast Asia as he saw fit.

The Soviet Union, meanwhile, had been placed in a new dilemma by the events in Laos. Soviet influence with the Pathet Lao had virtually disappeared, and Chinese influence with North Vietnam had been riding high since Liu Shao-chi's visit to Hanoi in April, 1963. Soviet statements condemned the United States for "provocative flights" over Laos and contended that Prince Souvanna Phouma's authorization for the flights, of which he had notified the Soviet Union and Britain on June 19, did not conform to the Declaration on the Neutrality of Laos.[27] On July 26, a communication from the Soviet Government to the participants in the Geneva Conference called for a reconvening of the Conference. It went on to state that, in the event that other states adopted a negative attitude to the Soviet proposal, the Soviet Union would have to reconsider the continuance of its function as Co-Chairman. A British mission finally hurried to Moscow to persuade the Soviet leaders not to relinquish their responsibility in Indochina. The fall of Khrushchev a few weeks later, however, and the start of the American bombing of North Vietnam ensured the continued Soviet commitment in Southeast Asia.

[27] See Appendix V.

The Paris Summit

On August 8, Prince Souphanouvong proposed in a message to Souvanna Phouma that a tripartite summit meeting be held in Paris to discuss the situation. After several weeks of preliminary negotiations, the meeting opened on September 21, 1964. It became clear from Souphanouvong's charges of American "aggression" (he claimed thirty-four American planes had been shot down) that the NLHS leader intended for the meeting to adopt his version of what had happened on the Plain earlier in the year. He said the Plain had been under the joint control of the NLHS and centrists ever since its capture from Phoumist forces in December, 1960. He argued that this state of affairs had been upset by the merger of Kong Le's army with the rightists under American pressure, which had led to further defections from Kong Le's forces to those of Deuan. Nevertheless, persons present at the meeting noted that Souphanouvong appeared cheerful and optimistic about the possibility of finding a settlement. Significantly, perhaps, he did not repeat his earlier statement withdrawing recognition from Souvanna Phouma as Prime Minister.

Prince Boun Oum had meanwhile departed for Nice, leaving the rightist delegation to be led by Ngon Sananikone, Minister for Public Works. Ngon returned home one morning at 4:00, after a round of nightclubbing, only to be awakened three hours later by an urgent telephone call from Souvanna Phouma. The latter had been meeting with Souphanouvong over breakfast and reported that the two of them had agreed to return control of the Plain to centrist forces. The Prime Minister asked agreement of the rightist faction to this plan, which would have involved, in Souphanouvong's words, "reintegration" of the centrist forces.

Ngon requested time to consult General Phoumi in Vientiane. He sent an urgent message to the general through the American Embassy in Paris, a perfectly normal practice, since the Lao did not have secure communications of their own. Phoumi refused to give his agreement, perhaps because he sensed that President Johnson was moving inexorably toward a harder line in the war. When Ngon informed the two princes, Souphanouvong became furious. Shaking his finger at Ngon, he exclaimed, "All right, you want to fight. We shall fight."[28] The meeting broke up without agreement on any substantive issue and in a poor atmosphere. An

[28] Conversation of the author with Ngon Sananikone, Vientiane, April 8, 1970.

opportunity to reopen negotiations may have been missed by a hair's breadth.

On June 23, 1965, the third anniversary of the formation of the National Union Government, the NLHS published a memorandum in which it was stated that "the present Vientiane authorities of whom Prince Souvanna Phouma is Prime Minister are in reality nothing but puppet authorities, antipopular, antinational, and 100 per cent in the service of the American policy of aggression."[29]

The NLHS position on the illegality of the Vientiane government continued to harden, so that by the seventh anniversary of the formation of the National Union Government in 1969 it was stated as follows:

> In the light of above-said facts and developments, we may come to the following conclusions:
>
> 1. The Laotian Tripartite National Coalition Government set up in 1962 has been completely sabotaged by the United States and their stooges; the tripartite form of 1962 has been abolished by them; hence, the 1961–62 tripartite agreements have also been scrapped.
>
> 2. The present Vientiane administration is definitely not the Tripartite National Coalition Government but only a product and a tool of U.S. neocolonialism and a completely illegal and antinational and antipopular administration.
>
> Prince Phouma, who heads that administration, is no longer the Prime Minister of the Tripartite National Coalition Government nor leader of the Neutralist Party. He has become a traitor, capitulationist, a follower of the United States and the Rightist Party, and a tool of the U.S. aggressors. His party also is no longer the Neutralist Party but has integrated itself into the Rightist Party and become its tail. Therefore the present Vientiane administration and Prince Phouma cannot speak in the name of the Tripartite National Coalition Government, have no quality to represent legally anyone in the settlement of any problems in the domestic as well as foreign relations of the country. They are only their own representatives.[30]

Improvement of the Ho Chi Minh Trail

From the autumn of 1964, the undeclared war between the United States and North Vietnam in Laos, which had been barely interrupted by the signing of the Geneva Protocol in 1962, gathered

[29] *Memorandum of the Central Committee of the Neo Lao Hak Sat on the Third Anniversary of the Signing of the Geneva Accords on Laos* (June 23, 1965) (n.p.: Neo Lao Hak Sat Editions, 1965).

[30] Memorandum dated June 23, 1969, broadcast by the NLHS radio in English on July 8, 1969.

momentum as the photographic evidence brought back by American reconnaissance planes revealed indisputable North Vietnamese intentions to enlarge their lines of communication through Laos to South Vietnam.

On October 16 and 17, American fighter-bombers bombed and strafed the area northeast of Tchepone claimed by North Vietnam as Huong Lap.[31] Whether the attack was in reply to the firing by the North Vietnamese on American reconnaissance planes or whether it was to protect Royal Lao Air Force planes bombing in that area was not clear. In response to a North Vietnamese Foreign Ministry statement demanding that the Royal Lao Government forbid the use of Laos by the United States as a base for attacks on North Vietnam, the Foreign Ministry in Vientiane recalled that the area belonged to Laos and said the government had never "allowed any foreign country to use the territory of Laos for military purposes or intervention in the internal affairs of other countries."[32] Nevertheless, the conflict was escalating rapidly.[33]

Aerial reconnaissance photos taken in September, 1964, by carrier-based aircraft under Operation Yankee Team had revealed large sheds, trucks, personnel, and concrete bunkers under construction on the Mu Gia Pass near the Laos border. With the end of the rainy season in November and December, the North Vietnamese undertook a massive effort to improve the network of trails known collectively as the Ho Chi Minh Trail. Existing paths were widened, river crossings strengthened, and new sections of road constructed so that trucks and other heavy vehicles could ply many parts of the Trail system from the Mu Gia Pass to the tri-border junction of Laos, Cambodia, and South Vietnam. The Trail as it existed at that time passed through Tchepone southward through Muong Nong and crossed the upper Kong River at Ban Bac. South of that river, a subsidiary route forked off to the northeast to Ban Tampril and thence into the A Shau Valley, which became an important staging area for supplies. The main route continued southward through extremely rugged mountainous country to Cha-

[31] Statement of the Democratic Republic of Vietnam Foreign Ministry, October 18, 1964.

[32] Lao Presse bulletin, Vientiane, November 12, 1964.

[33] According to *Hearings, IV*, the first American air strike not associated with reconnaissance missions occurred in October, 1964 (p. 476), the first request for bombing of the Trail occurred in January, 1965 (p. 481), and "both Prime Minister Souvanna Phouma and King Savang Vatthana endorsed United States air strikes against NVA [North Vietnamese Army] / Pathet Lao installations within Laos" (p. 371).

vane and beyond. In the early weeks of 1965, this improvement made it possible to equip all regular forces fighting in South Vietnam, who had been dependent on captured American small arms, with the Communist-bloc 7.62-mm. weapons system. Meanwhile, the movement of foot soldiers along the Trail also increased, so that by early 1965 the first entire regiments of North Vietnamese soldiers were identified in South Vietnam.

At the same time, North Vietnam's command structure of its forces along the Trail underwent a significant change. The frontier guard battalions[34] posted along the border of southern Laos, which had previously been attached to regional military headquarters in North Vietnam, were for the first time placed under a unified independent command. The new command, named *Doan* (Group) 559, controlled all frontier guard, Trail security, engineer, communications, and liaison troops, porters, and guides, as well as units of troops on the move down the Trail from its headquarters at Tchepone, and reflected the increased size and complexity of the Trail operations.

Greater use of the Trail led to greater food requisitioning and impressment of the local population for labor, which led to more frequent and intense attacks in southern Laos, as the North Vietnamese purposefully extended their control westward. This escalation, however, led to greater exposure of the North Vietnamese presence, which was verified by the Canadian and Indian members of the ICC at the Royal Lao Army Officer's School at Dong Hene (Savannakhet Province), which was attacked in March, 1965, and further confirmed by the capture of fifteen North Vietnamese prisoners, including a captain, near Thakhek the following November. According to Thomas Arbuckle, a journalist who witnessed the fighting at Thakhek, the North Vietnamese fled to a large cave in the karst northeast of the town. In this cave, thirteen of the men were trapped and captured by Lao troops. The North Vietnamese turned out to be from a provincial militia unit with orders to operate in Laos during the dry season and return to North Vietnam when the rains began.[35]

Americans on the Ground

While accompanying the Lao troops at Thakhek, Arbuckle observed an American captain and two sergeants, who appeared to be

[34] See p. 257, above.

[35] As of June 17, 1970, the Royal Government was holding 89 captured North Vietnamese prisoners.

engaged in radio communication with T-28's of the Royal Lao Air Force.[36]

The direct American military role in Laos had been growing simultaneously with that of North Vietnam, spurred on by the willingness of the Prime Minister to accept the delivery of American military supplies to two of the three factions and by his determination to oppose the intervention of one foreign power with that of another. The far-flung services of Air America, the pseudo-civilian airline, continued. Units of the rightist and centrist armies were given training at bases in Thailand under the auspices of the American military aid mission in that country.[37]

A small number of American military men fulfilled other missions that quietly helped the Royal Government to redress the imbalance between its means and those of its adversaries after the fighting of 1964. Some of these Americans were under the authority of the military attaché at the American Embassy, whose office had split amoeba-like into separate service offices and whose staff had grown from 8 in July of 1962 to more than 100 in 1969. Included in these were forward air controllers on temporary duty from Vietnam, who flew U.S. Air Force spotter planes, and advisers to Royal Lao Air Force T-28 squadrons.[38] Others engaged in clandestine operations from bases in South Vietnam and Thailand, and their presence in Laos was not officially admitted. Arbuckle, a journalist who took his duties more seriously than most and managed to piece together a fair picture of the extent of American involvement, came across an American in a single-piece green uniform running back from a lookout position on a rock outcrop in the vicinity of the Trail east of Saravane in August, 1965. Such men apparently acted as target spotters, and the intelligence they obtained made it possible to attack the traffic on the Trail, first by tactical bombing and later, when B-52's were introduced in 1965, by strategic bombing. They operated under the name of Studies and Observation Groups (SOG's) and were part of the Special Forces. A high-ranking American Special Forces officer in South Vietnam described privately how his men on a mission in Laos booby-trapped wicker baskets carried by porters on the Trail.

[36] Arbuckle's account to the author.

[37] *Hearings, IV*, p. 529.

[38] For a description of the various functions of these attachés, see *Hearings, IV*, pp. 514–16, and of the Air Force attachés, see *Ibid.*, pp. 465–66.

There were also bigger and more sophisticated operations, some of them a product of the decision to begin bombing North Vietnam. A U.S. Air Force detachment manned an isolated outpost atop Phou Pha Thi, a 5,860-foot peak west of Sam Neua town. The peak, protected by almost sheer cliffs on three sides and believed by the Meo to be a holy place, had been used as a counter-guerrilla base by the Royal Lao Army off and on since the first Indochina War. It was a natural site for a navigational beacon, and, when American planes from Thailand began bombing the Red River delta in 1966, a U.S. Air Force detachment was stationed there on a regular basis to guide the planes toward their targets.[39] It was also a meteorological and radio communications station, as well as a nest for refueling helicopters on search and rescue operations for air crews that had been shot down.[40]

In the south, American navigational beacons operated at Muong Phalane until December 25, 1967, and atop Phou Ka Te near Saravane until June 19, 1970, when they were overrun by the Communists.

Thai and Chinese Involvement

Thailand, for its part, continued to act in Laos on the basis of a consideration that had motivated governments in Bangkok since the nineteenth century: prevention of Vietnamese control of the left bank of the Mekong. Thai nationals had been active participants in the fighting in Laos on the side of the Vientiane government at least since the summer of 1964, and even earlier according to some Communist sources.[41] Arbuckle reports that he encountered a Thai with a Bangkok accent dressed in blue jeans at Ban Nam Bac in February, 1967.[42] To bolster the Lao capability in firepower, Thai artillerymen were moved into Laos and fought at Muong Soui before it fell in June, 1969. They were then evacuated to Thailand, only to reappear again at Long Cheng when that base

[39] For a good description of the appalling weather conditions encountered by these pilots, see Colonel Jack Broughton, *Thud Ridge* (Philadelphia: Lippincott, 1969).

[40] For purposes of cover, the men who manned the electronic equipment at Phou Pha Thi were described as Lockheed Aircraft Corporation personnel.

[41] See p. 275, above. Quang Minh, *Au Pays du Million d'Éléphants* (Hanoi: Éditions en Langues Étrangères, 1961), pp. 131–33, claims evidence that Thai pilots were flying AT-6's over the Plain of Jars as early as March, 1961.

[42] Arbuckle's account to the author.

came under threat of siege the following year. Reportedly, 280 artillerymen and 500 security troops were involved. In early 1970, a high official of the Thai Government admitted the presence of Thai "volunteers" in Laos.[43] Their involvement grew as the commitments in the secret war grew. But it was still only a fraction of the cost of a war that afforded far more geopolitical benefit to Thailand than to any other country, not to mention the direct financial benefits, paid by the United States, that the Thai Government derived from the stationing of Americans on its soil and its continued retention of the land transport monopoly to Laos.

Both Thailand and China, meanwhile, were improving road communications into and through Laos. The Thai Government, alarmed by the spread of insurgency in its northeastern and northern provinces, began to improve roads to several points on the Laos border. At the same time, another road was built from the Thai border to the capital of Sayaboury Province, which had once belonged to Thailand.

A much more ambitious program of road construction was undertaken by the Chinese. Having completed their initial roads in Phong Saly and Nam Tha,[44] they had started work in Luang Prabang Province, using engineers and security troops freed from duty in North Vietnam by the cessation of American raids in the northern part of that country. Beginning in September, 1968, taking advantage of the fact that the Pathet Lao had regained control of Ban Nam Bac, the last Royal Government outpost of significance in the region, the Chinese built southward from Ban Batene on the Yünnan border as far as Muong Sai, and thence in two directions, northeastward to Muong La and beyond to link up at Muong Khoua on the Hou River with the road built by the North Vietnamese from the Dien Bien Phu valley, and southwestward along the Beng River toward Pak Beng on the Mekong, only nineteen miles from the Thai border. Unarmed American planes that overflew the Chinese roads were visibly followed by the antiaircraft guns of ground crews on the alert but were not fired upon.

[43] Statement by Deputy Prime Minister Prapass Charusathiara at an informal press conference, reported in *Bangkok Post,* March 31, 1970. He is quoted as saying "We are brother races. A Laotian living in Korat goes home to fight. He is not a Thai Army soldier sent to fight there." His statement accords well with the ethnic realities. The exact nature and size of Thailand's commitment in Laos, however, has not been officially clarified by that government.

[44] See pp. 229–30, above.

MAP 5. Northwestern Laos Showing Chinese Roads

When Prince Souvanna Phouma was asked his opinion about the purpose of these Chinese roads, he replied they were "not meant for Lao tourism."[45]

The Fall of General Phoumi

The infighting within the rightist military command and Siho's paramilitary police erupted into violence once more in early 1965. General Phoumi had returned from attending the United Nations General Assembly toward the end of 1964 and, sensing that trouble was brewing, made another effort to patch things up among the generals. At a meeting in Luang Prabang in January, 1965, attended by Phoumi and all the generals, a compromise solution to the problem of the separate rightist and centrist armies was hammered out under which, for form's sake, the rightist army would be merged with the centrist army.

There was considerable surprise, therefore, when an obscure rightist colonel named Bounleut Saycocie took over the government radio station and the adjoining sports stadium on the evening of January 31 and demanded a reorganization of the army command, without wishing harm to the National Union Government. A communiqué issued by Bounleut on February 2, with the approval of Souvanna Phouma, stated that the Prime Minister and General Ouan Ratikon had agreed that a constructive solution would be put into effect to reaffirm the strength and unity of the army commanded by an effective staff.

A simultaneous attempt by Siho to move three companies of paramilitary police into Vientiane to "protect his interests" led to fighting with troops under General Kouprasith. The latter quickly mopped up scattered police resistance at points around the town, but the bulk of Siho's force occupied the General Staff Headquarters just outside the town, and this became the focus of the fighting.

General Phoumi, who had just celebrated his forty-fifth birthday with three straight days of festivities, remained in his house up to this moment attempting to find out what was happening. When he telephoned General Ouan, a voice with a Luang Prabang accent told him, "We are going to destroy you."[46] Reports were by now circulating in Vientiane that troops under General Khamkong from Paksane were moving toward Vientiane in support of General

[45] Lao Presse bulletin, Vientiane, February 6, 1970.

[46] Conversation of the author with General Phoumi in Bangkok, June 11, 1970.

Phoumi, and the latter received in quick succession visits from the Thai Ambassador and Ambassador Sullivan, each of whom pleaded with the general not to embark on an adventure that seemed to entail an uncertain outcome. Phoumi appeared noncommittal. Most sources agree that Khamkong's move from Paksane had been undertaken in league with Phoumi; but the latter may have intended it as a precautionary move.

In the harsh fighting that ensued, Kouprasith's soldiers in orange scarves took the offensive against Siho's white-scarved police, driving them out of the General Staff Headquarters, and against Khamkong's soldiers. Bounleut's soldiers, who had been relatively few in number, exchanged their blue scarves for orange ones. The fighting took the lives of only sixty civilians, a surprisingly small toll in view of the artillery exchanges; much of the population had evacuated the town before the fighting began. General Phoumi, accompanied by three or four other men, sensing that he had been isolated by the rightist generals, fled across the Mekong to Thailand in a small boat. Siho also fled.

In a press conference on February 8, General Ouan announced that there had been collaboration between Siho and Phoumi and that both would be judged according to the law. All armed forces were now loyal to the government, and the police would be reorganized; this reorganization marked the end of the Department of National Coordination. Further attempts by pro-rightist groups in Paksane and Thakhek during March and April proved unsuccessful.

The fates of Siho and Phoumi thereafter were completely different. The former journeyed to Ubol to consult a monk, who advised him that he would be lucky if he was in Pakse on a particular day. Siho crossed the Mekong and gave himself up to the commander of the Fourth Military Region in Pakse on June 17, 1966, after announcing his return to Laos in telegrams dispatched to all the Western ambassadors. He was taken to Phou Khao Khouei in government custody and was reportedly shot while attempting to escape. His life ended as he had lived it, violently.

As for General Phoumi, he retired to Songkhla by the seaside in southernmost Thailand, where he lived in a pleasant villa not far from the Governor's palace. In 1969, he was allowed to move to Bangkok, nearer Laos but still not too near. His enemies in Laos made no serious attempt to extradite him, and his many friends on both banks of the Mekong hoped that the passage of time would one day permit him decently to return to Vientiane. The court that tried him *in absentia* was unable to prove allegations of corruption in the use of public funds, and it appeared that the large private funds that he had spent had gone toward such ends as supporting the exchequer of the royal family. The monuments that this complex and often maligned man left behind included a huge triumphal arch in Vientiane and a casino in Savannakhet, both unfinished, but also the broad avenues that gave Vientiane at least the aspect of a modern city.

The escalation of the war produced a political feedback, in which the top levels of the military attempted to impose their views on the government. Following a pattern that became well established in South Vietnam during this same period, coup attempt followed coup attempt, for there was no effective way of putting a stop to the rival ambitions of the generals. The Lao Army staff continued to demonstrate an incompetence that was appalling by Western standards but did quite well in private business. While the average Lao soldier was lucky to get his pay[47] and rations, the generals built themselves villas and accepted lucrative positions as directors of bowling alleys and other ventures. Formerly they had driven Volkswagens; now they drove Mercedes. While the centrists were so far down the list of supply priorities that they were still armed with World War II carbines, the members of the General Staff armed their bodyguards with the latest M-16 rifles. The generals, in short, went on "farming on the backs of the people," as Kong Le described it.

The pressure from the rightist military for merger of the rightist and centrist armies was reflected among the politicians as well. The seats for the NLHS Cabinet members continued to be kept open for their possible return to the government. But this in turn imposed a ceiling on the political ambitions of young rightists with whom tripartitism was unpopular. Convocations to Cabinet meetings continued to be addressed to the offices of the absent ministers, and the minutes of each Cabinet meeting recorded their absence.

[47] The extremely low pay of all ranks in the Royal Lao Army, when compared with the high cost of the American bombing, gave rise to a question about the economics of the way in which the war was being fought. A private received pay ranging from 2,500 to 6,496 kip ($5.00 to $12.99) per month, a captain from 12,540 to 27,415 kip ($25.08 to $54.83). A single sortie by an American aircraft over northern Laos cost $3,190 (*Hearings, IV,* p. 556). This meant that for the cost of a sortie by an American aircraft a Royal Lao Army company could be kept in the field for ten weeks.

Within Souvanna Phouma's Neutralist Party,[48] there was a division of opinion between those who wanted to preserve it as a separate organization and those who favored merging it with other political parties in order to form a unified nationalist party for the day when the political contest with the NLHS would be resumed.

As the date of fresh elections to the National Assembly approached, the government, realizing that the NLHS would boycott them and refuse to allow voting in the areas under Pathet Lao control, introduced an amendment to Article 25 of the Constitution setting aside one-third of the seats by royal proclamation in case of extraordinary circumstances. This case would be the agreement of the NLHS to re-enter the national union pending the holding of genuine countrywide elections.

Elections were held on July 18, 1965, with voting limited mainly to officials and village chiefs. In the new Cabinet announced on September 6, Souvanna Phouma held the portfolios of Defense and Foreign Affairs, Souphanouvong remained the NLHS Deputy Prime Minister, and Leuam Insisiengmay, a southerner, was the rightist Deputy Prime Minister and Minister of Education. General Phoumi's old portfolio of Finance had been taken over by Sisouk na Champassak.

Following a budget crisis in the autumn of 1966, the National Assembly was dissolved and fresh elections were held on January 1, 1967, again under NLHS boycott. About 80 per cent of the registered electorate (i.e., the electorate in the government-held areas) voted. An Assembly that supported the policies of Prince Souvanna Phouma was returned to power, with the majority of the deputies expressing readiness to join a national front of all non-Pathet Lao political tendencies, to be headed by the Prime Minister.

Thao Ma's Raid and Kong Le's Departure

The chaotic relations between the General Staff and the regional military commanders and the anomalous situation of separate rightist and centrist forces in the field, frequently with little or no cooperation taking place between them, led to further violence in 1966.

As a result of its bombing of the Ho Chi Minh Trail, the Royal

[48] On its first anniversary on May 26, 1962, the Neutralist Party had counted 32,747 active members, both civilian and military. (Figure supplied by General Soukan Vilaysarn, the party's secretary-general.)

Lao Air Force had acquired unprecedented influence. Its commander, General Thao Ma, rated by American observers as one of the most skilled pilots in Laos, came into conflict with regional military commanders elsewhere in the country, particularly over their requisitioning of his small fleet of C-47 transport planes to fly private errands. After one such argument, allegedly involving a shipment of opium, General Ouan ordered General Thao Ma to move his headquarters from Savannakhet to Vientiane. The latter refused the order, precipitating a confrontation. Ambassador Sullivan flew to Savannakhet to try to reason with Thao Ma, but on October 21 the latter led a surprise bombing raid over Vientiane in his T-28's; the first bomb hit General Kouprasith's office at the General Staff Headquarters, but the general had not yet arrived and thus escaped injury. Other bombs fell over a wide area, killing more than thirty persons, a record for such a short action by a Lao military unit in a town. Both Thao Ma and Colonel Bounleut Saycocie, who was also implicated, fled to Thailand.

Meanwhile, the unresolved conflict over whether or not to integrate the rightist and centrist forces had finally resulted in another unfortunate departure from Laos, that of General Kong Le.

The centrist army was by now scattered over the far reaches of Laos in understrength battalions.[49] It received weapons from the United States and field training in Thailand, like the rightist army, and, in addition, selected training from the French Military Mission in Laos, which continued functioning as it had when the centrists had been on the Plain of Jars. Centrist finances and logistics were handled separately from those of the rightist army. Centrist commanders habitually overstated the numbers of men on their payrolls and engaged in other corrupt practices. An experiment of placing the centrists under the rightist regional military commanders, with centrist liaison officers at the latter's headquarters, failed when the centrists discovered that they were considered little more than a nuisance and were given no responsibilities. Only in southern Laos, where centrist forces were integrated into a mixed mobile group, did cooperation work out, and this success was ascribed to the fact that the local commander of centrist forces was a relative of the regional commander. The main irritant, however, between the rightists and the centrists was the question of officer ranks. Centrist officers had promoted themselves several grades during their alliance with the Pathet Lao (Kong Le himself had

---

[49] This arrangement had the advantage, from the generals' point of view, of minimizing the risk that these troops would take part in a coup.

risen from the rank of captain to that of general overnight), and these new grades were not recognized by the rightists.

Kong Le opposed the pressure from the rightists for integration of the two armies, which he feared would lead to the disappearance of the centrist army. In this sentiment, he had the support of the majority of his men. As the infighting among the rightist generals for "a share of the pie" (as one American observer put it) grew in intensity, Kong Le began to feel personally insecure and at one point sought safety in the Indonesian Embassy in Vientiane. He then left Vientiane[50] and subsequently settled in Paris. He remained loyal to Souvanna Phouma to the last. Ambassador Sullivan had never appreciated the fact that Kong Le was the kind of man with whom the United States had to identify, if its aid in the struggle against the Pathet Lao was to have any meaning for the Lao. The little general's departure was a loss for both Laos and the United States.

Colonel Sompeth Sotfavanh, who replaced Kong Le as Commander-in-Chief of the centrist army on March 20, 1967, was a very different sort of man. Following the example set by the rightist generals, he obtained the funds to build a large concrete house in Vientiane, something Kong Le had never had or needed. It was widely said in Vientiane that the price of Sompeth's agreement to the integration of the centrist army was $20,000 and a King's commission that legalized his grade. Nevertheless, when the Communists captured Muong Soui in June, 1969, it was revealed that half of the soldiers on Sompeth's payroll were nonexistent; as a result of this scandal, Prince Sengsouvanh Souvannarath, son of former Prime Minister Souvannarath and a nephew of Souvanna Phouma, was brought back from Paris, promoted to the rank of general, and placed in command of the centrist army over Sompeth. The planned integration of the centrists and rightists never materialized; morale among the centrist troops, however, declined, and corruption spread like wildfire through the ranks, eroding the old discipline that Kong Le had once instilled.

On the economic front, the successful operation of the Foreign Exchange Operations Fund,[51] supported by the United States, Brit-

[50] General Thao Ma appears to have been under the impression that he could count on Kong Le to turn against the generals once Kouprasith had been killed. But Thao Ma did not know that Kong Le had left Laos four days before the bombing raid. (Conversations of the author with Thao Ma and Bounleut Saycocie in Bangkok and Kong Le in Paris during 1968 and 1969.)

[51] See p. 228, above.

ain, France, Australia, and Japan, made the kip one of the most stable monetary units in the world. Although the budget deficit continued to be large, it was covered from year to year by foreign aid to the Royal Government. When large numbers of refugees began arriving in government-controlled territory, as a result of the North Vietnamese offensives in northern Laos, the Royal Government agreed to convert their "Souvanna kip" at par value for Vientiane kip. The NLHS administration continued to print its own money after 1962, and this was not recognized by the government in Vientiane.

TABLE 4

CONTRIBUTIONS TO FOREIGN EXCHANGE OPERATIONS FUND, 1964–69*
(*In Millions of Dollars*)

	1964	1965	1966	1967	1968	1969
United States	4.0	5.2	13.7	13.8	16.1	16.6
United Kingdom	1.7	1.7	1.7	1.7	1.7	1.7
France	1.7	1.3	1.7	1.7	1.7	1.7
Australia	0.4	0.4	0.8	0.6	0.8	0.7
Japan	—	0.5	1.7	1.7	1.7	1.7
Laos	—	2.8	—	—	—	—
Total	7.8	11.9	19.6	19.5	22.0	22.4

* *Source:* U.S. AID, Vientiane.
Note: Figures are for calendar years.

TABLE 5

VIENTIANE CONSUMER PRICES, 1964–69*
(12-month average of consumer price indexes of Lao and European households in Vientiane published by the Royal Lao Government Statistical Office)

1964	100.7
1965	113.2
1966	128.1
1967	136.1
1968	143.3
1969	148.9

* *Source:* U.S. AID, Vientiane.

13.

The Secret War

In 1966 and 1967, a situation approaching a military stalemate developed in Laos. The Communists were still solidly entrenched on the Plain of Jars and along the Ho Chi Minh Trail but were apparently unwilling or unable to field the additional men that a sustained offensive would have required. The rightist army, with precious American air support, held on to its positions and was able to make some tentative pushes. Thus, in July, 1966, it recaptured the valley of Ban Nam Bac and, during 1967, reached the approaches of Sam Neua town itself. In the latter part of 1967, however, North Vietnam began receiving and ferrying toward the battlefield the fresh supplies of Soviet and Chinese arms destined for the Tet Offensive the following year. A portion of these supplies was consigned to Communist forces in Laos, where a dry-season offensive of unprecedented breadth opened in mid-January, 1968.

The most dramatic action took place at Ban Nam Bac, the valley town far to the north of Luang Prabang that was famed for its oranges. The battle developed over several months, with both sides contesting control of the ridgelines that afforded the best defenses. The clashes of ground patrols were accompanied by artillery exchanges, and some extremely accurate mortaring compelled the government troops to displace their command post on two occasions. At the height of the battle for control of a key ridge dominating the southern side of the valley with its single airstrip, a U.S. Air Force captain piloting a C-46 transport rigged up his own contraption for chuting 500-pound bombs out the open door by visual aiming. Once the Communists were within mortar range of the airstrip, landings at Ban Nam Bac had to be abandoned altogether. The besiegers drew the noose tight on January 13, 1968, and sent the defenders fleeing into the hills, leaving their artillery pieces behind.[1]

Other Communist thrusts menaced government positions near Paksane, Saravane, and Attopeu. The Communists drove government troops out of Lao Ngam in the northern foothills of the Bolovens Plateau, thereby gaining a commanding hold on a region crisscrossed with trails and rich in produce. The valley of the Done River as far as Pakse came within the sphere of Pathet Lao requisitioning and recruiting activity. Lao Ngam became the terminus of new camouflaged roads that generally followed the line of Route Nationale 23 south from Muong Phine, then broke off and crossed the Done River at a series of fords downstream from Saravane. The capture of Thateng allowed the Communists to link up Lao Ngam with a new embarkation point near Ban Phone thirty miles south of the old mountain trail terminus of Ban Bac on the Kong River. Following the Tet Offensive, launched in South Vietnam on January 31, 1968, North Vietnamese traffic in Laos reached a record peak in March when 17,000 trucks were believed by American sources to be operating along the Trail as Hanoi bent all efforts to sustain the "generalized offensive" strategy in the South.

Vang Pao's War

Thanks largely to Air America, the loyalist Meo were assured the rice and salt without which they could not have gone on denying control of much of the mountain country of northern Laos to the Communists. As indefatigable as the North Vietnamese infantry themselves, these irregulars became the closest thing to a people's army on the government side. Their commander, Major General Vang Pao, was by far the most colorful figure the secret war produced.

Vang Pao's war had begun in 1945, when, at the age of thirteen, he offered his services as an interpreter to the tiny handful of Free French officers and men who had parachuted onto the Plain of Jars from December, 1944, onward, with the mission of secretly fostering popular resistance against the Japanese. These resistance fighters, who had been trained in India, received arms and radios by night parachute drops at isolated clearings at which they rendezvoused under cover of hunting wild game to deceive the Japanese. After March 9, 1945, they faded back into the mountains to escape arrest and, after blowing up a few strategic bridges, began to pre-

[1] This was the third time the Communists had captured Ban Nam Bac. The previous occasions had been in April, 1953, and in April, 1961.

pare redoubts from which to launch the planned French reoccupation.

Vang Pao recalls[2] working with a Captain Bichelot, who had responsibility for all the region east of the Plain, including the 4,500-foot-high plateau of Nong Het, which was Vang Pao's home. Vang Pao and the other Meo loyal to the pro-French Toubhy Lyfong[3] received arms from Bichelot's supply drops. Recruit Vang Pao's first fight against the Vietnamese occurred after the Japanese surrender, when local Vietnamese residents armed with Japanese weapons, and others coming up Route 7 from Nghe An, tried to take control of Xieng Khouang Province before the French occupation troops arrived. Later, following the arrival of French forces, Vang Pao joined in the task of providing decent burials for the dozens of Frenchmen killed by the Japanese and their Vietnamese or Meo collaborators. He then set off for Luang Prabang and helped clear Xieng Ngeun of Chinese Nationalist occupation troops before freeing King Sisavang Vong from the siege of his royal palace by the local representatives of the Lao Issara government.

When the brief French–Viet Minh *modus vivendi* of March 6, 1946, broke down, Vang Pao was back in the Meo and Black Thai country east of Xieng Khouang town and south of Route 7, helping the overstretched French organize counter-guerrilla forces, a task that called for both military and civilian skills. He recalls that in March, 1950, he decided that the French attempts to destroy the Viet Minh network of informers, propagandists, and guerrillas by a show of force were getting nowhere. One day, coming into a Meo village where a marriage ceremony was taking place, Vang Pao struck up a conversation with some of the villagers, asking them what their life was like and what they needed most. Shortly, Vang Pao found he was getting replies like "The Viet Minh came here and asked for food" or "We are forbidden to go to Xieng Khouang," and, after several more hours of this, the villagers were pointing out the house where the local Viet Minh platoon slept in the village when they were off duty. This became his approach thereafter.

Good luck came Vang Pao's way when, with the help of a kindly French officer, he was accepted for officer's training at Dong Hene, where the French had begun forming the new Lao Army. He graduated seventh out of a class of fifty-six. On the day Dien Bien Phu fell, Lieutenant Vang Pao was in Sam Neua Province, having led

[2] Vang Pao was kind enough to furnish the author with these details of his life in a conversation in Vientiane, April 19, 1970.

[3] See p. 155, above.

300 men as part of a vain last-minute attempt ordered by the French High Command to break through to the trapped garrison from the south.

In 1960, Vang Pao, although not yet commander of the Second Military Region, had command of the strategic Plain of Jars and was responsible for its adherence to General Phoumi in the civil war. Vang Pao was also involved in the arrest of General Amkha.[4] The rapidity of Kong Le's move in force eastward along Route 7, along with the signal failure of the defenders to destroy the key bridge over the Nam Ngum River east of Muong Soui, doomed the Phoumists' hopes of holding the Plain. Behind Kong Le's troops, carrying brand-new Russian weapons, came two battalions of North Vietnamese infantry that had parachuted into Muong Soui on December 30 and immediately taken in hand the fortification of the Plain to forestall any Phoumist counterattack. In the mountains around the Plain, the irregulars, under Vang Pao's dynamic leadership (similar in many ways to Kong Le's), began developing the harassing tactics that proved so successful in tying down the North Vietnamese troops.

The Meo irregulars were paid directly by the CIA, a system that removed them, and other irregular forces in southern Laos known as "special guerrilla units" (SGU's), from the vicissitudes of the general staff labyrinth. The irregulars received their pay, at least. Their headquarters were at Long Cheng, near Sam Thong. Each military region commander had a deputy in charge of irregulars, who reported to Long Cheng. Many of the CIA men involved in the support of these irregular mercenaries were in Laos under the cover of the American economic aid mission, and had been since 1962.[5]

Relations between the irregulars and the regulars were sometimes tense; an officer whom Vang Pao caught selling to the Pathet Lao Air America rice that he had received by mistake was found with a bullet between the ears. The fact that Vang Pao, who was a highly emotional man, did not succumb to the age-old temptation of leading the Meo into rebellion against the government (he possessed the prestige and the means to do so had he wished, including

[4] See p. 161, above.

[5] The link with the CIA was established over the personal objection of the Administrator of the Agency for International Development, Dr. John A. Hannah, who, when asked if the CIA was using the economic aid mission in Laos as a cover, replied: "This was a decision that was made back in 1962 and by administrations from now until then, and it is the only place in the world that we are" (June 7, 1970).

his own Meo radio station) was unusual and to his credit. On the contrary, in a rare gesture due largely to Vang Pao's personal magnetism, King Savang Vatthana paid a royal visit to Long Cheng and moved at ease among tribal subjects whom his family had traditionally disdained. The Meo performed a service of inestimable value to the lowland Lao by holding the mountains of the north against the North Vietnamese, a service for which they were unlikely to receive much gratitude. The great pity for the Americans was that they were never able to instill the same motivation in the Royal Lao Army.

The Capture of Phou Pha Thi

In Sam Neua Province, the North Vietnamese had made several unsuccessful attempts to drive the Americans off Phou Pha Thi, from which bombers were directed onto targets in the Red River delta. The position appeared so inaccessible that the North Vietnamese outfitted some of their antiquated Russian Antonov biplanes to carry mortar shells with which to bomb the radio and radar antennas on the summit. The lumbering craft made easy targets, and their raids were little better than suicide missions; the exuberant Americans at Phou Pha Thi gave visitors pieces of the wreckage of two of the biplanes as souvenirs.

By February, 1968, however, the North Vietnamese high command meant business and launched three battalions of the 766th Regiment against Phou Pha Thi. They took the airstrip and fought their way up the last slopes in hand-to-hand combat. The place was defended by Meo and Thai irregulars. Heavy bombing had not been able to prevent the North Vietnamese from building a road through the jungle to the foot of the peak. As the ring tightened around them, twelve U.S. Air Force technicians abandoned their van and, using ropes, lowered themselves down the almost sheer cliff face to their rear and sought shelter in caves. One by one they were killed by grenades dropped over the edge of the cliff by the North Vietnamese above. A thirteenth American, a ground air controller, slipped through the North Vietnamese lines and was later rescued by helicopter. On March 11, the handful of Americans and their loyal Meo guards, on whom the men in the air had depended for so long, were no more. Twenty days later, President Johnson announced that the United States was halting all bombing of the northern part of North Vietnam.

In the same speech in which he announced the partial bombing halt, President Johnson renewed his appeal for negotiations. The appeal was heeded, and, on April 3, the Hanoi leaders, flushed with the impact on American public opinion of the Tet Offensive, accepted the invitation to talks "to determine the total and unconditional cessation of bombing" of North Vietnam. On May 13, as Communist forces launched another onslaught on Saigon and other cities in South Vietnam, the two men who had led their countries' delegations at Geneva in 1961, Ambassador Averell Harriman and Minister without Portfolio Xuan Thuy, sat down at the same table together in Paris.

After three years of American bombing, North Vietnam's roads, railroads, and bridges had been pounded so badly that traffic rolled on by-passes, a network of parallel roads requiring great manpower to build and maintain. The countryside of the hardest-hit southern provinces of North Vietnam, near the demilitarized zone, resembled a moonscape. The bombing had not halted the movement of supplies and men southward through North Vietnam and into Laos, but it had interfered with this movement and elicited a herculean response.

Having decided to call a halt to the bombing of northern North Vietnam, which was the most heavily defended part of the country, President Johnson sought a *quid pro quo* for ending the bombing of the southern part of North Vietnam as well. He wished to end the bombing for two reasons. First, he had waited long for a step that would allow history to record him as a President more concerned with a just peace than with a just war. Second, he knew that a bombing halt would help the Democratic Party politically in the Presidential and congressional elections.

By a quirk of fate, and surely unintentionally, it was Prince Souvanna Phouma who gave the world the news that the United States had, indeed, made the decision to halt totally the bombing of North Vietnam. On October 25, after a meeting with Sullivan, the Prince announced that the Ambassador had informed him of the imminent bombing halt, but without disclosing the date. At that moment, the final signals were still being exchanged among Washington, Saigon, and Paris. The bombing halt went into effect on November 1.

The 1969 Monsoon Offensive

The war in Vietnam was far from finished, however. North Vietnam's leaders apparently made a crucial decision for a military-political gamble in Laos almost immediately after they had been relieved of the strain imposed upon them by the American bombing.

In December, Vang Pao and his hardy Meo launched a successful operation to reoccupy the old guerrilla base at Phou Pha Thi. The North Vietnamese drove them off again in January, 1969, and, on March 1, two battalions of the North Vietnamese 174th Regiment, which is recruited from the Tay Bac region of northwestern North Vietnam, and three battalions of the 148th Regiment succeeded in driving Vang Pao out of another guerrilla base thirty-five miles to the southwest at Na Khang, killing the *chao khoueng* (provincial governor) of Sam Neua in the fighting. In the leapfrog ground war in Laos, in which there is an extremely narrow margin of troops available in any one place at any one time for offensive actions (as opposed to forces tied down in portering and securing trails), these operations showed that the Communists had more men in northern Laos than they had had in previous dry seasons.

Up to that point, the North Vietnamese had followed their usual practice of moving individual elements of the 316th Division such as the veteran 174th Regiment, back and forth across the border, always retiring to North Vietnam at the onset of the rains. The new situation alarmed the government, because it was obvious that the Communists, after pinching off the last government strongholds in Sam Neua Province, intended to have all elements of the 316th Division in the Plain of Jars region at the start of the rainy season. These forces would be used to implement the political goal of the offensive proclaimed by the Communists, which was to reoccupy in the name of the NLHS and "patriotic neutralists" all the territory up to the 1961 ceasefire line, which in northern Laos would have implied a considerable falling back for the Vientiane government. In the event, the North Vietnamese failed to achieve this goal, but their effort demonstrated they were now prepared for the first time to undertake and sustain a major offensive in Laos during the rainy season, and the revelation came as quite a shock to the government.

Air power remained the quickest and most effective means of blocking this North Vietnamese thrust forward across the Plain of Jars into the mountains.[6] During the month of March, therefore,

[6] The American Ambassador in Vientiane had final authority to approve or disapprove air strikes by American aircraft over Laos, even though many of the targets of these strikes were pinpointed by American intelligence analysts in Thailand or South Vietnam. The criteria applied by the American Ambassador in Vientiane were essentially political in nature. (See *Hearings, IV*, pp. 457–59.)

the number of air sorties over Laos rose dramatically. From a previous figure of about 20 each day, flown mostly by the T-28's of the Royal Lao Air Force, it rose to about 200, flown mostly by aircraft of the U.S. Air Force based in Thailand. This was at a time when dust and smoke haze covers northern Laos and makes observation of the ground extremely difficult.

On the night of March 11, North Vietnamese sappers attacked the airfield at Luang Prabang, which was one of those used for T-28's. Vang Pao saw that the next point to come under menace from the forces gathered on the Plain of Jars would be Muong Soui, which was garrisoned by centrist troops. To delay this expected attack, he launched a raid on Xieng Khouang town, which was only lightly held by the Pathet Lao but had considerable political significance, since it was the traditional provincial capital. (Following its abandonment of Xieng Khouang, the Royal Lao Government had moved its provincial administration to the new defended town of Sam Thong southwest of the Plain.) The raid succeeded in diverting Communist forces temporarily from Muong Soui. However, the forces available to the Communists were superior in number, and they resumed their siege of Muong Soui in June, finally wresting it from government hands on June 27. Smaller forces were sent ahead to probe government defenses around Sala Phou Khoun, effectively blocking the Royal Road, which had been reopened to civilian traffic only the previous month.

At this point, Vang Pao again demonstrated his uncanny ability to surprise the enemy tactically by moving small forces rapidly to threaten enemy supply lines. Moving his men as usual by Air America planes, Vang Pao quickly landed two battalions in the rough mountain country west of Nong Het and north of Route 7 and two more south of the road. At the same time, American aircraft began intensive bombing of the Plain, hitting for the first time towns like Khang Khay and Ban Ban, in which the North Vietnamese had constructed gasoline depots and antiaircraft gun emplacements.

At Muong Soui, the Communists failed to react to this threat to their supply lines; instead of immediately withdrawing the main portion of their force at Muong Soui so as to conserve food, they proceeded to launch a regiment-sized attack against a small centrist outpost several miles away, whereupon Vang Pao began moving his forces forward onto the Plain. To his astonishment, he met little or no resistance. Outposts that had been manned by the Pathet Lao were found abandoned, apparently because of the lack of rice. Caches were discovered containing large quantities of arms and ammunition—some 7,500 tons in all—which had been stockpiled in relative security since 1961.

The North Vietnamese had allowed themselves to be strategically outmaneuvered. They had reacted too slowly to Vang Pao's initial moves to cut Route 7, and they had been caught by the rains without adequate supplies, especially food. Their failure to defend the Plain and the forced evacuation of their unviable garrison from Muong Soui cost them considerable political prestige with the Pathet Lao. Their situation was not made any happier by the seizure by police in Vientiane of a map of the base at Long Cheng, the headquarters of the CIA-supported irregular forces in Laos, as it was being delivered to the North Vietnamese Embassy in an Embassy car; it had been procured by a Black Thai agent within the base. The incident led to the expulsion from Laos of the second secretary of the Embassy. The desire of the North Vietnamese for revenge against Vang Pao was readily understandable.

Simultaneously with this success on the Plain, other government troops moved east along Route 9 in Savannakhet Province. As they advanced toward Muong Phine, which had long been in Pathet Lao hands, they found the countryside strangely deserted. When they arrived on the outskirts of Muong Phine and told the people there that they were government soldiers, the people were incredulous: The only soldiers they had seen for five years had been Pathet Lao and North Vietnamese. After the government troops withdrew again (it would have been an impossible task to defend the place), the 2,500 civilians who had reappeared in the town, mainly women and old men, announced to the returning Pathet Lao commissars in a body that they had made up their mind to leave the town. They would go toward the Mekong and find rice land on which to settle. The commissars could try to prevent their departure, but their mind was made up. All 2,500 departed safely in full view of the dumbfounded commissars.

The 1970 Offensive

The North Vietnamese got the following dry-season campaign off to an early start by marching onto the Plain of Jars again in mid-February, 1970, before even the opium harvest had been completed. Although there was little sustained fighting, and they advanced much as a high-pressure center moves into a low-pressure zone,[7] they were taking no chances this time. They were no longer relying on the Pathet Lao to do half the job and brought into action elements of a second North Vietnamese division, the 312th, which they hoped would allow them to spread their men more densely. An illustration of what this meant in practical terms was afforded by the 316th Division's attempt to drive government forces out of Sam Thong in March. The division numbered 10,000 men in all, but Western military observers estimated that no more than 2,000 of them ever got anywhere near Sam Thong itself, because the rest were walking back and forth between the forward supply caches behind the front line and the large depots that had been re-established on the Plain, carrying sacks of rice, munitions, and other supplies to keep the 2,000 on the front line in business. To complicate the North Vietnamese supply and labor schedules further, the government had had the foresight to evacuate nearly 20,000 civilians from the northern rim of the Plain just before the offensive began.

The strength of the 1970 offensive was such as to force the Meo irregulars to fall back in a broad arc, and no one was certain of the solidity of the centrist garrison in the Vang Vieng valley. By March, the forward units of the 316th Division, such as the 174th Regiment, were looking down on the airfield at Sam Thong from the surrounding hills, and the 42,000 civilians who had settled in the region were forced to abandon their homes, schools, and shops and take to the hills once again, creating a vast new burden for the government.

From the government's point of view, the prospects seemed grim. Should Souvanna Phouma be reduced to holding the 1961 ceasefire line, he would be in the position of sharing with the rightists control of the territory that the rightists had controlled exclusively in 1961. In Phong Saly Province, General Khammouane

[7] Total government dead on the Plain were 31, mostly in the initial onslaught. As in 1959, the world press gathered in Vientiane and proceeded to send out exaggerated accounts of the fighting. At one point, a military briefing officer reported that 4,000 enemy soldiers were involved in the offensive on the Plain, and this was reported by the news agencies, through a misunderstanding, as a 4,000-strong attack on a command post at the Plain of Jars airfield; the actual number of attackers there was 400. There was also one B-52 raid in the vicinity of Ban Ban on February 17, which justifiably created a stir. Most of the press stories were written at the swimming pool of the new Lane Xang Hotel, which had become a hub of activity, where journalists, American pacifists on their way to or from Hanoi, and the wives of American prisoners of war who were intent on seeing North Vietnamese and NLHS representatives rubbed elbows and exchanged stories.

Boupha had accepted the title of Supreme Commander of Patriotic Neutralist Forces in Northern Laos, and, in the South, the Communists were doing their best to dislodge Souvanna Phouma's grip on the last enclaves under centrist control.

"A Barren Zone"

By 1970, despite the full weight of American bombing operations, the Ho Chi Minh Trail was carrying truck traffic at record levels: 15,000 trucks were sighted during December, 1969; 25,000 during January, 1970; 45,000 during February. Besides improving a road network west of the mountains, thereby avoiding the great engineering difficulties involved in keeping mountain passages open and also making their roads suitable for high-speed traffic, the North Vietnamese had taken steps to reduce the effectiveness of the American bombing.

Hanoi had received large numbers of trucks from the Soviet Union and the East European countries. Adapting the system they had used for infiltrating men down the Trail, the North Vietnamese divided up the length of each truck route into twenty-mile sections. Each section was assigned its own equipment and work teams, whose mission was to keep that section operating, and maintained its own security forces, who were thoroughly familiar with the surrounding country and the location of government outposts. The presence of Special Forces patrols reconnoitering the Trail was signaled by means of wooden clappers of the type hung around the necks of buffaloes.

The trucks normally moved only when there was no sound of aircraft, and then only when camouflaged by tree branches tied to wooden frames. The drivers knew the locations of lay-bys in thickets or under rock overhangs in which to hide from observation or reconnaissance planes. Since bridges quickly became targets, underwater ramps were constructed of logs and stones. To cross wider rivers, bamboo rafts were kept moored to the river banks under cover of overhanging trees. In some places, stream beds were used for roadways to avoid leaving telltale tire tracks. On sections where there were particularly difficult fords, specially built trucks with high axles and oversize tires were used.

Ingenious warning signals had been rigged to cope with the problem of aerial observation. The signal for an approaching plane, for instance, had developed from a sentry's rifle shot to a system of flashing lights designed to indicate a plane's line of approach so that moving traffic could take appropriate evasive action. Decoys were set up by day and blinking red and white lights by night to deceive pilots into jettisoning their bombs. By 1970, some sections of the Trail were protected by Soviet SAM missiles, and all sections had antiaircraft guns.

The pounding of the Trail by B-52's had never been the subject of any specific agreement between Souvanna Phouma and the American Embassy; the most that could be said was that the Prince did not object. He described the eastern region of southern Laos as "a barren zone" and said "The war there is an affair between the Americans and the North Vietnamese."[8] His position that his government exercised no authority over the people who controlled the region through which the Trail passed allowed him to claim that he therefore exercised no authority over the means of warfare used there, including the American bombing.

As the American bombing made the movement of supplies along the Trail more hazardous (some of the bombs, in order to discourage repair gangs, were equipped with delayed-action fuses timed to detonate hours after they had buried themselves in the ground), the North Vietnamese engineers opened up a supplementary channel of supply through Cambodia. Known as the Sihanouk Trail, it involved a combination of roads and waterways. Large amounts of rice reached troops fighting in the Central Highlands of South Vietnam by this route. The goods were collected at the Mekong River port of Stung Treng and sent up the Kong River by motorized sampans, crossing the border between Cambodia and Laos at approximately the halfway point. Once inside Laos, the goods were transferred to trucks plying newly built roads parallel to the Cambodian border. Needless to say, such an operation involved considerable skill in planning of finances, motor repair, and manpower. The North Vietnamese also put into operation a number of small airstrips in this region for special courier flights, while on the right bank of the Mekong, in Sithandone Province, they operated a large base on flat ground covered by triple-canopy jungle near the trijunction of the borders of Laos, Cambodia, and Thailand.

American Opinion Reacts

Both on the ground and in the air, Americans were deeply involved in Laos, but even as late as the summer of 1969 the American public had been told very little about all this.

---

[8] Interview with the author in Vientiane, March 28, 1970. The description "barren zone" is not strictly accurate, as the Trail area is inhabited by numerous Kha tribes.

This situation stemmed from the fact that the United States has been extremely cautious about accusing North Vietnam of violating the Geneva agreement. Even though American intelligence had detected the large numbers of North Vietnamese troops remaining in Laos beyond the withdrawal deadline, it was not until the summer of 1964 that a formal charge of violating the accords was brought. Up to then, India and other countries had urged the United States not to make a *casus belli* of the North Vietnamese presence because, they said, it would simply lead to a total collapse of the Geneva settlement without producing any gains for the United States. Even after the renewed fighting in May, 1964, and the photographic evidence of North Vietnamese involvement, Souvanna Phouma wanted the United States to say publicly as little as possible about its actions,[9] and the United States was anxious to avoid provoking an ICC finding that it had violated the accords.[10]

While occasional articles in the American press alluded to the secret war in Laos, it was relatively easy for the American Embassy to maintain an official curtain of silence over the clandestine activities. Ambassador Sullivan asked the small handful of Western correspondents in Vientiane to observe discretion in their reporting on the grounds of Soviet sensitivity to publicity given American activities.[11]

The danger here, Sullivan believed, was that such publicity might force the Administration into an official admission of activities in violation of the Geneva agreement, and that this would damage, perhaps irreparably, the Soviet-American agreement on the neutrality of Laos reached by Kennedy and Khrushchev at their meeting in Vienna in 1961.[12] The main Soviet concern was to prevent Chinese hegemony over the Communist movements of Southeast Asia, especially the Vietnamese, and this seems to have been the reason why the new collective leadership that succeeded Khrushchev in October, 1964, reversed the latter's moves to disengage from responsibilities in Indochina. Official confirmation by

[9] *Hearings, IV*, p. 370.

[10] *Hearings, IV*, pp. 399 and 593.

[11] "It's one of the few areas of agreement we have with them," he told one reporter.

[12] As Sullivan put it on October 22, 1969: "What we would like to preserve is the presumption that, at the time when we can see re-established the prospects for a fulfillment and for the reinstigation, reinstitution of the 1962 agreements, the Soviets would maintain a position that Laos should be a neutral state and throw their weight behind the continuation of a status of neutrality for Laos." (*Hearings, IV*, p. 590.)

the United States Government that it was using its own men and aircraft against the Pathet Lao and North Vietnamese would force the issue of the solidarity of the Soviet Communists with the fraternal parties. It might push the Soviet Union in the direction already taken by the North Vietnamese and Chinese, who had signified their disapproval of Prince Souvanna Phouma's government by withdrawing their ambassadors from Vientiane and by maintaining that their embassies were accredited to the King of Laos, and who signified their contention that the Geneva agreement was not being respected by stopping, after 1963, their payments for the upkeep of the ICC. A situation had been created in Soviet-American relations, therefore, in which the Russians turned a blind eye to American violations of the Geneva agreement, and the Americans turned a blind eye to Soviet arms deliveries to North Vietnam, some of which went to the Pathet Lao.

The government offensives on the Plain of Jars and in Savannakhet Province in September, 1969, however, by their very success, stirred concern in the United States about the official silence surrounding American involvement on the side of the government. Outside reporters who again flocked to Laos did not respect the tacit agreement between the American Embassy and the press. As a result, speculation arose within the U.S. Congress, on the eve of a congressional inquiry into the extent of American commitments to the Lao Government, that "another Vietnam" might develop in Laos.

Congressional attempts to close off the authority vested in the President to send American troops to Laos, as they had been sent to South Vietnam, did nothing to change the policy of "protective reaction" under which American commanders in South Vietnam had for several years been allowed to make limited crossings of the border into Laos in order to silence North Vietnamese artillery or disrupt troop concentrations.[13] At the beginning of May, 1970, this policy was extended to what a Defense Department spokesman described as "reinforced protective reaction" when American aircraft struck at a supply buildup on the Nghe An side of the Barthélémy Pass, which had not been hit since the halt of the bombing of North Vietnam. A second such series of raids occurred on No-

---

[13] The principal spokesman for such congressional foreclosure was Senator John Sherman Cooper of Kentucky. However, when the author asked Defense Secretary Melvin Laird at a press conference in Saigon on February 11, 1970, whether the policy of protective reaction had been changed as a result of congressional action, Laird replied "No."

vember 21, 1970, near the DMZ, the Ban Karai Pass, and the Mu Gia Pass. As the effective range of SAM batteries positioned just inside North Vietnam extended some 25 miles into Laos, American aircraft were authorized by the Defense Department to attack North Vietnamese antiaircraft installations when the aiming radar of such installations "locked on" to aircraft flying over Laos, as well as when it "locked on" to reconnaissance planes overflying North Vietnam. A number of such "protective reaction" strikes occurred during 1970.

The increasingly frequent and well-publicized visits to Vientiane of wives and mothers seeking information about downed American air crews also helped stir a mood of public uneasiness.[14] Finally, on March 6, 1970, at Key Biscayne, Florida, President Nixon issued a statement that contained the first official announcement of air operations over Laos.

Although it had been known unofficially for some time that air operations were taking place, information was scanty because American reporters were not allowed to interview pilots at their bases in Thailand. Flight plans circumvented Vientiane and other Laotian cities; and when pilots and helicopter crews were killed in Laos, their families were notified that their deaths had occurred in "Southeast Asia."

Much of this unofficial air and ground activity was finally put on the record by the Nixon Administration in hearings held before a Senate subcommittee in October, 1969, and released to the public after March 6, 1970. The Administration continued to insist on secrecy, however, concerning some of the most far-reaching aspects of American involvement. These included the CIA's support for irregular forces (the Meo and SGU's, principally), participation of nationals of allied countries (such as Thailand and South Vietnam)

[14] According to official American figures, almost 380 American planes had been lost in Laos between 1964 and September 28, 1969, most of them in southern Laos (*Hearings, IV,* p. 478), and about 200 U.S. military personnel, most of them airmen, had been killed in Laos in the 1962–69 period, with 200 more missing or captured (*Hearings, V,* p. 827).

State Department spokesman Robert McCloskey said on December 22, 1970, that American requests to the Pathet Lao for information about prisoners had met with no response. A very few prisoners have escaped. One, Dieter Dengler, a U.S. Navy pilot, kept alive by eating leeches after escaping from a camp in the Tchepone region in July, 1966. Although seriously dessicated by lack of drinking water and at times unconscious, Dengler managed to spell out an S.O.S. sign with flare parachutes he collected and was picked up by a helicopter.

in operations in Laos, the costs and scope of air operations over northern Laos, and cumulative military aid totals.[15]

Partial Eclipse of the NLHS

While the United States was having these difficulties, the secret war was also creating problems for the NLHS. The North Vietnamese direction of the war on the Plain of Jars and the Ho Chi Minh Trail had the effect of overshadowing the role of the Pathet Lao. There was hardly a person in the so-called liberated zone who did not have personal experience of the North Vietnamese presence. The continual disruptions caused by American bombings and the large-scale movements of population (there were an estimated total of 700,000 displaced persons in Laos by the beginning of 1970, many of them belonging to the mountain tribes), which compounded the natural difficulties of great distances, poor communications, sparse settlement, and absence of social grievances, impeded the organizational work of the NLHS.

After the formation of the coalition government in 1962, the NLHS infrastructure in Vientiane Province, for instance, which had been well developed during the preceding years, began to deteriorate. One possible explanation lies in the fact that Vang Pao's Meo guerrillas, sitting astride the natural communication route between Vientiane and the NLHS base area in Sam Neua, became a serious obstacle to communication.

Meanwhile, in its bases, the NLHS was having to nurture the political and military development of the "patriotic neutralists" and at the same time to conceal the directing hand of the North Vietnamese in the NLHS as best it could. Almost the only young men the "patriotic neutralists" recruited into their ranks, according to the reports of defectors made in 1969, were several hundred of the more than 2,000 former Royal Lao Army soldiers taken prisoner after the collapse of their positions at Ban Nam Bac. A Political Consultative Conference, with the participation of the NLHS and the "patriotic neutralists," was held in October, 1965. On the opening day, the NLHS Central Committee announced that it had decided to call its army the "Laotian People's Liberation Army" in order to mark the twentieth anniversary of the Laotian revolution.

The "patriotic neutralists" made use of the same administrative hierarchy as the Royal Lao Government—*chao khoueng* (provin-

---

[15] See letter from Walter H. Pincus to Senator Stuart Symington reproduced in *Hearings, IV*, pp. iii–iv. For the SGU's, see above, p. 296.

MAP 6. Communist Administrative Subdivisions of Laos

* The name "Taven Ock" on this map means literally "Sun Up" in Lao, and therefore this province is sometimes referred to in English-language Pathet Lao radio broadcasts as "Eastern Province."

cial governor), *chao muong* (district officer), and so on down the line. The corresponding NLHS officials were called *neo khoueng, neo muong,* and so forth. North Vietnamese advisers were assigned to the *neo khoueng*s, the *neo muong*s, and the different departments of the administration, and, of course, to the provincial committees of the Phak Pasason Lao.[16] The North Vietnamese advisory effort with the NLHS was channeled through *Doan* (Group) 959, which had its headquarters at Gia Lam just outside Hanoi and received its orders from the Central Committee of the Lao Dong Party. According to reports from the "liberated zone," the North Vietnamese advisers in Laos viewed their counterparts with the same feelings a teacher bears toward his pupils but observed polite and correct relations that allowed them to get the job done.

TABLE 6

PATHET LAO FORCES AS OF SEPTEMBER 15, 1969*

Province	Battalions	Men
Nam Tha	3	700
Phong Saly	2	650
Luang Prabang	20	5,935
Sayaboury	6	1,120
Vientiane	3	625
Borikhane	none confirmed	
Sam Neua	14	3,755
Xieng Khouang	24	5,105
Khammouane	13	3,240
Savannakhet	7	1,715
Saravane	5	1,600
Wapikhanthong	1	325
Sedone	2	700
Champassak	3	650
Attopeu	4	1,125
Sithandone	3	1,025
Total	110	28,270
Command and Support Troops		16,400
Over-all Total		44,670

* *Source:* American estimates.

Descriptions of life in the hills of Sam Neua by the small number of Western and Japanese visitors revealed the grim hardship of a

16 A 1970 estimate put the membership of the Phak Pasason Lao at 10,000.

militarized society in the grip of a seemingly endless struggle. Prince Souphanouvong and the other NLHS leaders lived and worked in the shelter of the caves in which northern Laos abounds. Women and children tilled their fields at night in order to avoid marauding aircraft. The towns had been flattened by repeated raids. Hardly a brick house was left standing in the towns of the Plain of Jars. Souvanna Phouma, during a flying visit there in December, 1969, inspected the ruins of his old house at Khang Khay.

Caught in this maelstrom, Prince Souphanouvong was unable to admit, even to his intimate associates, that he harbored doubts about his decision to stake the future on the Vietnamese Communists. In his ability to endure lay his entire strength. Only by emerging from the war as the undisputed leader of the resistance could he hope to pry the NLHS from the stranglehold of the Vietnamese. In such a situation, the line between patriotism and treason is a thin one. In September, 1969, a year after the mysterious death in Sam Neua of his eldest son, the Moscow-educated Ariya, the fifty-seven-year-old Prince went to Hanoi for the funeral of his mentor, Ho Chi Minh.

New Moves Toward Negotiations

It should be remembered that North Vietnam's principal short-term interest in Laos was to gain unimpeded use of the Ho Chi Minh Trail, that "barren zone" that was the lifeblood artery of the revolution in South Vietnam. Not only did the bombing tie up a greater number of North Vietnamese troops than ordinarily would have been needed to keep the supply routes open in Laos, but the damage to Communist supply lines placed a definite limitation on how far the Pathet Lao could push. For these reasons, Hanoi sought to maneuver the Americans into a position where they would have to cease bombing the Trail.

Although the bombing of areas other than the Trail inconvenienced the Pathet Lao,[17] from the North Vietnamese point of view it did not matter much, because they had no intention of pushing far (as far as the Mekong Valley, for instance). The extent to

---

[17] It served the purposes of NLHS propaganda, however. Western newspapers in March, 1970, widely published a photograph of Prince Souphanouvong in knee boots with a striped towel tied around his waist, digging trenches in Sam Neua. The Pathet Lao claimed to have destroyed 1,521 U.S. aircraft in the air and on the ground between May 17, 1964, and August 22, 1970.

which they were willing to help the Pathet Lao push outward its lines of control had always depended on their judgment of priorities. The recital in the West of figures of thousands of North Vietnamese troops in Laos tended to create the impression that General Giap was willing to pour unlimited manpower into Laos in order to conquer it. On the contrary, Giap's true interest lay in keeping as few of his men as possible in Laos, for a North Vietnamese soldier in the Hou River Valley was only fractionally productive compared to a North Vietnamese soldier on the Ho Chi Minh Trail or one inside South Vietnam itself.

The American bombing of the Ho Chi Minh Trail, therefore, affected North Vietnam's prime short-term interest in Laos, and it had always been evident that, in order to get this bombing of the Trail stopped, Hanoi would be willing to make concessions elsewhere in Laos. The only question was whether concessions in Laos interested the Americans, for the bombing of the Trail was an American affair, as Souvanna Phouma repeatedly said, and the Americans seemed likely to want to obtain concessions in South Vietnam rather than in Laos for its cessation.

Nevertheless, in 1969 there was one attempt by Souvanna Phouma to explore the possibility of some sort of settlement in Laos and one attempt by Hanoi to obtain an end of the bombing of the Trail. Perhaps encouraged by the start of the four-way negotiations on Vietnam in Paris, which had opened in January, Souvanna Phouma dispatched a letter to Souphanouvong in Sam Neua in February by the hand of the Soviet Ambassador, Viktor Minin, who traveled by ICC plane as far as Hanoi and thence by road to Sam Neua.

The next move was made by Le Van Hien, Hanoi's Ambassador to Laos. North Vietnam, like China, had left only a chargé d'affaires at the head of its embassy in Vientiane after the NLHS had taken the position that Prince Souvanna Phouma had merged his faction with the rightists and the coalition no longer existed in its original form. Hien returned to Vientiane in May on what he described as a "special mission" and had an interview with the Prime Minister. He reportedly offered a *quid pro quo* for Souvanna Phouma's withdrawal of permission for the American bombing of the Trail; North Vietnam would halt its offensive in northern Laos, would begin to withdraw some troops, and would be willing in due time, though not necessarily immediately, to discuss a political compromise. In reply, Souvanna Phouma drew attention to the military situation in Laos and to the North Vietnamese intervention which, he said, had gone on since 1959. "We are ready to stop the bombing if the North Vietnamese withdraw," he told reporters after his interview with Hien. "We are ready to reduce the intensity of the bombing if we see a progressive withdrawal of North Vietnamese troops."[18]

Souvanna Phouma then offered to separate the situation along the Trail, where he had no control over the American bombing, from the situation elsewhere in the country. "We want to separate the Laos and Vietnam problems," he said. "I am happy the National Liberation Front has submitted its ten-point program. I am happy also that President Nixon has submitted his eight-point program."[19] The North Vietnamese Ambassador, however, showed no interest in Souvanna Phouma's offer to go to Hanoi in order to negotiate a withdrawal of North Vietnamese troops from other areas of Laos in return for a halt to the American bombing everywhere but along the Trail.[20] The conclusion of the interview was that any arrangements that might lead toward peace in Laos would still inextricably involve other countries on both sides in the war.

Souvanna Phouma returned once again to the idea of neutralizing the Plain of Jars, this time moving closer to a proposal that Souphanouvong had made at the Paris summit. At the beginning of February, with the new North Vietnamese offensive imminent, the Prime Minister proposed that control of the Plain be turned over to "all neutralist forces,"[21] the first time he had taken official cognizance of the role of the "patriotic neutralists."

In his statement on Laos on March 6, 1970, President Nixon disclosed that he had written to Prime Ministers Kosygin and Wilson proposing consultations among the Geneva signatories. That same day, however, the NLHS Central Committee issued a five-point statement, "On the Subject of a Political Solution to the Laos

---

[18] *The New York Times,* May 21, 1969.

[19] *Ibid.* The ostensible purpose of the Ambassador's visit had been to seek support for the ten-point NLF program, which had been presented at the Paris conference on May 8, 1969. When the NLF was transformed into the Provisional Revolutionary Government of the Republic of South Vietnam (PRGRSV) a month later, on June 8, the Royal Lao Government did not recognize it. The Saigon government had closed its embassy in Laos on November 8, 1962, the day Hieu had presented his credentials, but had reopened it on March 18, 1964, under American pressure. Vientiane, therefore, had embassies from both Hanoi and Saigon.

[20] Interview with the author in Vientiane, March 28, 1970.

[21] Lao Presse bulletin, Vientiane, February 6, 1970.

Problem." The statement amounted to the first new negotiating proposal from the NLHS in five years.

Following the North Vietnamese pattern for opening negotiations with the United States in 1968, the NLHS statement demanded that Souvanna Phouma call a halt to the bombing as a gesture of his "sincerity" so that negotiations might begin. As for the format such negotiations might take, the NLHS did not insist on retaining the tripartite representation at the negotiating table but merely said that a political consultative conference should be held "among the interested Laotian parties in a spirit of national concord, equality, and mutual respect" for the purpose of forming a provisional coalition government. This government then would organize "free and democratic" elections for a National Assembly and a "democratic government of national union." Pending reunification of the territory of Laos, the parties would pledge themselves to avoid the use of force to infringe on the zone of control of the other parties. "Pro-American forces must withdraw immediately from areas they have illegally occupied, and must return the people they have forced to leave their villages and pay compensation for all losses they have sustained."[22] These negotiating proposals were forwarded by Prince Souphanouvong to both Prince Souvanna Phouma and Khamsouk Keola, leader of the "patriotic neutralists."

The NLHS statement afforded an opportunity for Prime Minister Kosygin, in replying to Nixon's letter, to reject the proposed consultations among the Geneva signatories and to insist that the first step toward restoring peace in Laos should be consultations among the political forces of the country.[23] Before the proposal for negotiations among the Lao could be explored further, however, a constitutional *coup d'état* took place in Cambodia on March 18, 1970.

The sudden removal of Prince Norodom Sihanouk in Cambodia deprived the Communists of the important landing and transit rights for war supplies that had been granted them after Sihanouk had recognized the newly proclaimed Provisional Revolutionary Government of the Republic of South Vietnam (PRGRSV). This development induced the Vietnamese Communists to tighten the links among the Indochinese revolutionary movements. The formation of an Indochinese united front was announced by Le Duan in Moscow on April 21, and a conference was held in southern China

---

[22] "Statement of the Central Committee of the NLHS on· the Subject of a Political Solution to the Laos Problem" (mimeographed), March 6, 1970, p. 3.

[23] *International Herald Tribune,* March 16, 1970.

on April 24 and 25, attended by Premier Pham Van Dong, representing North Vietnam; Nguyen Huu Tho, representing the PRGRSV; Prince Sihanouk, whom the Vietnamese Communists still regarded as Head of State of Cambodia, representing the National United Front of Kampuchea (Cambodia); and Prince Souphanouvong and Khamsouk Keola, representing the "patriotic forces" in Laos.[24] The conference ended with a joint declaration, which stated:

> Proceeding from the principle that the liberation and the defense of each country are the business of its people, the various parties pledge to do all they can to give one another reciprocal support according to the desire of the party concerned and on the basis of mutual respect.[25]

One of the first concerns of the Vietnamese Communists was to restore their supply route to South Vietnam, in view of the loss of their Cambodian transit rights and the selective blockade of the Cambodian coastline by the South Vietnamese navy. Now they were forced into total dependence on the Trail, and a move to reorganize its operation, the third such reorganization, was put under way. They now had to use the Trail to funnel traffic southwestward into Cambodia as well as southeastward into the Central Highlands. In effect, this meant reversing the traffic flow on the old Sihanouk Trail, a fairly simple proposition, because they could now follow the direction of flow of the main waterway linking Laos and Cambodia, the Kong River. To accomplish this, however, they had to remove the last remaining obstacle along that waterway, the Royal Lao Army garrison at Attopeu. This they did on the nights of April 28 and 29.

Attopeu, the easternmost Lao settlement in Laos and a provincial capital, had long been the scene of one of those accommoda-

[24] The appearance of Princes Sihanouk and Souphanouvong on the same platform was not without its ironies. In view of the historic Lao claim to Stung Treng, where there was still considerable attachment to Laos despite Sihanouk's measures to colonize the region with Khmers and prohibit the speaking of Lao, the NLHS had delayed recognizing Cambodia's borders as demanded by Sihanouk. On May 23, 1968, Sihanouk said at a press conference: "Everyone knows that the Viet Minh are behind the Pathet Lao." Three weeks later, referring to the Lao claim to Stung Treng, he said that if Souphanouvong came into his hands he would "have him shot immediately" (Phnom Penh Radio, June 13, 1968). The NLHS formally recognized Cambodia's frontiers in October, 1968, more than one year after North Vietnam and the NLF had done so.

[25] *Vietnam Courier* (Hanoi), May 4, 1970.

tions so common in the Indochina fighting. Since 1963, the town, with a population of about 5,000, had been cut off from road communication with the Mekong Valley, and the Pathet Lao controlled the river both above and below the town. The North Vietnamese, however, had scrupulously built their supply routes around the town and had left the two battalions of Royal Army troops in splendid isolation defending a town that was militarily indefensible. To venture more than a few miles out of town in any direction was a risky proposition, and after a few sharp fights in which patrols of government troops were mercilessly cut down by North Vietnamese in entrenched positions, the local commander learned that the limits of the accommodation under which his men lived did not extend far and occupied himself thereafter with administrative and business matters.

One morning in April, it was discovered that Pathet Lao agents had posted notices around the town during the night warning the inhabitants that the town would soon be taken over by the Pathet Lao. When the attack came a few nights later, all the key outlying positions fell almost immediately, but there was some sharp fighting at a battalion command post near the airfield west of the town. The *chao khoueng,* a colonel, who was in Pakse when the attack came, helicopered back to Attopeu to what he knew was a hopeless situation; when Pathet Lao agents with loudspeakers announced from across the river on the second night that all who put down their arms would be allowed to evacuate the town safely, he needed little persuasion to accept the offer and led a column of 400 men out on the sole escape route, to the north along the base of the Bolovens Plateau. The Pathet Lao and North Vietnamese proceeded to burn down all military installations after they took control but left civilian homes undamaged. One of their first acts was to requisition approximately 100 boats and send them down the Kong River to North Vietnamese transport units on the Cambodian border. The Royal Government lodged a protest with the ICC over the capture of Attopeu.[26]

In the words of its Foreign Minister, South Vietnam had accepted

[26] This protest brought to more than fifty the number of such protests to the ICC since 1963. In addition, the Royal Government had sent more than twenty letters to the Co-Chairmen protesting violations of the Geneva agreement by North Vietnam, and the Chairman of the Ceasefire Committee had recorded more than 3,600 violations of the ceasefire in more than 600 letters. (Lao Presse bulletin, Vientiane, June 1, 1970.)

the Geneva Protocol on Laos "without harboring any illusions."[27] The ensuing nine years of war in South Vietnam amply justified that reservation and, on February 8, 1971, President Nguyen Van Thieu announced to his people that South Vietnamese forces had entered Laos in the Tchepone region in an attempt to disrupt the operations on the Ho Chi Minh Trail. With the Cambodian sea route barred to the Communists and with assurances in hand of U.S. logistical and air support, the temptation to cut the Trail had finally proved too great to resist.[28]

[27] Closing speech by Foreign Minister Vu Van Mau of the Republic of Vietnam at the Geneva Conference, July 21, 1962.

[28] See below, Chapter 14., pp. 357–58.

14.

Vietnam, Laos, and the Hegemony of Indochina

The conflict that has torn Laos for the past twenty-five years is more than a mere civil war and has many ingredients of foreign intervention. One of these ingredients is the Vietnamese impingement on affairs in Laos, which extends back well before the advent of Communism in Vietnam. A second of these ingredients is the intervention of a powerful outsider, the United States, in a conflict that is the modern equivalent of centuries-old dynastic rivalries and cultural absorption.

These two major ingredients of foreign intervention cannot be considered in the same perspective. To attempt to do so is to pose the question of who is the aggressor in Indochina, which is at once the root of interpretation of the conflict and an insoluble problem. While it may be true that in all wars each side affirms it is fighting for a righteous cause, probably never before have the perspectives on the war and its aims and methods been farther apart than in Indochina. Instead of considering these two massive foreign interventions, which have been at the root of the conflict in Laos, in the same light, therefore, it is necessary to consider each within its own perspective.

First, the intervention of the Vietnamese. Although they trace their origins to migrations from the north, the Lao and the Vietnamese have undergone completely different evolutions, and their cultures today are visibly different. The geography of Indochina and the channeling of successive waves of religious influences have played major parts in the evolution of different societies and ways of life in Laos and Vietnam. Yet the two peoples have continued to live as close neighbors, not only nation to nation but frequently house to house.

In the context of the flow of Southeast Asian history, the Communist regime that established itself in Hanoi in 1954 inherited the expansionist drive of its predecessors. Its aim of establishing hegemony over the former French Indochina is well documented and has recently been confirmed by the actions of this regime, not only in Laos but also in Cambodia and Thailand. The various aspects of the Vietnamese intervention in Laos can therefore be summed up as follows: (1) the historic role played by the Vietnamese attempting to guide the 1945 revolution in Laos along the lines of the revolution in Vietnam; (2) the Vietnamese interpretation of their country's border with Laos and their use of Laotian territory for their own national ends, particularly the reunification of Vietnam; and (3) the persistent efforts of the Vietnamese Communists to foster the development of fraternal Parties in Indochina that would be totally subservient to the Vietnamese Party.

The Vietnamese Role in the 1945 Revolution

In 1943, the six chief towns of Laos counted 30,300 Vietnamese inhabitants.[1] Many had been attracted by posts in the French colonial administration and others by the profits to be made in business. With their numerous families, northern Annamese for the most part,[2] they soon formed important communities in the principal administrative and commercial centers. The Vietnamese had a preponderant voice over the Lao in such departments of the administration as public works, postal and telegraph, customs, and even police.

Although the loyalty of the Vietnamese was first to Vietnam, second to Laos, and only third to France, the French judged the employment of Vietnamese to be a satisfactory arrangement; the French officials who had been sent out to Indochina for the purpose of turning the colonies to value found the Lao too easy-going and

[1] Eric Pietrantoni, "La Population du Laos en 1943 dans son Milieu Géographique," *Bulletin de la Société des Études Indochinoises* (Saigon), XXXII, 3 (1957), pp. 223–43. The six towns were Vientiane, Thakhek, Savannakhet, Pakse, Luang Prabang, and Xieng Khouang, and their total population was 51,150.

[2] Except for the Tonkinese workers at the Phonthiou and Boneng tin mines.

without the technical skills of the Vietnamese.[3] In the relative somnolence of the Protectorate, a routine surveillance by the French Sûreté sufficed to prevent the outbreak of revolt. For if the Vietnamese had a notorious knack for finding out about the most secret matters almost as soon as they occurred, they had little prospect of stirring up agitation so long as French rule was accepted by the majority of the Lao.

Thus, French rule bound Laos to Vietnam, for the employment of Vietnamese in Laos was but the extension of a more general policy.[4] It was in Vietnam that the French concentrated their investments to develop the resources of Indochina. Commerce from Laos was directed toward the seaports of Tourane and Saigon instead of toward Bangkok. The French had drawn up plans for constructing a railroad through the mountains from Vinh to Thakhek, but the Lao opposed these plans, fearing an influx of Vietnamese immigrants into the Mekong Valley. Prince Phetsarath himself opposed another French scheme to colonize the Bolovens Plateau with Vietnamese plantation labor. Lao students in search of higher education went to Vietnam. Some, like Prince Souphanouvong, married Vietnamese.

As part of their effort to counterbalance the psychological shock of the French defeat in 1940 and the stationing of Japanese troops in Indochina, the French began in 1941 to pay greater attention to the formation of Lao cadres as part of an attempt to foster a Lao national spirit. High-ranking Lao civil servants were for the first time made *chao khoueng* and *chao muong* under the orders of the French Residents. This reform helped to assuage the growing complaints from the Lao over the policy of favoritism shown to the Vietnamese.

The Japanese coup of March 9, 1945, changed the situation radically. In the days following the imprisonment of the French Senior Resident and all French citizens in the towns of Laos, the Japanese occupation authorities decreed severe penalties for anyone found assisting the few French who had managed to elude

[3] Years later, American officials seem to have come to the same conclusion. Of the 1,925 non-Americans employed in the U.S. AID mission in Laos in 1969, 509, or almost one-third, were third-country nationals, mostly Thai and Filipino. (*Hearings, IV,* p. 571.) When asked about the French employment of Vietnamese, many Lao say that it was due to the fact that the Vietnamese were good at flattering the French.

[4] See Paul Doumer, *L'Indochine Française* (Paris: Vuibert et Nouy, 1905), pp. 291, 309.

arrest and who were organizing resistance centers in the country-side. This decree provoked the desertion from the French of large numbers of the Garde Indochinoise, a native police force which in Laos was made up mostly of Vietnamese.

Neither the Vietnamese community nor Prince Phetsarath was foolish enough to believe at that late date in a Japanese victory, but both were moved by their own aims to take advantage of the Japanese-sponsored proclamation of the independence of Laos on April 8. The Vietnamese, who had heard of the organization of the Viet Minh in China, were far-sighted enough to offer their services to the Japanese in return for arms. Phetsarath, on the other hand, saw in the Japanese coup the means to prevent the Vietnamese from getting their hands on an independent Laos; taking advantage of the fact that the Japanese commander in Laos had promised not to interfere in the internal affairs of the country, Phetsarath undertook on his own initiative as Prime Minister to replace Vietnamese members of the civil service with Lao and to send the Vietnamese and their families down river to Thakhek.

The opposition between the Vietnamese and Phetsarath in the days following March 9 led to a virtual paralysis of the work of the ministries in Vientiane. The Lao civil servants loyal to Phetsarath were at odds with the Vietnamese technicians, who claimed to be acting with Japanese support and who looked upon the Lao with contempt. In the provinces, the situation varied. At Savannakhet, the Vietnamese denounced the *chao muong* to the Japanese for attempting to get his hands on the weapons of the Garde Indochinoise, whereas all he had tried to do was to assert his normal governing authority. At the village level, for the most part, the Lao notables went about their routine without giving much attention to Japanese demands, especially in the way of taxes and coolie labor, an attitude that was of immense benefit to the Frenchmen who parachuted into Laos from Liberators flying from fields in British India to strengthen the anti-Japanese resistance.[5]

Meanwhile, in Thailand, the United States and Britain had clandestinely supported the creation of a Free Thai movement against the Japanese. Given the ethnic identity of the Lao on the left bank of the Mekong with the people living on the right bank under the administration of the Bangkok government, it is not surprising that

[5] Two officers of this courageous resistance, waged in the name of Free France, have written firsthand accounts. They are L.-H. Ayrolles, *L'Indochine Ne Répond Plus* (Saint-Brieuc: Prud'homme, 1948), and Michel Caply (pseudonym), *Guérilla au Laos* (Paris: Presses de la Cité, 1966).

a Free Lao movement formed in June, 1944, under the cover of and with the support of the Free Thai movement. Its leader was Oun Sananikone, scion of the great Sananikone family of Vientiane with ties of marriage to the Abhays of southern Laos.

Oun had crossed into Thailand in 1941 at the time of the French-Thai conflict, having seen in this conflict an opportunity to win the independence of Laos from France. Following the Japanese mediation of the conflict, Oun settled in Bangkok and was given an official position in the Military Security Department. He was joined there by supporters coming from Laos, notably the professor of Pali and linguist Maha Sila Viravong, who began an exhaustive examination of the archives dealing with Laos in the Bangkok libraries; Oudon Sananikone, who studied journalism; and Dr. Phouvong Nosavan, a classmate of Oun's from medical school in Hanoi.

Oun was in secret contact with American and British agents, and his original plan was to arrange for OSS agents and arms to be parachuted into Laos, since Thailand came under the authority of the British South East Asia Command. In the event, he had to attempt to implement his plans from bases in northeastern Thailand. Free Lao emissaries crossed the river to contact such Lao as Dr. Phouvong's brother, Phoumi Nosavan, a Boy Scout leader; Ou Voravong; and Khong Vongnarath, all at Savannakhet. At Thakhek, Pheng Sananikone became an adherent, but his brother Ngon refused. Singkapo Chounlamany also joined but later left to follow Souphanouvong, like Phoumi Nosavan.[6] Another recruit to the ranks of the Free Lao was Chao Sisoumang Sisaleumsak, who had been in Saigon at the time of the March 9 coup and who hurried to Pakse aboard a commercial truck, there raising the Lao flag and upbraiding the youth of the town for cooperating with the Vietnamese in complicity with the Japanese. The Free Lao were less successful at Paksane, where their principal contacts, Kou Voravong and Nouphat Chounlamany, informed the Free French, who suspected Oun of attempting to create a "Greater Laos" under the sponsorship of the Bangkok government; the French rewarded Kou Voravong by naming him *chao khoueng* in place of Phaya Khammao at Vientiane. Vientiane, the official residence of the Viceroy and the seat of the Prime Minister and his government, was hos-

[6] See p. 77, above. Khong Vongnarath was promoted to general in the Royal Lao Army in 1970, interestingly enough, a bare three weeks after he had abandoned Attopeu, the capital of the province of which he was governor, to the Communists.

pitable ground for the Free Lao and harbored an affiliated association called the Lao Pen Lao ("Laos for the Lao"). Oun debarked at Savannakhet immediately after the Japanese surrender, and there he met Souphanouvong.

At the moment when Japan surrendered and the sovereignty of Laos appeared up for grabs, therefore, there were in existence in the main towns along the Mekong two distinct groups bent on achieving independence. On the one hand, there were the Vietnamese, who had the advantage of Japanese encouragement and who had already begun to organize and acquire arms, and who supported Souphanouvong because a Vietnamese government in Laos was an impracticality. On the other, there were the adherents of the Free Lao, who hoped to receive arms from the United States (the British quietly dropped their support of the Free Lao following the arrival in the river towns of the first emissaries of the Free French resistance, who promptly got in touch with the British agents in Thailand). As long as Phetsarath, who was personally popular with the Lao civil servants and, despite his conservative nature, inclined toward independence, remained in his post as Prime Minister and the King and Crown Prince were cut off in Luang Prabang, these two groups had a relatively free hand in mobilizing support against a French reoccupation.[7]

The problem confronting these independence-minded groups was that the Japanese troops were already withdrawing southward toward Saigon, and their place was to be taken not by American or British troops but by Chinese Nationalist troops north of the Sixteenth Parallel, which included all of Laos above Saravane. The Japanese, before withdrawing from many places, turned over their stocks of weapons, ammunition, and clothing, as well as confiscated civilian arms, bicycles, and radios kept in warehouses since March 9, to the Vietnamese, who would now be on their own and would have to calm Lao suspicions of their real intentions. As for the Free Lao, they would have to look to the Chinese, who were shortly to prove themselves extremely unreliable allies.

The task facing the handful of Free French resistance officers and men when they emerged from their camps in the Laotian bush was thus an awesome one. They had orders to reoccupy the towns,

[7] The author owes much of his understanding of the relations between these two groups to his conversations over a long period of time with Oun Sananikone and with Tran Van Dinh and Pham Xuan Giai, both members of Prince Souphanouvong's bodyguard at the time these events occurred, and with Colonel William Law, U.S. Army.

maintain order, disarm the civilian population, gear up the administration once again, and take in their charge all French prisoners, many of them women and children, who were in a pitiful state as a result of their imprisonment since March 9. To accomplish all this, the Free French had their own small force and their Lao supporters, their good faith in the deep-seated loyalty to France of the population, and their wits. Their wartime allies were now occupied elsewhere, the British in Malaya and Burma, and the Americans in the Philippines and China. Moreover, the Free French were prohibited by the terms of the agreement reached at the Potsdam Conference, at which they were not represented, from accepting the Japanese surrender, an honor that fell to the Chinese, who were then eagerly crossing the border from Yünnan.

The critical point in terms of political authority was Luang Prabang, the seat of the monarchy, a fact the French were quick to see. Major (promoted to Lieutenant Colonel when he was named Commissaire de la République a few days afterward) Hans Imfeld, who had made his jungle base at Ban Ping Ho in the Dong Ngon Massif northwest of the royal capital, landed at Luang Prabang at 6 P.M. on August 29 and found that the town had already been evacuated by the Japanese.[8] On his way down river, Imfeld, an artillery officer of Swiss origin, held a brief conference with Crown Prince Savang Vatthana at the latter's residence. The Crown Prince reaffirmed the attachment of the King and his Court to France and implored Imfeld to intervene with the Allies to revoke the decision to admit into Laos a Chinese occupation army that he believed would spread ruin and disaster. The local population was already building canoes in which to flee from the Chinese.

Imfeld held full powers from his superior officers in Calcutta and was in radio communication with them. On August 30, he had his first audience with Sisavang Vong, and the King handed him a solemn declaration affirming that the Protectorate over the Kingdom of Luang Prabang had never ceased to exist. The King, however, expressed reservations about the French-sponsored Indochinese Federation, which he feared would further entrench Vietnamese dominance over the other peoples of Indochina, and asked that France take steps to secure the rapid restitution of Sayaboury, where Thai troops were parading in plain sight of Luang Prabang across the river, and of the right bank of Champassak.

The King and his Prime Minister were deeply split over the latter's insistence that, first, the Vichy Government had gone out of

[8] Caply, *op. cit.*, p. 241.

existence and thus the French were not legally entitled to restore the Protectorate, and second, the provinces of southern Laos should be unified with Luang Prabang. In Vientiane, the atmosphere of nascent nationalism had become highly charged as a result of inflammatory propaganda distributed mainly by the Vietnamese. On August 24, Phetsarath was compelled to decree strict measures for preserving law and order; the carrying of arms and the display of any political flag were forbidden on maximum penalty of death. The Prime Minister, who was in close touch with Phaya Khammao and the Free Lao liaison agents in the town, hoped that a political settlement to determine the future status of Laos could be worked out by an inter-Allied commission, which he hoped would soon arrive in Vientiane.[9] When he learned, therefore, that the King had handed a French agent a declaration stating that the Protectorate was still in force, and when he received no answer from Luang Prabang to his request for authority to issue a proclamation attaching the southern provinces to the Kingdom of Luang Prabang, Phetsarath was furious.

Phetsarath was now blocked on two sides. On the one hand, his quarrel with the King deprived him of full authority to deal with an explosive situation and forced him more and more to give way to the agitators who were urging him to take matters into his own hands, even at the risk of breaking relations with the King. On the other, there was still no sign of the hoped-for inter-Allied commission which, Phetsarath felt certain, would decide against France. This situation gave the Vietnamese, who had been fanning the flames of popular agitation, the opportunity they needed to overcome Phetsarath's hesitations. Discreet assurances were passed to the Prime Minister by a Viet Minh agent in Vientiane that support would be forthcoming from Vietnam, where the Viet Minh were taking power. The primary intermediary of this promised support was none other than Phetsarath's young half-brother, Prince Souphanouvong, who at that very moment was preparing to march across the Annamite Mountains with a Viet Minh bodyguard of fifty men.

Long before Ho Chi Minh proclaimed the establishment of the Democratic Republic of Vietnam on September 2, the Viet Minh had taken an active interest in the land beyond the Annamite Chain. Ho himself was active in Siam during 1928–29 on behalf of

[9] See Phetsarath's telegram to *chao khouengs* of August 28 and his proclamation to the French population of September 1, quoted in Caply, *op. cit.*, pp. 251–52.

the Vietnam Revolutionary Youth Association and visited Udorn, Sakhorn Nakhorn, Mukdaharn, and Nong Khai; he returned there briefly in March, 1930, to spread the word of the founding of the Indochinese Communist Party at Hong Kong the previous month.[10]

Immediately after the March 9 coup, Viet Minh agents in Laos began distributing anti-French propaganda and urging the members of the Garde Indochinoise to prepare to fight should the French attempt to reassert their sovereignty over Laos. The Viet Minh even fomented rebellion among the members of this force who had withdrawn from Laos with the Free French into China and succeeded in getting most of them to desert. When Japan surrendered, these militia units were already in control of towns like Thakhek and Paksane, where the red and yellow-starred flag of Ho's republic flew. The Viet Minh also were strong at Kam Keut and Nape, where they persuaded Japanese troops to help them repulse the Free French.[11] Farther south, the Viet Minh maintained access to Vietnam through their control of the towns of Naphao and Tchepone, which the Free French did not attempt to reoccupy with their meager forces.

Politically, the Viet Minh had formed a network of spies that operated in the Vietnamese communities in the towns of Laos. When the Free Lao movement emerged as the first Lao political group that might lead an independence movement, they infiltrated it to turn it to their own design and prevent it from securing a monopoly of popular support. Their agent in this was Kaysone Phomvihan.[12]

Discussions were held between Souphanouvong and the Free Lao. The latter, responding to Phetsarath's appeal for the unification of Laos, had created a "Committee for Free Laos" under Oun, who had received the title Governor of the South.[13] This committee was reshuffled following the discussions at Savannakhet and renamed on October 8 the "Committee for Independent Laos" (Khana Lao Issara), with Phetsarath as Honorary President. Souphanouvong as President, and Oun as Vice President. The first step

[10] See Le Manh Trinh, "Dans le Kouang Toung et au Siam" in *Souvenirs sur Ho Chi Minh* (Hanoi: Éditions en Langues Étrangères, 1962).

[11] Caply, *op. cit.,* p. 264.

[12] See pp. 72–74, above.

[13] The heir to the defunct throne of Champassak, Prince Boun Oum, had thrown in his lot with the French. He believed that immediate independence would turn Laos into a battleground between Siam and Vietnam. (Conversation with the author in Champassak, May 3, 1970.)

toward establishment of an independent government of Laos had been taken. The same day, Souphanouvong signed an order in the name of this committee creating a liberation army. Because of some confusion among the Lao civil servants as to the exact authority of this committee, Souphanouvong issued a clarifying circular to all *chao khouengs* on October 11, saying there was no conflict of function between this and the Defense Committee that had been established in Vientiane the previous day and promising to go to Vientiane to merge the two groups. This he did at the end of October, after he had visited Thakhek, which was the town in Laos with the largest community of Vietnamese and which, as the terminal of the roads leading from the Keo Neua and Mu Gia passes over the mountains, served as Vietnam's gateway to the Mekong Valley. The liberation army at Thakhek comprised 1,500 armed Vietnamese and Lao.

On arrival at Vientiane, Souphanouvong was made Commander-in-Chief of the Armed Forces and immediately announced the conclusion of a "Military Convention" with Hanoi which, in effect, "gave a decisive voice at every level to the Vietnamese cadres who had come from Hanoi in the guise of 'technical advisers.' "[14] Souphanouvong now had under his personal control the armed defectors of the Garde Indochinoise, who henceforth acted in the name of the Lao Issara government that had been formed earlier in October under the premiership of Phaya Khammao.

Souphanouvong also acted to get full control of the services of the police and intelligence agencies. His decree of November 1

---

[14] Caply, *op. cit.,* p. 314. Caply, who witnessed these events, furnishes much evidence that, although the Viet Minh did not actually hold official positions in the Lao Issara government, they worked actively to control its policies through their "technical advisers." For the Viet Minh version *cf.* p. 24, footnote 4, above.

Oun, who was made Minister of National Economy, claims that the decision to make Souphanouvong Commander in Chief was agreed to in a private arrangement among the three princely brothers. After the inauguration of the government, Souphanouvong spent most of his time at Thakhek instead of at Vientiane.

The key Vietnamese members of Souphanouvong's entourage were: Le Phung Thoi, Le Thieu Huy (who was killed at Thakhek in Souphanouvong's boat), Hoang Xuan Binh, and Nguyen Van Thuong, who all came from Hanoi; Tran Van Dinh, Doan Thuan, Tran Khanh Thanh, Tran Van Que (who was wounded in the leg at Thakhek in Souphanouvong's boat), Nguyen Van Tue, Tran Ba, and Nguyen Chuong, who all came from Hué; Pham Xuan Giai, who came from Savannakhet; and Pham Xuan Phong, who came from Thakhek. (Conversations of the author with Pham Xuan Giai in Vientiane in 1970.)

stated that the intelligence section of the armed forces was henceforth the central organ for all services having to do with the Police, Sûreté, and Military Intelligence for all levels in Laos. Article 3 of this decree entrusted the use of all information to "the chief of the Intelligence Section in complete agreement with his technical advisers"; Article 4 gave the "technical advisers" the power to interrogate prisoners; Article 5 required "one or more of his technical advisers" to be present when the chiefs of the Intelligence Section released a prisoner; and Article 8 stated bluntly: "The Lao chief of the Intelligence Section of the General Staff will make no decision without consulting his technical advisers, who, officers of the personal bodyguard of His Highness Prince Souphanouvong, are experienced specialists in this important matter."[15]

While Thakhek was in the hands of armed Vietnamese and while Vientiane was under strong Vietnamese influence through the presence of the "technical advisers," the situation at Luang Prabang was different. The royal capital had virtually no Vietnamese residents, and there the Lao Issara could conduct affairs on their own. An emissary of the Free Lao, Prince Sisoumang, had already bicycled up the Royal Road to organize support; on arrival, he began forming units of young men to support the independence movement.[16] The air drops of arms promised him by the OSS officers with whom he had had contact failed to materialize, however, and so other sources had to be found, for Sisoumang and his supporters possessed exactly six pistols among them.

On the night of November 4, without waiting for the arrival of a stronger armed force dispatched from Vientiane under the command of Sing Ratanasamay, who had opposed the French since 1941 and had returned from Thailand to become the Defense Minister in the Lao Issara government, Prince Sisoumang's young men struck. With Chinese occupation troops (who had begun arriving in Luang Prabang late in September) maintaining a cordon around the house where Imfeld and his small group had established their command post, they forced the barracks of the Gardes Civiques, gaining access to a large quantity of arms and ammunition, some of which were afterward dispatched to Xieng Khouang, Sam

[15] The full text of this amazingly frank decree is given in Caply, *op. cit.,* pp. 315–17.

[16] Conversation of the author with Chao Sisoumang in Vientiane, April 21, 1970. Sisoumang says he was halted outside Vientiane by a band of armed Vietnamese and it was thanks to his knowledge of their language that he was able to obtain permission to pursue his journey.

Neua, and Vientiane. Then, led by Tiao Boungnavath, the chief delegate in Luang Prabang of the Lao Issara government, who ostentatiously knocked over the statue of Pavie on the way, they marched on the Royal Palace. There was some shooting in the air by the excited youths, and King Sisavang Vong was informed that, since he had refused a request from the government that he abdicate voluntarily, he had been deposed by order of the government. A triumphant telegram was dispatched to inform the government of this "*coup de force* unprecedented in the annals of the Kingdom."[17] The Lao Issara also managed to get their hands on 200,000 piastres in cash, which Imfeld had entrusted to Kampheuane Tounalom to give the King; the money was sent to Vientiane to replenish their government's nearly depleted treasury.

Finding that he was powerless to reverse the situation, Imfeld left Luang Prabang a few weeks later. He had received a last desperate plea from Savang Vatthana for 300 French paratroopers to be dropped on the Plain of Jars to block the expected advance into Laos of Viet Minh troops; the paratroopers were not available.[18] There were only forty Europeans living in Luang Prabang at the time.

The situation in Xieng Khouang was even more confused than elsewhere.[19] On April 12, four days after the Japanese-sponsored declaration of independence, Vietnamese at Khang Khay announced a decision taken at a secret meeting to proclaim a *phu* (prefec-

[17] Quoted in Caply, *op. cit.*, p. 318. Caply's account was confirmed by General Ouan Ratikon in a conversation with the author in Vientiane on June 3, 1970. Ouan, who was at that time a sergeant in the French Army and under Imfeld's orders, formed three companies of soldiers at Luang Prabang and gave them arms that Imfeld had received by parachute. After the arrival of the Chinese, however, Ouan's soldiers withdrew into the forest and buried their arms. They then returned to Luang Prabang, where they were won over to the Lao Issara cause by Chao Sisoumang's propaganda. After participating in the storming of the Royal Palace on the night of November 4, Ouan ordered the buried arms dug up and handed over to the Lao Issara.

[18] After he became King, Savang Vatthana retained this pessimism as to the future of Laos. At his father's funeral in 1961, he remarked to Prince Sihanouk of Cambodia: "Alas, I am doomed to be the last King of Laos."

[19] Much of the following account is based on a conversation of the author with Chao Say Kham in Vientiane, May 9, 1970. A direct descendant of Chao Noi, Chao Say Kham has been *chao khoueng* of Xieng Khouang since 1946. The Lao Issara killed one of his young brothers in 1946, and the Viet Minh killed an elder brother who was serving in the French Army in 1947.

ture), restoring the allegiance to Annam of 1832. The governor of this newly proclaimed *phu* was stated to be Le Xuan Phy, a technician of public works. A Vietnamese had managed to obtain the post of key-keeper to the Japanese armory in that town, and, as a result, the Vietnamese were able to back up their proclamation with stolen Japanese arms. However, a pro-French secretary, Chao Say Kham, was able by means of a youth corps he had organized to prevent the Vietnamese from taking over Xieng Khouang town with its seals of the provincial administration until the arrival of the French, who immediately began to deal with the Viet Minh reinforcements moving up Route 7 from Nghe An. The *chao khoueng* of the province, who had cooperated with bad grace with the Free French agents during the Japanese occupation, abandoned his post to join the Lao Issara supporters in Luang Prabang as soon as he heard of Sing's planned march. The balance of forces was made more precarious by the fact that the Meo (yet another important element of the population, who considered that they lived neither in Laos nor in Annam but in their own Meo kingdom), while in majority sympathetic to the French, harbored a minority faction that supported the Viet Minh.

Sing led his attacking column of 100 men, mostly Lao but also some Thai from Sayaboury, onto the Plain of Jars on November 26. Sing's advance coincided with scattered actions by Viet Minh partisans, who were surprised and badly beaten by a small group of Frenchmen and Lao and Meo supporters at Nong Het under the command of Lieutenant Gauthier, one of L.-H. Ayrolles's group. With pro-French Meo guarding the trails over the border from Vietnam and Gauthier blocking Route 7, the Viet Minh were unable to do much to help Sing, who succeeded in capturing Xieng Khouang town on November 28, only to lose it again to the French on January 26, 1946.

The OSS agents sympathized with the Vietnamese and the Lao, even to the extent of undermining the French, and it is interesting to speculate whether there would have been war in Indochina twenty-five years later had the independence movement succeeded in enlisting international support. The OSS disbanded, however, and American policy was dictated by the need to save Western Europe from the threat of Communist takeover. The British, on the other hand, instinctively sympathized with the French and helped them reassert French sovereignty, at first covertly, but later more overtly and in contravention of the authority of their South East

Asia Command.[20] The inter-Allied commission on which Phetsarath had pinned his hopes never materialized.

In retrospect, the consequences of the Potsdam decision to have the Chinese occupy Indochina north of the Sixteenth Parallel, in the absence of any sort of inter-Allied understanding of what the political future of Indochina was to be, seem to confirm the judgment of the Lao in 1945 that the Chinese occupation was sheer folly. Whatever may have been in the mind of President Truman at Potsdam, the slim chance that the Chinese might have constituted a force for independence in Laos rapidly vanished as the Chinese set about eating the country into a food crisis, extorting money from its merchants, and even making a clumsy attempt to annex the northwestern region of Laos to the Republic.[21] Before closing this extraordinary chapter, the Chinese were actually to betray the Lao Issara at their last foothold of Ban Houei Sai, selling once again to the highest bidder, the French.

Once the fortunately short-lived Chinese occupation had come to a close[22] and British forces had withdrawn from southern Indochina, the stage was left to the French and the Viet Minh with their

[20] The authority of SEAC during this period is defined in Vice Admiral the Earl Mountbatten of Burma, *Post Surrender Tasks; Section E of the Report to the Combined Chiefs of Staff by the Supreme Allied Commander South East Asia 1943–1945* (London: HMSO, 1969) as follows:

At the Potsdam Conference, the Combined Chiefs of Staff had allotted to SEAC that part of French Indo-China lying south of 16° North, and by this arbitrary division the northern half of the country was occupied by Chinese forces (p. 285).

. . . .

On the 1st October, I received a telegram from the Chiefs of Staff, altering my instructions and informing me that I was to use British Indian troops to give assistance to the French throughout the interior of Southern F.I.C., so long as this did not prejudice my primary responsibility for Saigon (p. 288).

Clearly, the authority of SEAC did not extend north of the Sixteenth Parallel at any time. A development that greatly influenced the feeling of the British toward the French was the attempted massacre by the Viet Minh of French citizens in Saigon during September, which was thwarted by British Indian troops.

[21] Caply, *op. cit.,* pp. 244–45.

[22] The Chinese occupation forces undertook to withdraw by March 31, 1946, under the terms of a French-Chinese agreement signed on February 28.

clients in Laos and Cambodia. The French reoccupation of Laos, effected under conditions of great frustration for the French, virtually emptied the river towns of their Vietnamese population. The leaders of the Lao Issara government also fled across the river. But the resistance to the French was to grow again, and the independence that had been missed in 1945–46 was eventually born in the flames of the first Indochina War.

The sudden removal of French rule from Laos in World War II meant the disappearance of a cohesive political force. Some Lao were tempted to look across the Mekong to their brethren on the Korat Plateau; others began thinking in terms of amalgamating their northwestern region with Yünnan. Within the Lao independence movement itself, which incorporated the elite of the country, the rapid and dramatic sequence of events resulted in an almost random apportioning of loyalties, with members of the same family often finding themselves on opposing sides, as was the case with Souvanna Phouma and his brothers and with the large Sananikone family. Paradoxically, it was the Vietnamese who emerged in this time of troubles in the position of wanting to hold together what had been French Indochina, with the provision that they would replace the French as its masters.[23]

The Vietnamese claim was not an empty one. In the name of independence, they had, after all, spilled Vietnamese blood to prevent the fragmentation of Laos. At Thakhek in March, 1946, the spilling of blood had been particularly heavy[24] and occurred *after* the *modus vivendi* between the Viet Minh and the French in Vietnam. Young Vietnamese, who had originally enrolled in the Mixed Forces[25] with the hope of going to France to complete their education, instead spent the war patrolling Laos, which they got to know

[23] For an excellent compendium of the history of these conflicting forces, see Hugh Toye, *Laos: Buffer State or Battleground* (London: Oxford University Press, 1968), Chapters I and II, which are based on Colonel Toye's extensive perusal of the literature and on his personal observations of the problem while serving as military attaché at the British Embassy in Vientiane.

[24] The battle of Thakhek remains to this day the bloodiest engagement in the modern history of Laos. According to eyewitness accounts, 3,000 persons were killed in the town. Many of the casualties occurred when the British Spitfires supporting the French forces strafed the market place and the river banks where thousands were trying to get away across the river.

[25] A component of French forces in Indochina, the Mixed Forces came under the command of the Annam-Laos Brigade, with headquarters at Hué, and were regular military troops, unlike the Garde Indochinoise.

intimately. If the exact outline of what the leaders of the Viet Minh had in mind for the future of Laos remained somewhat blurred, the fact was that here and now sections of the Lao and the Vietnamese were fighting a common enemy, the French.[26]

The Border Question

Adding to the historical ambiguities in the relationship between Laos and Vietnam, and in part derived from them, are the physical ambiguities surrounding the border between the two countries. The border does not follow the watershed precisely. Nor can it be described precisely as an ethnic border. The borders of present-day Laos can hardly he said to correspond to the limits inhabited by the Lao. There are approximately six times as many Lao living across the Mekong in northeastern Thailand as there are on its left bank. There are an estimated 20,000 Lao living in Cambodia.[27] Laos's borders with Vietnam, Cambodia, and China run through mountainous areas inhabited by tribesmen rather than Lao, Vietnamese, Khmers, or Han, and, in the past, this fact has often bedevilled relations between Laos and Vietnam.

The first attempts to fix the border for political purposes appear to have been made where there existed a frequented trail or road over the mountains. Thus, one of the oldest border treaties in existence is the 1364 agreement between the King of Lan Xang and the King of Annam, which fixed the boundary in the vicinity of the Ai Lao Pass. Under the reign of Souligna Vongsa came the famous border treaty fixing the boundary according to whether the houses of the inhabitants were built on stilts or on the ground. This served the purpose until the arrival of the French, when more precise means of delimitation were called for. Pavie furthered the work of border definition on his last mission to Laos.

On December 27, 1913, the Governor General of Indochina signed a decree establishing a commission to define the boundaries

[26] An interesting sidelight on how national feelings among the Vietnamese transcend political divisions is the fact that, on Ho Chi Minh's death in September, 1969, many Vietnamese in Vientiane were seen wearing the swatch of black mourning cloth.

[27] Jean Delvert, *Le Paysan Cambodgien* (Paris and The Hague: Mouton, 1961), p.16. For the extent of the Lao-inhabited areas of northeastern Cambodia, see the ethnolinguistic map in *Bulletin de la Société de Etudes Indochinoises*, XXVII, 1 (1952), facing page 5. Lao was the *lingua franca* of Darlac and Stung Treng as recently as 1955, according to Lucien Coudoux, who traveled from Ban Me Thuot to Stung Treng on foot and by oxcart in that year.

of Annam and Laos. This commission met at Hué during 1914 and on March 21, 1914, published its report. On the basis of this report, the Governor General decreed on October 12, 1916, that the border in the Ai Lao Pass area would be defined as follows: "The border starts from elevation 1221 and runs N-S along the 115.78 meridian grades East of Paris to its meeting with bench mark 1020.82 meters at Dong Ta Puc."[28] This represents a distance of 21 miles. This is one of the very few sections that has been defined according to international grid measurements.

By and large, therefore, the French left the independent Lao and Vietnamese governments a common political border that, while it follows *grosso modo* the watershed of the South China Sea and the Mekong River, reflects accurately neither geography nor ethnography and furthermore is defined according to the international grid along only a fraction of its great length.

Aside from this, the border situation is further complicated by the fact that different principalities or provinces lying along its length became attached at various times in the past to various authorities by the French, who prided themselves on their systematic administration and were eager to open up the alleged riches of these territories to economic exploitation. After the French had succeeded in expelling the Siamese from all the left-bank territories in 1893 by enforcing the claims of Annam in Khammouane and Savannakhet and of the Khmer monarchy farther south, they followed up with a ten-year-long attempt to reorganize the territories thus acquired. It was not until 1904, with the attachment of Darlac and Stung Treng to Annam and Cambodia, respectively, that Laos assumed the shape it has today.[29] In the course of this attempt at reorganiza-

---

[28] "Note d'Information du Ministère des Affaires Étrangères du Royaume du Laos au Sujet des Relations Laos-RDVN," p. 2. Much of the information in the following section is derived from this source, which also contains valuable documentation relevant to the exchange of notes between Laos and North Vietnam with respect to charges of violations of North Vietnamese airspace in 1958 and 1959. Of twelve such incidents protested by Hanoi, the Lao Government accounted for all but four.

[29] Prince Boun Oum maintains (conversation with the author in Champassak, May 3, 1970) that Pavie wanted to attach all the territories that had once belonged to the Kingdom of Champassak to Cambodia but was prevented from doing so by Boulloche, who was named French Senior Resident in Laos at the end of 1895. A postal mark "Pakse, Cambodia" is in Boun Oum's possession. Sarin Chhak refers to a letter from Pavie in Hanoi to the French Minister of Foreign Affairs dated September 19, 1894, as evidence (*Les Frontières du Cambodge,* Paris: Dalloz, 1966, p. 39) and argues that, as France had acquired sovereignty of the territories by invoking the historic

tion, the border principalities were moved about like discs in a game of shuffleboard.

Of all the territorial ambiguities left unresolved by the French, none is more vexing than that of Xieng Khouang, the ancient kingdom whose fate it was to lie at fifteen days' march from Hué and forty days' march from Bangkok.[30] After its annexation to the Empire of Annam in 1832, Xieng Kouang was ruled as the Prefecture of Tran Ninh until 1848, when Chao Noi's eldest son, Chao Pho, was returned home from Hué following the accession there of Tu Duc. Although Annam still considered Tran Ninh a vassal, Chao Pho managed to resume the practice of paying tribute to both Luang Prabang and Annam. The invasion of the Ho ushered in another period of devastation and evacuation of the countryside. This was the state of affairs when the French asserted Annam's right to hold the kingdom in protectorate against the claim of Siam. By a decree of November 22, 1895, the French detached Xieng Khouang from Annam and attached it to Laos; there it has remained, albeit shakily, to the present day.

Similarly, Sam Neua, which lies northeast of Xieng Khouang, has a history of alternating attachment to rival entities on either side of the cordillera. Known in former times as Houa Phan, the territory was conquered in the sixteenth century by King Setthathirath of Lan Xang, who endowed it with many pagodas. When Lan Xang split up, Houa Phan went to Luang Prabang. The treaty of October 3, 1893, put an end to Siamese extension of influence in Houa Phan, which became French-protected territory. A decree dated June 6, 1894, divided the territory in two for administrative purposes and attached Sam Neua town and some other districts to

---

claims of the Khmer monarchy, which had antedated, and included, Champassak, it had no right to attach them to anyone but Cambodia. (France had originally attached them to Cochinchina.) If this argument were applied elsewhere, however, there would simply be no Laos at all south of the Ca Dinh River.

Texts of the 1904 decrees transferring Darlac and Stung Treng are reproduced in Khamchan Pradith, *Place Historique du Laos en Asie* (Vientiane: 1968), pp. 44–45. The situation of some of these territories was finally regularized by a presidential decree dated September 20, 1915, which had the effect of ratifying a series of prior administrative measures and was known as the "Decret Doumergue" after the then French Minister of Colonies, Gaston Doumergue.

[30] Charles Archaimbault, "Les Annales de l'Ancien Royaume de S'ieng Khwang," *Bulletin de l'École Française d'Extrême-Orient,* Tome LIII Fasc. 2 (Paris, 1967), p. 622.

Annam and Xieng Kho, Muong Het, Muong Son, and Hua Muong districts to Laos. Following a migration of people out of the Annam-administered areas, a decree of June 15, 1903, attached the entire territory to Laos, and another dated June 20, 1905, made Sam Neua the capital.[31] Until recent years, only a rough pony trail connected Sam Neua to the rest of Laos, and it was easier to travel to Hanoi than to Vientiane.

When the Democratic Republic of Vietnam came to power in Hanoi in 1945, it inherited the traditional Vietnamese interest in the mountainous territories to the west. It was not until 1954, however, that this government was in a position to enforce its claims. North Vietnam has been quite taciturn on the subject and, when pressed by the Lao, has put off the opening of negotiations. In a letter dated February 23, 1957, Premier Pham Van Dong assured Prince Souvanna Phouma as follows: "The border between Vietnam and Laos concerns all of Vietnam. In southern Vietnam there are numerous regions in dispute as in the north. Thus, in present circumstances, the time seems to be unfavorable for an over-all settlement of the question."[32] However, later that year, the Lao insisted on opening talks about a border violation by North Vietnam, and in these talks, the only negotiations known to have taken place, Hanoi behaved in a most curious way.

The negotiations arose out of North Vietnam's occupation of a small valley enclosing the headwaters of a tributary of the Song Ca River in Xieng Khouang Province, which encompasses the Plain of Jars, the dominant geographical feature of northern Laos.[33] The Plain constitutes one of the exceptions to the general rule regarding the lay of the border between Laos and Vietnam along the riverbed. From the Phou San Massif just to the northeast of the Plain, the Mat River rises and flows eastward to join the Song Ca, which flows into the South China Sea near Vinh. Due north of the Plain, the Nam Khan zig-zags its way to join the Mekong at Luang Prabang; as late as the 1920's it afforded travelers a means for completing the journey from Hanoi at a time when the road had not yet been extended west of the Plain. Finally, rising to the south

[31] André Boutin, "Monographie de la Province des Houa-Phan" *Bulletin des Amis du Laos* (Hanoi), No. 1 (July, 1937), pp. 71–72.

[32] "Note d'Information," *op. cit.*, p. 1.

[33] I am indebted to Thongsavat Vongsavanthong, the present *chao khoueng* of Vientiane Province, who was the leader of the Lao delegation to these negotiations, for furnishing me with this information in a conversation in his office in Vientiane on April 20, 1970.

of the Plain, two rivers, the Ngum and the Nhiep, flow into the Mekong, one below Vientiane and the other above Paksane, and their courses have become natural tracks for travelers and marching armies.

The valley occupied by North Vietnam lies in a north-south alignment close to the border of North Vietnam to the north of Nong Het. Administratively, the area is known as the *tasseng* of Chang and is accessible only by trails. The Royal Lao Army had withdrawn its garrison from Chang as part of a consolidation of positions after the 1954 armistice. The local inhabitants were alarmed to find that, after the withdrawal of the Lao soldiers, soldiers of the North Vietnamese Army entered the area "to assure the security of the region," as they put it. The North Vietnamese brought with them teachers, who began instructing the children of Chang in Vietnamese language and culture. Soon, a regular civil administration was functioning there. The local inhabitants, more alarmed than ever, reported this state of affairs to the *chao muong,* and the report reached the ears of the *chao khoueng.* At this, the Vietnamese accelerated their colonization, bringing in more and more civil servants and even settlers. The local inhabitants began to demand action, and in an exchange of letters the Lao and North Vietnamese governments agreed to open negotiations on the matter.

When the negotiations began in Nong Het in mid-1957, with mixed civilian and military representatives, the North Vietnamese claimed that the *tasseng* had belonged to them since the days of the old kings of Xieng Khouang and showed documents that the Lao took to be forgeries. When the Lao delegation produced the standard French map of Indochina, clearly showing Chang to be on the Lao side of the border, the North Vietnamese dismissed the map as an "imperialist legacy." After ten days of fruitless argument, the Lao delegation decided to take the matter to Hanoi. The delegation left for Hanoi in September, only to find that the same arguments were advanced by the other side. The Vietnamese were unable to answer Lao demands that they produce Vietnamese names for the peaks, streams, and various villages within the *tasseng.* During the course of these talks, which ended inconclusively, a curious incident occurred. One night the Vietnamese cut the power supply of the radio used by the Lao delegation to communicate with Vientiane. The Lao, seeing what had happened, rejected a Vietnamese suggestion that they use the Hanoi telegraph office instead. The leader of the Royal Lao Government delegation became the *chao khoueng* of Sam Neua Province in November, 1957, and when he asked an NLHS official there about Hanoi's attitude toward the border negotiations, the latter replied, "Oh, that's a small thing. When Laos is free they'll give it back to us again."

The Lao knew differently, however. Vietnamese immigration onto the Plain was encouraged in the days of the French and aroused the concern of the Lao. The Vietnamese made good vegetable farmers, and, in pre–World War II times, potatoes and gladioli were shipped by air to Hanoi from the Plain. Documents found in Xieng Khouang after eight years of Communist administration mention a special category of North Vietnamese advisers to the Neo Lao Hak Sat (NLHS) civilian administration called "Nghe An cadres," and plans for further Vietnamese colonization of the province are still apparently alive.[34] It is the Plain that Hanoi covets, in the words of Souvanna Phouma, "as a strategic base for its ideological and political expansion to the west."[35]

Premier Pham Van Dong's letter of February 23, 1957, implied that the Hanoi government was unwilling to see discussions take place in regard to the border between Laos and South Vietnam until Vietnam had been reunified. The provisional military demarcation line[36] in the vicinity of the Seventeenth Parallel, which had been settled on at the eleventh hour by the delegates at Geneva in 1954 as the point of partition, intersected at right angles the border between Laos and Vietnam along the section defined in the 1916 decree of the French Governor General. The western end of the demarcation line, which is defined in the 1954 Geneva agreements as following the parallel of the Vietnamese village of Bo Ho Su, lies slightly to the south of the Seventeenth Parallel. It was here that, in December, 1958, the clash occurred between a patrol of the Royal Lao Army and North Vietnamese soldiers who had taken up positions in a number of villages on the Laos side of the border.[37]

The region in question lies north of Route Nationale 9, which

[34] See Edwin T. McKeithen, *The Role of North Vietnamese Cadres in the Pathet Lao Administration of Xieng Khouang Province* (Vientiane: U.S. AID, 1970), pp. 2–4.

[35] Speech on the occasion of the twentieth anniversary of the Lao National Army, reported in Lao Presse, Vientiane, March 24, 1970. For Giap's view of the strategic importance of the Plain, see p. 259, above.

[36] Drawn on the 1:100,000 map of Indochina and known as Secret Document IC/42. Annex; 20 July 1954.

[37] See p. 115, above.

MAP 7. The Ho Chi Minh Trail, 1958

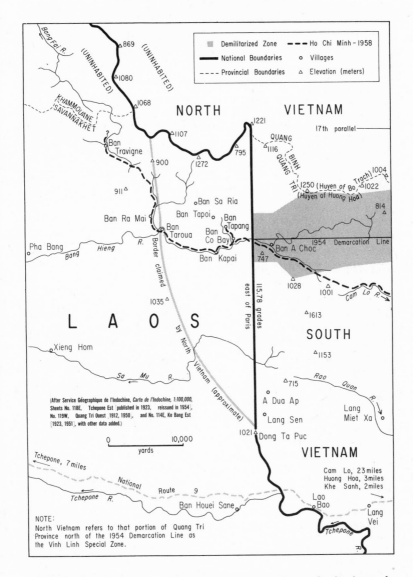

According to this map, the watershed follows the Laos-Vietnam border for as far south as its junction with the Quang Binh Province-Quang Tri Province boundary and then follows this boundary as far east as a point at approximately elevation 1004, where it drops south once more.

joins Quang Tri, Dong Ha, and Khe Sanh in Vietnam with Savannakhet in Laos through Tchepone, and at the headwaters of the Bang Hieng River. Its terrain is among the roughest in the Annamite Chain. The vegetation, fed by annual rainfall amounting to 160 inches or more, is lush; stream banks are overgrown with reeds that rot and effuse noxious smells into the dank, humid valley bottoms, while the higher ground produces a thick cover of elephant grass and brambles as high as a man. In the southern portion, there are dark forests, but farther north, where the whitish calcareous cliffs mark the beginning of the karst country, the vegetation is sparser. In the rainy season, the monsoon clouds coming up from the Gulf of Siam across the Korat Plateau shroud the valleys in mist for days on end. This forbidding country abounds in malarial mosquitoes, leeches, and scorpions, and the lowland Lao avoid the interior.

The province of Savannakhet, as it is known today, was inhabited long ago by Kha tribesmen called in the annals Pheng-My.[38] The Kha paid an annual tribute of elephants to the Court of Annam. During the fifteenth century, about the time of the establishment in Vietnam of the Le Dynasty, there occurred a migration of people coming from the north. These people were the Phou-Thai, and, unlike the Kha, they belonged to the Thai family and were Buddhists. At first their migration was a peaceful one, but later trouble developed between the Phou-Thai and Kha, and the latter sought refuge in the mountainous eastern region on the territory of the Vietnamese *phu* of Cam Lo.

The three principal notables of the Phou-Thai, who were brothers, applied to the ruler at Vientiane for titles to administer the new lands. At this time, Vientiane was enjoying a period of stability and the ruler willingly acceded to this request, which brought

---

[38] For the following account of historical events, the author has consulted Harmand (1879–80), Odendhal (1894), Lemire (1894), Lefèvre (1898), Pavie (1898–1919), Gosselin (1900), Picanon (1901), Reinach (1901), Damprun (1904), Dufrénil (1908), Malpuech (1920), Malleret (1936), Gentil (1950), Le Thanh Khoi (1955), Vella (1957), Bui Quang Tung (1958), Pensri Duke (1962), Wyatt (1963), and Toye (1968), works listed in the Bibliography at the end of this book. For spelling of place names, the author has relied on *Viet Nam, Cambodia, Laos and Thailand* (Washington: National Geographic Society, 1967) and the extremely detailed 1:100,000 map of the Service Géographique de l'Indochine rather than the spellings used in the above works, which use the Lao and Vietnamese versions (e.g. Muong Phalane is written Ba Lan in Vietnamese, Pha Bang is written Ta Bang, and so forth) indiscriminately, and furthermore contain variations among themselves.

under his domain a vast area far removed from his capital. The brothers were named *chao muong* of Muong Phong, Muong Vang, and Tchepone, respectively. About twenty years afterward, a fourth *muong,* Champhone (now Keng Kok) was created for the son-in-law of the *chao muong* of Muong Phong. To avoid troubles with either the Vietnamese or the Kha, the ruler of Vientiane commanded these notables to go on paying the prescribed tribute to the Court of Annam, which had dispatched a mandarin to Vientiane with the object of determining the ruler's intentions. Thus the acknowledgement of dual sovereignty was established at an early date.

Upon the disorders that followed the death of Souligna Vongsa in 1694, which resulted in the splitting up of the old Kingdom of Lan Xang and the capture of Vientiane by a Vietnamese army, Vietnamese suzerainty was extended to all the left bank of the Mekong and to the Korat Plateau as well. The *muongs* between the Annamite Chain and the Mekong came under the able organizing hand of the Vietnamese, still gloved, however, in the form of reliance on the local notables. New *muongs* were created at Muong Nong, Muong Phalane, Muong Phine, Xieng Hom, and Pha Bang. By 1828, the Le Dynasty had been succeeded, following a period of internal revolts, by the Nguyen Dynasty. Under the energetic administrator Minh Mang, the tributary *muongs* were renamed *chaus* and their notables became *tri-chaus.* The country of the nine *chaus* became known to the Vietnamese as the Ai Lao Dinh and was attached to the *phu* of Cam Lo. Minh Mang created a *huyen* of this *phu* at Lang Con and established a military post at Lao Bao on the Tchepone River.

In 1828, the Kingdom of Vientiane ceased to exist as a result of its disastrous war with Siam. Annam was forced to give up suzerainty over the Korat Plateau. Apparently angered by the refusal of one of the Vietnamese-appointed notables on the right bank of the Mekong to recognize this change of allegiance, the Siamese invaded the left-bank marches and occupied the *chaus* of Champhone, Muong Phong, and Muong Phalane, forcibly evacuating a large portion of their population to the right bank in the process. The *tri-chaus* took temporary refuge on the territory of Cam Lo. Vietnamese general Pham Van Dien succeeded in forcing the Siamese troops to retreat to the Mekong. But the Vietnamese had no interest in occupying lowlands that were kept practically emptied of their population by a series of Siamese raids into the six eastern *chaus.* The most ambitious period of Vietnamese expansion up to that time was at an end, and the commercial traders who had plied the tracks leading from Hué to Kemmarat on the Mekong disappeared. The Vietnamese Court, which had apparently not wanted war with Siam, maintained a Vietnamese notable with the local administrators in the safety of the upper valleys in each *chau,* where the Siamese were reluctant to venture. The only permanent population remained the Kha, who were quite at home in the mountains, where they came and went along the trails they knew perfectly, disappearing from the sight of any stranger "like ghosts, without so much as snapping a dead twig."[39]

The reign of the Emperor Tu Duc saw a systematization of the Vietnamese interest in the Laotian marches. Instead of attempting to drive the Siamese out of the three western *chaus* by force of arms, Tu Duc embarked on a more sensible policy of improving his communications with the six eastern *chaus,* mainly by road-building. There existed three main trails across the mountains between Cam Lo and the Mekong. One of these led from Lang Miet Xa through A Dua Ap to Xieng Hom, and Tu Duc had this built into a road between two and four meters wide, sufficient to allow two elephants to pass each other with ease. Charles Lemire, a French administrator who traveled along part of its length in 1892, said it had been surveyed to travel along ridge lines or mountain flanks in such a manner as to provide a virtually level journey, and it was a remarkable engineering job. The policy of the Vietnamese agents in the trans-mountain country at this time consisted of inducing the superstitious Kha and Phou-Thai to believe that the Vietnamese were the "sons of heaven" whose instructions carried religious sanction. The distribution of titles of nomination, especially, was made a ceremonial act in which the titles themselves were looked on as talismans so that the recipients kept them locked up, not daring to touch them without the ritual of a buffalo sacrifice, gathering the whole village lest terrible punishment ensue.

Tu Duc's successors had to cope with the French, and therefore Vietnamese intervention in the affairs of the people of the Ai Lao Dinh lessened somewhat after the emperor's death in 1883; the titles of nomination were no longer distributed, and the *huyen* at

[39] As described by the French explorer Dr. François-Jules Harmand, who traversed this region in July, 1877. (*Op. cit.,* 1880, p. 308.) The Vietnamese felt no more at home in the mountains than the Siamese or the Lao. The Ai Lao Dinh was particularly dreaded by them, and the Court of Annam maintained a penitentiary at Lao Bao until 1885. A Vietnamese proverb went: "For the Annamite to go as far as Ai Lao without risk, he must be preceded by an elephant."

Lang Con was abandoned. A revolt of regents at Hué occurred in 1885, sowing anarchy throughout much of central Annam. This was the opportunity the Siamese had been waiting for, and they lost no time in pushing again up into the mountain country. They proceeded to set up outposts at Muong Nong, Muong Phine, Tchepone, Muong Vang, Xieng Hom, and Pha Bang.

This strong Siamese presence soon provoked a reaction from the French, who had signed their treaty of protectorate with the Court of Annam in 1884 enabling them to place their Residents over the mandarin administrators of the various *phu*. Ironically, the palace revolt at Hué in 1885 had the effect of drawing the French into conflict with the Siamese earlier than might otherwise have been the case, because the rebel emperor, Ham Nghi, crossed the Ai Lao Pass and took refuge in the mountains; he was not hunted out until 1888. The French became fully awakened to the trouble they could expect from Ham Nghi's followers should they be permitted a mountain sanctuary from which to issue imperial edicts stirring up anti-French resistance in the coastal towns. Having fortified themselves first with research into the archives at Hué, completed in May, 1889, by Captain Luce, the French took up where Tu Duc had left off and began pressing Annam's historic claims to the territory west of the mountains all the way to the Mekong.

The Siamese, for their part, had been alerted to French intentions by Pavie's arrival at Luang Prabang in February, 1886. At the same time that Siamese *commissaires* set up outposts toward the mountains, the government in Bangkok offered to discuss the conflicting claims to the territory involved. In 1889, Pavie reached an agreement under which neither side was to move further forward until a frontier settlement could be negotiated. It must be remembered that even at this late date the French were only beginning to distribute to their own representatives in Indochina a map of the Lao country showing Annam's claims, thanks to prodding by Pavie and others, and were therefore at a great disadvantage in dealing with the Siamese, whom they saw as continuing a steady expansion eastward that had been set in motion by the Siamese liquidation of the Kingdom of Vientiane. Pavie's standstill agreement, of course, did not hold up for long.

In February, 1892, a French outpost was established for the first time at Lao Bao on the upper Tchepone River, barely a three-hour walk from Ban Houei Sane, the nearest Siamese outpost to the west. The Siamese replied by establishing outposts at Ban A Choc on March 11 and at A Dua Ap and at Lang Miet Xa, both

Kha villages, on March 20. They thereby effectively blocked all of the three passages through the mountains from Cam Lo to the Mekong. It seemed as if the showdown had arrived. On September 1, an expedition led by Lemire moved up the Cam Lo River valley and planted the tricolor at Ban A Choc; the Siamese garrison had decamped before the arrival of the French. It had consisted of a total of sixteen men, giving an idea of the numbers involved in this struggle for an empire. On the way up from the east, Lemire's Vietnamese assistants demolished the border marker set atop a mountain in the vicinity by the Lao agents of the Siamese. Lemire continued on to establish another French outpost at Pha Bang, also evacuated by its Siamese garrison.

The Siamese at Luang Prabang, meanwhile, had made life so miserable for the assistant Pavie had left in charge there while he conducted his reconnaissances, made rapid trips to Paris to stiffen the spine of the French Government, and attempted to maneuver the Siamese into negotiations, that the poor fellow committed suicide in March, 1893, in a fit of despondency that his government had forgotten him. In the same month at Bangkok, Pavie, fed up with the "interminable negotiations"[40] for a frontier settlement, peremptorily demanded the immediate evacuation of all Siamese outposts in the region, making it clear that France was claiming in the name of Annam all territory east of the Mekong from Khammouane southward. To enforce this claim, a French column under the command of the Vice-Resident at Dong Hoi, P. Dufrénil, and a young inspector of militia, Claude Garnier, departed on April 23 for Lao Bao. Six days later, this column occupied Ban Houei Sane, on May 2 Tchepone itself, and on May 4 and 10, the outlying posts of Xieng Hom and Muong Vang, respectively. Then the column continued its march westward, reaching Muong Phine on May 14 and, on May 21, occupying the camp at Muong Phong, where there had been 300 Lao and Siamese soldiers. On May 23, the column reached Song Khon on the lower Bang Hieng River, heading for the Mekong by the shortest route, and, on May 26, the tricolor floated in the breeze on the bank of the Mekong opposite Kemmarat. The French had made their point, and now they were there to stay. Hardly a shot had been fired, but before withdrawing the Siamese had set many villages afire.[41]

[40] Malleret, *op. cit.*, p. 72.

[41] The written orders sent to Dufrénil by De Lanessan on April 23, 1893, said: "You will make them [the Siamese officers] understand that they must turn things over to you. You will have recourse to force only in the event

French gunboat diplomacy at Bangkok finally produced the treaty with Siam, but on September 30, without waiting for the signing, Jean-Marie-Antoine de Lanessan, Governor-General of Indochina, signed a decree reorganizing the nine *chaus* into a province, administered from Hué, but with its capital at Song Khon.[42] On April 16, 1895, the capital was moved to the new town of Savannakhet on the Mekong opposite Mukdaharn and the province took the same name, being detached in that year from Annam and absorbed into what the French referred to as "Lower Laos," administered by a senior commander at Khong. It was not until twenty-one years later that the French actually defined the eastern boundary of Savannakhet Province, and then the 1916 line separated, at least on paper, Pha Bang and Xieng Hom from A Dua Ap and Ban A Choc. Farther south, the boundary followed the bed of the Tchepone River, leaving Lao Bao in Vietnamese territory.

With the countryside between the Mekong and the Lao Bao Pass largely denuded of it population, the French officials who arrived in the late nineteenth century to see to its administration and exploitation naturally thought of the advantages of Vietnamese colonization. The Siamese were tardy in living up to the commitment they had undertaken under Article 4 of the Franco-Siamese Convention of October 3, 1893, to permit the return of the Lao population to the left bank. Among the strongest French advocates of Vietnamese colonization was Dr. François-Jules Harmand, who wrote: "It is to the Vietnamese, shut in and stifled as they are between the sea and the mountains . . . that we must open the Me-

---

its use becomes imperiously necessary." (Dufrénil, *op. cit.,* p. 11.) The French had learned that there was a good deal of bluff to the Siamese policy. Soldiers of the Siamese *commissaire* in Khammouane had made an interesting confession when questioned by the French interpreters: "We received orders to come here and show ourselves when the French arrived. If they did not open fire, we were to stay. But if they fired, we were to flee." (Pavie, *Géographie et Voyages, VII,* p. 280.) About the same time, a French-officered column of Vietnamese occupied Stung Treng (April 3) and Khong (April 5), sending the Siamese fleeing. (*Ibid.,* p. 330.)

[42] The province of Khammouane was also formed as part of this administrative reorganization in 1893, after a French-officered column composed of Vietnamese soldiers had chased the Siamese out in May. The assassination by the Siamese of a French official in Khammouane on June 5, 1893, played into the hands of the lobby in Paris that had for years been advocating, without great success, the adoption of a forward policy against Siam. Full descriptions of the events in Khammouane may be found in Pavie and Gosselin, *op. cit.*

kong valley." Vietnamese immigration began in a serious way after the death of Tu Duc in 1883, and was encouraged by the French through an exemption from payment of taxes for three years. There is evidence that in the 1930's officials from Annam collected taxes from Vietnamese settlers in Laos, and the French sanctioned a triangular zone west of the 1916 line wherein Vietnamese could continue to settle.[43]

A French commission studied the feasibility in 1897 of building a railroad from Dong Ha to Savannakhet, but the French later decided that it would make more sense to link Thakhek with Tan Ap on the Trans-Indochina railroad through the Mu Gia Pass because of the exportable tin near Thakhek; the link was never completed, although the pylons for an aerial ropeway to bring construction supplies into the interior were erected through the Mu Gia Pass. In 1909, the Governor-General of Indochina spoke fondly of connecting up the motorable road existing then from Savannakhet as far as Muong Phine with Dong Ha, account being taken of the budgetary strains of such an enterprise. The benefits of Vietnamese labor would thereby, as the Governor-General saw it, be made available to a needy country "whose most beautiful provinces were formerly dependencies of the Court of Hué," and he regretted that the press of business had kept him from studying this project on the spot.[44]

In the upheaval following the March 9, 1945, coup, the Viet Minh clamped their hold on the Tchepone region and its people. The French, at first preoccupied with driving the rebels out of Savannakhet town, found, when they turned their attention to Tchepone, that the Viet Minh had burned the house of the French district officer to the ground. When a French administrator named Pierre Gentil visited the region in September, 1946, slogging his

[43] Acknowledgement is hereby made to Mark S. Pratt of the Foreign Service of the United States for his research on this matter. I am also grateful to Chansamone Voravong, Director of the National Geographic Service, Vientiane.

Gosselin, *op. cit.,* p. 96, mentions the tax exemption to attract immigrants. Harmand's words are from a report he made to the Quai d'Orsay dated November, 1892, quoted in Toye, *op. cit.,* p. 39.

For the French complaint against the Siamese fulfillment of the 1893 convention, see Pavie, *Géographie et Voyages, II,* pp. 252–53. The full text of the treaty and its convention is on pp. 247–49.

[44] "Discours prononcé par M. A. Klobukowski, Gouverneur Général de l'Indochine au Conseil Supérieur le 27 Novembre 1909" (Saigon: Imprimerie Commerciale Marcellin Rey, 1909), p. 28.

way along muddy trails between Kha and Phou-tai villages and fording swollen streams, he found many of the villages along the upper Bang Hieng similarly burned and the Viet Minh in firm control of the border itself. Gold was being freely smuggled across, and herds of cattle from the plains were being rustled to feed the growing Viet Minh army in Annam.

There is no question that the location of the Tchepone region almost at the geographic center of Indochina gives it military importance. The route of withdrawal of Viet Minh forces from the Central Highlands of South Vietnam, from Cambodia, and from southern Laos after the 1954 armistice lay through Tchepone. As they moved northward, they left behind buried caches of arms. Some of these caches were subsequently uncovered by Laotian paratroopers on the road leading to the Mu Gia Pass.

The first claim by the Vietnamese to the villages near the 115.78 meridian after the 1954 armistice was made not by the Hanoi government, however, but by the Saigon government. This occurred in 1957. But the responsible Laotian military commander, meeting his South Vietnamese opposite number, told him in no uncertain terms that the interests of South Vietnam would be better served by paying attention to the implications of the arms caches hidden by the Viet Minh than by asserting a claim over a poor and sparsely inhabited border district. Thereupon, the Laotian and South Vietnamese military commanders considered plans for the stationing of South Vietnamese troops, which were at that time better prepared than the Laotians to assume such a responsibility, along the axis of Route Nationale 9 inside Laos to interdict movement across that road to the south. President Ngo Dinh Diem of South Vietnam gave his assent to this plan.[45]

Diem was in fact fully alert to the vulnerability of his northern provinces to re-infiltration of Communist agents and supplies through this mountainous and untenable region. In an effort to exert more control here, he ordered his commander of the First Military Region, General Tran Van Don, to establish outposts in the mountains on the traditional pattern. Beginning in 1957, the South Vietnamese Army garrisoned Lao Bao and posted platoon-sized surveillance teams to remain at Ban A Choc astride the

---

[45] Private information to the author from the general officers involved in the talks on both sides. The Lao were also at that time anxious to make new maps on a scale of 1:50,000 with the aid of aerial photography to replace the old French maps on a scale of 1:100,000 drawn by ground parties.

northernmost of the three old trails across the mountains, to A Luoi and Tabat in the A Shau Valley to the south, and to twenty-odd other outposts farther south. The effort this decision represented may be imagined from the fact that the rice and other supplies needed to sustain these outposts were portered up by columns of men carrying back-packs, because no aircraft was then available for air-dropping purposes. Diem's government also began a program of training *montagnard* villagers at a school in Hué, since the *montagnards,* once won to the side of the government, were the world's best intelligence network in their hills.

Furthermore, an ambitious program to improve communications not only on the South Vietnam side of the border but also in Laos was launched by Diem with American financial support. Route 9 was to be widened, and the road from Muong Phine southward to Saravane was to be improved and extended as far as Attopeu, which was seen in Saigon as the key to the Central Highlands of South Vietnam. Then the South Vietnamese and the Lao, working simultaneously from Kontum and Attopeu, were to build a new road connecting these two towns. To complete the opening up of the mountain country that this plan envisaged, the South Vietnamese would link Kontum with the coast at two points, one at Mo Duc in Quang Ngai and the other south of Da Nang. Lastly, large airfields were to be built at Saravane and Attopeu. On the Lao side, implementation of these plans was entrusted to General Phoumi Nosavan, newly back from staff training in France. The road network was to be passable by jeep by early 1960. The surveying of the road from Attopeu eastward to the border of South Vietnam, the most difficult segment of the network, ran into a snag when it was pointed out to Phoumi that the trace that had been made ran across a corner of Cambodia, and the Cambodians objected to this. The shortest route between Attopeu and Kontum was the old trail explored by Prosper Odendhal through Dak Rode and was rated a nine-day walk. Phoumi's trace was shifted farther to the north to circumvent Cambodia.

This is where matters stood when, in December, 1958, a Laotian patrol discovered and exchanged fire with North Vietnamese soldiers occupying Ban Taroua, Ban Tapang, and Ban Kapai (the administrative headquarters of the *tasseng*). A statement broadcast by the Vietnam News Agency in Hanoi accused the Lao Government of "repeated military encroachments" into Quang Tri Province and the Tchepone administration of massing troops on the border "in the Huong Lap area" and of threatening to occupy some

Vietnamese places. "All this constitutes a threat to the security of the Vietnamese people who live along the Vietnamese-Laotian border," it said.[46]

The charges from Hanoi followed shortly the dispatch on December 22 of the latest in a series of letters from Premier Pham Van Dong to Diem in Saigon suggesting talks "at the earliest possible date" aimed at normalizing relations. A few days later, Dong dispatched a cable to Marshal Sarit protesting arrests and other "repressive measures" against Vietnamese residents in Thailand.[47] These exchanges also coincided with talk in Vientiane that the NLHS would be outlawed and with the establishment in Vientiane of a Nationalist Chinese consulate.

The Lao then received a cable from Dong on January 1, in which the North Vietnamese Premier protested the encroachment by the Royal Lao Army on "Taroua hamlet of Quang Tri Province" on the morning of December 31 and accused the Lao of opening fire on "Vietnamese guarding the hamlet."[48] In a new message on January 5, Dong proposed to Premier Phoui Sananikone that negotiations on the matter be opened in either Vientiane or Hanoi.[49] Phoui rejected this proposal, saying that Hanoi's claim was based on no material evidence. Phoui maintained that two companies of North Vietnamese soldiers had occupied the villages in question between December 23 and 29.[50]

In his messages to Phoui, Dong gave the following explanation of the North Vietnamese claim:

Concerning the village of Huong Lap, I should inform you that it actually belongs to the territory of the D.R.V. The D.R.V. is now in possession of necessary materials and evidence to prove this openly. Huong Lap village, which comprises 27 hamlets such as Co Bay, Taroua, and Travigne, belongs to Huong Hoa District, in Quang Tri Province.

---

[46] Vietnam News Agency, Hanoi, December 28, 1958, quoted in *Bangkok Post,* December 30, 1958. The statement also accused the Lao of violating North Vietnamese airspace farther north.

[47] *Bangkok Post,* January 9, 1959.

[48] *Bangkok Post,* January 3, 1959. Note that Dong's message confirmed the fact that there were Vietnamese under arms in the area.

[49] *Bangkok Post,* January 7, 1959. A dispatch from Washington in this same issue reported that American officials were taking a calm view and did not see the clash as a forerunner of an attack on Laos or Thailand.

[50] *Bangkok Post,* January 10 and January 12, 1959.

Its administrative history, covering various dynasties from the Le dynasty (1428–1789) to the Nguyen dynasty, the period of French occupation, and finally the present period under the regime of the D.R.V., testifies that Huong Lap has uninterruptedly been part of Vietnamese territory. Before 1945, this village was designated as Co Bay canton and belonged to Huong Hoa District of Quang Tri Province. After the people's democratic power was set up, the administrative committee of Quang Tri Province changed its name to Huong Lap village and made it an administrative division of Huong Hoa District.

Numerous proofs in our possession such as mandarins' tiles, seals, receipts of head taxes, tax and forced labor payment cards, and other administrative materials of Quang Tri Province and Huong Hoa District fully demonstrate that this region has at all times belonged to Vietnam's territorial patrimony.

A note circulated among members at the United Nations at the request of the Royal Government stated that the North Vietnamese had been in permanent occupation of an area near Tchepone since December 15.[51] An Associated Press dispatch, datelined Tchepone, said that troops of the opposing sides were facing each other across the Bang Hieng River and that Royal Lao Army reinforcements had arrived on the scene. The dispatch observed that the area of the confrontation was located at two days' march from Tchepone;[52] it might well have added that it was a hard two days' march.

Ban Travigne, the most northerly of the villages mentioned in the Lao Government's protest note, is situated in a wooded valley a bare 4,500 yards from the border of North Vietnam on the banks of a small stream that zig-zags in a northwesterly direction until it joins the Bang Fai River, a tributary of the Mekong in Khammouane Province. The country north of Ban Travigne is particularly rugged and rocky and is uninhabited for the most part.

The next village to the southeast, Ban Taroua, is reached by a footpath that crosses a forested divide at about 875 meters elevation and is situated on the upper reaches of the Bang Hieng River. Ban Taroua is about 9,750 yards from the border of North Vietnam.

Ban Kapai, the third village in question, is situated farther upstream and less than 4,000 yards from the border of *South* Vietnam.

Ban Tapang, yet another village reported to have been occupied

[51] *Bangkok Post,* January 20, 1959.
[52] *Ibid.*

by North Vietnamese troops at the same time, is situated slightly to the north and only 3,000 yards from the junction of the borders of Laos and North and South Vietnam.

A map published by Hanoi in 1964[53] showed Hanoi's version of the border, with Huong Lap marked and no cognizance taken of the 115.78 meridian. The version shown on this map, together with further repetitions of the claim to Huong Lap contained in North Vietnamese notes to the Royal Government of October 18 and November 5, 1964, which mentioned the additional villages of Ban Tapoi, Ban Saria, and Ban Ramai situated in the region, were rejected by the Royal Government on February 12, 1965.[54] Commenting on Hanoi's conduct with respect to its occupation of and subsequent claim to the *tasseng* of Kapai, the Royal Government said: "It is a case of an extremely clever annexationist policy."[55]

The border between Laos and Vietnam has never been the subject of a treaty. Pham Van Dong's letter of 1957 puts him on record as opposed to the negotiation of such a treaty, while the Lao seem inclined toward negotiations. With respect to the section of the border between Savannakhet and Quang Tri, the Lao can argue that Dong accepted their version at the 1954 Geneva Conference, since the map on which the Viet Minh and the French drew the provisional military demarcation line was a French map and showed the demarcation line ending at the 1916 north-south border line.

This raises the intriguing and highly important question of the status of that part of Huong Lap west of the 1916 line in the eyes of Hanoi. The demarcation line between North and South Vietnam extended, by definition of the armistice agreement signed by the Viet Minh and the French, to the Laos border. But realities on the ground were different. The line as drawn on the map at Geneva, the demilitarized zone as drawn on the map a few days later at meetings in Vietnam of representatives of a mixed military commission, and the subsequent inspection functions of the fixed ICC team stationed at the demilitarized zone, all ended at the 1916 north-south line. The North Vietnamese could therefore cross from North to South Vietnam through Huong Lap. Though they might

---

[53] *Ban Do Viet-Nam.* Hanoi. Drawn by the Topographic and Cartographic Office in June, 1964. Edited by the Cultural and Artistic Editions (Ministry of Culture). First edition: 50,000 copies. Printing completed on the presses of the Progress Press July 10, 1964. Scale 1:1,600,000.

[54] Lao Press Bulletin, Vientiane, February 13, 1965.

[55] *Ibid.*

be violating the terms of the armistice agreement in doing so (depending on one's answer to the question of whether the use of armed force to achieve ends that political means provided for at Geneva had failed to achieve was justified or not), there was no likelihood that their movement would be recorded as a violation, for it was of no concern to the ICC inspectors if they heard reports of persons moving southward in what the inspectors regarded as Laotian territory. The ICC was there to ensure compliance with the prohibition of movement across the demilitarized zone, not to defend the borders of South Vietnam.

Guided by Kha and Phou-Thai sympathizers, the 140,000 Viet Minh southerners who had been regrouped to the North in 1954 began moving through the defensive positions established by the North Vietnamese Army in Huong Lap on their way south.[56] Initially, they were veteran political cadres whose mission was to report back to Hanoi about conditions in the South; later, they were regular soldiers.[57] All, however, shared the single purpose that had been stated so eloquently and unequivocally by Dong at Geneva on July 21, 1954:

> Our heartfelt thoughts go out to the people of our country, whose great love for their nation and courage during the war will remain steadfast in the coming era of peace.
>
> The Conference set a date for our reunification. We shall win this unity, we shall win it as we have won the peace. No force in this world, whether internal or external, can force us off our path toward unity by means of peace and democracy. This will be the culmination of our national independence.
>
> People of Vietnam, fellow citizens of the south, victory is ours. The independence and unity of our country are in our hands; the

[56] The figure of 140,000 is given by Wilfred Burchett in *The Second Indochina War; Cambodia and Laos* (New York: International Publishers, 1970), p. 165, note, and includes "troops, cadres, and a few of their families."

[57] Giap's infantry was accustomed to the hardships of the forest and its trails; in January, 1954, the Viet Minh infantry had emerged from the forests around Kontum to threaten French control of the Central Highlands. (The author is indebted to Denis Warner, the Australian writer on Southeast Asia, for this observation.)

Bernard Fall analyzed Hanoi's complaints to the ICC of violations of Article 14C of the armistice agreement, which prohibits reprisals and guarantees democratic liberties, and concluded that the accuracy of Hanoi's information about even the most minute events in South Vietnam betrayed the existence of an operative network of agents in the South with just such a mission in the years 1957–59. (See Fall, *Viet-Nam Witness 1953–66,* New York: Praeger, 1966, p. 184.)

men devoted to peace and justice of the entire world are with us. Remember the words of Ho Chi Minh:

"The struggle is hard, but we are the ones who will win in the end. Long live peace; long live the unity of our country!"[58]

Diem's government, however, was preparing to defend the South. Operational cooperation between the South Vietnamese garrison at Lao Bao and the Royal Lao Army garrison at Ban Houei Sane was to be expanded under plans drawn up during 1958 so as to allow the formation of mixed patrols for intelligence missions. On these missions, the South Vietnamese soldiers were to wear Lao army uniforms, a stratagem that recalls the disguise donned by Souphanouvong's Vietnamese bodyguards in 1945.[59] Coordination between the staffs of the two governments was to be assured by the young South Vietnamese colonel Nguyen Van Thieu, who was attached to the headquarters of Third Military Region Commander General Sing Ratanasamay in Savannakhet. After General Phoumi became Secretary of State for Defense in the Phoui Sananikone government in January, 1959, the South Vietnamese were given *carte blanche* for joint operations in Laos. Soon ten teams of South Vietnamese Special Forces soldiers with ten men each and equipped with radios were operating in southern Laos.

In the autumn of 1959, however, when Phoumi visited Saigon on the occasion of South Vietnam's National Day (October 26), he met the chief of the U.S. MAAG mission, Lieutenant General Samuel T. Williams, who informed him that all funds for completion of the strategic communications program in Laos had been cut off. Williams could not give any reason for the cutoff. "Ask Diem," he said. Clearly, the decision by the Americans was beyond the purview of the MAAG. Phoumi next had a meeting with Diem, Don, Thieu, and all the high-level officers responsible for the South Vietnamese side of the program. "It's too late," Thieu announced. "The Communists are already infiltrating into South Vietnam."

[58] "Documents relatifs à la Conférence de Genève sur l'Indochine (21 juillet 1954)," *Notes et Études Documentaires*, No. 1,901, July 30, 1954, p. 9 (translated by the author). One is compelled to admire Ho's foresight in warning of the "hard struggle" for unity even on the day that struggle began. Strangely enough, Lacouture and Devillers, in both the French (1960) and English (1969) editions of their book on the 1954 Geneva Conference, dismiss this speech of Pham Van Dong's as "of relatively little interest."

[59] See Tran Van Dinh, "Laos: The Fiction of Neutrality," *New Republic*, February 24, 1968, p. 29.

From one day to the next, Diem had gone from unbridled enthusiasm to refusal even to discuss the matter further.[60]

What had happened? One theory is that some Americans who knew about the project became alarmed by the possibility that operations by South Vietnamese troops in Laos might provoke North Vietnam and urged that the idea be dropped. The irony of the outcome is evident today. Had Diem been given the means by the United States in 1959 to improve the security of his open border with Laos, it might not have been necessary a decade later to send American reconnaissance patrols into Laos to gather intelligence about North Vietnamese movements. The tragedy is that the decision to avoid involvement in southern Laos in 1959 did not keep the war from enveloping that region a decade later. For this was the origin of the Ho Chi Minh Trail.

The Long March to the South

An attack by Communist guerrillas on a road construction camp north of Kontum in October, 1960, obviously mounted with outside support, appeared to confirm the fears of Diem and his entourage. Then, beginning in the spring of 1961, the first specially trained cadres to graduate from the Xuan Mai camp near Hanoi were sent south along these forest trails to join the newly-constituted NLF.[61] When the United States accepted the challenge from Hanoi and became itself involved in the war, the trail network was improved and expanded and became the artery along which the lifeblood of the revolution in the South was pumped.

From the standpoint of geography, the distance from the Red River Delta in North Vietnam to the populous rice lands of the Mekong Delta in South Vietnam was shorter by way of Laos than by the old Mandarin Road along the coast, even if use of the latter had been available to the Communists after the 1954 partition. Getting across the mountains into Laos posed a problem, but travel through the sparsely inhabited eastern region of Laos seemed feasible. The passes across the mountains between Vietnam and Laos were similar to hundreds of other passes in the Annamite Chain

[60] This account is based mainly on interviews with Generals Tran Van Don and Phoumi Nosavan, who were of course both directly involved, and is corroborated by American sources.

[61] Interview of the author with Colonel Huynh Cu in Saigon, September 15, 1969. Colonel Cu, a native of Quang Ngai Province, was an instructor at Xuan Mai in 1965 and later defected from the Communists in South Vietnam.

MAP 8. The Ho Chi Minh Trail, 1970

Vinh

Keo Neua Pass
1,969 feet

Nape

NORTH VIETNAM

Mu Gia Pass
1,371 feet

AREA SHOWN IN
MAP No. 7

Ban Karai
Pass
1,500 feet

17 th Parallel

LAOS

Tchepone

Hue

SOUTH

THAILAND

0   25   50   75
miles

- - - - Ho Chi Minh Trail - 1970

VIETNAM

CAMBODIA

and were at relatively low elevations. But approaches to both sides of these passes lay through a wide strip of rugged terrain, often deeply cut by torrents and forested with thick jungle. Roads for vehicular and traffic had to be engineered in the most difficult conditions. In the northern sector, the North Vietnamese were able to use old roads through the Keo Neua and Mu Gia passes, which they improved during 1961 and 1962 under their aid agreements with Souvanna Phouma. In the southern sector, however, which ran through the area with the heaviest annual rainfall in Laos, new roads had to be built. Below the latitude of the demilitarized zone, there were similar obstacles to traffic from Laos into South Vietnam.[62]

Without the Trail, the Vietnamese Communists would not have been able to send the arms and ammunition to their supporters in the South that would permit them to take on first-line American divisions in battle. Without the Trail, the North Vietnamese could not have *trucked* the weapons used in their 1968 Tet Offensive against Hué to within *ten miles* of the Citadel, using the A Shau Valley as a forward storage depot, or for that matter to dozens of other points right down the length of South Vietnam. This feat was the military equivalent, from Giap's point of view, of sending his soldiers into battle ten miles outside Hanoi, rather than 500 or 800 miles away. Without the Trail, Giap could not have mounted the siege of the Khe Sanh, which captured headlines for weeks on end, while the American people asked themselves whether the Marines could hold out.

Many of those who embarked on the three-month march to South Vietnam died along the way of malnutrition or malaria. But for the survivors, the march was the most effective toughening imaginable, and they fought the American troops they met on the battlefields of the South with courage and determination. The Trail was like a precious jewel. Its construction, involving uncounted man-hours of labor over many years, and its year-round operation, involving an estimated 25,000 of the 40,000 North Vietnamese soldiers in Laos,[63] will rank perhaps as Giap's greatest contri-

[62] The low elevations of the passes through the Annamite Chain contrast with the high elevations of the passes through the Himalayan border between the North East Frontier Agency of India and China. The Route 9 crossing at Lao Bao was too close to the demilitarized zone to be of any use to the North Vietnamese, except for localized operations such as those against Khe Sanh. Tchepone on Route 9, however, became the headquarters for the operation of the entire Trail.

[63] Langer and Zasloff, *op. cit.,* p. 171.

bution to the Vietnamese Revolution, as great in its own way as the victory of Dien Bien Phu. Given the paucity of the means Giap had at hand, the operation of the Trail may be considered to be the most difficult feat of military logistics since the operation of the Burma Road in World War II.

To comprehend what this Vietnamese Long March represented for Giap's enemies with all the resources of modern technology at their disposal, one has to enter for a moment the insect world of Henri Fabre. Everyone has observed a column of ants hurrying along the ground, threading their way around pebbles, twigs, and leaves in their path, hardly halting for more than a second or two before pushing on, over or around every obstacle, as if driven by some invisible motor. It is not possible for the onlooker to know where they come from, or where they are going. Looking at them, one is conscious of watching a small section of a living, organic monster. One brings one's shoe down in their path, crushing a few of them and temporarily sowing confusion. Those coming from behind circle in feverish activity, and then the whole column pushes forward once more, trampling over the bodies of their slain comrades. The shoe represents the sudden appearance of a flight of American bombing planes overhead. If it is at night, one can imagine the pilots peering down at the rim of light cast by a flare or a searchlight, or at the blip on a radar screen picking up movement of metal bodies or the hum of motors on the ground below. But there is not one column of ants. There are dozens of such columns, and the eastern region of Laos is vast.[64]

To cut this lifeline had been a persistent temptation for the generals in Saigon. The advisability of making the attempt had always hinged on the cost, for it was not simply a question of having enough men in Laos to prevent movement, but of ensuring the safety of these men as well, and the specter of Dien Bien Phu was always in the background. An American military estimate in late 1967 was that it would require the commitment of an American army corps to cut the Trail for three months, and of half a million men—as many as the United States had committed in South Vietnam at the time— to keep it cut permanently.[65] Ambassador Ellsworth Bunker and

[64] In his statement on Laos on March 6, 1970, President Nixon reported that more than 500,000 North Vietnamese soldiers had used the Trail since 1964. Figuring three months' march per man, this represents 125,000 man-years of effort, a Long March of formidable proportions.

[65] Conversation of General Richard G. Stilwell, commanding General of Military Assistance Command, Thailand, with Kim Wilenson of United Press International in Bangkok.

General William C. Westmoreland had recommended from Saigon in that year in favor of such an operation in Laos,[66] but the Tet offensive had intervened and changed the priorities. By early 1971, however, South Vietnamese forces had improved to the point where they were judged to be able to assume the major responsibility across the border; the options available to the North Vietnamese were judged to be fewer and riskier than ever before; and, perhaps most important, with no expectation in the near term of a negotiated settlement, the Nixon administration was in a position to justify to American public opinion unreserved American logistical and air support for South Vietnamese troops in Laos, on the basis that it hastened the continuing withdrawal of American troops from South Vietnam by placing the Saigon government in an advantageous military position.

The temptation was thus given way to on February 8, 1971. The South Vietnamese called their incursion into Laos "Operation Lam Son 719." In deference to Congressional sentiment, no American ground troops were permitted in Laos. A sign reading "NO U.S. PERSONNEL BEYOND THIS POINT" was posted where Route 9 crossed the border, and an American correspondent wrote "NO NVA [North Vietnamese Army] BEYOND THIS POINT" on the back. The trouble was that, as with so much else in this frustrating war, the surgical cleanliness of the military plans laid in Saigon and Washington could not be duplicated diplomatically, and there were many loose ends left hanging. Prince Souvanna Phouma had not been consulted about the entry of South Vietnamese forces into Laos before it happened. Such prior consultation would have implied that Souvanna Phouma had agreed to the entry when it took place, whereas circumstances prevented him from either agreeing to it or protesting against it. In the event, he made no initial comment; the Royal Government issued a statement deploring the fact that foreign troops belonging to countries whose governments had signed the Geneva Protocol had chosen to make Laos their battlefield.[67] Souvanna Phouma's failure to agree to the entry appeared to contradict numerous statements by President Thieu himself that South Vietnam would not consider going into Laos in the absence of a formal request. As in 1959, military planning—this time at the last moment—was held up while the State Department weighed the possible reactions of North Vietnam.

[66] Ambassador Bunker, in conversation with author, December, 1970.
[67] Text in *Lao Presse,* Vientiane, February 8, 1971.

Fear of Encirclement and Communist Solidarity

Giap and his fellow officers, being landbound and having fought the French in a war of position and movement over land, were obsessed with the concept of territorial security. Giap's remark to Souvanna Phouma about the strategic value of the Plain of Jars, which itself was an appreciation inherited from the French,[68] betrays this obsession. As early as September, 1945, Ho Chi Minh himself had instructed the Viet Minh agents in Laos in the following terms:

> Laos must be kept out of the hands of the imperialists at all costs; if not, Vietnam can never stay independent. Hostile forces cannot be tolerated the length of the borders of Tonkin.[69]

In this regard, the Vietnamese Communist leaders were acting to safeguard the same interests as had the French when they looked across the mountains from Annam and Tonkin. At the very least, from Giap's point of view, Thai influence had to be prevented from implanting itself among the mountain peoples who, because of the elevation, extended their lands in some places almost to the sea, where the fingers of the Annamite Chain jutted across the narrow waist of Vietnam.

Finally, of course, the relationship between Laos and Vietnam has come to include an underpinning of Marxist dogma and Leninist discipline so far as the revolutionary movements of both countries are concerned. The overview of the common struggle against colonialism and neocolonialism, especially, provided the unifying force that transcended matters of national frontiers and justified the ultimate objective of the NLHS and Phak Pasason Lao, which was to bend the diverse and colorful peoples of Laos into the conformity exhibited by the drab and totalitarian society of North Vietnam.

As one observer in Laos has written:

> The NLHS seeks nothing less than a radical transformation of Lao society from a loosely structured hierarchical system to a tightly organized conformist society where the rather foreign concepts of persuasion and guilt are introduced as mechanisms of social control. They have pressed for economic equality by introducing progressive taxation and discouraging the conspicuous consumption that estab-

[68] See the description of the mission of the Free French guerrillas on the Plain of Jars in 1945 given by Ayrolles, *op. cit.*, p. 42.

[69] Quoted in Caply, *op. cit.*, p. 291.

MAP 9. Thai Insurgents' Infrastructure in Laos, 1969

lishes a wealthy villager's status. They have almost eliminated the "wasted resources" that are spent on *bouns,* marriages, funerals, and traditional celebrations. They have taken initial steps toward the communalization of property by establishing "public" padi, by closely controlling livestock sales and slaughter, and by introducing public ownership of livestock in the school system.[70]

This is the price to be paid for liberation from foreign rule. This is the North Vietnamese ambition that is perhaps the most alien to the Lao, the Meo, the Kha, and the other peoples of Laos, and it reveals the true meaning of the policy of the Indochinese Communist Party and its plans for an Indochinese federation.

Historically, the interests of the Vietnamese Communists have extended beyond the Mekong frontier of French Indochina to northeastern Thailand, which is part of Indochina proper. During their war against the French, the Vietnamese Communists drew on the support of the 40,000 Vietnamese who had settled in this region for war supplies. Nationalist rivals of the Viet Minh were also assassinated here.

By 1970, there was plentiful substantiated evidence that North Vietnam and China were supporting the development of insurgency in Thailand and making use of the territory of Laos for this purpose. The exact division of responsibilities remained unclear, but cadres from Thailand who had received training in North Vietnam and China passed through Laos on their way into Thailand, where they recruited new adherents. These men were trained at special camps in Laos under the supervision of North Vietnamese and Chinese instructors. A network of support bases had also been set up inside Laos along the border with Thailand. The security of the training camps, support bases, and infiltration routes used for passage back and forth across the border was provided by Pathet Lao and North Vietnamese forces. The pattern of these operations recalled North Vietnamese support of the Pathet Lao in Laos following the 1954 armistice.[71]

---

[70] Edwin T. McKeithen, *Life Under the P.L. in the Xieng Khouang Ville Area* (Vientiane: U.S. AID, 1969), mimeographed, pp. 2–3.

[71] For much valuable information on this subject, the author is indebted to Jack Foisie of the *Los Angeles Times.*

15.

The United States and Laos: The Flawed Bastion

The United States arrived late on the scene of the conflict in Laos. The first official representatives of the United States in Vientiane worked in tents pitched in an open field. It was a difficult moment in the history of Laos, the moment of transition from a French protectorate to an independent state, and the Americans immediately faced problems in their dealings with the French as well as with the Lao.

The Americans were inspired by no desire of material acquisition. Their whole approach reflected a generosity that never ceased to amaze European visitors to Vientiane. Politically, the strength of the Americans was their very difference from the French. But this was also a weakness in the sense that, lacking the long French experience, Americans were often clumsy in their dealings with the Lao. Where the French had been patient and willing to go along with the system, the Americans were impatient and intolerant. The Americans should perhaps have known that corruption would survive (and, with the arrival of American aid, increase markedly). They should have realized that the Lao do not see things in black and white and that moralistic judgments generated antagonism among their Lao friends, which led to such political absurdities as the alienation of Prince Souvanna Phouma in the autumn of 1960.

These new grievances and issues gave the Communists their chance. The leaders of the Hanoi regime portrayed, with devastating effect, the American presence in Laos in terms of the Leninist theory of neocolonialism, thereby undermining confidence among the friends of the United States in what had begun as a selfless attempt to foster the genuine independence of Laos.

Many explanations have been advanced for the U.S. failure to keep Laos and its people secure from the hands of the political commissar of Hanoi. Some say the United States was not firm enough, since it is a well-known fact that the Communists respect force. Others say the United States was too categoric in its opposition to any suggestion of a negotiated accommodation, that the bold phrases used by Administration spokesmen before Congressional committees were carried over into actual policy and torpedoed any chance of an accommodation short of outright military victory, which, of course, was out of the question.

An American who served in the Eisenhower Administration in negotiations with the Soviets in Europe has said, "Basically, we tried to solve a sociological problem by military means where we can't use our military." And there is some truth in that. The fact is that no single explanation totally accounts for the failure of the United States to achieve its goal in Laos—a viable state secure in its independence and livelihood. The outcome was determined by a number of mistakes committed (or simply permitted) by the United States and fully exploited by the Communists, plus a conjunction of unhappy circumstances. The American presidential election campaign of 1960 coincided with the most acute phase of the Laos crisis, marked by the establishment of a Soviet Embassy in Vientiane and the sending of Soviet aid to Souvanna Phouma. For the outgoing Administration, the penalties of sitting tight were less than those of shifting course. No fresh initiatives were forthcoming from Washington until the incoming Administration had its hands securely on the tiller.

By the summer of 1961, as we have seen, a very definite correlation had established itself between Pathet Lao aggressiveness and American unwillingness to escalate the conflict. The North Vietnamese, because they were in a position to adjust the pressure exerted by the Pathet Lao, could test their opponents' will to resist. The correlation that emerged, therefore, from the multiplicity of actions and words, input of arms, and threats from both sides, was precise almost to the single village or the length of roadway occupied by either side. Neither the pressure on the Communist side nor the resistance on the American side was constant; the former fluctuated with the estimation by the Hanoi leadership of risks involved, and the latter fluctuated in accordance with logistical obstacles, relations with the European allies, and was even affected by such factors as the changed mood of the President in the aftermath of the Bay of Pigs disaster. This neat correlation emerged, in any case, at a late stage of the conflict. It was an oversimplification, therefore, to argue that because Communist acquisition of new territory in Laos was proportionate to the "softness" of the American position, the solution to the predicament was a "hard" stand even at the expense of committing American forces.

In reality, the predicament was neither wholly circumstantial nor wholly a simple matter of an arithmetic equation. It is possible to identify a number of faults of omission or commission whose presence within the structure of American policy in Laos made inevitable its crumbling, regardless of the hardness of the material employed in its construction.

1. Nationalism was potentially the most powerful motivating force in the Indochina countries at the end of World War II. More than any other factor, the Viet Minh's monopoly of this appeal, coupled with the possession of a tightly organized machine to carry out orders, accounted for the Viet Minh success. Conversely, the United States failure to appreciate the significance of this force and to bend all its efforts toward making use of it contributed immensely to the governmental instability.

The evolution undergone by American thinking on the question of nationalism in Indochina can be summarized as follows: World War II saw frequent references to the fact that Americans attached supreme importance to the principle of self-determination of peoples. In the immediate postwar period, American actions subordinated this principle to other considerations. Finally, when the storm clouds gathered over Indochina and the United States found itself on the side of the colonial power, American statements tended to see in the vague and tardy concessions wrested from the French sufficient substance to satisfy the nationalist aspirations of the Indochinese peoples. Secretary of State Dean Acheson said American assistance to the French-sponsored governments in Indochina after 1950 was intended to help the Indochinese develop "genuine nationalism."[1] But who were the "genuine" nationalists? Members of the Lao Issara, who had formed their own government and proclaimed their own Constitution in 1945, were certainly genuine nationalists. The three princely brothers of Laos were genuine nationalists, and that is why the Viet Minh made efforts to win one of them to their ranks at the very time they were liquidating powerful

[1] Department of State Bulletin, June 18, 1950, pp. 877–78.

Vietnamese nationalist rivals in Hanoi and Saigon. And it was to the French, rather than to these men, that American help went. Therefore, in the eyes of the Indochinese nationalist leaders, the Viet Minh victory at Dien Bien Phu was a defeat for the United States as well as for France.

Once the United States had forfeited the issue, it was never able to grasp it firmly again. American officials could not comprehend how peasants armed with homemade shotguns who came into a village at night to ask for a handful of rice could be welcomed as patriots. The Pathet Lao, recognizing the potential mobilizing force of nationalism, directly involved the people in what they called the struggle against the foreigner. In this effort, they even succeeded in overcoming the "foreignness" of their Vietnamese advisers, whom they portrayed as friends of the people of Laos. The vast American aid mission in Laos seemed to confirm the Pathet Lao contention that their country had come under the yoke of a new form of colonialism—a preposterous distortion of motivations, but nonetheless effective propaganda. There were more Americans in Laos in 1961 than there had been Frenchmen under the Protectorate at the outbreak of World War II.

2. The United States allowed American disapproval of the Communist regime of Ho Chi Minh to become confounded with American opposition to the expansion of Vietnamese Communist power into Laos and South Vietnam. This led to a rigidity of approach in policy-making that did not permit taking into account such factors as Ho's historic mistrust of the Chinese. Such considerations would have given American policy much more flexibility in dealing with Ho's expansionist aims. During the critical period when policy for Laos was being formulated, State Department thinking bore many resemblances to the 1947 dictum of French Admiral d'Argenlieu that there could be no negotiating with Communists. For example, Assistant Secretary of State for Far Eastern Affairs Walter S. Robertson declared on January 13, 1955: "The Chinese Communists and, for that matter, the other Asian Communists such as the Viet Minh, may have points of conspicuous physical difference from the Russians, but as Communists they are all identical."[2]

While infiltration of North Vietnamese cadres into and through Laos could not be prevented without a direct military effort, which the United States was not prepared to undertake, the U.S. voluntarily renounced all possibility of communicating with Ho through

---

[2] Department of State Press Release No. 23, January 13, 1955, p. 3.

diplomatic channels, and of restraining him. North Vietnam was not treated as a state; it was ignored. Even its modest efforts to participate in Southeast Asian affairs on a nondiplomatic level—a recent example of which was its application to join the Economic Commission for Asia and the Far East (ECAFE) in March, 1962—were summarily rebuffed. The American attitude toward North Vietnam from 1954 to 1964 was one that past experience had shown went against all prospect of reward.

The British took a more pragmatic approach in their Far Eastern policy. They fought the Communist terrorists in Malaya, most of whom were Chinese, while they maintained their diplomats in Peking. Likewise, they maintained a consul in Hanoi, as well as their embassy in Saigon. It was their experience, they explained, that dictators could best be handled by keeping lines of communication open rather than by ignoring their control of their countries (a stand the British have maintained in regard to trading with Cuba, despite U.S. protests). The rationale behind the U.S. isolation policy was that South Vietnam should be built up as an internationally recognized and sovereign state and that the Communist government of North Vietnam, weakened by a deteriorating economic situation, should be permitted to be overthrown in the course of an internal rebellion. Leaving aside the question of whether the population of a country is more united behind a government facing hostility abroad, the policy adopted gave the Saigon regime a restricting power over American diplomacy in Indochina. No official contacts could take place between Washington and Hanoi, since this would undermine the Saigon regime's contention to be the sole legitimate government of Vietnam. North Vietnam had no alternative but to remain in the Sino-Soviet camp, and lacking other sources of food, Ho had an even more urgent need to annex the rice-rich south.

3. On the ground in Laos, American effectiveness was hamstrung by an inability to visualize situations in terms meaningful to the local population. Ambassador Parsons' attributing opportunities for corruption in the aid program to loss of confidence in the kip sounded logical on Wall Street but hardly made sense in Laos. American methods were applied to the solution of problems in an underdeveloped country where the practices of fifteenth-century Europe would have been more appropriate. In contrast to the relatively ineffective aid program mounted by Americans who shut themselves up in air-conditioned cubicles, a small aid program with a large impact was carried on at the same time in Cambodia by the Chinese Communists, whose engineers and workmen lived in barracks on

the construction sites of the factories they were building. A similar lack of rapport hampered American propaganda efforts. As General Heintges testified, "Do not forget . . . that 87 per cent of the population in Laos is illiterate. These people do not know what the word 'democracy' or 'communism' means."[3] The Pathet Lao, therefore, pitched their appeal on a level where it was meaningful—promising specific, visible benefits to the population and rejecting the sophistication of the Marxist-Leninist vocabulary in which their leaders conversed.

4. The United States, having taken an equivocal stand at the Geneva Conference in 1954 by unilaterally declaring that it would not impede the implementation of the accords, allowed itself to be bound by the most restrictive features of the Laos cease-fire agreement but made little or no effort to exploit the potential offered by that agreement's most favorable provisions. The United States abided by the Geneva prohibition against all foreign military missions in Laos except French, giving the French primary responsibility for training the American-financed Lao army, but benefited little from French experience in the field and proceeded on the basis of trial and error. (The French used their control over military training to reassure the Lao politicians who were nervous about American policy that they, the French, could restrain the Americans. The French maintained their military training mission at half strength, fulfilled their training responsibilities lackadaisically, and proclaimed on every side that they knew more about the situation in Laos than anyone else. This may well have been true, but with this dog-in-the-manger attitude on the part of the French and frustration on the part of the Americans, relations deteriorated steadily. When the best unit in the Lao army overthrew the "pro-American" government, its action was met with unconcealed French approval.)

5. The effect of the American aid program was bound to be disruptive. Nothing like it had ever been tried under the Protectorate. Its major effect was to exacerbate the disparities between the haves and the have-nots. Its results went against common sense. Chinese shops in Vientiane were well stocked with Scotch whisky, while a concrete floor for the capital's open-air market, a notable advance in sanitation benefiting some 60,000 people, was not provided until 1963. The Pathet Lao were able to make use of the visible difference between constructive aid and nonproductive aid in their propaganda. The aid program also exaggerated the isolation of a central

[3] *Hearings*, III, p. 2375.

government already one step removed from the countryside because its appointive authority stopped at the district level. The greater the accouterments of office in Vientiane, the less the government could understand the problems of the villages; the less it understood the villages, the less became its popular rapport; the less rapport, the more isolated it became; the more isolated, the more it had to be propped up by American aid; the more it depended on American aid, the less popular it became and the more isolated from the villages.

6. The vicious circle resulting from the increasing Vientiane-centeredness of the government meant that the Americans could do nothing to help extend the government's authority to the country-side, at the very time when the newly installed Communist government in Hanoi was engaged in consolidating its own authority and creating autonomous regions for its ethnic minorities. As the loss of authority in the countryside became greater, the process of Cabinet-making in Vientiane retained less and less meaning, and political parties, aside from the Neo Lao Hak Sat, atrophied into little more than high-sounding names. The single serious attempt at party-building on a reformist platform by non-Communists was made by a group of army officers and failed miserably. The United States must take a large portion of the blame for neglecting to emphasize the crucial importance of the interaction between local democracy and central authority. The Royal Government gradually came to realize that it had forfeited the ability to communicate with its own people, that it was a stranger in its own land. The Pathet Lao, on the other hand, studied the system of local government in minute detail, since this was the key to success in winning the allegiance of the people in the Lao-inhabited areas of the Kingdom. Prince Souphanouvong, for instance, garnered the most votes of any candidate in Vientiane Province in the 1958 election; yet he also felt quite at home walking up and down the country from village to village.

7. The Royal Government's authority did not extend at all into the territories of the mountain tribes, because of their almost total lack of previous political organization and the age-old animosities between them and the lowlanders. This precluded any real possibility of creating a sense of national unity. Not until 1961, when U.S. Special Forces detachments arrived in Laos, was any effort made to recruit these tribesmen into the army. American support for a national army composed almost entirely of Lao prolonged the separation; when the army appeared in the upland villages, even outside the Pathet Lao-controlled provinces of Sam Neua and Phong

Saly, it was feared as an army of foreigners rather than welcomed. For years, the tribesmen had been recruited into the Pathet Lao and given a cause to fight for. Their political indoctrination came from untiring Pathet Lao organizers like Sithone and Phay Dang, who traveled the jungle trails exploiting the fears and grievances of the Kha and the Meo. The French, whose military training mission had numerous contacts among the tribes, especially after 1959, made no effort to get the Royal Government to give specific assurances to the tribesmen that it would not prevent them from having a representative voice in the government. Pathet Lao propaganda was, therefore, able to tell the tribes that they were victims of discrimination.

8. On a strategic plane, the United States overestimated the possibilities of military offensives open to Communist China and North Vietnam, with disastrous consequences for the programming of aid to Laos that began in 1955. The program was weighted heavily on the side of military defense, to the neglect of civic action, an imbalance rooted in Washington's reassessment of Communist intentions in the aftermath of the Korean invasion of June 25, 1950. There are indications that a grand strategy of offense against positions of Western influence on the rim of Asia may have been discussed by Stalin and Mao Tse-tung in Moscow during their prolonged talks in the winter of 1949–50.[4] Stalin may have been favorably impressed by a Chinese desire to exploit their own revolutionary momentum by a three-pronged attack against South Korea, Taiwan, and Indochina. After all, it was apparently the Chinese who convinced Stalin that Ho Chi Minh's appeal for recognition of January 14, 1950 (to which the Chinese acquiesced on January 18), should be favorably treated even though it went against Soviet preoccupation with European politics. The Chinese could not have failed to appreciate the fact that recognition would allow the French to portray what was essentially a colonial war as an anti-Communist crusade in order to win material assistance from the United States, and they could hardly have been unhappy about the prospect of being begged for help by their fraternal Vietnamese comrades. However, the swift and decisive American riposte to the invasion of South Korea warned Moscow and Peking that the United States would henceforth act to

---

[4] See, for example, Marshall D. Shulman, *Stalin's Foreign Policy Reappraised* (Cambridge, Mass.: Harvard University Press, 1963), p. 141. The likelihood that the Soviet Union was then poised to spread its control, by force of arms if necessary, in Europe, the Middle East, and Asia was discussed in a National Security Council paper called NSC-68 in early 1950 (*The New York Times*, April 13, 1964).

prevent the use of Red armies in outright attempts at territorial aggrandizement. After this warning, Moscow and Peking were compelled to re-examine the possibilities of offensive operations of the Korean type. After Stalin's death, in 1953, it is doubtful that the Soviets would have supported an effort by Chinese ground troops in Indochina on the side of the Viet Minh unless it had been provoked by direct American intervention on the side of the French. After 1954, North Vietnam, despite its army's success in fighting a superior enemy, was hardly eager to risk the gains sealed by the Geneva settlement by mounting an invasion of Laos. Reports from observers who had contact with the Viet Minh delegation at Geneva indicate that the Viet Minh welcomed the settlement as a respite in which to consolidate their power at home; other accounts have sought to make it appear that the Viet Minh accepted the cease-fire unwillingly and only at Soviet Foreign Minister Molotov's insistence. The evidence seems irrefutable that the United States based its program of aid to Laos on premises that may have been valid in 1950 but were no longer valid in 1955.

9. In seeking to deter the military threat to Laos represented by its two stronger Communist neighbors, the United States based its planning on the protective "umbrella" provided by SEATO, apparently disregarding the fact that General Giap's guerrillas had prevailed over the 350,000-man French Expeditionary Corps in spite of the possibility of American intervention with nuclear weapons. The United States took over support of the Lao Territorials from the French on the supposition that the army was the only effective nation-building force in Laos. When this army found itself engaged in warfare against the Pathet Lao beginning in 1955, however, the U.S. proceeded to fashion it into a national army on the model of the French Army. Little or no attention was paid to defense against the village-by-village infiltration and subversion that had played such a predominant role in the Viet Minh success. Unfortunately, from the American point of view, the atypical battle of Dien Bien Phu served to reinforce the obsession with frontal attack. The Royal Lao Army inherited the barbed-wire and mud-fort mentality of the men responsible for that disaster. The Vietnamese Communists, on the other hand, retained their thousands of bicycles, whose mobility they had come to appreciate in the Tonkin highlands. The French repeatedly warned the American PEO that the tanks and artillery given the Royal Lao Army were well suited to fighting set-piece battles on the Korat Plateau or in the Mekong Delta, places where the Lao would probably not be called upon to fight, but were of little value in Sam Neua Province.

Dulles contemplated a conference of experienced leaders of Southeast Asia after ratification of the SEATO treaty to discuss how to meet the threat of "people's war"; however, the project was abandoned after the death of President Magsaysay of the Philippines. If it had taken place, the Royal Lao Army might have been in a better position to cope with the guerrilla tactics it later faced.

10. The creation of this army introduced an unstabilizing, rather than a stabilizing factor. Not until January, 1960, was an effort made to draw the soldiers into civic action,[5] and so the Royal Lao Army was one of the least politicized in the world. Even the soldiers of the Foreign Legion had constructed kilns to bake bricks in the villages where its men were stationed in Laos; after 1954, the Royal Lao Army did none of this public-relations work, unlike the Pathet Lao. Rare was the officer, like Kong Le, who made his troops pay for food taken from local civilians. Most officers had little rapport with their own troops, and less with the people; the Phoumist officers at Nam Tha were in the forefront of the flight to the Mekong, leaving their men behind to fend for themselves. Defections were commonplace. But despite their lack of political sense, these officers had ambitions that could be translated into political action. First there was the attempted putsch in December, 1959, and eight months later the Kong Le *coup d'état,* brought off successfully by a small group of junior officers in protest against the politics of an allegedly corrupt government, whose leading Cabinet minister was a general officer. The Pentagon had originally advised the State Department that a Lao army of any size would have little military value in furthering the mutual-security policy of the United States in Southeast Asia. The Royal Lao Army, which had been supported by the United States primarily for political reasons, grew from a force level of 23,600 in 1955, to 30,000 four years later, and to 48,000 in another four years. At the same time, the territory it controlled shrank. The attempted putsch of April, 1964, one of whose leaders was a twenty-eight-year-old general, was evidence that the United States had allowed the army to develop along lines far from the initial intention of assisting Laos attain a stable nationhood.

11. The complexity of Communist motivations and the difficulty of predicting Communist actions are incontrovertible, but they constitute no explanation for the lack of foresight in so many American actions. The formal commitment of the United States toward Laos and South Vietnam, as well as toward Thailand, was

---

[5] *Hearings,* III, p. 2385.

clearly worded in the SEATO treaty. Nevertheless, this was a commitment with strictly limited ends. The United States, in the case of subversion in Laos, was legally obligated only to consultations. Therefore, in hard policy terms, the United States had no *obligation* to be led deeper and deeper into an involvement from which it derived no immediate gain (such as military bases) and raised the stakes more and more. The extent of U.S. control over the economy of Laos, for instance, led to the paradoxical situation that, if America threatened to cut off aid in order to pressure the Lao government, it could virtually bring about the downfall of the Vientiane government (at least, until the advent of economic aid from the Soviet bloc). The certain long-range effect of such an aid cut-off, however, was to halt the flow of hard goods into the country to soak up money paid out to the administration and army, and thus to produce a runaway inflation that might very well drive the country into the arms of the waiting Communists. The theory was that by exerting pressure on the Lao government, the United States could "polarize" the political situation to the point where there were only Communists and anti-Communists. This theory failed to consider that only the Communist side in this neat dichotomy possessed a widespread apparatus of obedience in the countryside. The United States was involved with all sectors but the one that counted most—the people. Again, the experience of the French in 1946 could have been instructive.

12. The American "country team" in Laos was a many-headed animal, analyzing the situation from many different viewpoints and producing as many interpretations. The military mission, for instance, had few illusions about the "bastion" concept of Laos, which found favor among the political experts of the State Department. Most of the military regarded the Royal Lao Army as a makeshift force that liked to ride at high speeds along the country's few paved roads and had a penchant for night-clubbing and new cars—all of whom might decide at a moment's notice not to fight when faced with a strong enemy, particularly a Vietnamese enemy. After it became evident that the invasion from China or North Vietnam would not, after all, take place, the American military viewed their role in Laos as a holding operation to give the "pro-Western" governments of Thailand and South Vietnam more time to solidify their own positions. What the military did not understand was that the greater the gains made by the Pathet Lao in the countryside, the less became the inclination of the Thais to bind themselves to the American alliance and the greater their inclina-

tion became to adopt "neutralism" themselves. The State Department understood the fears of the Bangkok government better than the military, which helps to explain why its spokesmen put a façade of boldness on an operation that the military knew to be much less than a do-or-die proposition. As for the CIA, its able agents in the field accumulated an encyclopedic knowledge of the country and its people that appears to have been carefully studied by neither the Pentagon nor the State Department. The result was that while the men in Laos possessed accurate knowledge, in many cases those in Washington were talking to one another at cross-purposes, at least until President Kennedy began studying the details and reaching his own decisions on that basis. When the United States finally accepted the proposal in 1961 that Laos should be neutralized, if such neutralization was still possible, the contrast with the previous bold façade was so great that the impression gained widespread currency in the United States that Washington was "losing" Laos.

13. The "country team" system, accepted as the least unsatisfactory of the several possible organizational methods of implementing policy, in Laos reduced the Ambassador's authority to a point where it was no longer commensurate with the degree of American involvement. Theoretically, the Ambassador was advised by the mission heads of the various agencies operating in the field—the economic-aid mission, the military-aid mission, and the CIA. In practice, each of these missions functioned on its own initiative, maintained its own channels of communication to Washington, and had at its disposal a share of the American funds being expended in Laos. The Ambassador often had cause to wonder how much autonomy the members of his team enjoyed in dealing with the Lao. In 1959, the State Department protested a promise the PEO head gave to the Lao Defense Minister for more funds for army salaries, although this promise had been approved along the line of PEO's chain of communications to the Pentagon. The set-up was potentially dangerous because a skilled politician could play one agency off against another, or use the actions of one agency for his own internal political purposes against the wishes of another agency. The support given General Phoumi in the autumn of 1960 by the Defense Department and the CIA was used by the General as evidence that the United States was backing him in the contest for allegiance between himself and Souvanna Phouma, although the State Department had made distinct reservations on this score.

The adoption of General Phoumi by the Defense Department

and the CIA led to a foreign-policy predicament not unlike that faced by the United States in China in the late 1940's. "The reactionaries in the Government have evidently counted on substantial American support, regardless of their actions," General George C. Marshall reported after the failure of his Chinese mediation mission. In the delicate negotiations for a coalition government in Laos in 1961 and 1962, President Kennedy attempted to make it clear that a political figure's standing in relation to the needs of his country—rather than his professions of anti-Communism—was the proper criterion for American backing. This reflected a nobility of purpose that had previously been sadly lacking in American actions in Indochina.

If the Ambassador could on occasion curb the agency representatives on his "team," the fact remained that his advice to Washington on the formulation of policy carried little weight there, and he was sometimes reduced to the role of titled messenger boy for the policy-makers in the State Department. At one point in October, 1960, Ambassador Brown was receiving telegrams from Washington informing him bluntly that aid to Laos was being cut off, or was being turned on again. It was Brown's task to acquaint the Prime Minister as best he could with the reasons for these sudden stops and starts. Frequently the Prime Minister had already got wind of Washington's action through news dispatches. The decisions were Washington's, and they were based on a broad view that attached greater importance to the effects of American actions on allies elsewhere in the Pacific than to their effect inside Laos.

The Ambassador's authority was further undermined at critical junctures by the flying trips made by high-ranking State Department officials. The usefulness of such missions was limited by their brevity and by the inordinate amount of publicity they received. Both characteristics conflicted with an old Oriental notion that bargaining, if it is to be serious, should proceed quietly and only after several days of polite preliminaries. Such American visitors to Laos thus arrived with their bargaining position already undercut, and departed with little more understanding of the problem than they had possessed when they arrived. Their observations of Vientiane, Luang Prabang, and the countryside in between as seen from an airplane window left them still trying to come to grips with Laos. Souvanna Phouma managed to survive more than one "tough talk" process, which added to his prestige among the Lao.

14. The switch from a policy of consistency without victory to one of inconsistency without defeat caused bewilderment in Laos

and in surrounding nations. Compelled to choose which among the princely politicians of Laos to support, just as the French had done sixty years before them, the Americans at first formed their closest relationships with those they viewed as anti-Communists, in the belief that these men had the best prospect of leading their country to nationhood and stability. American support was the *sine qua non* of political power in Laos, and in one case it allowed a general in rebellion to prevail over a prince who had been three times Prime Minister. All-out support of this nature alienated those who felt that the wisest policy for their country was one of disentanglement and reconciliation rather than one of commitment and repression. However, the course of Washington's diplomacy soon shifted again, making possible a *rapprochement* with the protagonists of reconciliation. Of course, this stranded the men who had previously been hailed for their anti-Communism.

One man who had particular reason for wonderment at American actions was King Savang Vatthana. During the attempted putsch in January, 1960, he had been confronted with the ambassadors of all the Western powers, who, in a united voice, argued against the advisability of permitting a military dictatorship, even one that proclaimed itself reformist in platform, in favor of the preservation of parliamentary institutions. Three years later, he witnessed the U.S. failure to advance similar arguments when the Pathet Lao declared their intention to disregard the actions of this same parliament because it was known to have been packed by anti-Communists at the previous election.

The reactions of men like King Savang Vatthana went deeper than bitterness. They felt that Washington was treating their country like a political football. But they also wondered at the coherence of American policy in Southeast Asia. In surrounding countries as well, many leaders wondered whether the day might not come when they, too, might be left high and dry, their U.S. support suddenly withdrawn. In the long run, this is certain to be one of the most damaging effects of American actions in Laos. By contrast, the Chinese, the North Vietnamese, and the Pathet Lao gave an appearance of constancy to their actions, by cloaking their policy in the mantle of "support for the people of Laos," in 1964 as in 1954. There was nothing in the series of Communist statements on Laos to match the fluctuation in American statements, which at one time described Laos as a bastion of freedom and at another as a neutralist state. (This is not to say, of course, that the Communists have not shifted their affections frequently in dealing with the multiplicity of personalities offered by the Indochinese states. For instance, Peking once viewed Prince Sihanouk as the "puppet king of Cambodia." This characterization was dropped after Bandung and after Sihanouk abdicated the throne in 1955 to take an active part in Cambodian politics.)

15. For Americans, there were always too few hard facts to go by in Laos. And when there were facts, they gave rise to divergent, not to say contradictory, interpretations.

The 1959 crisis provided the first of many examples of how facts became exaggerated and their interpretations distorted. To describe the return to Laos of NLHS cadres trained in North Vietnam and the entry of selected North Vietnamese units in support of Pathet Lao troops as an invasion, an impression assiduously fostered for diplomatic reasons by the Royal Government and the State Department and uncritically accepted by the Western press, was to miss the point entirely. Unlike the operations by Giap's divisions in Laos in 1953 and 1954, which had been intended to tie down *men* on the French side to make possible what Giap perceived to be the climactic engagement of the war, and which therefore could accurately be described as invasions, Giap's 1959 operations consisted exclusively of covert support for the Pathet Lao, intended to secure control over *territory*. Given the limitations of territorial control in the mountain country of Laos, his objective was and is to drive the government forces out of their isolated jungle footholds in the regions of Laos that interested North Vietnam. Because Giap could not afford to tie down a great number of his troops to accomplish this, he sent agents to spread rumors of thousands of Vietnamese on the march.

This tactic, a traditional one in Vietnamese warfare,[6] was inexpensive as long as the Royal Government remained unable to prove that there was no substance to the rumors. And the North Vietnamese, as Phoui Sananikone observed at the time, were "much too smart to let themselves get caught in a flagrant violation." Among the easy-going Lao, the rumor-spreading tactic was doubly effective.[7] In the nineteenth century, King Anourouth's ill-fated march on Bangkok had been inspired in part by a rumor that the British

[6] The phantom army, or *nghi binh,* was one of the three elements of the ancient Vietnamese army. See Douglas Pike, *War, Peace and the Viet Cong* (Cambridge, Mass.: MIT Press, 1969), p. 120.

[7] Caply, *op. cit.,* p. 265, reports that rumors swept the town of Kam Keut in September, 1945, that 30,000 Vietnamese were marching down from Nape.

Navy was about to attack that city. Anourouth in turn used the rumor to gain entrance to Korat on the pretext that his army had been summoned to Bangkok to help fight the British and to persuade the Lao living in Siam to return home in the belief that the British were about to conquer Bangkok.[8]

The North Vietnamese campaign of 1959 had three principal objectives: first militarily, following the breakdown of the first coalition and the resumption of open fighting between the Pathet Lao and government forces, to re-create a solid base area for the Pathet Lao on the North Vietnamese border like the one given up in 1957; second, politically, to warn the Royal Government of the consequences of tying itself too closely to the Americans; and third, insofar as the attacks in Khammouane and Savannakhet provinces were concerned, to secure control over the border strip essential for communication to South Vietnam.

Bernard Fall has documented several cases of the exaggeration by the press that became commonplace in reporting the 1959 crisis. He quotes an Associated Press dispatch:

> The government is dropping hundreds of paratroopers on Sam Neua's Muong Peun fortress, surrounded by deep palisades and depending entirely on air drops for its supplies.
>
> Observers say the fortress looks like the famed battlegrounds of Dien Bien Phu, where the French failed in the last major battle of the Indochinese war.

From his own visit to Muong Peun during this period, Fall was able to describe the outpost as "two little bamboo and wood barracks constructed on a small hillock overlooking the surrounding plain, encircled by a six-foot-high breast of sand bags and wooden planks which were surrounded in turn by a few harmless strands of barbed wire," and he reported that on August 21 two sticks of paratroopers, which would normally comprise a total of 48 men, were dropped there without incident other than a few fractured ankles.[9]

[8] Vella, *op. cit.*, p. 81.

[9] Fall, *Anatomy of a Crisis*, pp. 129–130. Even Fall sometimes allowed his thinking to get muddled. In the same passage, he makes a surprising comment, "the Communist probe on Muong Peun was more likely to impress the armchair strategists outside of Laos, who still tended to look at jungle warfare in European terms of overland communication lines," which appears intended to minimize the significance of the abandonment of Muong Peun to the enemy. The North Vietnamese were an infantry army and depended almost exclusively on overland communication lines. Thus,

The misleading picture of what was happening in Laos in 1959 was thus based on a faulty view of the situation, the product of press reporting. Because the Lao army, which was running the show, stood to benefit materially in terms of increased American aid, and because the American Government wished to persuade Congress and the American public to finance such aid, neither government did anything to correct the impression of a North Vietnamese invasion.

When the new coalition government was established in 1962, it enjoyed widespread sympathy, even though it was soon seen to be unworkable. The resumption of fighting in Laos in 1963 did not attract much attention, being overshadowed by the more dramatic events in South Vietnam, where President Diem had been overthrown in a coup d'état. The high-level expressions of concern and flying missions to Vientiane of the Eisenhower Administration days were no longer in vogue. The U.S. Defense Department managed to impose a total blackout on information about American aircraft losses in Laos from June 7, 1964, to March 10, 1970. It was a quiet war, a forgotten war as some called it.

The American news agencies, which maintained large staffs in South Vietnam from 1965 to 1970, did not keep a single staff correspondent in Laos on a permanent basis for any significant portion of that period. As a result, there was virtually no reporting on the handful of Americans on the ground, supported by air crews, who probably did more per man than anyone else in the war, through their efforts to hinder North Vietnamese movements down the Trail, to keep the number of American deaths in South Vietnam from rising above the 40,000 killed since mid-1965. Then the North Vietnamese offensives of 1969 and 1970 raised anew all the critical issues of perception that had been raised in 1959.

Press correspondents newly arrived in Vientiane chafed under restrictions, adopted by the Lao Government under pressure from the American Embassy, that kept them from traveling in the country and that prohibited military officers from talking to the press. As in 1959, the press was in the dark. Since it was impossible for correspondents to talk to the men who were fighting the war—the Lao and Meo on the ground and the American pilots in the air—it was inevitable that their attention should focus on the

---

their probe on Muong Peun was an extremely significant indicator of their intentions, though not in the sense in which the armchair strategists saw it. His comment that "the fall of Muong Peun would not have materially affected the defense of Sam Neua," which was twenty miles away and also depended on air supply, is correct but irrelevant.

clandestine activities of the Americans, about which there had been the darkest suspicions ever since the Pathet Lao outcry about Air America in 1962.

As the reporter population in Vientiane soared yet again to a hundred the impression was created that Laos threatened to suck the United States into a "new Vietnam." The large figure of North Vietnamese troops in Laos that was so uncritically bandied about by Administration spokesmen and the press alike gave the wrong picture once again. But because the misleading picture suited the purposes of the Lao generals and of the American Embassy, no effort was made to correct it. The press accepted it and reported it in 1970 as in 1959.

In the absence of hard facts to go by, newspapers normally known for their sense of responsibility fell back on the time-honored expedient of describing Laos as a never-never land where events followed no logic and were not worthy of serious attention in any case. A typical example described a "psychedelic political power struggle between fractured Centralists and splintered Neutralists, Rightists and crypto-Communists, which might tell you a great deal about the significance of the military byplay if you could somehow wrap your mind around it, and having done that, take it seriously."[10]

In view of the state public opinion on the war had reached by 1970, it can readily be seen that almost any factual revelations about American actions in Laos would have led to a new flood of press stories about escalation (a highly ambiguous word), which in turn would have set off a fresh Congressional uproar, which in turn would have made life for the President even more unbearable than it already was. Thus, the illusions of Laos were perpetuated by the Royal Government, the United States, and the press.

Since the signing of the 1962 Geneva agreement, American policy has been aimed at minimizing the effects of these "flaws in the bastion," while the North Vietnamese have been trying to maximize their effects. These efforts constitute the context of the present conflict, the contest of wills in Laos.

[10] *Washington Post,* March 2, 1970.

16.

The Contest of Wills

Since the departure of the French, there have been two radically different perceptions of the situation in Laos: North Vietnam and the United States started from different premises and have interpreted events in a different manner. Thus, when they exchanged accusations, it was as if they were talking about two different worlds, for there was total misunderstanding between them.

North Vietnam's perspective emerged from a history of Vietnamese intervention across the Annamite Mountains, the interests that the Indochinese Communist Party and the Viet Minh pursued in acting beyond Vietnam's frontiers, and the temptations that followed the collapse of the French empire in Indochina, with its aspirations for unity, its preferential role for the Vietnamese, and its plans for an Indochinese federation. Hanoi saw the conflict in Laos as part of an American scheme to perpetuate the partition of Vietnam. It regarded the United States as France's successor in Indochina, as an aggressive and colonialist power that was intervening in an area where the Americans had no right to be and the Vietnamese belonged.

After 1954, the leaders of North Vietnam began to work for the reunification of their divided country in accordance with the principles of sovereignty and unity that they had succeeded in writing into the Geneva agreement. They acted with confidence and consistency in what they believed to be a legitimate and noble enterprise, and, in this task, they insisted that Laos had a vital role to play. They brought young men from Laos and South Vietnam to Hanoi for indoctrination and training.

But the ambitions of the North Vietnamese and their Pathet Lao and Viet Cong allies soon came into conflict with American policies toward the area. Contrary to their predictions and their experience with the French, the North Vietnamese discovered that the Americans did not give way to the logic and strength of the North Vietnamese position but instead, through either blindness or stubbornness, only saw Hanoi's undeniable but never openly confessed objective of hegemony in Indochina. Wherever the North Vietnamese chose to expand the war, the Americans prolonged it, and their misreading of American determination was to become the Achilles' heel of their entire enterprise.

The U.S. perspective, on the other hand, emerged from a different historical tradition. Americans, having won their independence from a colonial power in a revolutionary war, had an equally strong distaste for foreign intervention. President Roosevelt's determination not to let the French back into Indochina after World War II had truly reflected the wellsprings of American character, and American aid to the newly independent governments of Laos and South Vietnam had been generous. To the United States, foreign efforts to subvert the governments of Laos and South Vietnam were abhorrent, and the operations of North Vietnamese Army units in Laos and South Vietnam were intolerable, particularly because North Vietnam's violation of the 1954 armistice provisions in South Vietnam and of the 1962 neutralization agreement in Laos affronted American respect for contracts and fair play. Although Washington might act indecisively and wastefully, while Hanoi's every step was the result of painstaking discussion and collective decision, U.S. policy-makers were of one mind in regarding Hanoi's behavior as a direct challenge to the traditional American belief that justice will prevail in the world.

It is only against this background of a tradition of fair play and justice that the American commitment of half a million men to the Vietnam war can be understood, not to speak of aid programs intended to "win hearts and minds." The failure of such programs to elicit an American-style response was one of the biggest disappointments to Americans in Indochina. On a tactical level, the Americans with their ill-defined purposes were at a disadvantage *vis-à-vis* the skilled bluffers in Hanoi with their panoply of front organizations in South Vietnam, Laos, and Cambodia. Hanoi never mentioned the presence of its troops in Laos, yet certain units of the North Vietnamese Army had a generation of experience in Laos. The Vietnamese Communists feigned ignorance of the Ho Chi Minh Trail, yet when their soldiers on the Trail wanted to know how Laos permitted it, they told them it was a temporary arrangement.[1] This was a charade, but if one accepted it, it was indeed plausible to imagine that the United States was the aggressor in Laos. Hanoi's version of events, so often adopted by the intellectuals of the antiwar movement to support their arguments, was just as logical in its own way (allowing for the habitual gross exaggeration of statistics for internal propaganda purposes) as the reporting in the Western press. The only difference was that, in the one view, the pilot of an American jet was bombing Laotian villagers in violation of the 1962 Geneva Agreement, while, in the other, he was destroying a fuel depot where the North Vietnamese refueled their trucks on their way south.

The gap between these two contradictory perspectives remained constant with the passage of time. In 1958–59, the "forward policy" adopted by the Royal Government with American encouragement led to clashes with North Vietnam. Hanoi thereupon enunciated its position that "peace in Indochina is indivisible,"[2] but the United States still separated the Laos problem from that of South Vietnam until the actual breakdown of the Geneva agreements of 1962.[3] From 1964 on, as the fighting in Laos resumed on a bigger scale and the situation in South Vietnam deteriorated and then spread into Cambodia in 1970, the United States accepted the fact that the Indochina War was one. Much of the American effort in Indochina was directed against traffic along the Ho Chi Minh Trail, which made sound military sense but complicated the problem of finding a political settlement in Laos.[4] By 1970 North Vietnam no longer recognized the government in Vientiane as the tripartite coalition government established in 1962. Hanoi's position implied that it was responsible only to the Pathet Lao faction for whatever use it made of the areas of Laos controlled by that faction. The inevitable consequence of this position was renewed conflict between North Vietnam and the United States in Laos (also, after 1970, in Cambodia).

[1] The 316th Division, for example, took part in the 1953 invasion; its 174th Regiment was employed by Giap in both the 1959 and 1970 offensives. A North Vietnamese prisoner captured at Dong Hene in March, 1965, said his unit was only "borrowing the road" in Laos to reach South Vietnam. (Quoted in Langer and Zasloff, *op. cit.*, p. 184.)

[2] See p. 112, above.

[3] See p. 276, above.

[4] As President Nixon put it in his statement on Laos of March 6, 1970: "As Commander-in-Chief of our Armed Forces, I consider it my responsibility to use air power to interdict this flow of supplies and men into South Vietnam and thereby avoid a heavy toll of American and allied lives."

People's War

The formula employed to wage this war was by and large the one that the Viet Minh had used in their successful war against the French. It incorporated the same mixture of military and political ingredients, in which civil war and foreign intervention become confounded and strategic ends can be attained by a coup d'état as readily as by a military victory, and the same strategy of pitting opposing forces one against the other that Ho Chi Minh had perfected in his dealings with his enemies and rivals in Vietnam since the 1930's.

There is no question that the North Vietnamese made good soldiers. Armed only with bamboo spears, they had received their baptism of fire while assaulting French machine gun positions. The North Vietnamese mounted their operations with an efficiency that was equaled only by their minute planning. When an unfriendly witness stumbled by accident on one of these operations, as occurred in the case of a British nurse who was on the road between Thakhek and Paksane when North Vietnamese troops were crossing it, death was meted out quickly.

The military theory of this war has been well described as "people's war," a phrase used by Giap to match his description of his soldiers as a "people's army." Giap represented the North Vietnamese soldier in his highest form; as a student, according to a classmate, he used to spend hours poring over maps, and it is little wonder that he later turned the wars he waged into wars of geography. Giap and his fellow officers learned other lessons from the history of their country's numerous wars against the Chinese, from the peasants' revolts, or from the operations of secret societies.

Most of their knowledge came from what they themselves did. They learned from the French paritsans of 1945 how to prepare jungle bases and cache food and arms, to ambush convoys and patrols, to keep liaison by courier. The French had always attached great importance to territorial representation and the fact of the existence of legitimate government, even one in exile or of a provisional character. De Gaulle's example impressed the Vietnamese, as did the order he sent to General Sabattier "to keep hold of a piece of the territory of Indochina, no matter how small." In their war against the Americans, the Viet Minh first formed the NLF, a maze of paper organizations, and gradually added to it. It is little wonder that they counted the seating of a separate NLF delegation at the Paris conference table opposite the Saigon delegation as a victory. The next step was to enfold the NLF within the PRGRSV and surround the latter with all the apparatus of a functioning government at home and abroad.

This was also a war in which an important key to success lay in relating men to ideas and then identifying men with territory. Here the Vietnamese secret societies provided a precedent, for though their methods resembled nothing so much as protection rackets, such methods had application in political warfare in setting up parallel administrations. Success lay in demonstrating credibly that the resistance governed a particular village, a district, a province. No matter if the boundaries of the village, district or province did not coincide with the enemy's; the gerrymandering of such administrative units (again the supreme importance of a knowledge of geography) became a standard practice of the Viet Minh, the Viet Cong, and the Pathet Lao. Only in this sense can one understand the pique of the Pathet Lao at having a group of guerrillas under the orders of the government in Vientiane sitting atop a mountain only twenty miles from Sam Neua after the regrouping of the Pathet Lao forces in that province in 1955; the Pathet Lao regarded the province as *theirs* and the government guerrillas as bandits who represented no legitimate authority.

Physical resources sometimes had to be commandeered when they could not be acquired voluntarily. "People's war" was a particularly brutal form of warfare; not even the private lives of those involved were spared. Bernard Fall has pointed out that at least 10,000 Lao and tribesmen left Phong Saly and Sam Neua provinces for North Vietnam after these provinces had been temporarily integrated with the rest of Laos in November, 1957; here was the raw material of which the revolution was made.

The general rule held that the regular army had to be protected at all times by the regional troops and self-defense forces. This rule was observed at the battle of Thakhek in 1946 and in the campaign the North Vietnamese waged in 1970 to protect their sanctuaries in Cambodia; the number of bodies left on the battlefield usually gave rise to an exaggerated estimate of the damage inflicted on the Communists' regular army.

Human lives were the most important single resource, but the revolution required other resources as well, and some of them were bizarre. The dollar of the American soldier was needed to purchase arms and medicines or to pay the rent on an NLF information office in a European capital. Counterfeit currency also had its use, as was discovered when crates of the Cambodian 500-riel note were found in the ransacked PRGRSV Embassy in Phnom Penh.

The mental resources of the Vietnamese Communists were made up of a fierce pride in being Vietnamese, a people with 4,000 years of recorded history, and the high motivation that comes from thorough indoctrination. Ho once upbraided a young revolutionary for despairing of ever being able to propagate the revolution among the Vietnamese of Mukdaharn, who lived in utter poverty and moreover gambled away what little money they had managed to save. "You forget you are dealing with Vietnamese like yourself," Ho told the young man, "Vietnamese in misery and who don't even have a fatherland."[5] At times this national pride bordered on arrogance, especially in an intellectual like Giap. Even Peking complained about the "arrogant" behavior of the Vietnamese.

The single-minded determination of the guerrilla fighter or the agent behind enemy lines is by far the most important mental resource of the revolutionary.[6] In the jungle, the job of the guerrilla requires full concentration every minute and, above all, discipline, which permits the split-second timing of operations and the careful coordination of military with political action. The Free French depended on their rear headquarters in Calcutta, which sent them orders in Laos to take action or, equally important, *not* to take action. (The general order sent to all groups in Laos on April 16, 1945, not to engage the enemy, which was obeyed reluctantly, later permitted the groups that had avoided detection to strike with maximum surprise.) Likewise, the Vietnamese Communists depended on their array of rear headquarters, often so baffling to the uninitiated foreigner, to assure coordination. Perhaps the most significant statement contained in the 1959 United Nations subcommittee report was the observation that "certain of these hostile operations must have had centralized coordination." The most dramatic example of such coordination, of course, was the 1968 Tet offensive in South Vietnam.

The Vietnamese Communists used their skills at deception to help compensate for other resources they lacked.[7] The highest art

---

[5] Trinh, *op. cit.,* p. 113.

[6] Probably the best description of the mental attitude of the guerrilla fighter remains F. Spencer Chapman, *The Jungle Is Neutral* (London: Chatto & Windus, 1949).

[7] Two examples illustrate North and South Vietnamese skills in deception. For many years, the Soviet government had wished to learn about NLF high command headquarters in South Vietnam. Ivan Shedrov, Hanoi correspondent of *Pravda,* was eventually permitted to visit an NLF underground command post. There, he met Mrs. Nguyen Thi Dinh, deputy commander of the NLF army. During the interview, Mrs. Dinh was busy answering telephone calls and apparently giving orders to all battle fronts. The

of "people's war" was to accomplish much with very little. In Laos, the North Vietnamese were able to maintain a constant threat, although they rarely had any men available for offensive operations, a reality that contradicted the picture propagated by the Royal Government and the United States.[8] To maintain this threat, the North Vietnamese ensured that every porter and engineering soldier they sent to Laos was combat-ready. Some very bitter fighting went on in the back hills of Sam Neua and Xieng Khouang, places where the *status quo* was most brittle, but it involved small units, not divisions, exchanging fire.

Sudden *changes* in the *status quo* were crucial in Laos, for they immediately affected Princes Souvanna Phouma and Souphanouvong, each of whom had a keen sense of balance. The American use of bases in Laos, such as Phou Pha Thi, for operations against North Vietnam particularly bothered Souvanna Phouma, for he foresaw that it would increase North Vietnamese pressure on his half-brother Souphanouvong to upset the *status quo* between their two forces. The danger of a change in the balance of forces was far more important for the practical Lao than the fact that the use of such bases by the United States clearly violated the Geneva agreement.

The war in Laos had a great deal more accommodation to it than many of those who attempted to report it realized. The Pathet Lao, the "forest men" as villagers called them, prevented the government in Vientiane from extending its roots into vast areas of the countryside and exerted an influence born of a mixture of fear and respect on thousands of people in the nominally government-held towns. For its part, the government maintained its flag and authority in many places that were completely indefensible from the

---

Vietnamese later had a good laugh; the command post was not the real NLF headquarters; the telephone calls had advised Mrs. Dinh how to answer Shedrov's questions. An American columnist, equally naive, was regularly taken on tours of the Mekong Delta to report on the progress of pacification in South Vietnam. He saw no evidence of Viet Cong and concluded that they had abandoned even their oldest strongholds. But a mile ahead of his touring vehicle, armored personnel carriers were clearing the road. In each case, the Vietnamese were eager to receive a continued flow of foreign aid.

[8] Langer and Zasloff, *op. cit.*, p. 171, have estimated that North Vietnam had no more than 14,300 men available for military operations in all of Laos outside the Trail area. Figuring that four men must porter for each man on the firing line, 2,860 men would have been available for combat, about the equivalent of a regiment.

military point of view and were manned, in addition, by soldiers who had no intention of making a last-ditch stand. At the same time, the Pathet Lao needed certain commodities that could only be secured in the government-held towns, such as flashlight batteries, kerosene, and bicycles. One frequently saw well-stocked shops, owned by Vietnamese and Chinese for the most part, in towns that, like Attopeu, were completely surrounded for years by the Pathet Lao and North Vietnamese, where the only transport was by air. In many lesser towns and villages, if the local government military commander was not in actual communication with the local Pathet Lao commander, a tacit agreement existed between the two men not to stir things up, for this would have meant mopping-up operations in the forest, bombing strikes by pilots from the town, followed by retaliatory mortar attacks on the town, its evacuation, and other disruptions that would be of no benefit to either side, since the Pathet Lao did not possess the means to defend the town if they captured it (in fact, most of the towns in Pathet Lao–held territory were completely deserted), any more than the government had the means to prevent its capture.

Western observers tended to be shocked by what they viewed as the cynicism of the Vietnamese Communists' politico-military strategy. The agreement between the PRGRSV and Prince Sihanouk, permitting the former to use Cambodian territory "until the end of the war" appears in Western eyes a masterpiece of cynicism. But one can understand it if one recalls the experiences of the Vietnamese with their former French rulers. Ha Van Lau, later to be the negotiator with the French and the Americans, enlisted in the French forces in 1940 in hopes of getting to France to finish his studies; instead, his one-year enlistment was arbitrarily extended following the Franco-Thai conflict, and he spent the war in Laos. The French had "bought on credit" from him; he in turn saw nothing cynical about "buying on credit" from the Sihanouks of the world.

Vietnamese and Americans in Laos Compared

The Vietnamese Communists, being good Marxists, interpreted the relationship between the Americans and their "lackeys" in Laos as one founded on purely selfish motives and therefore basically unstable. The Lao would flatter and fool the Americans as soon as they had had a taste of the benefits of the American presence, and the Americans would not be able to trust the Lao. An element of force would enter into the equation, and the relationship would be vitiated. There were exceptions, and frequently the Communists put a price on their head. An Indiana farmer named Edgar Buell lived among the Meo of Xieng Khouang Province for ten years, and he trusted them as they trusted him.[9] Buell had started out in Laos as an International Voluntary Service volunteer; another IVS volunteer in Champassak Province was assassinated by the Pathet Lao, and Prince Boun Oum commented "I'd rather lose the lives of 1,000 of our Lao than the life of one such American." But mostly the American presence took the form of bureaucracy rather than human contact. The disinterestedness of the Americans in Laos differed markedly, of course, from the attitude that had been taken by French colonial officials and thus might have been turned to political advantage. Whereas the French had occasionally gone to extraordinary length to "go native," the Americans tended to live in a world apart from the Lao and interest themselves only in technical problems. This was quickly perceived by the middle-level Lao officials. The Americans wasted inordinate time in meetings (almost as much an obsession with the Americans as with the Communists) and followed routine to the point of absurdity. Edicts issued by American career bureaucrats interfered with travel by young Americans along "insecure" roads, in disregard of the effect such measures had on the morale of the population. Americans assassinated by the Pathet Lao were sometimes not replaced, an error that doubled the value of such an assassination for the Pathet Lao but that remained unperceived by men in air-conditioned offices. Although many knowledgeable Frenchmen had remained in Laos as teachers, missionaries, and military observers, they were rarely consulted by busy Americans, and so the Americans were fated to repeat the painful lessons taught to the French.

In Vientiane, the life of the American Embassy revolved around the tiny group of politicians and generals at the apex of the vast money-making machine that was the army with the control it had acquired by selling everything from wooden ammunition crates to permits for wealthy Vietnamese and Chinese merchants to evacuate towns threatened by the Communists. Americans in Vientiane tended to discuss the problems of Laos in terms of statistics and the profusion of acronyms to which the American presence had given birth, mistaking their norms for Lao norms, programs for

[9] Buell's story has now been written by Don A. Schanche in *Mister Pop* (New York: McKay, 1970).

progress, and the enthusiasm of the elite for the enthusiasm of the masses. Only the Lao who had money were in favor of continuing the war, for the American attempt to "win the hearts and minds of the peasants" had failed dismally, and the moneyed elite had the least to lose from a Communist takeover, because they could afford to go abroad.[10] In talking with Americans in the field in Laos, especially the military attachés whose job it was to deal with the Royal Lao Army, one sometimes detected an inner rage, not at their mission, to which they were completely dedicated, but at their Lao "counterparts" who could not be made to share the same dedication.

The relations between the North Vietnamese and their Lao allies were completely different. The North Vietnamese went to considerable lengths to conceal the presence of their soldiers and political cadres, but on the whole they managed to exert greater influence over the Pathet Lao than did the Americans over the Royal Government. North Vietnamese advisers and troops in Laos were quartered apart from the Pathet Lao, and their relations with the local population were kept to a strict minimum. In 1962, a member of the French Military Mission on the Plain of Jars wandered off in search of a buffalo for his mess, was arrested by the Pathet Lao, and underwent interrogation by a French-speaking North Vietnamese officer, but such glimpses of the North Vietnamese running things were the exception.

North Vietnamese cadres in Laos at all levels adopted the attitude that they were engaged in helping a younger brother, and, while this was trying at times, it was nevertheless a noble ideal. This attitude explains the great patience of the North Vietnamese and their efforts to fit into the local scene. It was common, for instance, for North Vietnamese cadres working among the primitive tribes along the Ho Chi Minh Trail to adopt tribal customs, even filing their teeth and putting ear plugs in their ears. A French teacher on the Plain of Jars, who observed North Vietnamese soldiers unloading a truck, recalls the high spirits with which they tackled their job, conversing in loud voices and singing, an attitude that contrasted rather sharply with American doubts about

[10] The supply of money, arms and other appurtenances of war, moreover, stimulated appetites. The general who commanded one of Laos's five military regions complained to the author that he did not have enough helicopters, transport planes and guns, and so the Lao soldier did not fight as well as in the days of the French Union (forgetting that these appurtenances had been virtually nonexistent then).

whether or not the Lao would manage to pull through and whether their work would have any lasting value. Each side had its own view of what a just peace would mean for Laos, but the essential question of the war was how long each side could hold out, and here the mental attitude was all-important.

The War in American Eyes

For the Vietnamese Communists, there was another vital ingredient of success, however. Even with their organizational ability, their cleverness, their *sang froid,* and the material support of the socialist camp, the North Vietnamese leaders still realized that they could not hope to win the war solely in Indochina; they would have to extend the battle front to the United States, as they had done in the case of France. The North Vietnamese needed to mobilize American opinion against the war.

The actions of their government in Indochina and the arguments produced to justify these actions were not easily understood by the American people. The conflict seemed far away, its origins were obscure, and its outcome could affect them little. Moreover, they had been told by Defense Secretary Robert S. McNamara that the war would soon be over and, later, by their President that peace was certain once the opposing sides had agreed to sit down at the conference table. When Secretary of State Dean Rusk told them in 1967 how very deeply the United States had become involved in Indochina, following the crucial decision in 1950 to side with the French against the Viet Minh by providing material aid, and how Giap's victory would constitute the most damaging humiliation ever suffered by the United States, they saw him as a warmonger.[11]

[11] The Secretary hardly discouraged this impression with his unfortunate remark about "one billion Chinese armed with nuclear weapons" (1967), which recalled the Bismarckian "yellow peril" instead of suggesting serious diplomacy. Dean Rusk was an Assistant Secretary of State when the crucial decision to give aid to the French was made. His superior, Dean Acheson, has written that the decision was taken only after "hesitation" and that "all of us recognized the high probability of this result [i.e., French defeat by the Viet Minh] unless France swiftly transferred authority to the Associated States and organized, trained, and equipped, with our aid, substantial indigenous forces to take over the main burden of the fight." (*Present at the Creation; My Years in the State Department* [New York: Norton, 1969], pp. 672–73.) The State Department about this time characterized Ho Chi Minh as "the mortal enemy of native independence in Indochina" (*Department of State Bulletin,* February 13, 1950, p. 244), which must surely rank as one of the most mistaken evaluations of a foreign situation ever made by any government. Some members of the American mission in Indochina

North Vietnam calculated, therefore, that the United States was conducting a losing policy in Indochina and, when confronted with its many dilemmas, would throw up its hands in despair and, like France in 1954, accept a dictated armistice that would leave the Communists in a monopoly position. Hanoi had capable and intelligent men who read everything that was published in the United States concerning the war and paid particular attention to the interaction of press reports and congressional pressure on the Executive.[12]

Some of the dilemmas that Hanoi perceived did indeed give rise to the most profound moral agony in the United States. After having totally encouraged Saigon to flout the provision in the 1954 Geneva Agreements for elections in 1956, U.S. acquiescence in the brutal murder of President Ngo Dinh Diem, the man who had been the instrument of that policy, was unquestionably immoral. And the politicians who a few years later called for the overthrow of the general who succeeded Diem and continued his policies at American behest were doubly immoral.

A similarly agonizing dilemma was created by the official American silence about violations of the 1962 Geneva agreement in Laos. While this practice served to defuse congressional opposition to these activities in the short term,[13] it built up future issues of far graver import: The policy of official secrecy was undermining the confidence of the people in their government. The public feared that what the government was not telling it about Laos, some hints

---

in 1950 argued forcefully, though unsuccessfully, that American aid to the governments of the Associated States should not be channeled through the French, as the French insisted.

[12] Phan Hien, the director of the American Desk in the Foreign Ministry in Hanoi, told the author in Paris in 1968 that he read the *Congressional Record* every day. In talking with the North Vietnamese delegates in Paris, it was touching to see how much faith they placed in the domestic American opposition to the war. It was also interesting to observe their satisfaction at the schemes, some of them obviously impractical, advanced by American politicians to disentangle the United States from Indochina without actually admitting defeat, since this spectacle confirmed Hanoi's leaders in their view that the American effort in Indochina was a desperate one and bound to fail.

[13] For complaints about how little the Executive kept Congress informed of American involvement in Laos, see remarks of Senator Stuart Symington in *Hearings, IV*, p. 435. Symington was a member of both the Senate Foreign Relations Committee and the Armed Services Committee. See also remarks of Senator J. William Fulbright in *Ibid.*, p. 547, and *Hearings, V*, p. 673.

of which were getting into the press, could foreshadow a new and unexpected disaster.[14] This was not the case, since both sides had limited interests in the conflict in Laos, but the American people had no way of judging this, and so the impression spread that Laos could become "another Vietnam."

The most appropriate comment on the effects of the practice of official silence about American activities in Laos came from Senator Stuart Symington, the Chairman of the Subcommittee on U.S. Security Agreements and Commitments Abroad of the Senate Foreign Relations Committee, who observed that "speculative news stories, Communist propaganda, irresponsible political charges, are poor substitutes for reliable information on a subject of such importance."[15]

The practice of official silence dated back to the first American action that contravened the spirit of the Geneva agreement—the re-establishment, in October, 1962, of a military mission disguised as an economic aid team. The silence was extended in 1964 to cover such activities as the American reconnaissance flights and air strikes that Souvanna Phouma had requested. The Prince's original motive in asking for silence on these matters was undoubtedly his wish to return to a mutual observance of the provisions of the Geneva agreement as the basis for a settlement in Laos. As time went on, another factor emerged. It seemed likely that the rightists, especially the Army General Staff, whose interests the United States had fostered, would rationalize an abnormal situation by ousting Souvanna Phouma and replacing him with one of their own men, should the Prince officially condone American violations and thereby downgrade the Geneva agreement; on the other hand, a rightist coup would make a return to the Geneva agreement impossible.

Ambassador Sullivan's request that press correspondents observe discretion in reporting on American activities in Laos, on the grounds that publicity would embarrass the Russians, was aimed at

---

[14] On February 11, 1969, a military attaché, Captain Joseph K. Bush, Jr. was killed in an attack at Muong Soui, and his death went virtually unnoticed, except for a report on February 13 and an obituary on February 15 in his hometown newspaper, The *Temple Telegram* (Texas). On March 6, 1970, President Nixon stated that "no American stationed in Laos has ever been killed in ground combat operations." On March 8, 1970, the story of how Bush had died was made public in the *Los Angeles Times,* and it forced an official correction the next day.

[15] *Hearings, IV,* p. 366.

heading off an official admission of such activities. As Sullivan later explained the situation:

> A senior Soviet official, for example, has said that insofar as he reads things in newspapers or hears statements and allegations about U.S. operations, he does not have to take any official cognizance of them. But if they are made directly by U.S. officials he does have to take cognizance of them, and this will color, to some extent, the Soviet attitude toward Souvanna Phouma's neutrality and toward the retention of the understandings which underlie the agreement between ourselves and the Soviets for the neutrality of Laos.[16]

The North Vietnamese method of political warfare against the United States consisted of spotlighting all the contradictions in U.S. policy maneuvers in Indochina. One contradiction that particularly tickled the fancy of the men in Hanoi was that the United States appeared to be supporting a coalition government in Laos while opposing the formation of one in South Vietnam, as demanded by the PRGRSV. As one American writer pointed out, "If we are serious about resisting aggression, why fight it at great cost in one small country and ignore it—or all but ignore it—in an adjacent small country? . . . If we are serious about self-determination, why defend it on only one side of a border drawn for administrative purposes by some French bureaucrats in the last century?"[17]

A somewhat similar quandary, involving the extension into Laos of the so-called McNamara Line—a barrier against infiltration from North Vietnam into South Vietnam—was never resolved. With men and supplies slipping into South Vietnam at alarming levels, the United States had built a barrier against the most direct infiltration route across the eastern end of the demilitarized zone. Militarily, its extension to the Mekong River in Laos made sense, because such a barrier would have cut off the Trail and forced Hanoi's leaders to find alternative methods of retaining their contact with

---

[16] *Hearings, IV,* p. 399. Unlike Hanoi and Peking, Moscow had not taken the position that Souvanna Phouma's government no longer was the tripartite coalition established as a result of the negotiations of 1961 and 1962. The Soviet Union, in dealing with Souvanna Phouma, however, stuck by Hanoi's line up to 1970 that a settlement in Laos would have to wait until a "final settlement" had been reached in Vietnam. It will be recalled that this position had been repudiated by the Phoui Sananikone government in 1959 (see p. 116, above), but neither Hanoi nor Moscow had had diplomatic relations with Laos at the time.

[17] Richard H. Rovere, "Letter from Washington," *The New Yorker,* March 21, 1970.

the South. The extension of the McNamara Line would be costly, its advocates granted, but over the long term the cost of bombing the Trail was proving to be much higher. On the other hand, the cost of constructing the barrier had to be added to the cost of past bombing.

The ideal time for the construction of such a barrier would have been in the years of truce that followed the 1954 Geneva Conference. If men had known then what the later war would cost, an effective barrier, equipped with electronic sensor devices, could have been constructed economically along the entire length of the border between Laos and North Vietnam, just inside Laos. This was never done, of course, and the infiltration across the open border began. To meet this threat, the Lao Government adopted the "forward policy" that led to clashes on the ground and charges of border violations from North Vietnam.

During the debate on the extension of the McNamara Line, however, Prince Souvanna Phouma and Ambassador Sullivan registered their opposition to the plan on the grounds that it would probably induce North Vietnam to launch large-scale ground attacks in northern Laos and might even lead to the Communist takeover of the entire northern part of the country, a development that would have required an American response. Once again, American behavior in Indochina revealed to the men in Hanoi the inscrutability of American logic.

Both Sides Locked In

By early 1969, the war in South Vietnam had cost the Communists half a million dead. This was without doubt a far heavier price than the Lao Dong Party had expected it would have to pay for South Vietnam when, at its Third Congress in 1960, it decided to embark on the struggle for the South. Conversely, this heavy sacrifice increased the North Vietnamese commitment to the struggle.[18]

On the American side as well, the costs of the war had been heavy and the sacrifices made for it stood as a mortgage of the American involvement. The conflict that had divided the Vietnamese had also divided the Lao. As one American Senator declared, "We have involved the Laotians to such an extent that we

[18] "We have paid an enormous price for our victory," Pham Van Dong told the French journalist Jacques Decornoy in 1970 (*Le Monde,* December 2, 1970). The figure of half a million Communist dead was admitted by Vo Nguyen Giap in an interview in Hanoi with Oriana Fallaci, published in the *Los Angeles Times,* April 13, 1969.

have created an obligation which is most difficult for us to get out of at the present time."[19]

The only way out obviously lay through some form of negotiated political settlement. Incredible as it seems in retrospect, the first official communication between the United States and North Vietnam after the former closed its consulate in Hanoi in 1955 was to be a formal protest delivered to Hanoi through the ICC following the Gulf of Tonkin incidents in August, 1964. For the next six years, the United States and North Vietnam largely talked past each other about a war that held them both locked in.

President Kennedy, however preoccupied he was with Laos, never turned his full attention to Vietnam, where the American dilemma was becoming apparent about the time that the foreign ministers in Geneva were signing the Laos agreement.[20] While the United States and North Vietnam argued about the origins of the crisis in Laos, the American delegation failed to explore the possibility of negotiating with Hanoi about South Vietnam.[21] Only one private meeting between the American and North Vietnamese representatives in Geneva took place, and it occurred at the end of the fourteen months of negotiations.[22] The discussion about the situation in South Vietnam was without result. Afterward, Colonel Ha Van Lau remarked to a high Quai d'Orsay official in Geneva, "*Maintenant, c'est la guerre.*"[23] The North Vietnamese Foreign

[19] Senator Mike Mansfield in *Congressional Record*, December 15, 1969, p. S16753.

[20] Schlesinger, *op. cit.*, p. 997.

[21] For an indication of how little thought was given by the Kennedy Administration to the idea of negotiating with North Vietnam, see the joint memorandum on the Vietnam situation sent by Harriman, leader of the American delegation in Geneva, and John Kenneth Galbraith, Ambassador to India, to President Kennedy, dated April 2, 1962, quoted in Galbraith, *Ambassador's Journal* (Boston: Houghton-Mifflin, 1969), pp. 342–44.

[22] The meeting was arranged at the suggestion of James Barrington, a high-ranking official of the Burmese Foreign Ministry. Present on the North Vietnamese side were Foreign Minister Ung Van Khiem, who had just arrived from Hanoi to sign the Laos agreement; Xuan Thuy, the leader of Hanoi's standing delegation in Geneva; and Colonel Ha Van Lau, the veteran of the 1954 conference. Present on the American side was Sullivan. The meeting in Barrington's hotel room lasted about one hour. Personal conversation of the author with one of those present.

[23] Personal conversation of the author with the official concerned in Paris in 1968.

For confirmation by a well-informed writer that the North Vietnamese representatives in Geneva were willing to talk about the situation in South Vietnam, provided the NLF was represented, see Georges Chaffard, *Les Deux Guerres du Vietnam* (Paris: La Table Ronde, 1969), pp. 260–63.

Ministry had put out a feeler for a conference on South Vietnam in January, 1962, but the establishment by the United States of its Military Assistance Command in Saigon the following month appears to have convinced Hanoi of an American determination on war. The Viet Cong were held off balance by the new American helicopter tactics in South Vietnam in the first half of 1962, and Hanoi certainly foresaw that the United States would use the special majority ICC report on Vietnam published on June 2, which condemned North Vietnam for violation of the 1954 armistice, as justification for increased American military involvement.

Almost imperceptibly, the United States was being sucked into a war in South Vietnam that it had avoided in Laos, stepping into that "military and political quagmire without bottom" of which De Gaulle had warned Kennedy at their meeting in 1961.[24] Each step was small enough so that its consequences were insufficient to force a reappraisal of the line of march, but each added inexorably to the commitment. Kennedy and his senior advisers clung to their conviction that the Russians could be induced to influence Hanoi to "call off"[25] the Viet Cong; in this they badly underestimated Hanoi's freedom of maneuver and determination.

While the Viet Minh undoubtedly welcomed the end of the first Indochina War, they had yielded to considerable Soviet pressure at Geneva in 1954.[26] Again, in 1962, the North Vietnamese signed an agreement on Laos under great Soviet pressure.[27] Harriman and Sullivan, Kennedy's negotiators at Geneva, failed to appreciate that

[24] Charles de Gaulle, *Mémoires d'Espoir; Le Renouveau 1958–1962* (Paris: Plon, 1970), p. 269.

[25] The phrase is Galbraith's.

[26] The Soviet Union in 1954 was more interested in seeing the French Government defeat the project for the European Defense Community (EDC) than in helping the Viet Minh quibble with the French about where the demilitarized zone in Vietnam should be.

[27] By the summer of 1962, the question of negotiations with the imperialists had become one of the central issues of the deepening Sino-Soviet split. For the markedly different reactions of Moscow and Peking to the signing of the agreement on Laos, see p. 221, above. Chinese Foreign Minister Marshal Chen Yi bluntly told a Western diplomat at Geneva, "Ten years later it [Laos] will be Communist. We are patient. We can wait." (Quoted by C. L. Sulzberger in *The New York Times,* June 18, 1962.) In comparison to the Soviet view of the Laos agreement as a good augury, the Chinese view that it was merely a step toward "liberation" proved to be more accurate. The Chinese argument against big-power dealings at the expense of small countries bore particular relevance for Vietnam.

this Soviet pressure, which was later viewed as a source of shame by the proud Vietnamese, made Hanoi *less* rather than *more* likely to let its actions be influenced by the Russians again.[28] Once the United States began bombing North Vietnam, the Russians were obliged, whether they liked it or not, to help a fellow member of the socialist camp; this was a poor position from which to bargain.The Russians passed on part of the bill for aid to North Vietnam to the East Europeans and must have held many of the same feelings toward the men in power in Hanoi as the United States held toward those in power in Saigon. In return for Russian support, Hanoi used opportunities such as the invasion of Czechoslovakia in 1968 to give the Russians immediate verbal support and thereby accumulate credit. Interventionists themselves, they found little difficulty in reconciling themselves to the invasion, unlike their comrades in Western Europe.

Yet the neutralization agreement on Laos represented a risk for everyone concerned, and especially for North Vietnam. In the face of the ominous signs in South Vietnam, Hanoi had reason to read the Kennedy Administration's actions in Laos in the weeks following the signing at Geneva as equivocal. American military advisers departed. Air America remained. There was no retaliation against North Vietnamese military movements on the Plain of Jars. American military deliveries were resumed to the rightist army. Each side, conscious of the keystone position of Laos in Indochina, was watching the other's moves there for an indication of intentions in South Vietnam, while the coalition in Vientiane hung at the edge of the precipice.

In the end, it was the increased tempo of the fighting and the rising stakes in South Vietnam that prevailed. The North Vietnamese did not move out of eastern Laos as they had promised to do. Souvanna Phouma construed their continued presence as a reversal of previous agreements and as a threat to his government, and he saw nothing wrong in asking for further American aid, which had

[28] According to the author's own observations, the relations between Harriman and the North Vietnamese negotiators, when they met again at the official conversations between North Vietnam and the United States in Paris in 1968, were almost invariably polite, almost courtly. When Harriman was replaced by Henry Cabot Lodge in January, 1969, the North Vietnamese even complimented Harriman for his relatively "realistic" views on the problem of Indochina, although, as they were far too polite to note, Harriman had pinned his hopes of a negotiated settlement on the good offices of the Russians.

the effect of further impeding a political settlement. The termination of the Soviet airlift to Kong Le's troops left them at the mercy of the Pathet Lao forces they were facing and the North Vietnamese who armed those forces. In Vientiane, Souphanouvong and the other NLHS ministers found themselves skating on thin ice as the Prime Minister, incensed at the North Vietnamese perfidy, took Cabinet affairs into his own hands, and the guns boomed once more on the Plain of Jars.

Hanoi sacrificed the coalition as the price for securing control of the Ho Chi Minh Trail, by proxy of the Pathet Lao. The coalition had already ceased to be effective, however, a year before the NLHS, Hanoi, and Peking withdrew their recognition of the National Union Government in the summer of 1964.

Two opportunities to reopen negotiations were lost during 1964. Prince Sihanouk proposed in April that a conference be called to deal with Laos and also prepare for an international meeting "to deal with . . . the whole of the former Indochina." This met with no response. Then, only a few days after the Gulf of Tonkin incidents, Prince Souphanouvong suggested a new meeting of the three Lao princes. When they eventually met in France, he proposed turning over control of the Plain of Jars to a reintegrated, centrist force. This suggestion was vetoed, with American knowledge, by the rightist faction, even though it represented an important concession from Giap's position in a declaration to Souvanna Phouma in Hanoi barely five months previously.

Diplomacy having failed, the leaders in Washington and Hanoi turned to force. There followed in rapid succession the North Vietnamese preparation of the Trail to carry truck traffic, the reorganization of North Vietnamese forces along the Trail, and the appearance of the first regular North Vietnamese Army regiments in battle in South Vietnam. On the American side, there were the first air strikes not associated with reconnaissance, the start of intensive bombing of the Trail, the bombing campaign against North Vietnam, and the commitment of American ground troops to South Vietnam. All these things happened in the space of a few months, and they certainly reinforced the hand of presidential advisers in Washington, like Walt Rostow, who favored "teaching Hanoi a lesson." In spite of the first doubts about the efficacy of counterinsurgency techniques and associated gadgetry, and more broadly about the ability of a democratic society like that of the United States to cope with the moral consequences of such a war, the conflict had already reached the stage of a "test of will,"[29] and President Johnson obviously saw it as such.

Still, American diplomacy in Laos continued to rely on the perceived ability of the United States to persuade Moscow to influence Hanoi, despite the declining Soviet involvement in Indochina and rising Chinese influence with Hanoi to the detriment of the Soviet Union. When Harriman made another trip to Moscow in 1963 to try to persuade Khrushchev to live up to the heavy responsibility the Soviet Union had assumed as Co-Chairman, Khrushchev seemed bored with the subject and asked Harriman irritably why Washington bothered so much about Laos.[30] Before he was overthrown in the following year, Khrushchev threatened to resign the responsibility of Co-Chairman.

Harriman and Sullivan knew much about the Russians and little about the Chinese, and, in the conflict between the two Communist powers, they thought that Washington and Moscow had a basis for a mutuality of interest in Indochina. As Sullivan explained it:

> While not prepared to oppose Hanoi openly, the U.S.S.R. has played a restraining role and given indications that it would prefer neutralist solutions in Laos and Cambodia in order to provide buffers between the Vietnamese and Thai peoples. Conflict between the Vietnamese and Thai would facilitate the extension of Chinese and reduce Soviet influence. Moscow may fear that a major North Vietnamese victory on the peninsula would increase the pro-Maoist tendencies in Hanoi and its satellite Communist movements.[31]

After he became Ambassador to Laos, Sullivan sought to keep the Russians engaged there. Actually, the Russians had no choice in the matter, once they had decided to reverse Khrushchev's course of disengagement, if it is true, as Sullivan said, that they feared polarization of the situation in Laos would benefit the Chinese. When he was asked afterward to give an example of Russian restraining influence in Laos, Sullivan could point only to

---

[29] The phrase was used by Administration spokesmen to describe the February 7, 1965, retaliatory air attack against North Vietnam. (*The New York Times,* February 8, 1965.) In his speech announcing his decision to send American troops into Cambodia, President Nixon said: "It is not our power but our will and character that is being tested tonight." (April 30, 1970.)

[30] Schlesinger, *op. cit.,* p. 517.

[31] *Hearings, IV,* p. 374.

"measures that have not been taken by them,"[32] and to assurances from the Soviet Ambassador to Laos and other Soviet officials.[33]

Distracted as they were by their fear that the Soviet Union "might decide to scrap the basic understanding"[34] with the United States for the neutrality of Laos, and by the Soviet Union's alleged concern "because of the Chinese desire to benefit by a scrapping of the neutrality status so that they might have an extension of this power and hegemony into the South,"[35] Harriman and Sullivan simply failed to take China and its concerns into account. They overlooked China's interest in the genuine neutralization of Laos and in preventing, if possible, the emergence on its border of a strong North Vietnam with undisputed hegemony over South Vietnam, Cambodia, and Laos. China had had some 4,000 years of involvement in Indochina. Souvanna Phouma and the French, among others, repeatedly pointed out that no settlement would last if it did not have the concurrence of China.[36] Moreover, Harriman and Sullivan discarded any possibility of influencing Hanoi through Peking.

With so quixotic an approach to the problem of neutralization of Laos foremost in the minds of their senior advisers, Presidents

[32] *Ibid.*, p. 451.

[33] *Ibid.*, p. 451. During his term as Ambassador to Laos (December, 1964, to March, 1969), Sullivan appears to have been influenced to some extent by the close personal relationship that existed between himself and Boris Kirnossovsky, the Soviet Ambassador in Laos for much of that time.

Sullivan admitted doubts in October, 1969, about the *willingness* of the Soviets to exercise a restraining influence in Laos. He told the Senate subcommittee: "They certainly, in private conversations, say that this is their policy, and we have no reason to believe that within the limits of their willingness to execute such a policy it is not their ultimate policy." The Senators in their questioning failed, however, to ask him for his evaluation of the *ability* of the Soviets to exercise a restraining influence. (*Hearings, IV*, p. 451.)

At one time, Sullivan believed that American-Soviet understanding could by itself settle problems not only in Laos but elsewhere, without mentioning China. Immediately after the signing of the Laos agreement, he called the agreement "a template for a pattern of peace which would have not only significance for Southeast Asia but for the rest of the world." (*Hearings, IV*, p. 430.)

[34] *Hearings, IV*, p. 590.

[35] *Hearings, IV*, p. 591.

[36] In making known its withdrawal of recognition of the Vientiane government on June 9, 1964, Peking had explicitly warned that the Lao civil war would resume (see p. 276 , above).

Kennedy[37] and Johnson were doomed to fail in their search for a lasting negotiated settlement. It was only in January, 1970, with the Nixon Administration's resumption of the interrupted Warsaw talks with China, that a settlement in Indochina once again came within the realm of possibility. This neglect of China's position is all the more paradoxical in view of U.S. efforts to avoid involving China in hostilities. American pilots bombing North Vietnam were under orders not to penetrate a buffer zone along the China border. When the Chinese began to construct roads into Laos from Ban Tatene in the autumn of 1968, Air America planes flew over the construction sites, but hostile action against the roads and their builders was forbidden. The American crews reported that they were followed by antiaircraft guns on the ground, but the guns held their fire. These facts show that understanding on at least a limited scale was possible.

Under the tacit understanding between Washington and Moscow, the former turned a blind eye on Soviet arms deliveries to North Vietnam, part of which were transferred to the Pathet Lao, while the latter turned a blind eye on American violation of the Geneva Protocol. The arrangement had the advantage to the Russians of being completely costless. Their main strategic concern was the limitation of Chinese influence with the Communist movements of Indochina, and their main tactical policy was to continue to support Souvanna Phouma as leader of the Laos coalition. They were able to cite Pathet Lao and North Vietnamese reports of American actions in Laos in violation of the Geneva Protocol, without ever bringing into question the continued validity of this protocol, because the American actions were not officially admitted by Washington. The citing of these reports, together with the evidence of their arms aid, enabled the Russians to maintain solidarity with Hanoi and with the other Communist movements of Indochina, while their support of a neutralist government in Vientiane brought them benefits in their relations with the Third World. The Russians were so cocksure in Laos that the amiable station chief of the KGB in Vientiane, Viktor Zhukov, was heard on occasion to speak openly about the presence in Laos of the North Vietnamese Army.

The arrangement was not quite so costless for the United States.

[37] President Kennedy appeared to be on the verge of making some changes in United States relations with China when he was assassinated. See Roger Hilsman, *To Move a Nation* (Garden City, N.Y.: Doubleday, 1967).

In violation of Clause 2 (i) of the Geneva Protocol forbidding the use of "the territory of the Kingdom of Laos for interference in the internal affairs of other countries," North Vietnam had 40,000 soldiers in Laos, most of them manning the Trail to South Vietnam.[38] Admitting failure to ensure respect for one of the key provisions of the agreement on neutralization of Laos, Harriman told the North Vietnamese in 1968: "Not for a day have you carried out the provisions of the 1962 Agreements."[39]

The sequence of events that led North Vietnam to maintain its forces in Laos in spite of the Geneva agreements and to withdraw its recognition of Prince Souvanna Phouma's government as the original coalition reflected a judgment in Hanoi that the coalition in Laos was not worth saving. An argument could be made, however, that the coalition was worth saving from Hanoi's point of view and that in sacrificing it Hanoi was committing a costly error. Not only was Hanoi throwing away the opportunity to demonstrate that a coalition could work in South Vietnam, where the nationalist political forces were strongly prejudiced against it on the basis of their fate under the 1945–46 coalition with Ho Chi Minh, but Hanoi was also refusing the advantages that would accrue to it from having its partisans in the Vientiane government. Under the guise of supporting the neutrality of Laos, Prince Souphanouvong would have been in a position to mobilize international opinion against American violations of the Geneva agreements. On the basis of the tripartite agreements, he could have insisted on vetoing the American bombing of the Ho Chi Minh Trail and even the permitting of American overflights of Laos to bomb North Vietnam, actions of inestimable value to Hanoi. This was the sort of policy the North Vietnamese leaders elected to follow with respect to Cambodia for eight years until it collapsed with Prince Sihanouk's overthrow. But this required more foresight than the leaders in Hanoi possessed; in 1963 and 1964, they knew neither how long the war would last nor what it would cost them.

The remorseless logic with which the conflict escalated made it no less a tragedy for those on whose soil it was fought, and Laos suffered disproportionately high human costs. There were grounds for outrage at a war that swallowed up boys of thirteen and fourteen as well as grown men. Many were killed or maimed by the

[38] Figure given by Harriman in the Paris talks, June 5, 1968.

[39] Statement at the 17th Session of the Official Conversations between the United States and the Democratic Republic of Vietnam in Paris, August 14, 1968.

mines and booby traps that had been scattered with unthinking abandon by both sides. According to official figures, 3,900 members of the Royal Lao Army were killed during 1969, mostly in small-scale ambushes and shellings; this number is the proportional equivalent of 300,000 American deaths. By 1969, the war had taken the lives of 15,000 Lao and produced 18,000 casualties among the Meo.[40] It had also made 700,000 persons, or a quarter of the population, homeless at least once.

A Vietnamese friend living in Vientiane remarked that, while he thought the Vietnamese probably deserved the horrors of the war in their own country, the Lao were innocent of design and had done nothing to deserve the war that engulfed them. Anyone who knows the Lao realizes they are at heart an undemanding people, satisfied with life as they find it in an admirably balanced natural environment, and devoted to the pleasures of family life. Though a small number of them have been corrupted[41] by their contact with the developed countries, they mean no harm to the Vietnamese. Some American liberals have concluded that the intelligent, industrious, and prolific Vietnamese have earned the right to dominate Indochina. But to suggest that the United States should therefore turn over the Lao to the North Vietnamese is to advance a frankly colonialist argument.

While no one would argue that the Lao should be absolved of responsibility for the war in their country, the burden of responsibility falls heavily on others. The performances of Britain and the Soviet Union as Co-Chairmen of the Geneva Conference, and of India, Canada, and Poland as members of the ICC, present as miserable a record of failure as any to be found in the history of international peace-keeping. In the advanced stage of its paralysis in 1970, the ICC was unable even to bring itself to record the American violations of the 1962 agreement that had been officially announced by President Nixon on March 6. The decreasing succor that the so-called nonaligned nations have brought to the preservation of neutrality in Laos is a good measure of their moral influence in a polycentric world, a trend particularly marked by the abdication of post-Nehru India from such leadership. As India's impact on Southeast Asia has declined, Japan's has risen steadily. It should also be pointed out, without intending any moral judg-

[40] *Hearings, IV,* p. 454.

[41] Not only by governments, either. The correspondent in Laos of Japan's largest newspaper paid $200 to General Kouprasith to give him an interview in March, 1970.

ment, that, whereas the United States went to the aid of the French in their hour of need in Indochina, under difficult conditions and against the advice of some wise men, the United States received no sympathy from General de Gaulle in its hour of trial in the same region.

Enforceable Neutralization

The survival of a Laos that is not a colonial possession occupied by European or American garrisons, a Vietnamese fief in a Communist-dominated Indochinese federation, or a vassal of China depends on the effective neutralization of Laos by international consent. Souphanouvong has had to rely on the Vietnamese in his quest for power, and Souvanna Phouma has found that "neutralism" alone is not enough to preserve Laos's independence. As I have said, neutralization rather than neutralism is the only possible way to extricate Laos from the currents of big-power politics.

The neutralization of Laos obviously presents greater problems than does, for instance, the neutralization of Finland, which has existed as a sovereign state on the border of the Soviet Union since World War II with a coalition government that includes Communists. In Finland, if a stranger asked a villager the way to a strategic installation in wartime, the Finn would immediately try to telephone the police. In Laos, however, there are no police in most of the villages. Then, too, the villagers have little concept of modern statehood and little contact with central authority; they tend to deal with strangers on a strictly local basis, and often this has meant evacuating their villages and fleeing into the hills. I once watched a Lao employee of U.S. AID standing on the front porch of the AID office in Pakse pointing out to two Lao soldier friends the location of each American office in the small compound—the offices of the Army and Air Attachés, the CIA, the Requirements Office, and so forth. Laos is, after all, a country where there are few secrets, and even the CIA considers itself lucky if it can pick up half as much information as is carried in the head of the local village chief.

Despite these internal deficiencies, the situation of Laos remains susceptible to neutralization, and indeed this is the only way of restoring a durable peace. The real reasons for the failure of the 1962 attempt are external rather than internal: (1) the virtual disappearance of Soviet influence on the situation after the termination of the Soviet airlift and North Vietnamese actions to squeeze off Soviet supplies to Kong Le, and the simultaneous rise of Chinese influence with Hanoi, circumstances in which the American failure to find another dynamic to make the 1962 agreement work deprived neutralization of any chance of success; (2) the breakdown of international machinery for supervising in Laos the implementation of the agreement; and (3) above all, the failure to find a political settlement in South Vietnam.

Under present conditions, any settlement in Laos in isolation from Vietnam is impossible. The wars in Vietnam, Laos, and Cambodia have come to resemble communicating receptacles in which the level of fluid in one is affected by any change in the level of fluid in any of the others. American delegates in Paris in 1968–69 found that they could not negotiate a settlement in Vietnam without at the same time negotiating about Laos. The Lao factions were faced with a Sisyphean task in trying to reach a settlement after 1965, when a major portion of the war in Laos, the American bombing of the Trail, was entirely outside their control.

This is not to say, however, that the only way to a settlement lies in a grand conference of all concerned to discuss the entire Indochina situation. In fact, there are a number of objections to such an ambitious conference. Two of these are the difficulty of obtaining the participation of all the interested parties and the inadaptation to public negotiation of fundamentally divergent interpretations of the causes of the conflict. Private negotiations, on the other hand, if possible on a bilateral basis, may offer a better chance of exploring and reaching compromises. Private negotiations allow each side to stick to its own interpretation of the conflict, while a settlement could, if so agreed, be put into effect without public acknowledgment of certain actions that would simply be unilaterally verified by the other side. To succeed, such negotiations must include, in one manner or another, all the interested parties, and their progress must be coordinated.

Thus, for example, the Pathet Lao has demanded a total halt to American bombing before it will agree to resume political negotiations with the Vientiane government, and it seems hardly likely that they will drop this demand unilaterally unless they are on the point of surrender. But the United States has viewed the bombing of the Trail as essential to the protection of American and South Vietnamese forces in South Vietnam and therefore would require a *quid pro quo* before ending the bombing. The Paris conference offers a forum in which these positions can be discussed, but guarantees may be required from China or the Soviet Union. The pattern of negotiation leading to a political settlement in Laos might then involve, *concurrently,* the Paris conference, the Warsaw talks between American and Chinese Ambassadors, talks in Washington between the American Secretary of State and the Soviet Ambassador, as well as a meeting of the factions in Laos.

The neutralization of Laos, and possibly of the other countries of Indochina, has become part of a vast international diplomatic operation whose beginnings can still be perceived only dimly in 1970. Peace in Indochina, like the war, is indivisible.

A Note About Place Names in Laos

Place names in Laos are intimately linked to descriptive geography. Thus, a place name is usually a combination of words signifying real things. Ban Na, from *ban* = village and *na* = rice field, is the name of a village rich in rice. Muong Kheung, from *muong* = town and *kheung* = halfway, is a town located midway between two others. Phou Nok Coc, a mountain northeast of the Plain of Jars overlooking Route 7, can be rendered in English as Woodpecker Ridge, from *phou* = ridge or mountain, *nok* = bird, and *coc*, indicating the sound a woodpecker makes. Pak Hou and Paksane are the towns situated at the mouths (*pak*) of the Hou River and the Sane River, respectively. The Keo Neua Pass, from *Keo* = Vietnam and *neua* = north, is the pass leading to northern Vietnam. While some words, like *ban* = village and *houei* = stream, are found from the extreme north of Laos all the way to the extreme south, and even in Cambodia and the Central Highlands of South Vietnam (e.g., Ban Me Thuot), there are some geographical variations. For example, the common word for river is *nam* in the north (e.g., Nam Tha, Nam Ngum) and *se* in the south (e.g., Se Bang Fai, Se Done, Se Kong). This book uses the English version (e.g., Ngum River, Kong River). According to the Lao, some place names appearing on maps of Laos are deformations. Thus the Hin Boun River, which flows through the chalk hills north of Thakhek, and the town of Pak Hin Boun at its confluence with the Mekong, should correctly be written Hin Poun, from *hin* = rock and *poun* = lime, meaning "rock from which lime is made, or limestone." The deformation resulted from the inability of the Vietnamese interpreters employed by French cartographers to pronounce the word Poun.

APPENDIX I. THE LAO MONARCHY

(Based on Paul Le Boulanger, *Histoire du Laos Français* [Paris: Plon, 1931] and Katay Don Sasorith, *Le Laos* [Paris: Berger-Levrault, 1953].)

Kings of Lan Xang[1]	Reign
Fa Ngoun	1353–1373
Sam Sen Thai *or* Oun Hueun	1373–1416
Lan Kham Deng	1416–1427
Phommathat	1428–1429
Kham Tem *or* Pak Houei Luong	1429–1430
Sai *or* Mune Sai	1430
Khai or Fa Khai	1430–1433
Kon Kham or Kong Keo *or* Chieng Sa	1433–1434
Yukhon	1434–1435
Kham Keut	1435–1438
Sai Tiakaphat	1438–1479
Theng Kham *or* Souvanna Palang	1479–1486
La Sen Thai *or* La Nam Sen Thai	1486–1496
Som Phou	1496–1501
Lu Phe Sai *or* Visoun	1501–1520
Phothisarat	1520–1548
Sai Setthathirath	1548–1571
Sen Soulinthara (first reign)	1571–1575
Maha Oupahat	1575–1580
Sen Soulinthara (second reign)	1580–1582
Nakhone Noi	1582–1583
Interregnum	*1583–1591*
Nokeo Koumane	1591–1596
Thammikarath	1596–1622
Oupagnouvarath	1622–1623
Phothisarat	1623–1627
Mone Keo	1627
Oupagnouvarath	Dates unknown
Tone Kham	Dates unknown
Visai	Dates unknown
Souligna Vongsa	1637–1694

[1] Until the reign of Sai Setthathirath, the royal capital was Luang Prabang. Subsequently, it was moved to Vientiane.

Tian Thala	1694–1700
Nantharath	1700
Sai Ong Hue	1700–1707

In 1707, the Kingdom of Lan Xang split up into three separate kingdoms, the Kingdom of Vientiane, the Kingdom of Luang Prabang, and the Kingdom of Champassak.

Kings of Vientiane	*Reign*
Sai Ong Hue (nephew of Souligna Vongsa)	1707–1735
Ong Long	1735–1760
Ong Boun	1760–1778
Interregnum	*1778–1782*
Nan	1782–1792
In	1792–1805
Anourouth or Anou[2]	1805–1828

Kings of Luang Prabang	*Reign*
Kitsarat (grandson of Souligna Vongsa)	1707–1726
Khamone Noi	1726–1727
Inta Som	1727–1776
Sotika Koumane	1776–1781
Vong	1781–1787
Interregnum	*1787–1791*
Anourouth	1791–1817
Manta Tourat	1817–1836
Souka Seum	1836–1851
Tiantha	1851–1872
Oun Kham	1872–1887[3]
Zakarine	1894–1904
Sisavang Vong[4]	1904–1959
Savang Vatthana	1959–present

Kings of Champassak	*Reign*
Soi Sisamout (nephew of Souligna Vongsa)	1713–1737
Saya Koumane	1737–1791
Fay Na *or* Sairaja Khati Vongsa	1791–1811

[2] Anourouth died in Bangkok in 1835 after having attempted in vain to restore his throne in Vientiane, which had been sacked by the Siamese in 1827.

[3] An interregnum followed the sacking of Luang Prabang by Thai tribesmen from the Tonkin border region in 1887; Pavie confirmed the rights of the royal house of Luang Prabang after establishment of the French Protectorate in 1893.

[4] Under the terms of the Provisional Constitution of October 12, 1945, Sisavang Vong agreed, at the insistence of the Lao Issara provisional government, to exercise sovereignty over a unified Laos having virtually the same borders as the country has today; the exercise of this sovereignty was confirmed by the French in the *modus vivendi* of August 27, 1946.

Chao Nou	1811
Interregnum	*1811–1813*
Phromma Noi	1813–1817
Chao Nho	1817–1826
Chao Houy	1826–1840[5]
Chao Nak	1841–1850
Chao Boua	1852
Chao Kham Nhai *or* Youtti Thammathone	1856–1858
Kham Souk *or* Youtti Thammathone II	1863–1900

[5] The Siamese court, which appointed the vassal rulers of Champassak, permitted the throne to remain vacant for varying periods of time after 1840.

APPENDIX II. PRIME MINISTERS OF LAOS

Prince Souvannarath	March 15, 1947–March 25, 1948
Prince Boun Oum na Champassak	March 25, 1948–February 24, 1950
Phoui Sananikone	February 24, 1950–October 15, 1951
Prince Souvanna Phouma	November 21, 1951–October 20, 1954
Katay Don Sasorith	November 25, 1954–February 13, 1956
Prince Souvanna Phouma	March 21, 1956–July 23, 1958
Prince Souvanna Phouma (Caretaker)	July 23, 1958–August 18, 1958
Phoui Sananikone	August 18, 1958–December 30, 1959
Kou Abhay (P)	January 6, 1960–June 3, 1960
Prince Somsanith	June 3, 1960–August 14, 1960
Prince Souvanna Phouma	August 16, 1960–December 11, 1960 (W)
Prince Souvanna Phouma	August 16, 1960–June 11, 1962 (C)
Prince Boun Oum na Champassak	December 15, 1960–June 11, 1962 (W)
Prince Souvanna Phouma (P)	June 11, 1962–present

NOTE: (P) = Provisional government
        (W) = Western recognition
        (C) = Communist recognition

Appendix III. Final Declaration of the Geneva Conference on the Problem of Restoring Peace in Indochina, July 21, 1954[1]

Participants: Cambodia, The Democratic Republic of Vietnam, France, Laos, The People's Republic of China, The State of Vietnam, The Union of Soviet Socialist Republics, The United Kingdom and The United States of America.

1. The Conference takes note of the agreements ending hostilities in Cambodia, Laos and Vietnam and organizing international control and the supervision of the execution of the provisions of these agreements.

2. The Conference expresses satisfaction at the ending of hostilities in Cambodia, Laos and Vietnam; the Conference expresses its conviction that the execution of the provisions set out in the present declaration and in the agreements on the cessation of hostilities will permit Cambodia, Laos and Vietnam henceforth to play their part, in full independence and sovereignty, in the peaceful community of nations.

3. The Conference takes note of the declarations made by the Governments of Cambodia and of Laos of their intention to adopt measures permitting all citizens to take their place in the national community, in particular by participating in the next general elections, which, in conformity with the constitution of each of these countries, shall take place in the course of the year 1955, by secret ballot and in conditions of respect for fundamental freedoms.

4. The Conference takes note of the clauses in the agreement on the cessation of hostilities in Vietnam prohibiting the introduction into Vietnam of foreign troops and military personnel as well as of all kinds of arms and munitions. The Conference also takes note of the declarations made by the Governments of Cambodia and Laos of their resolution not to request foreign aid, whether in war material, in personnel or in instructors except for the purpose of the effective defense of their territory and, in the case of Laos, to the extent defined by the agreements on the cessation of hostilities in Laos.

5. The Conference takes note of the clauses of the agreement on the cessation of hostilities in Vietnam to the effect that no military base under the control of a foreign State may be established in the regrouping zones of the two parties, the latter having the obligation to see that the zones allotted to them shall not constitute part of any military alliance and shall not be utilized for the resumption of hostilities or in the service of any aggressive policy. The Conference also takes note of the

[1] Miscellaneous No. 20 (1954), *Further Documents Relating to the Discussion of Indo-China at the Geneva Conference, June 16–July 21, 1954,* Cmd. 9239 (London: HMSO, August, 1954).

declarations of the Governments of Cambodia and Laos to the effect that they will not join in any agreement with other States if this agreement includes the obligation to participate in a military alliance not in conformity with the principles of the Charter of the United Nations or, in the case of Laos, with the principles of the agreement on the cessation of hostilities in Laos or, so long as their security is not threatened, the obligation to establish bases on Cambodian or Lao territory for the military forces of foreign Powers.

6. The Conference recognizes that the essential purpose of the agreement relating to Vietnam is to settle military questions with a view to ending hostilities and that the military demarcation line is provisional and should not in any way be interpreted as constituting a political or territorial boundary. The Conference expresses its conviction that the execution of the provisions set out in the present declaration and in the agreement on the cessation of hostilities creates the necessary basis for the achievement in the near future of a political settlement in Vietnam.

7. The Conference declares that, so far as Vietnam is concerned, the settlement of political problems, effected on the basis of respect for the principles of independence, unity and territorial integrity, shall permit the Vietnamese people to enjoy the fundamental freedoms, guaranteed by democratic institutions established as a result of free general elections by secret ballot. In order to ensure that sufficient progress in the restoration of peace has been made, and that all the necessary conditions obtain for free expression of the national will, general elections shall be held in July 1956, under the supervision of an international commission composed of representatives of the Member States of the International Supervisory Commission, referred to in the agreement on the cessation of hostilities. Consultations will be held on this subject between the competent representative authorities of the two zones from July 20, 1955, onwards.

8. The provisions of the agreements on the cessation of hostilities intended to ensure the protection of individuals and of property must be most strictly applied and must, in particular, allow everyone in Vietnam to decide freely in which zone he wishes to live.

9. The competent representative authorities of the Northern and Southern zones of Vietnam, as well as the authorities of Laos and Cambodia, must not permit any individual or collective reprisals against persons who have collaborated in any way with one of the parties during the war, or against members of such persons' families.

10. The Conference takes note of the declaration of the Government of the French Republic to the effect that it is ready to withdraw its troops from the territory of Cambodia, Laos and Vietnam, at the request of the Governments concerned and within periods which shall be fixed by agreement between the parties except in the cases where, by agreement between the two parties, a certain number of French troops shall remain at specified points and for a specified time.

11. The Conference takes note of the declaration of the French Government to the effect that for the settlement of all the problems connected with the re-establishment and consolidation of peace in Cambodia, Laos and Vietnam, the French Government will proceed from the principle of respect for the independence and sovereignty, unity and territorial integrity of Cambodia, Laos and Vietnam.

12. In their relations with Cambodia, Laos and Vietnam, each member of the Geneva Conference undertakes to respect the sovereignty, the independence, the unity and the territorial integrity of the above-mentioned States, and to refrain from any interference in their internal affairs.

13. The members of the Conference agree to consult one another on any question which may be referred to them by the International Supervisory Commission, in order to study such measures as may prove necessary to ensure that the agreements on the cessation of hostilities in Cambodia, Laos and Vietnam are respected.

DECLARATION BY THE ROYAL GOVERNMENT OF LAOS, JULY 21, 1954

(Reference: Articles 4 and 5 of the Final Declaration)

The Royal Government of Laos is resolved never to pursue a policy of aggression and will never permit the territory of Laos to be used in furtherance of such a policy.

The Royal Government of Laos will never join in any agreement with other States if this agreement includes the obligation for the Royal Government of Laos to participate in a military alliance not in conformity with the principles of the Charter of the United Nations or with the principles of the agreement on the cessation of hostilities or, unless its security is threatened, the obligation to establish bases on the territory of Laos for military forces of foreign Powers.

The Royal Government of Laos is resolved to settle its international disputes by peaceful means so that international peace and security and justice are not endangered.

During the period between the cessation of hostilities in Vietnam and the final settlement of that country's political problems, the Royal Government of Laos will not request foreign aid, whether in war material, in personnel or in instructors, except for the purpose of its effective territorial defense and to the extent defined by the agreement on the cessation of hostilities.

DECLARATION BY THE ROYAL GOVERNMENT OF LAOS, JULY 21, 1954

(Reference: Article 3 of the Final Declaration)

The Royal Government of Laos,

In the desire to ensure harmony and agreement among the peoples of the Kingdom,

Declares itself resolved to take the necessary measures to integrate all citizens, without discrimination, into the national community and to guarantee them the enjoyment of the rights and freedoms for which the Constitution of the Kingdom provides;

Affirms that all citizens of Laos may freely participate as electors or candidates in general elections by secret ballot;

Announces, furthermore, that it will promulgate measures to provide for special representation in the Royal Administration of the provinces of Phong Saly and Sam Neua during the interval between the cessation of hostilities and the general elections of the interests of nationals of Laos who did not support the Royal forces during hostilities.

APPENDIX IV. COMMUNIQUÉS OF THE SECOND PARATROOP BATTALION[1]

Communiqué No. 1. All compatriots! The High Command of the Revolution informs the people that as of 0300 hours August 9 it has held in its hands all civil and military powers. The population is urged to remain calm and to continue work as usual and to respect the laws of the country.

CAPTAIN KONG LE

Communiqué No. 2. The High Command of the Revolution informs the people that the military *coup de force* is aimed at safeguarding and consolidating the Nation, the religion, the Throne, and the Constitution. The revolutionary group will apply justice and friendship to all those who remain quiet, continue their usual occupations, and observe all national laws and regulations. The revolutionary group will recognize all human rights. The revolutionary group will struggle against bribery, reorganize the parliamentary system and cleanse the administrative machinery. The revolutionary group will oppose foreign intervention in the country's military affairs and will expel all foreign bases. In the field of foreign policy, the revolutionary group recognizes the provisions of the Charter of the United Nations, and assumes the task of maintaining a neutral policy and entertaining friendly relations with neighboring countries. The revolutionary group intends to respect all agreements that have been signed by the Royal Government. In the field of economic affairs, the revolutionary group will encourage trade and industry in order to raise the people's living standards. The revolutionary group intends to accept aid from foreign countries, provided no strings are attached to this aid.

CAPTAIN KONG LE

[1] Broadcast by Radio Vientiane, August 9, 1960.

APPENDIX V. DECLARATION ON THE NEUTRALITY OF LAOS[1]

The Governments of the Union of Burma, the Kingdom of Cambodia, Canada, the People's Republic of China, the Democratic Republic of Vietnam, the Republic of France, the Republic of India, the Polish People's Republic, the Republic of Vietnam, the Kingdom of Thailand, the Union of Soviet Socialist Republics, the United Kingdom of Great Britain and Northern Ireland and the United States of America, whose representatives took part in the International Conference on the Settlement of the Laotian Question, 1961–1962;

Welcoming the presentation of the statement of neutrality by the Royal Government of Laos of July 9, 1962, and taking note of this statement, which is, with the concurrence of the Royal Government of Laos, incorporated in the present Declaration as an integral part thereof, and the text of which is as follows:

The Royal Government of Laos, being resolved to follow the path of peace and neutrality in conformity with the interests and aspirations of the Laotian people, as well as the principles of the Joint Communiqué of Zurich dated June 22, 1961, and of the Geneva Agreements of 1954, in order to build a peaceful, neutral, independent, democratic, unified and prosperous Laos, solemnly declares that:

(1) It will resolutely apply the five principles of peaceful coexistence in foreign relations, and will develop friendly relations and establish diplomatic relations with all countries, the neighboring countries first and foremost, on the basis of equality and of respect for the independence and sovereignty of Laos;

(2) It is the will of the Laotian people to protect and ensure respect for the sovereignty, independence, neutrality, unity, and territorial integrity of Laos;

(3) It will not resort to the use or threat of force in any way which might impair the peace of other countries, and will not interfere in the internal affairs of other countries;

(4) It will not enter into any military alliance or into any agreement, whether military or otherwise, which is inconsistent with the neutrality of the Kingdom of Laos; it will not allow the establishment of any foreign military base on Laotian territory, nor allow any country to use Laotian territory for military purposes of interference in the internal affairs of other countries, nor recognize the protection of any alliance or military coalition, including SEATO;

[1] Treaty Series No. 27 (1963), *Declaration and Protocol on the Neutrality of Laos, Geneva, July 23, 1962,* Cmnd. 2025 (London: HMSO, May, 1963).

(5) It will not allow any foreign interference in the internal affairs of the Kingdom of Laos in any form whatsoever;

(6) Subject to the provisions of Article 5 of the Protocol, it will require the withdrawal from Laos of all foreign troops and military personnel, and will not allow any foreign troops or military personnel to be introduced into Laos;

(7) It will accept direct and unconditional aid from all countries that wish to help the Kingdom of Laos build up an independent and autonomous national economy on the basis of respect for the sovereignty of Laos;

(8) It will respect the treaties and agreements signed in conformity with the interests of the Laotian people and of the policy of peace and neutrality of the Kingdom of Laos, in particular the Geneva Agreements of 1962, and will abrogate all treaties and agreements which are contrary to those principles.

This statement of neutrality by the Royal Government of Laos shall be promulgated constitutionally and shall have the force of law.

The Kingdom of Laos appeals to all the States participating in the International Conference on the Settlement of the Laotian Question, and to all other States, to recognize the sovereignty, independence, neutrality, unity and territorial integrity of Laos, to conform to these principles in all respects, and to refrain from any action inconsistent therewith.

Confirming the principles of respect for the sovereignty, independence, unity and territorial integrity of the Kingdom of Laos and non-interference in its internal affairs which are embodied in the Geneva Agreements of 1954;

Emphasizing the principle of respect for the neutrality of the Kingdom of Laos;

Agreeing that the above-mentioned principles constitute a basis for the peaceful settlement of the Laotian question;

Profoundly convinced that the independence and neutrality of the Kingdom of Laos will assist the peaceful democratic development of the Kingdom of Laos and the achievement of national accord and unity in that country, as well as the strengthening of peace and security in Southeast Asia;

1. Solemnly declare, in accordance with the will of the Government and people of the Kingdom of Laos, as expressed in the statement of neutrality by the Royal Government of Laos of July 9, 1962, that they recognize and will respect and observe in every way the sovereignty, independence, neutrality, unity and territorial integrity of the Kingdom of Laos.

2. Undertake, in particular, that

(a) they will not commit or participate in any way in any act which might directly or indirectly impair the sovereignty, independence, neutrality, unity or territorial integrity of the Kingdom of Laos;

(b) they will not resort to the use or threat of force or any other measures which might impair the peace of the Kingdom of Laos;

(c) they will refrain from all direct or indirect interference in the internal affairs of the Kingdom of Laos;

(d) they will not attach conditions of a political nature to any assistance which they may offer or which the Kingdom of Laos may seek;

(e) they will not bring the Kingdom of Laos in any way into any military alliance or any other agreement, whether military or otherwise, which is inconsistent with her neutrality, nor invite or encourage her to enter into any such alliance or to conclude any such agreement;

(f) they will respect the wish of the Kingdom of Laos not to recognize the protection of any alliance or military coalition, including SEATO;

(g) they will not introduce into the Kingdom of Laos foreign troops or military personnel in any form whatsoever, nor will they in any way facilitate or connive at the introduction of any foreign troops or military personnel;

(h) they will not establish nor will they in any way facilitate or connive at the establishment in the Kingdom of Laos of any foreign military base, foreign strong point or other foreign military installation of any kind;

(i) they will not use the territory of the Kingdom of Laos for interference in the internal affairs of other countries;

(j) they will not use the territory of any country, including their own, for interference in the internal affairs of the Kingdom of Laos.

3. Appeal to all other States to recognize, respect and observe in every way the sovereignty, independence and neutrality, and also the unity and territorial integrity, of the Kingdom of Laos and to refrain from any action inconsistent with these principles or with other provisions of the present Declaration.

4. Undertake, in the event of a violation or threat of violation of the sovereignty, independence, neutrality, unity or territorial integrity of the Kingdom of Laos, to consult jointly with the Royal Government of Laos and among themselves in order to consider measures which might prove to be necessary to ensure the observance of these principles and the other provisions of the present Declaration.

5. The present Declaration shall enter into force on signature and together with the statement of neutrality of the Royal Government of Laos of July 9, 1962, shall be regarded as constituting an international agreement. The present Declaration shall be deposited in the archives of the Governments of the United Kingdom and the Union of Soviet

Socialist Republics, which shall furnish certified copies thereof to the other signatory States and to all the other States of the world.

In witness whereof, the undersigned Plenipotentiaries have signed the present Declaration.

Done in two copies in Geneva this twenty-third day of July one thousand nine hundred and sixty-two in the English, Chinese, French, Lao and Russian languages, each text being equally authoritative.

U THI HAN (Burma), NHIEK TIOULONG (Cambodia), H. C. GREEN (Canada), CHEN YI (China), UNG VAN KHIEM (Democratic Republic of Vietnam), M. COUVE DE MURVILLE (France), V. K. KRISHNA MENON (India), A. RAPACKI (Poland), VU VAN MAU (Republic of Vietnam), DIRECK JAYANAMA (Thailand), A. GROMYKO (Union of Soviet Socialist Republics), HOME (United Kingdom), DEAN RUSK (United States)

PROTOCOL TO THE DECLARATION ON THE NEUTRALITY OF LAOS

The Governments of the Union of Burma, the Kingdom of Cambodia, Canada, the People's Republic of China, the Democratic Republic of Vietnam, the Republic of France, the Republic of India, the Kingdom of Laos, the Polish People's Republic, the Republic of Vietnam, the Kingdom of Thailand, the Union of Soviet Socialist Republics, the United Kingdom of Great Britain and Northern Ireland and the United States of America;

Having regard to the Declaration on the Neutrality of Laos of July 23, 1962;

Have agreed as follows:

Article 1. For the purposes of this Protocol

(a) the term "foreign military personnel" shall include members of foreign military missions, foreign military advisers, experts, instructors, consultants, technicians, observers and any other foreign military persons, including those serving in any armed forces in Laos, and foreign civilians connected with the supply, maintenance, storing and utilization of war materials;

(b) the term "the Commission" shall mean the International Commission for Supervision and Control in Laos set up by virtue of the Geneva Agreements of 1954 and composed of the representatives of Canada, India and Poland, with the representative of India as Chairman;

(c) the term "the Co-Chairmen" shall mean the Co-Chairmen of the International Conference for the Settlement of the Laotian Question, 1961–1962, and their successors in the offices of Her Britannic Majesty's Principal Secretary of State for Foreign Affairs and Minister for Foreign Affairs of the Union of Soviet Socialist Republics respectively;

(d) the term "the members of the Conference" shall mean the Governments of countries which took part in the International

Conference for the Settlement of the Laotian Question, 1961–1962.

Article 2. All foreign regular and irregular troops, foreign para-military formations and foreign military personnel shall be withdrawn from Laos in the shortest time possible and in any case the withdrawal shall be completed not later than thirty days after the Commission has notified the Royal Government of Laos that in accordance with Articles 3 and 10 of this Protocol its inspection teams are present at all points of withdrawal from Laos. These points shall be determined by the Royal Government of Laos in accordance with Article 3 within thirty days after the entry into force of this Protocol. The inspection teams shall be present at these points and the Commission shall notify the Royal Government of Laos thereof within fifteen days after the points have been determined.

Article 3. The withdrawal of foreign regular and irregular troops, foreign para-military formations and foreign military personnel shall take place only along such routes and through such points as shall be determined by the Royal Government of Laos in consultation with the Commission. The Commission shall be notified in advance of the point and time of all such withdrawals.

Article 4. The introduction of foreign regular and irregular troops, foreign para-military formations and foreign military personnel into Laos is prohibited.

Article 5. Note is taken that the French and Laotian Governments will conclude as soon as possible an arrangement to transfer the French military installations in Laos to the Royal Government of Laos.

If the Laotian Government considers it necessary, the French Government may as an exception leave in Laos for a limited period of time a precisely limited number of French military instructors for the purpose of training the armed forces of Laos.

The French and Laotian Governments shall inform the members of the Conference, through the Co-Chairmen, of their agreement on the question of transfer of the French military installations in Laos and of the employment of French military instructors by the Laotian Government.

Article 6. The introduction into Laos of armaments, munitions and war material generally, except such quantities of conventional armaments as the Royal Government of Laos may consider necessary for the national defense of Laos, is prohibited.

Article 7. All foreign military persons and civilians captured or interned during the course of hostilities in Laos shall be released within thirty days after the entry into force of this Protocol and handed over by the Royal Government of Laos to the representatives of the Governments of the countries of which they are nationals in order that they may proceed to the destination of their choice.

Article 8. The Co-Chairmen shall periodically receive reports from the Commission. In addition the Commission shall immediately report to the Co-Chairmen any violations or threats of violations of this Protocol, all significant steps which it takes in pursuance of this Protocol, and also any other important information which may assist the Co-Chairmen in carrying out their functions. The Commission may at any time seek help from the Co-Chairmen in the performance of its duties, and the Co-Chairmen may at any time make recommendations to the Commission exercising general guidance.

The Co-Chairmen shall circulate the reports and any other important information from the Commission to the members of the Conference.

The Co-Chairmen shall exercise supervision over the observance of this Protocol and the Declaration of the Neutrality of Laos.

The Co-Chairmen will keep the members of the Conference constantly informed and when appropriate will consult with them.

Article 9. The Commission shall, with the concurrence of the Royal Government of Laos, supervise and control the cease-fire in Laos.

The Commission shall exercise these functions in full cooperation with the Royal Government of Laos and within the framework of the Cease-Fire Agreement or cease-fire arrangements made by the three political forces in Laos, or the Royal Government of Laos. It is understood that responsibility for the execution of the cease-fire shall rest with the three parties concerned and with the Royal Government of Laos after its formation.

Article 10. The Commission shall supervise and control the withdrawal of foreign regular and irregular troops, foreign para-military formations and foreign military personnel. Inspection teams sent by the Commission for these purposes shall be present for the period of the withdrawal at all points of withdrawal from Laos determined by the Royal Government of Laos in consultation with the Commission in accordance with Article 3 of this Protocol.

Article 11. The Commission shall investigate cases where there are reasonable grounds for considering that a violation of the provisions of Article 4 of this Protocol has occurred.

It is understood that in the exercise of this function the Commission is acting with the concurrence of the Royal Government of Laos. It shall carry out its investigations in full cooperation with the Royal Government of Laos and shall immediately inform the Co-Chairmen of any violations or threats of violations of Article 4, and also of all significant steps which it takes in pursuance of this Article in accordance with Article 8.

Article 12. The Commission shall assist the Royal Government of Laos in cases where the Royal Government of Laos considers that a violation of Article 6 of this Protocol may have taken place. This assistance will be rendered at the request of the Royal Government of Laos and in full cooperation with it.

Article 13. The Commission shall exercise its functions under this Protocol in close cooperation with the Royal Government of Laos. It is understood that the Royal Government of Laos at all levels will render the Commission all possible assistance in the performance by the Commission of these functions and also will take all necessary measures to ensure the security of the Commission and its inspection teams during their activities in Laos.

Article 14. The Commission functions as a single organ of the International Conference for the Settlement of the Laotian Question, 1961–1962. The members of the Commission will work harmoniously and in cooperation with each other with the aim of solving all questions within the terms of reference of the Commission.

Decisions of the Commission on questions relating to violations of Articles 2, 3, 4, and 6 of this Protocol or of the cease-fire referred to in Article 9, conclusions on major questions sent to the Co-Chairmen and all recommendations by the Commission shall be adopted unanimously. On other questions, including procedural questions, and also questions relating to the initiation and carrying out of investigations (Article 15), decisions of the Commission shall be adopted by majority vote.

Article 15. In the exercise of its specific functions which are laid down in the relevant articles of this Protocol the Commission shall conduct investigations (directly or by sending inspection teams), when there are reasonable grounds for considering that a violation has occurred. These investigations shall be carried out at the request of the Royal Government of Laos or on the initiative of the Commission, which is acting with the concurrence of the Royal Government of Laos.

In the latter case decisions on initiating and carrying out such investigations shall be taken in the Commission by majority vote.

The Commission shall submit agreed reports on investigations in which differences which may emerge between members of the Commission on particular questions may be expressed.

The conclusions and recommendations of the Commission resulting from investigations shall be adopted unanimously.

Article 16. For the exercise of its functions the Commission shall, as necessary, set up inspection teams, on which the three member-states of the Commission shall be equally represented. Each member-state of the Commission shall ensure the presence of its own representatives both on the Commission and on the inspection teams, and shall promptly replace them in the event of their being unable to perform their duties.

It is understood that the dispatch of inspection teams to carry out various specific tasks takes place with the concurrence of the Royal Government of Laos. The points to which the Commission and its inspection teams go for the purpose of investigation and their length of stay at those points shall be determined in relation to the requirements of the particular investigation.

Article 17. The Commission shall have at its disposal the means of communication and transport required for the performance of its duties. These as a rule will be provided to the Commission by the Royal Government of Laos for payment on mutually acceptable terms, and those which the Royal Government of Laos cannot provide will be acquired by the Commission from other sources. It is understood that the means of communication and transport will be under the administrative control of the Commission.

Article 18. The costs of the operations of the Commission shall be borne by the members of the Conference in accordance with the provisions of this article.

(a) The Governments of Canada, India and Poland shall pay the personal salaries and allowances of their nationals who are members of their delegations to the Commission and its subsidiary organs.

(b) The primary responsibility for the provision of accommodation for the Commission and its subsidiary organs shall rest with the Royal Government of Laos, which shall also provide such other local services as may be appropriate. The Commission shall charge to the Fund referred to in sub-paragraph (c) below any local expenses not borne by the Royal Government of Laos.

(c) All other capital or running expenses incurred by the Commission in the exercise of its functions shall be met from a Fund to which all the members of the Conference shall contribute in the following proportions:

The Governments of the People's Republic of China, France, the Union of Soviet Socialist Republics, the United Kingdom and the United States of America shall contribute 17.6 per cent each.

The Governments of Burma, Cambodia, the Democratic Republic of Vietnam, Laos, the Republic of Vietnam and Thailand shall contribute 1.5 per cent each.

The Governments of Canada, India and Poland as members of the Commission shall contribute 1 per cent each.

Article 19. The Co-Chairmen shall at any time, if the Royal Government of Laos so requests, and in any case not later than three years after the entry into force of this Protocol, present a report with appropriate recommendations on the question of the termination of the Commission to the members of the Conference for their consideration. Before making such a report the Co-Chairmen shall hold consultations with the Royal Government of Laos and with the Commission.

Article 20. This Protocol shall enter into force on signature.

It shall be deposited in the archives of the Governments of the

United Kingdom and the Union of Soviet Socialist Republics, which shall furnish certified copies thereof to the other signatory States and to all other States of the world.

In witness whereof, the undersigned Plenipotentiaries have signed this Protocol.

Done in two copies in Geneva this twenty-third day of July one thousand and nine hundred and sixty-two in the English, Chinese, French, Lao and Russian languages, each text being equally authoritative.

U Thi Han (Burma), Nhiek Tioulong (Cambodia), H. C. Green (Canada), Chen Yi (China), Ung Van Khiem (Democratic Republic of Vietnam), M. Couve de Murville (France), V. K. Krishna Menon (India), A. Rapacki (Poland), Vu Van Mau (Republic of Vietnam), Direck Jayanama (Thailand), A. Gromyko (Union of Soviet Socialist Republics), Home (United Kingdom), Dean Rusk (United States), Q. Pholsena (Laos)

Appendix VI. Action Program of the Neo Lao Hak Sat[1]

1. To unite all the people, unite various nationalities [tribal groups], strata, religious communities, political parties, patriotic personalities, and intellectuals, including individuals in the Royal Family and Buddhist monks and nuns who favor peace and neutrality, regardless of their political tendencies, beliefs and religion, also organizations and individuals who were formerly forced by the United States to follow it but now favor a policy of peace and neutrality; and to strive to consolidate and strengthen the alliance and mutual assistance between the Neo Lao Hak Sat and the patriotic Neutralist forces.

2. To struggle against the United States imperialists and their followers—the traitors—for a correct implementation of the 1962 Geneva agreements and the agreements reached among the three parties of Laos; to defend and consolidate the coalition government so as to fully carry out the political program aimed at restoring peace, building national concord, and consolidating the independence of the country; first of all to demand that the United States imperialists and their satellites withdraw all their troops from Laos, stop the introduction of weapons and war material into Laos and all acts of intervention in Lao affairs under whatever form and in whatever fields, and not set up military bases on Lao territory; to demand that the Phoumi Nosavan group put an end to aiding operations encroaching upon and terrorizing

[1] Adopted at the Second National Congress of the Neo Lao Hak Sat in Sam Neua Province, April 6–11, 1964, and reported by Vietnam News Agency (Hanoi), April 13, 1964.

the people and withdraw their troops to the positions existing when the 1962 Geneva agreements were signed; to demand that the Phoumi Nosavan group strictly implement the agreements concluded among the three parties: first of all to organize the mixed police and to neutralize Vientiane and Luang Prabang so as to restore the normal activities of the coalition government, and then to continue the tripartite negotiations in order to settle pending questions and other problems of the fatherland and people.

3. To correctly carry out the policy of peace and neutrality ensured by the Geneva agreements, implement the independent foreign policy on the basis of the Five Principles of Peaceful Coexistence, to establish diplomatic relations with all countries on an equal footing, receive aid without any conditions attached from all countries regardless of their political regimes, provided the latter respect the sovereignty and independence of Laos and sincerely help Laos' national construction; to actively support all movements for peace, democracy, and social progress, and the national liberation movement of all the Asian, African, and Latin American countries, and actively contribute to the safeguarding of peace in Southeast Asia and the world.

4. To heighten the spirit of self-reliance and at the same time make full use of assistance without any conditions attached from various countries to build an independent and self-supporting economy under the leadership and unified management of the coalition government; to wipe out the vestige of local despots and trade monopolies, and at the same time to help people develop production, tap forest products and natural resources, expand exchanges of goods, develop handicrafts, and build industry; to eliminate speculation and hoarding, oppose corruption and misuse of power to grab goods and economic monopolies; to help the peasants develop cultivation and livestock breeding; to encourage the improvement of cultivation and protection of crops, thus helping the peasants to raise their income; to help the workers to get jobs, to improve their living conditions, and create a regime of social insurance so as to enable them to restore and develop the national economy; to stimulate and help the traders and industrialists to invest in construction and commerce which benefit the national economy and the people's life; to create conditions for students and pupils to study and develop their abilities to serve the fatherland; to provide intellectuals, office employees, cultural workers, and artists with suitable jobs and security so that they may serve the people.

5. To organize and build a national army and police force to defend the independence of the fatherland and the security of the people; to help soldiers and policemen to come close to and help the people; to forbid all repression of the people by the army and the police; to ensure political rights and due pay for soldiers; to cancel the regime of ill treatment of soldiers and policemen; to work out a policy to improve the living conditions of wounded soldiers' and war martyrs' families.

6. To carry out all the democratic rights of the citizens as provided for by the 1947 Constitution, thus enabling them to devote all their abilities to serve national construction; first of all to release all political detainees and ensure the life and property of the people; to stop all acts of discrimination and reprisal against patriotic individuals and organizations in the areas temporarily controlled by the Phoumi Nosavan group, especially Vientiane.

7. To respect and defend the Throne, build and consolidate national solidarity, and realize national harmony and unification; to carry out the policy of national union, thus helping the various nationalities [tribal groups] to live on an equal footing and carry out mutual assistance, improving their living standards, helping each other in studying; to oppose all schemes of sowing discord among the nationalities [tribal groups] and ensure the legitimate rights of foreign residents in Laos.

8. To assure equality between men and women; help women in all fields so as to enable them to develop their ability to catch up with men; to help confined mothers and protect children.

9. To develop progressive national culture; to devote attention to education and develop both primary and secondary educational systems and other popular educational schools; to help all the people, especially the mountain people, to learn to read and write; to protect and develop good ethics; to strictly oppose the depraved and obscurantist culture of the United States and its henchmen; to eliminate gambling and other social vices; to respect freedom of belief, oppose all schemes to sabotage and split up religions; to protect pagodas and respect Buddhist priests.

10. While the United States imperialists have not yet given up their schemes to eliminate the Neo Lao Hak Sat and other patriotic forces, to turn Laos into a neocolony, a war-provocative base, and to turn the Lao people into their slaves, all the people of Laos have the task of defending and consolidating the liberated areas, strengthening the Neo Lao Hak Sat forces, helping to consolidate the other patriotic forces, resolutely smashing all schemes to encroach upon and occupy the liberated areas and to send bandits to disturb and sabotage these areas. The people of Laos must actively carry out all tasks which benefit the people and must bring them a happy life so as to help them build the liberated areas into a firm basis for the people's struggle for peace, neutrality, independence, democracy, unity, and prosperity.

APPENDIX VII. ZURICH COMMUNIQUÉ, JUNE 22, 1961[1]

As agreed between them on 18 June last, the three Princes, Souvanna Phouma, Boun Oum and Souphanouvong, being the high repre-

[1] Miscellaneous No. 25 (1965), *Documents Relating to British Involvement in the Indo-China Conflict 1945–1965*, Cmnd. 2834 (London: HMSO, December, 1965), pp. 174–76.

sentatives of the three parties in Laos, met at Zurich on 19 June and thereafter to discuss the problem of achieving national concord by the formation of a Government of National Union. The three Princes discussed successively the political program of the provisional Government of National Union and its immediate tasks.

With regard to these two matters, the Princes agreed as follows:

I. Political Program

The Kingdom of Laos is resolved to follow the path of peace and neutrality in conformity with the interests and aspirations of the Laotian people and with the Geneva Agreements of 1954, in order to build a peaceful, neutral, independent, democratic, unified and prosperous Laos. A provisional Government of National Union will be formed, which will give effect to this policy of peace and neutrality, by carrying out the following political program:

Domestic policy:

(1) To implement the ceasefire agreement concluded between the three parties concerned in Laos and to see that peace is restored in the country.

(2) To give full effect to democratic freedoms for the benefit of the people and to abrogate all provisions contrary to such freedoms; to bring back into force the law on the democratic freedoms of citizens and the electoral law approved by the National Assembly in 1957.

(3) To preserve the unity, neutrality, independence and sovereignty of the nation.

(4) To ensure justice and peace for all citizens of the Kingdom with a view to appeasement and national concord without discrimination as to origin or political allegiance.

(5) To bring about the unification of the armed forces of the three parties in a single National Army in accordance with a program agreed between the parties.

(6) To develop agriculture, industry and crafts, to provide means of communication and transport, to promote culture and to concentrate attention on improving the standard of living of the people.

Foreign policy:

(1) Resolutely to apply the five principles of peaceful co-existence in foreign relations, to establish friendly relations and to develop diplomatic relations with all countries, the neighboring countries first and foremost, on the basis of equality and the sovereignty of Laos.

(2) Not to join in any alliance or military coalition and not to allow the establishment of any foreign military base on Laotian territory, it being understood that a special study will be made of what is provided in the Geneva Agreements of 1954; not to allow any

country to use Laotian territory for military purposes; and not to recognize the protection of any alliance or military coalition.

(3) Not to allow any foreign interference in the internal affairs of Laos in any form whatsoever; to require the withdrawal from Laos of all foreign troops and military personnel, and not to allow any foreign troops or military personnel to be introduced into Laos.

(4) To accept direct and unconditional aid from all countries that wish to help Laos build up an independent and autonomous national economy on the basis of respect for Laotian sovereignty.

(5) To respect the treaties and agreements signed in conformity with the interests of the Laotian people and of the policy of peace and neutrality of the Kingdom, in particular the Geneva Agreements of 1954, and to abrogate all treaties and agreements which are contrary to those principles.

II. Immediate Tasks

The provisional Government of National Union will carry out the following immediate tasks:

(1) Formation of a Government delegation to take part in the International Conference on the Settlement of the Laotian Question.

(2) Implementation of the ceasefire and restoration of peace throughout the country.

(3) Fulfillment of the undertakings entered into on behalf of Laos at the International Conference on the Settlement of the Laotian Question and faithful execution of the agreements concluded between the three parties concerned in Laos.

(4) Release of all political prisoners and detainees.

(5) Holding of general elections to the National Assembly for the formation of the definitive Government.

(6) During the transitional period, the administrative organs set up during the hostilities will be provisionally left in being.

As regards the formation of the Government of National Union the three Princes agreed on the following principles:

(1) The Government of National Union will include representatives of the three parties and will be provisional.

(2) It will be formed in accordance with a special procedure by direct designation and nomination by His Majesty the King, without reference to the National Assembly.

Exchanges of views on this matter will be continued between the three Princes at further meetings, in order to achieve national reconciliation as soon as possible.

PRINCE BOUN OUM
PRINCE SOUVANNA PHOUMA
PRINCE SOUPHANOUVONG

Bibliography

OFFICIAL SOURCES

Agreements and Decrees Prior to 1954

Terms of French Treaty of Protectorate over Laos, August 29, 1941: ADMIRAL DECOUX. *A la Barre de l'Indochine: Histoire de Mon Gouvernement General (1940–1945)*. Paris: Plon, 1949. P. 297.

Text of statement to the Lao Issara by King Sisavang Vong: *The New Asia* (Bangkok), No. 8, March 10, 1946.

Text of royal decree proclaiming Provisional Constitution of October 12, 1945: *Tin-Vietnam (Vietnam News)*, No. 4, July 14, 1946.

Text of Constitution of May 11, 1947: KINGDOM OF LAOS. *The Lao Constituent Assembly, March 15–May 10, 1947*. Saigon: Imprimerie Française d'Outre-Mer, 1948. Pp. 99–108.

Text of Franco-Lao General Convention of July, 1949: *Documentation Française* (Paris), No. 1241, December 7, 1949.

Text of decree dissolving the Lao Issara: KATAY DON SASORITH. *Le Laos*. Paris: Berger-Levrault, 1953. Pp. 131–35. Communiqué announcing dissolution: *Bangkok Post*, October 26, 1949.

Treaty of Amity and Association Between France and Laos: ALLAN B. COLE (ed.). *Conflict in Indo-China and International Repercussions; A Documentary History, 1945–1955*. Ithaca, N.Y.: Cornell University Press, 1956. Pp. 192–93.

1954 Geneva Conference

CMD. 9186. MISCELLANEOUS No. 16 (1954). *Documents Relating to the Discussion of Korea and Indo-China at the Geneva Conference, April 27– June 15, 1954*. London: HMSO, June, 1954.

CMD. 9239. MISCELLANEOUS No. 20 (1954). *Further Documents Relating to the Discussion of Indo-China at the Geneva Conference, June 16–July 21, 1954*. London: HMSO, August, 1954.

International Control Commission

CMD. 9445. LAOS No. 1 (1955). *First Interim Report of the International Commission for Supervision and Control in Laos, August 11– December 31, 1954*. London: HMSO, May, 1955.

CMD. 9630. LAOS NO. 2 (1955). *Second Interim Report of the International Commission for Supervision and Control in Laos. January 1–June 30, 1955.* London: HMSO, November, 1955.

CMND. 314. LAOS NO. 1 (1957). *Third Interim Report of the International Commission for Supervision and Control in Laos, July 1, 1955–May 16, 1957.* London: HMSO, December, 1957.

CMND. 541. LAOS NO. 1 (1958). *Fourth Interim Report of the International Commission for Supervision and Control in Laos, May 17, 1957–May 31, 1958.* London: HMSO, October, 1958.

Message No. 35 of 16 September 1965 from the International Commission for Supervision and Control in Laos to the Co-Chairmen of the Geneva Conference. No place of publication, no date, mimeographed.

1961–62 Geneva Conference

CMND. 1828. LAOS NO. 1 (1962). *International Conference on the Settlement of the Laotian Question, May 12, 1961–July 23, 1962.* London: HMSO, October, 1962.

CMND. 2025. TREATY SERIES NO. 27 (1963). *Declaration and Protocol on the Neutrality of Laos, July 23, 1962.* London: HMSO, May, 1963.

U.S. Congress

COMMITTEE ON FOREIGN AFFAIRS, HOUSE OF REPRESENTATIVES. *Mutual Security Program in Laos: Hearings Before the Subcommittee on the Far East and Pacific, May 7 and 8, 1958.* (85th Cong., 2d sess.) Washington: Government Printing Office, 1958.

COMMITTEE ON FOREIGN RELATIONS, SENATE. *Background Information Relating to Southeast Asia and Vietnam.* 5th rev. ed. Washington: Government Printing Office, March, 1969.

COMMITTEE ON THE JUDICIARY, SENATE. *Refugee and Civilian War Casualty Problems in Indochina: A Staff Report Prepared for the Use of the Subcommittee to Investigate Problems Connected with Refugees and Escapees, September 28, 1970.* Washington: Government Printing Office, 1970.

Hearings, I: COMMITTEE ON GOVERNMENT OPERATIONS, HOUSE OF REPRESENTATIVES. *United States Aid Operations in Laos: Hearings Before the Foreign Operations and Monetary Affairs Subcommittee, March 11–June 1, 1959.* (86th Cong., 1st sess.) Washington: Government Printing Office, 1959.

Hearings, II: COMMITTEE ON GOVERNMENT OPERATIONS, HOUSE OF REPRESENTATIVES. *United States Aid Operations in Laos: Seventh Report by the Committee, June 15, 1959.* (86th Cong., 1st sess.) Washington: Government Printing Office, 1959.

Hearings, III: COMMITTEE ON ARMED SERVICES, SENATE. *Military Cold War Education and Speech Review Policies: Hearings Before the Special Preparedness Subcommittee, Part 5, April 16, 17, 18, 19; May 11 and 14, 1962.* (87th Cong., 2d sess.) Washington: Government Printing Office, 1962.

Hearings, IV: COMMITTEE ON FOREIGN RELATIONS, SENATE. *United States Security Agreements and Commitments Abroad: Kingdom of Laos: Hearings Before the Subcommittee on United States Security Agreements and Commitments Abroad, Part 2, October 20, 21, 22, and 28, 1969.* (91st Cong., 1st sess.) Washington: Government Printing Office, 1970.

Hearings, V: COMMITTEE ON FOREIGN RELATIONS, SENATE. *United States Security Agreements and Commitments Abroad: Kingdom of Thailand: Hearings Before the Subcommittee on United States Security Agreements and Commitments Abroad, Part 3, November 10, 11, 12, 13, 14, and 17, 1969.* (91st Cong., 1st sess.) Washington: Government Printing Office, 1970.

Department of State

Aggression from the North: The Record of North Vietnam's Campaign to Conquer South Vietnam. Washington: Government Printing Office, February, 1965.

American Cooperation with Laos: A Vital Link in the Chain of Mutual Security. Report of the Director, U.S. International Cooperation Administration, U.S. Operations Mission to Laos, Vientiane, July, 1959.

A Threat to the Peace: North Viet-Nam's Effort to Conquer South Viet-Nam. U.S. Department of State Publication No. 7308 (in 2 parts). Washington: Government Printing Office, December, 1961.

Briefing Notes on the Royal Kingdom of Laos. Vientiane: USIS, May, 1959.

Comments by the Department of State and ICA on the Report of the House Committee on Government Operations. Washington: Government Printing Office, 1959.

Economic Cooperation Agreement and Notes between the United States of America and Laos. Treaties and Other International Acts Series, No. 2344. Washington: Government Printing Office, 1952.

Laos Fact Sheet: Mutual Security in Action. U.S. Department of State Publication No. 6842. Washington: Government Printing Office, 1959.

Mutual Defense Assistance in Indochina, Agreement between the United States of America and Cambodia, Laos and Vietnam. Treaties and Other International Acts, Series, No. 2447. Washington: Government Printing Office, 1953.

The Situation in Laos. Washington: Department of State, September, 1959.

United Nations

Report of the Security Council Sub-Committee, under Resolution of 7 September 1959. New York: United Nations Security Council, November, 1959.

Report on Laos Recommends U.N. Development Aid. Bangkok: Economic Commission of Asia and the Far East (ECAFE), Press Release No. L/29, December, 1959.

Great Britain

CMND. 2834. *Documents Relating to British Involvement in the Indo-China Conflict 1945–1965.* London: HMSO, 1965.

Laos: Basic Facts and Figures. Reference Division, Central Office of Information. London: HMSO, 1958.

Laos: Political Developments, 1958–60. Reference Division, Central Office of Information. London: HMSO, 1960.

Laos. Reference Division, Central Office of Information. London: HMSO, 1961.

Laos: Political Developments, 1961. Reference Division, Central Office of Information. London: HMSO, 1961.

Laos. Reference Division, Central Office of Information. London: HMSO, 1967.

MOUNTBATTEN OF BURMA, VICE ADMIRAL THE EARL. *Post Surrender Tasks; Section E of the Report to the Combined Chiefs of Staff by the Supreme Allied Commander South East Asia 1943–1945.* London: HMSO, 1969.

China

A Chronicle of Principal Events Relating to the Indo-China Question, 1940–1954. Peking: Shih-chieh Chih-shih (World Culture), 1954.

Concerning the Situation in Laos. Peking: Foreign Languages Press, 1959.

North Vietnam

Les Peuples Indochinois Vaincront. Hanoi: Éditions en Langues Étrangères, 1970.

The Problems Facing the Democratic Republic of Viet Nam in 1961. Hanoi: Foreign Languages Publishing House, n.d.

France

L'Affaire du Laos (1954–1962). Paris: Notes et Études Documentaires No. 3011, July 23, 1963.

Annuaire Statistique de l'Indochine. Hanoi and Saigon: Direction des Affaires Économiques, Service de la Statistique Générale, 1927–49.

Conventions Inter-États Conclues en l'Application de l'Accord Franco-Laotien du 19 Juillet 1949. Saigon: Imprimerie d'Extrême-Orient, 1951.

L'Évolution de la Situation au Laos; Chronologie (Juin 1962-Avril 1963). Paris: Notes et Études Documentaires No. 3189, May 10, 1965.

Notice sur le Laos Français. Gouvernement Général de l'Indo-Chine. Hanoi: Schneider, 1900.

Laos

Annuaire Statistique du Laos. Vientiane: Ministère des Finances, de l'Économie et du Plan, Direction de la Statistique, yearly from 1950.

L'Ingérence Nord-Vietnamienne au Laos. Vientiane: Ministère des Affaires Étrangères, 1964.

Lao Presse, Agence d'Information Télégraphique. Vientiane. (Daily from 1953.)

Livre Blanc sur les Violations des Accords de Genève de 1962 par le Gouvernement du Nord Vietnam. Vientiane: Ministère des Affaires Étrangères. 1965; *Idem*, 1969; *Idem*, 1970.

Mémorandum du Comité Central du Neo Lao Hak Sat à l'Occasion du 23 Juin 1969; Déclaration du Comité Central du Neo Lao Hak Sat et Déclaration des Forces Neutralistes Patriotiques Lao à l'Occasion du 7e Anniversaire de la Signature des Accords de Genève de 1962 sur le Laos. Documents Officiels, Éditions du Neo Lao Hak Sat, 1969.

Political Program of the Neo Lao Hak Sat (Lao Patriotic Front). Neo Lao Hak Sat Publications, 1968. (Text of the Political Program adopted at the Extraordinary Congress of the Neo Lao Hak Sat, October 31, 1968.)

Programme d'Action des Forces Neutralistes Patriotiques Lao. Imprimerie Lao Hak Sat, 1970.

Text of 1955 ceasefire agreement in Sam Neua and Phong Saly: *Accord sur la Cessation de Tous Actes Hostiles dans les Provinces de Sam Neua et Phongsaly*. Vientiane, 1955.

Text of Plain of Jars Agreement: *Lao Presse*, June 13, 1962.

Text of Zurich Communiqué of June 22, 1961: CMND. 2834, pp. 174–76.

South Vietnam

Accords et Conventions entre la République du Viêt-Nam et le Royaume du Laos Signés à Vientiane le 11 Juin 1959. Saigon: IFOM, n.d.

Thailand

Thailand: How Thailand Lost Her Territories to France. Bangkok: Department of Publicity, 1940.

Australia

Laos; Select Documents on International Affairs No. 16. Canberra: Department of External Affairs, April, 1970.

GEOGRAPHY, HISTORY, ETHNOGRAPHY, AND GENERAL DESCRIPTION

ABHAY, NHOUY. Aspects du Pays Lao. Vientiane: Ministère de l'Education Nationale, Éditions Comité Littéraire Lao, 1956.

ARCHAIMBAULT, CHARLES. La Cérémonie du Nouvel An à Bassac. Ithaca, N.Y.: Cornell University Press, forthcoming.

―――. "L'Histoire de Campasak," Journal Asiatique, CCLIX (1961), 519–95.

―――. "Les Annales de l'Ancien Royaume de S'ieng Khwang," Bulletin de l'École Française d'Extrême-Orient, LIII Fasc. 2 (1967), 557–673.

―――. "Religious Structures in Laos," The Journal of the Siam Society, LII Part 1 (April, 1964).

AUVRAY, GEORGES. "Les Voies de Pénétration au Laos," Bulletin des Amis du Laos, 1 (1937), 45–57.

AYABE, TSUNEO. The Village of Ban Pha Khao, Vientiane Province: A Preliminary Report. (Laos Project, Paper No. 14.) Los Angeles: Department of Anthropology and Sociology, University of California, 1961. (Mimeographed.)

AYME, G. Monographie du Ve Térritoire Militaire. Hanoi: Imprimerie d'Extrême-Orient, 1930.

AYMONIER, ÉTIENNE. Voyage dans le Laos. 2 vols. Paris: Leroux, 1895.

―――. Notes sur le Laos. Saigon: Imprimerie du Gouvernement, 1885.

BARTHÉLÉMY, COMTE PIERRE DE. En Indo-Chine 1894–1895; Cambodge—Cochinchine—Laos—Siam Méridional. Paris: Plon, 1899.

―――. En Indo-Chine 1896–1897; Tonquin—Haut-Laos—Annam Septentrional. Paris: Plon, 1901.

BELAKOWICZ, Z. DE. "Notes sur Deux Peuples du Darlac (Laos): les Radés et les Khas Pi," Revue Indochinoise, 1906, pp. 129–41, 225–45.

BERVAL, RENÉ DE. Kingdom of Laos: The Land of the Million Elephants and of the White Parasol. Saigon: France-Asie, 1959.

BOUTIN, ANDRÉ. "Monographie de la Province des Houa-Phan," Bulletin des Amis du Laos, 1 (1937), 69–119.

BRODRICK, ALAN H. Little Vehicle: Cambodia and Laos. London: Hutchinson, 1949.

434 · BIBLIOGRAPHY

BRUK, S. I. *The Peoples of Indochina*. Translated from the Russian. (U.S. Joint Publications Research Service, Publication No. 6914.) Washington: March 14, 1961.

BUI QUANG TUNG. "Chao Anou, Roi de Vientiane: à travers les Documents Vietnamiens," *Bulletin de la Société des Études Indochinoises*, XXXIII, 4 (1958), 401–6.

Bulletin de l'École Française d'Extrême-Orient. (Hanoi, quarterly 1901–57; Paris, from 1957.)

Bulletin de la Société des Études Indochinoises. Saigon. (Quarterly from 1883.)

Bulletin des Amis du Laos. Hanoi. (4 issues, 1937–1940.)

Bulletin des Amis du Royaume Lao. Vientiane. (Quarterly from 1970.)

Bulletin des Amis du Vieux Hué. Hanoi. (Quarterly, 1914–1944.)

Bulletin Économique de l'Indochine. Saigon. (Monthly from 1898.)

Bulletin Statistique du Laos. Vientiane: Ministère des Finances, de l'Économie et du Plan, Direction de la Statistique. (Quarterly from 1950.)

CADY, JOHN F. *The Roots of French Imperialism in Eastern Asia*. Ithaca, N.Y.: Cornell University Press, 1954.

Carte Ethnolinguistique d'Indochine. Hanoi: École Française d'Extrême-Orient, 1949.

CHEMINAUD, GUY. *Mes Chasses au Laos*. Paris: Payot, 1939.

CHUMSAI, M. *History of Laos*. Bangkok, 1960. (Typescript.)

COEDÈS, GEORGE. *Les États Hindouisés d'Indochine et d'Indonésie*. Paris: E. de Boccard, 1964.

COLANI, MADELEINE. *Mégalithes du Haut-Laos (Hua Phan, Tran Ninh)*. 2 vols. Hanoi: École Française d'Extrême-Orient, 1935.

COLONNA, M. "Monographie de la Province de Saravane," *Bulletin des Amis du Laos*, 2 (1938), 81–121.

CONDOMINAS, GEORGES. *Essai sur la Société Rurale Lao de la Région de Vientiane*. Vientiane: Ministère des Affaires Rurales, 1962. (Mimeographed.)

COOLIDGE, HAROLD J., and ROOSEVELT, THEODORE. *Three Kingdoms of Indochina*. New York: Crowell, 1933.

COUSSOT, ALFRED, and RUEL, HENRI. *Douze Mois chez les Sauvages du Laos*. Paris: Challamel, 1898.

DAMPRUN, M. "Monographie de la Province de Savannakhet," *Bulletin de la Société des Études Indochinoises*, 47 (1904), 23–71.

DEYDIER, HENRI. *Introduction à la Connaissance du Laos*. Saigon: IFOM, 1952.

———. *Lokapâla: Génies, Totem et Sorciers du Nord Laos*. Paris: Plon, 1954.

DOBBY, E. H. G. *Southeast Asia*. 7th ed. London: University of London Press, 1960.

DOUMER, PAUL. *L'Indochine Française*. Paris: Vuibert et Nouy, 1905.

DUFRÉNIL, P. "La Prise de Possession du Laos en 1893," *Revue Indochinoise*, X (July–December, 1908), 11–33 and 115–20.

EMBREE, JOHN F., and THOMAS, WILLIAM L., JR. *Ethnic Groups of Northern Southeast Asia.* (Southeast Asia Studies.) New Haven, Conn.: Yale University Press, 1950.

FIASSON, JEANNINE. *Au Laos avec Mes Hommes et Mes Éléphants.* Paris: Julliard, 1961.

France-Asie. Saigon and Tokyo. (Monthly and bimonthly from 1946.)

FRANCK, HARRY A. *East of Siam: Ramblings in the Five Divisions of French Indo-China.* New York: Century Press, 1926.

GARNIER, FRANCIS. *Voyage d'Exploration en Indo-Chine.* Paris: Hachette, 1885.

GAUDILLOT, CLAUDE, and CONDOMINAS, GEORGES. *La Plaine de Vientiane: Rapport d'Étude, I-III.* Paris: Bureau pour le Développement de la Production Agricole, 1959.

GOSSELIN, CAPITAINE. *Le Laos et le Protectorat Français.* Paris: Perrin, 1900.

GUILLEMET, EUGÈNE. *Sur les Sentiers Laotiens.* Amiens: Yvert, 1929.

HALL, D. G. E. *A History of South-East Asia.* 2d ed. London: Macmillan, 1964.

HALPERN, JOEL M. *Government, Politics, and Social Structure in Laos: A Study of Tradition and Innovation.* (Southeast Asia Studies, Monograph Series, No. 4.) New Haven, Conn.: Yale University Press, 1964.

————. *The Lao Elite: A Study of Tradition and Innovation.* Santa Monica, Calif.: The RAND Corporation (RM-2636-RC), November 15, 1960.

————. (Laos Project.) Los Angeles: Department of Anthropology and Sociology, University of California, 1961: *The Role of the Chinese in Lao Society—1959* (No. 1); *Capital, Savings and Credit among Lao and Serb Peasants: A Contrast in Cultural Values* (No. 2); *Population Statistics and Associated Data* (No. 3); *American Policy in Laos* (No. 6); *Laotian Educational Statistics* (No. 7); *Government Statistics* (No. 8); *Laotian Agricultural Statistics* (No. 9); *Laotian Health Statistics* (No. 10); *Economic and Related Statistics Dealing with Laos* (No. 11); *The Natural Economy of Laos* (No. 17); *Laos Profiles* (No. 18); *The Rural and Urban Economies* (No. 19); *Laotian Health Problems* (No. 20); *Government, Politics and Social Structure of Laos: A Study in Tradition and Innovation* (No. 21). (Mimeographed.)

HARMAND, DR. FRANÇOIS-JULES. "Le Laos et les Populations Sauvages de l'Indo-Chine," *Le Tour du Monde,* 38 (1879), pp. 1–48, and 39 (1880), pp. 241–320.

Indo-China. Geographical Handbook Series, Naval Intelligence Division London: 1943.

Indochine Sud Est Asiatique. Paris and Saigon. (Monthly, 1951–1954.)

IWATA, KEIJI. "Boloban Kogen no Jinbun Chiri" ("Descriptive Geography of the Bolovens Plateau"), *Jinbun Kenkyū* (*Studies in Cultural Science*), XI, No. 2 (1960), 46–70.

———. *Ethnic Groups in the Valley of the Nam Song and Nam Lik.* (Laos Project, Paper No. 15.) Los Angeles: Department of Anthropology and Sociology, University of California, 1961. (Mimeographed.)

———. *Minority Groups in Northern Laos—Especially the Yao.* (Laos Project, Paper No. 16.) Los Angeles: Department of Anthropology and Sociology, University of California, 1961. (Mimeographed.)

IZIKOWITZ, KARL GUSTAV. *Lamet: Hill Peasants in French Indochina.* Goteborg: Etnografiska Museet, 1951.

JANSE, OLOV R. T. *The Peoples of French Indochina.* (Smithsonian Institution War Background Studies, No. 14.) Washington: Government Printing Office, 1943.

KAHIN, GEORGE MCTURNAN (ed.). *Governments and Politics of Southeast Asia.* 2d ed. Ithaca, N.Y.: Cornell University Press, 1964.

La Revue Française. No. 203 (October, 1967). Special issue entitled "Le Laos."

LAFONT, PIERRE BERNARD. *Aperçus sur le Laos.* Vientiane: Comité de l'Alliance Française au Laos, 1959.

LANDON, KENNETH P. *Southeast Asia: Crossroads of Religions.* Chicago: University of Chicago Press, 1949.

———. "Thailand's Quarrel with France in Perspective," *Far Eastern Quarterly,* I, No. 1 (November, 1941), 25–42.

LE BAR, FRANK M.; HICKEY, GERALD C.; and MUSGRAVE, JOHN K. *Ethnic Groups of Mainland Southeast Asia.* New Haven, Conn.: Human Relations Area Files Press, 1964.

LE BAR, FRANK M., and SUDDARD, ADRIENNE (eds.). *Laos: Its People, Its Society, Its Culture.* New Haven, Conn.: Human Relations Area Files Press, 1960.

LE BOULANGER, PAUL. *Histoire du Laos Français.* Paris: Plon, 1931.

LE THANH KHOI. *Le Viêt-Nam; Histoire et Civilisation.* Paris: Les Éditions de Minuit, 1955.

LEFÈVRE, DR. E. *Un Voyage au Laos.* Paris: Plon, 1898.

LEMIRE, C. *Le Laos Annamite; Régions des Tiém (Ailao), des Moïs et des Pou-Euns (Cam-Mon et Tran-Ninh) Restituées en 1893.* Extrait de la Revue de l'Anjou, Angers-Paris, 1894.

MALLERET, LOUIS, "Auguste Pavie, Explorateur et Conquérant Pacifique," *Bulletin de la Société des Études Indochinoises,* XXII, 2 (1947), 79–92.

———. "Charles Lemire ou la Foi Coloniale," *Bulletin de la Société des Études Indochinoises,* XI, 4 (1936), 1–98.

MALPUECH, U. "Historique de la Province de Savannakhet," *Revue Indochinoise*, 7–8 (July–August, 1920), 1–26.

MANICH, M. L. *History of Laos*. Bangkok: Chalermnit, 1967.

MOUHOT, HENRI. *Travels in the Central Parts of Indo-China (Siam), Cambodia, and Laos, during the Years 1858–1859, and 1860*. London: J. Murray, 1864.

ODENDHAL, PROSPER. "Les Routes de l'Annam au Mé-Kong (de Hué à Saravane et à Attopeu)," *Revue Indochinoise*, 7 (1894), pp. 131–61, and 8 (1894), pp. 1–50.

PARMENTIER, HENRI. *L'Art du Laos*. 2 vols. Hanoi: École Française d'Extrême-Orient, 1954.

PAVIE, AUGUSTE. *À la Conquête des Coeurs*. Paris: Presses Universitaires de France, 1947.

——. *Mission Pavie en Indochine, 1879–1895*. 10 vols. Paris: Leroux, 1898–1919.

PELACOT, CAPITAINE DE. "Le Tran-Ninh Historique," *Revue Indochinoise*, 1906, pp. 569–80, 661–65, 755–67.

PENSRI, SUVANICH. *Les Relations Entre la France et la Thaïlande (Siam) au XIXe Siècle d'Après les Archives des Affaires Étrangères*. Bangkok: Chalermnit, 1962.

PICANON, EUGÈNE. *Le Laos Français*. Paris: Challamel, 1901.

PIETRANTONI, ERIC. "La Population du Laos de 1912 à 1945," *Bulletin de la Société des Études Indochinoises*, XXVIII, 1 (1953), pp. 25–38.

——. "La Population du Laos en 1943 dans Son Milieu Géographique," *Bulletin de la Société des Études Indochinoises*, XXXII, 3 (1957), pp. 223–43.

POUVOURVILLE, ALBERT DE. *Études Coloniales, l'Affaire de Siam 1886–1896*. Paris: 1897.

——. *Auguste Pavie*. Paris: Larose, 1933.

PRADITH, KHAMCHAN. *Place Historique du Laos en Asie*. Vientiane: 1968.

REINACH, LUCIEN DE. *Le Laos*. 2 vols. Paris: A. Charles, 1901.

Revue Indochinoise. Hanoi (1893–1925).

ROUX, COLONEL HENRI. "Quelques Minorités Ethniques du Nord Indochine," *France-Asie*, No. 92–93 (January–February, 1954), pp. 131–419.

SAVINA, F. M. *Histoire des Miao*. Hong Kong: Imprimerie de la Société des Missions Étrangères de Paris, 1930.

SCHAAF, C. HART, and FIFIELD, RUSSELL H. *The Lower Mekong; Challenge to Cooperation in Southeast Asia*. Princeton, N.J.: Van Nostrand, 1963.

Sud-Est. Saigon. (Monthly from 1949.)

Thailand: How Thailand Lost Her Territories to France. Bangkok: Department of Publicity, 1940.

THOMPSON, VIRGINIA, and ADLOFF, RICHARD. *Minority Problems in Southeast Asia*. Stanford, Calif.: Stanford University Press, 1955.

———. "Laos: Background of Invasion," *Far Eastern Quarterly*, 22, No. 6 (1953), 62–66.

VELLA, WALTER F. *Siam Under Rama III*. Locust Valley, N.Y.: Augustin, 1957.

VERCEL, ROGER. *Francis Garnier à l'Assaut des Fleuves*. Paris: Albin Michel, 1952.

VIRAVONG, MAHA SILA. *History of Laos*. (U.S. Joint Publications Research Service, Publication No. [N.Y.] 712.) Washington: October 1, 1958.

WENK, KLAUS. *The Restoration of Thailand Under Rama I, 1782–1809*. Tucson: University of Arizona Press, 1968.

WYATT, DAVID K. "Siam and Laos 1767–1827," *Journal of Southeast Asian History*, IV, 2 (September, 1963), 12–32.

CONTEMPORARY POLITICS AND WARFARE

AYROLLES, L.-H. *L'Indochine Ne Répond Plus*. Saint-Brieuc: Prud'homme, 1948.

BERGOT, ERWAN. *Mourir au Laos*. Paris: Éditions France-Empire, 1965.

BOUN OUM NA CHAMPASSAK, PRINCE. "Allocution à l'Occasion de la Signature des Conventions Franco-Laotiennes," *France-Asie*, No. 46–47 (January–February, 1950), pp. 629–31.

BURCHETT, WILFRED G. *The Furtive War: The United States in Vietnam and Laos*. New York: International Publishers, 1963.

———. *Mekong Upstream*. Hanoi: Red River Publishing House, 1957.

CAPLY, MICHEL (pseud.). *Guérilla au Laos*. Paris: Presses de la Cité, 1966.

CHAFFARD, GEORGES. *Les Deux Guerres du Vietnam*. Paris: La Table Ronde, 1969.

CHALERMNIT PRESS CORRESPONDENT. *Battle of Vientiane 1960*. Bangkok: Chalermnit, 1961.

CHASSIN, L.-M. *Aviation Indochine*. Paris: Amiot-Dumont, 1954.

China News Analysis. Hong Kong. (Weekly since 1953.)

CLOSE, CAPTAIN DONALD. "The Battle at Nam Tha," *Marine Corps Gazette*, February, 1965.

COLE, ALLAN B. (ed.). *Conflict in Indo-China and International Repercussions; A Documentary History, 1945–1955*. Ithaca, N.Y.: Cornell University Press, 1956.

CROZIER, BRIAN. "Peking and the Laotian Crisis: An Interim Appraisal," *China Quarterly*, No. 7 (July–September, 1961), pp. 128–37.

―――. "Peking and the Laotian Crisis: A Further Appraisal," *China Quarterly*, No. 11 (July–September, 1962), pp. 116–23.

CZYZAK, JOHN J., and SALANS, CARL F. "The International Conference on Laos and the Geneva Agreement of 1962," *Journal of Southeast Asian History*, VII, No. 2 (1966), 27–47.

"Der Kurs Moskaus und Pekings in der laotischen Krise." Unsigned article in *Neue Zürcher Zeitung*, January 3, 1961.

DEVILLERS, PHILIPPE. *Histoire du Viêt-nam de 1940 à 1952.* Paris: Éditions du Seuil, 1952.

DISCHAMPS, J. M. *Tam Tam sur le Mékong avec les Guérillas Laotiens.* Saigon: C. Ardin, 1948.

DOMMEN, ARTHUR J. "Neutralization Experiment in Laos," *Current History*, February, 1965.

―――. "Laos: The Troubled 'Neutral,'" *Asian Survey*, January, 1967, pp. 74–80.

―――. "Laos in the Second Indochina War," *Current History*, December, 1970.

DUPARC, CHARLES-HENRI. "Le Problème Politique Laotien," *Politique Étrangère*, XII (November, 1947), 529–56.

DUSKIN, LIEUTENANT COLONEL EDGAR W. "Laos," *Military Review*, March, 1968, pp. 3–10.

EDEN, ANTHONY. *The Memoirs of Anthony Eden: Full Circle.* Boston: Houghton Mifflin, 1960.

EISENHOWER, DWIGHT D. *The White House Years: A Personal Account 1956–1961; Waging Peace.* Garden City, N.Y.: 1965.

ELY, PAUL. *L'Indochine dans la Tourmente.* Paris: Plon, 1964.

EPSTEIN, ISRAEL, and FAIRFAX-CHOLMELEY, ELSIE. *Laos in the Mirror of Geneva.* Peking: New World Press, 1961.

FALL, BERNARD B. "The International Relations of Laos," *Pacific Affairs*, XXX (March, 1957), 22–34.

―――. *Le Viet-Minh, 1945–1960.* Paris: Armand Colin, 1960.

―――. "Reappraisal in Laos," *Current History*, XLII (January, 1962), 8–14.

―――. "The Pathet Lao," in Robert A. Scalapino (ed.). *The Communist Revolution in Asia.* Englewood Cliffs, N.J.: Prentice-Hall, 1965, pp. 173–97.

―――. *Anatomy of a Crisis: The Laos Crisis of 1961.* New York: Doubleday, 1969.

―――. *Hell in a Very Small Place.* New York: Lippincott, 1966.

―――. "Problèmes des États Poly-Ethniques en Indochine," *France-Asie*, No. 172 (March–April, 1962), pp. 129–52.

FIELD, MICHAEL. *The Prevailing Wind: Witness in Indo-China.* London: Methuen, 1965.

GENTIL, PIERRE. *Remous du Mékong.* Paris: Charles Lavauzelle, 1950.

GRONIER, MAURICE. *Riz et Pruneaux; avec les Commandos dans la Brousse d'Indochine.* Paris: Émile-Paul, 1950.

HALPERN, A. M., and FREDMAN, H. B. *Communist Strategy in Laos.* Santa Monica, Calif.: The RAND Corporation (RM-2561), June 14, 1960.

———. "The Emergence of an Asian Communist Coalition," *The Annals of the American Academy of Political and Social Science,* CCCXLIX (September, 1963), 117–29.

HAMMER, ELLEN. *The Struggle for Indochina.* Stanford, Calif.: Stanford University Press, 1954.

HONEY, P. J. *Communism in North Vietnam.* Cambridge, Mass.: The M.I.T. Press, 1963.

JOEL, CLARK. "The Foreign Exchange Operations Fund for Laos: An Interesting Experiment in Monetary Stabilization," *Asian Survey,* March, 1966, pp. 134–49.

JONAS, ANNE M., and TANHAM, GEORGE K. "Laos: A Phase in Cyclic Regional Revolution," *Orbis,* V (Spring, 1961), 64–73.

KARPIKHIN, A. "The U.S.A. Sabotages the Geneva Agreements on Indochina," *International Affairs* (Moscow), August, 1959, pp. 57–62.

KATAY, THAO. *Le Laos.* Bangkok: Éditions Lao Issara, 1948.

KAUFMAN, RICHARD H. "The Asian Gold Trade," *Asian Survey,* May, 1965, pp. 233–44.

KEMP, PETER. *Alms for Oblivion.* London: Cassell, 1961.

KHOMAN, THANAT. "Which Road for South East Asia?" *Foreign Affairs,* XLII, No. 4 (July, 1964), 628–39.

KOJEVNIKOV, V. A., and POPOVKINA, R. A. *Laos Today: A Reference Book.* Moscow: Academy of Sciences of the U.S.S.R., Asian People's Institute, Publishing House "Nauka," 1966.

LACOUTURE, JEAN, and DEVILLERS, PHILIPPE. *End of a War: Indochina 1954.* New York: Praeger, 1969.

LANCASTER, DONALD. *The Emancipation of French Indo-China.* London: Oxford University Press, 1961.

LANGER, PAUL F., and ZASLOFF, JOSEPH J. *North Vietnam and the Pathet Lao: Partners in the Struggle for Laos.* Cambridge, Mass.: Harvard University Press, 1970.

LÉVY, ROGER. *L'Indochine et Ses Traités.* Paris: Hartmann, 1947.

McALISTER, JOHN T., JR. "Mountain Minorities and the Viet Minh: A Key to the Indochina War," in Peter Kunstadter (ed.). *Southeast Asian Tribes, Minorities and Nations.* Princeton, N.J.: Princeton University Press, 1967. Pp. 771–846.

McKEITHEN, EDWIN T. *Life Under the P.L. in the Xieng Khouang Ville Area.* Vientiane: USAID, 1969. (Mimeographed.)

———. *The Role of North Vietnamese Cadres in the Pathet Lao Administration of Xieng Khouang Province.* Vientiane: USAID, 1970. (Mimeographed.)

MARCHAND, JEAN. *Le Drame Indochinois.* Paris: Peyronnet, 1953.

MEEKER, ODEN. *The Little World of Laos.* New York: Charles Scribner's Sons, 1959.

Mittasone. Vientiane. (Quarterly from 1967.)

MODELSKI, GEORGE A. *International Conference on the Settlement of the Laotian Question, 1961–62.* Canberra: Department of International Relations, Research School of Pacific Studies, Australian National University, 1962.

NAVARRE, HENRI. *Agonie de l'Indochine.* Paris: Plon, 1956 and 1958.

NAVILLE, PIERRE. *La Guerre du Viêt-nam.* Paris: Éditions de la Revue Internationale, 1949.

NUECHTERLEIN, D. E. *Thailand and the Struggle for Southeast Asia.* Ithaca, N.Y.: Cornell University Press, 1965.

NUTT, ANITA LAUVE. *Troika on Trial—Control or Compromise?* Study prepared for the Office of International Security Affairs, U.S. Department of Defense, September, 1967.

ORGWALD. *Tactical and Organizational Questions of the Communist Parties of India and Indo-China.* The Pan-Pacific Worker, 1933.

OSBORN, G. M. T. "Government and the Hill Tribes of Laos," in Peter Kunstadter (ed.), *Southeast Asian Tribes, Minorities and Nations.* Princeton, N.J.: Princeton University Press, 1967. Pp. 259–70.

PACE, ERIC. "Laos: Continuing Crisis," *Foreign Affairs,* XLIII, No. 1 (October, 1964), 64–74.

PHAM VAN DONG. "The Foreign Policy of the Democratic Republic of Vietnam," *International Affairs* (Moscow), July, 1958, pp. 19–22.

PHAN NGHI. *Vuot Truong Son (Trekking Through the Annamite Chain).* Saigon: n.p., 1966.

QUANG MINH. *Au Pays du Million d'Éléphants.* Hanoi: Éditions en Langues Étrangères, 1961.

ROCHET, CHARLES. *Pays Lao, le Laos dans la Tourmente.* Paris: 1946.

ROCOLLE, PIERRE. *Pourquoi Dien Bien Phu?* Paris: Flammarion, 1968.

ROY, JULES. *La Bataille de Dien Bien Phu.* Paris: Julliard, 1963.

SABATTIER, GENERAL G. *Le Destin de l'Indochine, Souvenirs et Documents, 1941–1951.* Paris: Plon, 1952.

SARDESAI, D. R. *Indian Foreign Policy in Cambodia, Laos, and Vietnam 1947–1964.* Berkeley: University of California Press, 1968.

SASORITH, KATAY DON. *Le Laos.* Paris: Berger-Levrault, 1953.

SCHLESINGER, ARTHUR M., JR. *A Thousand Days.* Boston: Houghton Mifflin, 1965.

SHAPLEN, ROBERT. "Letter from Laos," *The New Yorker,* May 4, 1968.

SIMMONDS, E. H. S. "Independence and Political Rivalry in Laos 1945–61," in Saul Rose (ed.). *Politics in Southern Asia.* London: 1963.

———. "The Independent State of Laos," *The World Today,* October, 1957.

———. "A Cycle of Political Events in Laos," *The World Today,* February, 1961.

———. "Power Politics in Laos," *The World Today,* December, 1962.

———. "Breakdown in Laos," *The World Today,* July, 1964.

SISOUK NA CHAMPASSAK. *Storm Over Laos*. New York: Frederick A. Praeger, 1961.

SIVARAM, M. *Mekong Clash and Far East Crisis*. Bangkok: 1941.

SOUVANNA PHOUMA. "Le Laos, avant-garde du monde libre," *France-Asie*, No. 164 (November–December, 1960), pp. 1427–34.

———. "Le Laos: Le Fond du Problème," *France-Asie*, No. 166 (March–April, 1961), pp. 1824–26.

STAROBIN, JOSEPH R. *Eyewitness in Indochina*. New York: Cameron and Kahn, 1954.

TANHAM, GEORGE K. *Communist Revolutionary Warfare: The Vietminh in Indochina*. New York: Frederick A. Praeger, 1961.

TOYE, HUGH. *Laos: Buffer State or Battleground*. London: Oxford University Press, 1968.

TRAN NGOC HUNG. "The Role of the Indo-Chinese Communist Party in the Evolution of the Viet Minh: 1945–1951," *Australian Quarterly*, September, 1954, pp. 87–98.

VO NGUYEN GIAP. *Dien Bien Phu*. Hanoi: Foreign Languages Publishing House, 1962.

———. *People's War, People's Army*. Hanoi: Foreign Languages Publishing House, 1961; New York: Frederick A. Praeger, 1962 (facsimile edition).

VONGVICHIT, PHOUMI. *Laos and the Victorious Struggle of the Lao People Against U.S. Neo-Colonialism*. Neo Lao Hak Sat Publications, 1969.

WARD, J. THOMAS. "U.S. Aid to Hill Tribe Refugees in Laos," in PETER KUNSTADTER (ed.). *Southeast Asian Tribes, Minorities and Nations*. Princeton, N.J.: Princeton University Press, 1967, pp. 295–306.

WISE, DAVID, and ROSS, THOMAS B. *The Invisible Government*. New York: Random House, 1964.

WOLFKILL, GRANT (with ROSE, JERRY). *Reported to be Alive*. London: W. H. Allen, 1966.

ZAGORIA, DONALD S. *The Sino-Soviet Conflict, 1951–1961*. Princeton, N.J.: Princeton University Press, 1962.

ZUKROWSKI, WOJCECH. "I Was Kong Le's Shadow," *Literaturnaya Gazeta* (Moscow), February 28 and March 2, 4, and 7, 1961.

EXTENDED BIBLIOGRAPHIES

CORDIER, G. *Bibliotheca Indosinica: Dictionnaire Bibliographique des Ouvrages Relatifs à la Péninsule Indochinoise*. Vol. I (1912), cols. 997–1084; vol. IV (1915), cols. 2789–2806. Paris: Imprimerie Nationale, 1912–15.

HALPERN, JOEL M. *Bibliography of Laos and Related Areas to 1961.* Edited by JOHN McKINISTRY. Berkeley, Calif.: Center for Southeast Asian Studies, University of California, 1962. (Mimeographed.)

HAY, STEPHEN N., and CASE, MARGARET H. *Southeast Asian History: A Bibliographic Guide.* New York: Frederick A. Praeger, 1962.

HOBBS, CECIL. *Southeast Asia: An Annotated Bibliography of Selected Reference Sources.* Washington: U.S. Library of Congress, Orientalia Division, 1952.

KENE, THAO. *Bibliographie du Laos.* Vientiane: Ministère de l'Éducation Nationale, Éditions Comité Littéraire Lao, 1958.

KEYES, JANE GODFREY. *A Bibliography of North Vietnamese Publications in the Cornell University Library.* (Southeast Asia Program, Data Paper No. 47.) Ithaca, N.Y.: Department of Asian Studies, Cornell University, September, 1962.

LAFONT, PIERRE BERNARD. *Bibliographie du Laos.* Paris: École Française d'Extrême-Orient, 1964.

Index

DATE DUE